· THE ·
CHURCH
IN · THE
TWENTIETH
CENTURY

THE CHURCH IN THE TWENTIETH CENTURY

RICHARD O. COWAN

BOOKCRAFT

SALT LAKE CITY, UTAH

Library of Congress Catalog Card Number: 84-71986
ISBN 0-88494-541-3

First Printing, 1985

Printed in the United States of America

Contents

Maps and Charts

Description or Title

Preface

The twentieth century has been one of the most significant eras in the history of The Church of Jesus Christ of Latter-day Saints. Surely it would have been wonderful to live in the days of Joseph Smith and to associate with him personally. Likewise, to accompany the pioneers in their westward trek would have been an unforgettable experience. Yet the challenges and opportunities of the twentieth century hold a unique excitement. To the casual observer the primary theme of recent Latter-day Saint history is worldwide growth. This work will show that there have also been many other significant developments in Church organization, programs, and activities. Even though the Lord has worked through fallible human beings and institutions, I am convinced that his hand can be seen, not only in specific incidents where inspired guidance was obvious, but also in the overall progress of his kingdom during the present century. Thus we do not need to look only to past ages for examples of divine direction or assistance.

I have encountered a number of interesting challenges while researching and writing this book. Even though I have written from the perspective of faith, I have also wanted to follow high standards of historical scholarship. I do not believe that one necessarily excludes the other. In addition, writing contemporary history has its advantages and disadvantages: There may be an abundance of public sources such as newspapers, but more reflective personal sources such as journals or correspondence are less likely to be available to the historian. In some cases the researcher himself may have been intimately involved in the events he must describe, but at the same time he lacks the perspective necessary to assess their long-term importance. Furthermore, writing about individuals who are still living requires particularly sensitive judgment. Despite these challenges, I have found the preparation of this book to be an especially rewarding work.

My interest in this topic is of long standing. After finishing my Ph.D. in American history at Stanford University in 1961, I joined the religion faculty at Brigham Young University, where I was asked to specialize in researching and teaching LDS history from 1900 onward. This book is an outgrowth of that assignment.

I am indebted to many persons who have provided assistance without which this work could not have been completed. Larry C. Porter, who at the time was chairman of the Department of Church History and Doctrine at BYU, directed me to write a text on twentieth-century Church history; afterward he encouraged me to submit my manuscript for publication. Research assistants, particularly David F. Boone and Frank Alan Bruno, have made a major contribution. Personnel at the Historical Department of the Church have also been cooperative and helpful. Many typists and editors have played a key role in moving this project forward. Most recently, I have appreciated the valuable help from Bookcraft's editorial department: George Bickerstaff has insightfully and graciously pointed out ways the manuscript could be polished, while Andy Allison has assisted in the selection of illustrations and in other ways has helped move the manuscript toward publication. To all these individuals I express my deep gratitude.

It is my hope that this history of The Church of Jesus Christ of Latter-day Saints in the twentieth century will be a source of information, interest, and especially inspiration to all who read it.

1 The Turn of the Century: Lorenzo Snow

As the twentieth century dawned, Lorenzo Snow was sustained as Prophet, Seer, and Revelator, and President of the Church of just over 250,000 Latter-day Saints—only a small fraction of what the Church's membership would be during the later twentieth century. Many of these early Saints had personally experienced the hardships of pioneering in the deserts and had suffered through the persecutions that had been so common in the nineteenth century. Some forty-three stakes and nineteen missions were functioning. Missionaries were teaching the restored gospel in the United States, Canada, western Europe, and the islands of the Pacific. Because about five out of every six Latter-day Saints lived in the predominantly Mormon Intermountain area of the western United States, however, the Church's influence elsewhere was limited. The Church's four temples were all located in Utah. The twentieth century would see The Church of Jesus Christ of Latter-day Saints expand far beyond these modest dimensions.

On Tuesday, January 1, 1901, the opening day of the new century, President Snow addressed a special New Year's Day audience in the Salt Lake Tabernacle. Having played a key role

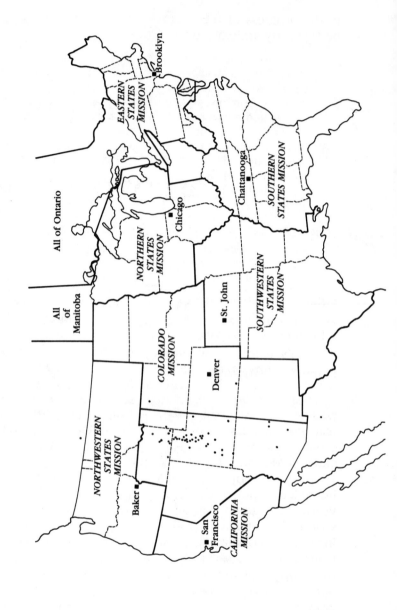

Missions and Stakes of the Church
U.S. and Canada 1900

in the progress of the Church almost since its beginning, he now eagerly anticipated the future:

> I hope and look for grand events to occur in the twentieth century. At its auspicious dawn, I lift my hands and invoke the blessings of heaven upon the inhabitants of the earth. May the sunshine from above smile upon you. May the treasures of the ground and the fruits of the soil be brought forth freely for your good. May the light of truth chase darkness from your souls. May righteousness increase and iniquity diminish as the years of the century roll on. May justice triumph and corruption be stamped out. And may virtue and chastity and honor prevail, until evil shall be overcome and the earth shall be cleansed from wickedness. Let these sentiments, as the voice of the "Mormons" in the mountains of Utah, go forth to the whole world, and let all people know that our wish and our mission are for the blessing and salvation of the entire human race. May the Twentieth Century prove the happiest as it will be the grandest of all the ages of time.[1]

Although President Snow's hopes have not been fully realized even yet, he did see the Church take substantial strides toward achieving the strength needed to fulfill its worldwide mission.

Lorenzo Snow's Earlier Life

Lorenzo Snow was eighty-four years of age when he assumed the leadership of the Church. No other President had reached such an advanced age at the time of entering this office. President Snow's long life had been filled with experiences that prepared him for his prophetic call.

Although opportunities for formal schooling were quite limited in frontier Ohio, Lorenzo Snow loved to read and yearned for an education. After completing one term in high school, he attended Oberlin College, a nearby Presbyterian institution. Lorenzo Snow would be the first President of the Church to have had any college education. He taught school for a season in Ohio and would later organize the Polysophical Society to promote cultural refinement and learning among the early pioneers in Utah. This society was a forerunner of the Mutual Improvement Associations.

1814	April 3: Born in Mantua, Ohio
1831	Heard Joseph Smith preach (age 17)
1835	Entered Oberlin College (21)
1836	Attended Hebrew school in Kirtland; baptized (22)
1837-40	Mission in Kentucky and Ohio; taught school
1840	Received revelation on nature of God and man (26)
1840-43	Mission to Great Britain, during which he gave copy of the Book of Mormon to Queen Victoria (26-29)
1846-48	Leading role in pioneers' crossing of the plains
1849	Called to the Twelve and on mission to Italy (35)
1852	Organized Polysophical Society (38)
1853	Called to preside over Saints in Brigham City (39)
1864	Restored to life after drowning in Hawaii (50)
1872-82	Served as president of Utah Territorial Legislative Council (58-68)
1873	Participated in rededication of Holy Land (58)
1873-77	One of seven counselors to President Brigham Young (59-63)
1885	Arrested on charge of polygamous cohabitation (71)
1888	Participated in Manti Temple dedication (74)
1893	Became president of Salt Lake Temple (79)
1898	Met the Savior in Salt Lake Temple; sustained as President of the Church (84)
1899	Inspired to reemphasize tithe paying (85)
1901	Sent Elder Heber J. Grant to open Japanese Mission; died October 10 in Salt Lake City, Utah (87)

Lorenzo's first contact with the restored gospel came at the age of seventeen when he went to hear Joseph Smith preach in Hiram, Ohio, just four miles from his home. Four years later Lorenzo was receptive when his sister Eliza, who had joined the Church a few months earlier, wrote from Kirtland and invited him to visit her and attend the Hebrew school that was being opened there by the Mormons. This gave him the opportunity to become acquainted with Joseph Smith and other Church leaders, and in June 1836 he was baptized.

Deep personal spirituality would characterize Lorenzo Snow throughout his life, and this trait was manifested early. He later recalled:

> Some two or three weeks after I was baptized, one day while engaged in my studies, I began to reflect upon the fact that I had not obtained a *knowledge* of the truth of the work—that I had not realized the fulfillment of the promise "he that doeth my will shall know of the doctrine," and I began to feel very uneasy. I laid aside my books, left the house, and wandered around through the fields under the oppressive influence of a gloomy, disconsolate spirit, while an indescribable cloud of darkness seemed to envelop me. I had been accustomed, at the close of the day, to retire for secret prayer, to a grove a short distance from my lodgings, but at this time I felt no inclination to do so. The spirit of prayer had departed and the heavens seemed like brass over my head. At length, realizing that the usual time had come for secret prayer, I concluded I would not forego my evening service, and, as a matter of formality, knelt as I was in the habit of doing, and in my accustomed retired place, but not feeling as I was wont to feel.
>
> I had no sooner opened my lips in an effort to pray, than I heard a sound, just above my head, like the rustling of silken robes, and immediately the Spirit of God descended upon me, completely enveloping my whole person, filling me, from the crown of my head to the soles of my feet, and O, the joy and happiness I felt! No language can describe the almost instantaneous transition from a dense cloud of mental and spiritual darkness into a refulgence of light and knowledge, as it was at that time imparted to my understanding. I then received a perfect knowledge that God lives, that Jesus Christ is the Son of God, and of the restoration of the holy Priesthood, and the fulness of the Gospel. It was a complete baptism—a tangible immersion in the heavenly principle or element, the Holy Ghost; and even more real and physical in its effects upon every part of my system than the immersion by water; dispelling forever, so long as reason and memory last, all possibility of doubt or fear.[2]

It was in Nauvoo that Lorenzo received by personal revelation a knowledge of man's potential destiny:

> The Spirit of the Lord rested mightily upon me—the eyes of my understanding were opened, and I saw as clear as the sun

at noonday, with wonder and astonishment, the pathway of God and man. I formed the following couplet which expresses the revelation, as it was shown to me, . . . "As man now is, God once was: As God now is, man may be."[3]

Lorenzo Snow played a key role in the westward migration of the Mormon pioneers. Then, in 1849, he was called to the Quorum of the Twelve and appointed to open a mission in Italy. After only two weeks' preparation, he left his wives and families and traveled east with the first group of missionaries sent from the Rocky Mountain area.

Elder Snow and his companions arrived in Italy in 1850. Despite initial discouragement, he prayed fervently for the Italian people and for his own success. This success did not come easily, however. Only after Elder Snow had exerted his great faith in healing a young boy were the missionaries able to open the door, albeit just a crack, to missionary work in Italy.

In 1853 he was called to preside over the settlements in Box Elder County of northern Utah, where he named the principal settlement Brigham City in honor of President Young. He lived in this region for over forty years, although he did accept frequent assignments to travel elsewhere. Under his leadership, the Saints developed a series of cooperative enterprises that brought prosperity to the area. Here he gained valuable economic experience that would give him needed perspective when, as President of the Church, he would confront the challenge of an overwhelming debt.

Elder Snow accepted several assignments to travel overseas. This broadened his appreciation of the Church's worldwide mission. While filling a special assignment in Hawaii in 1864, he drowned when the small boat in which he was riding capsized. After fifteen or twenty minutes his lifeless body was finally found and taken from the water. His companions administered to him and continued praying as they worked over him. Finally they felt impressed to apply mouth-to-mouth resuscitation, a life-saving technique not commonly known at that time, and his life was restored.

In 1872-73 he toured Europe and the Near East with a group of General Authorities and others. President Brigham Young had instructed the group:

The Presidents of the Church

Name	Presided as Apostle	Served as President	Age when called	died
1. Joseph Smith		1830-1844/14 yrs	24	38
2. Brigham Young	3.5 yrs	1847-1877/30 yrs	46	76
3. John Taylor	3 yrs	1880-1887/7 yrs	71	78
4. Wilford Woodruff	1.7 yrs	1889-1898/9 yrs	82	91
5. Lorenzo Snow	11 days	1898-1901/3 yrs	84	87
6. Joseph F. Smith	7 days	1901-1918/17 yrs	62	80
7. Heber J. Grant	4 days	1918-1945/26.5 yrs	62	88
8. George Albert Smith	7 days	1945-1951/6 yrs	75	81
9. David O. McKay	5 days	1951-1970/19 yrs	77	96
10. Joseph Fielding Smith	5 days	1970-1972/2.5 yrs	93	95
11. Harold B. Lee	5 days	1972-1973/1.5 yrs	73	74
12. Spencer W. Kimball	4 days	1973-	78	

. . . We desire that you observe closely what openings now exist, or where they may be effected, for the introduction of the Gospel into the various countries you shall visit. When you get to the land of Palestine, we wish you to dedicate and consecrate that land, that it may be blessed with fruitfulness, preparatory to the return of the Jews, in fulfillment of prophecy and the accomplishment of the purposes of our Heavenly Father.

On March 2, 1873, Elder Snow and the others ascended the Mount of Olives and, in compliance with President Young's instructions, offered a solemn prayer blessing the Holy Land. Elder Snow's son later asserted that "few experiences in the long and eventful life of Father were of greater interest and brought more joy to his soul than this trip."[4]

Spiritual experiences continued to characterize Elder Lorenzo Snow's ministry. On March 9, 1891, through his great faith in the power of the priesthood, he raised a young woman from the dead. Ella Jensen of Brigham City had been dead for two hours when he commanded her to "come back and live," declaring, "your mission is not ended." She lived to become the mother of eight children.

Upon the dedication of the Salt Lake Temple in 1893, Lorenzo Snow was named to be its first president. He had earlier worked on the construction of the Nauvoo Temple and officiated in sacred ordinances there, and had participated at the cornerstone's laying and the public dedication of the Manti Temple. His great spirituality and love of people well qualified him for this new calling. He enjoyed his service in the temple until he was released upon becoming President of the Church in 1898.

Selection as President of the Church

Two important principles relative to succession in the Presidency of the Church were clarified as Lorenzo Snow assumed that office and during his administration. One of these points dealt with how soon the new President should take office, and the other defined how that person should be selected.

Immediate Reorganization of the First Presidency

Following the deaths of the first three Presidents of the Church, the Council of the Twelve Apostles had presided for prolonged periods of times before the new President took office. As early as 1892, however, President Wilford Woodruff instructed that there should not be another of these lengthy "apostolic presidencies" following his death. Elder Lorenzo Snow, President Woodruff's successor, recorded his instructions as follows:

> He said, and spoke with much feeling and energy, "I have an important request to make of you which I want you to fulfill. A few months ago while on a visit to St. George I came near dying. I have no lease of my life, and know not how soon I may be called away, and when I go I want you, Brother Snow, not to delay, but organize the First Presidency. Take George Q. Cannon and Joseph F. Smith for your counselors; they are good, wise men of experience."

Of course I was much surprised, and said, "President Woodruff, am I to receive this as a revelation?" I do not call to mind the words of his answer, but they were such as gave me the impression that he wanted me to regard it as such. Without thought or thinking of the impropriety of such questions, I continued: "President Woodruff, is this the place I am to occupy?" He hesitated a moment, then replied, "It is according to the order . . ."[5]

The authority of these instructions was later confirmed through a sacred experience Elder Snow had in the Salt Lake Temple. In 1898, as President Wilford Woodruff became critically ill, Lorenzo Snow grew extremely worried. The Church was unable to pay even the interest on its heavy debt. Elder Snow's son recorded:

My father went to his room in the Salt Lake Temple . . . knelt at the sacred altar in the Holy of Holies in the House of the Lord and there pled to the Lord to spare President Woodruff's life, that President Woodruff might outlive him and that the great responsibility of Church leadership would not fall upon his shoulders. Yet he promised the Lord that he would devotedly perform any duty required at his hands. At this time he was in his eighty-fifth year.[6]

Elder Snow was in Brigham City when he received notice of President Woodruff's death on September 2, 1898. The Apostle immediately returned to Salt Lake City and went to his room in the temple.

President Snow . . . repaired again to the same sacred altar and poured out his heart to the Lord. He reminded the Lord how he pled for President Woodruff's life to be spared, that President Woodruff's days would be lengthened beyond his own; that he might never be called upon to bear the heavy burdens and responsibilities of the Church. "Nevertheless," he said, "Thy will be done. I have not sought this responsibility but if it be Thy will, I now present myself before Thee for Thy guidance and instruction. I ask that Thou show me what Thou wouldst have me do."

After finishing his prayer he expected a reply, some special manifestation from the Lord. So he waited,—and waited—and waited. There was no reply, no voice, no visitation, no manifestation.[7]

Disappointed, he left the sacred room, and walked through the celestial room out into the large corridor. Here he received a glorious manifestation, which he later described to his granddaughter. She wrote:

> One evening while I was visiting grandpa Snow in his room in the Salt Lake Temple, I remained until the door keepers had gone and the night-watchmen had not yet come in, so grandpa said he would take me to the main front entrance and let me out that way. He got his bunch of keys from his dresser. After we left his room and while we were still in the large corridor leading into the celestial room, I was walking several steps ahead of grandpa when he stopped me and said: "Wait a moment, Allie, I want to tell you something. It was right here that the Lord Jesus Christ appeared to me at the time of the death of President Woodruff. He instructed me to go right ahead and reorganize the First Presidency of the Church at once and not wait as had been done after the death of the previous presidents, and that I was to succeed President Woodruff."
>
> Then grandpa came a step nearer and held out his left hand and said: "He stood right here, about three feet above the floor. It looked as though He stood on a plate of solid gold."
>
> Grandpa told me what a glorious personage the Savior is and described His hands, feet, countenance and beautiful white robes, all of which were of such a glory of whiteness and brightness that he could hardly gaze upon Him.
>
> Then he came another step nearer and put his right hand on my head and said: "Now, granddaughter, I want you to remember that this is the testimony of your grandfather, that he told you with his own lips that he actually saw the Savior, here in the Temple, and talked with Him face to face."[8]

On September 13, the Apostles met to discuss Church finances in the wake of President Woodruff's death. Elder Francis M. Lyman referred to "President Woodruff's feelings, as expressed on different occasions during his administration, to the effect that whenever he died, the First Presidency of the Church should be organized without delay." Elder Lyman then declared, "And if the Lord should manifest to you, President Snow, that it was the proper thing to do now, I am prepared to not only vote for the Trustee-in-trust, but for the President of the Church." The others present concurred, and

Lorenzo Snow was unanimously sustained as the new President of the Church.

President Snow then arose and acknowledged that "there was no use in his making excuses as to [his] inability, etc., to assume the vast responsibilities involved in the position to which he had been elected [called]. He felt that it was for him to do the very best he could and depend upon the Lord. He knew the action taken by the Council was according to the mind and will of the Lord who had shown and revealed to him several days ago that the First Presidency should be organized before the next conference." Before calling for a formal vote, President Snow explained: "I have not mentioned this matter to any person, either man or woman. I wanted to see what the feelings of the brethren were. I wanted to see if the same spirit which the Lord manifested to me was in you. I had confidence in you that the Lord would indicate to you that this was proper and according to his mind and will."[9]

Seniority Among the Twelve

As early as 1887 Elder Wilford Woodruff had given his reasons for believing that the president of the Twelve would always become the new President of the Church:

> . . . when the President of the Church dies, who then is the Presiding Authority of the Church? It is the Quorum of the Twelve Apostles (ordained and organized by the revelations of God and none else). Then while these Twelve Apostles preside over the Church, who is the President of the Church[?] It is the President of the Twelve Apostles. And he is virtually as much the President of the Church while presiding over Twelve men as he is when organized into the President of the Church, and presiding over two men.[10]

Elder John A. Widtsoe has explained:

> This is a wise procedure. It places at the head of the Church the Apostle who has been longest in service. He is known well to the people and trusted by them. He himself knows the procedure of Church affairs. He is no novice to be trained for the position. He can call to his assistance, in addition to his counselors, any helpers from among the priesthood of

the Church. It eliminates the shadow of politics from the operations of the Council.

Should there be any deviation from the practices of the past, it would come by revelation to the President of the Twelve, who by virtue of his presidency, holds the keys of authority committed to this quorum of the priesthood. However, President Woodruff declared that in his opinion, the President of the council would never be set aside for someone else in appointing a president of the Church.[11]

More recently, Elder Spencer W. Kimball testified:

Even when a powerful leader dies, not for a single instant is the Church without leadership, thanks to the kind Providence who gave his kingdom continuity and perpetuity. . . .

The moment life passes from a President of the Church, a body of men become the composite leader—these men already seasoned with experience and training. The appointments have long been made, the authority given, the keys delivered. For [a few] days, the kingdom moves forward under this already authorized council. No "running" for position, no electioneering, no stump speeches. What a divine plan! How wise our Lord, to organize so perfectly beyond the weakness of frail, grasping humans. . . .

People talk about precedent. If it is precedent, it has become such by the repetition of the revealed order since the beginning.[12]

President Harold B. Lee further testified that the President of the Church, like all other officers, must (in the words of the fifth article of faith) "be called of God by prophecy and by the laying on of hands by those who are in authority. . . ." One's call as President of the Church actually begins when he is ordained and set apart as a member of the Quorum of the Twelve Apostles.

Each apostle so ordained under the hands of the President of the Church, who holds the keys of the kingdom of God in concert with all other ordained apostles, has given to him the priesthood authority necessary to hold every position in the Church, even to a position of presidency over the Church. . . .

Immediately following the death of a President, the next ranking body, the Quorum of the Twelve Apostles, becomes the presiding authority, with the President of the Twelve automatically becoming the acting President of the Church until a President of the Church is officially ordained and sustained in his office.

Early in this dispensation, because of certain conditions, the Council of Twelve continued to preside as a body for as long as three years before the reorganization was effected. As conditions in the Church became more stabilized, the reorganization was effected promptly following the passing of the President of the Church.[13]

The foregoing statements clearly indicate that upon the death of a President of the Church, the senior Apostle succeeds him in that office. During Lorenzo Snow's administration, Church leaders had the opportunity to clarify how seniority among the Twelve should be determined.

Brigham Young, Jr., had been ordained an Apostle in 1864, and Joseph F. Smith received a similar ordination two years later. Because there were no vacancies in the Twelve at the time, however, these two men were not immediately sustained as members of the Quorum. In 1867 Joseph F. Smith was called to fill a vacancy in the Twelve, and a year later Brigham Young, Jr., filled another vacancy in that same quorum. Thus when the President of the Twelve died in 1899, the question arose as to which of these two men was the senior Apostle.

On April 5, 1900, at a meeting held in the Salt Lake Temple, the First Presidency and the Twelve unanimously decided that "the acceptance of a member into the Council or Quorum of the Twelve fixed his rank or position in the Apostleship," that "the Apostles took precedence from that date they entered the quorum," and that "ordination to the Apostleship under the hands of any Apostle other than to fill a vacancy in the quorum, and authorized by the General Authorities of the Church, did not count in precedence." Hence Joseph F. Smith ranked ahead of Brigham Young, Jr., among the members of the Twelve. Finally, it was decided that "if the First Presidency were dissolved by the death of the President, his counselors having been ordained Apostles in the Quorum of the Twelve would resume their places in the quorum,

The First Presidency and the Quorum of the Twelve Apostles about 1899: (top row, from left) Anthon H. Lund, John W. Taylor, John Henry Smith, Heber J. Grant, Francis M. Lyman, George Teasdale, Marriner W. Merrill; (middle row, from left) Brigham Young, Jr., George Q. Cannon, Lorenzo Snow, Joseph F. Smith, Franklin D. Richards; (bottom row, from left) Matthias Cowley, Abraham O. Woodruff. (Church Archives)

according to the seniority of their ordinations into that quorum."[14]

Overcoming Church Debt

A major challenge that faced the Church as Lorenzo Snow assumed the presidency in 1898 was a debt that exceeded $1.25 million. Historian Leonard Arrington has explained the circumstances that led to this predicament: The Church initially went $300,000 into debt as a direct result of the 1887 Edmunds-Tucker Anti-Bigamy Act, which provided for the confiscation of Church property. Furthermore, the Church established a defense fund to help with legal fees and court costs of those being prosecuted for living in plural marriage, and it assumed the responsibility of caring for the families of men who were imprisoned. At the same time, members became reluctant to make financial contributions to the Church, fearing that these funds would be seized by the government. Thus, annual tithing income fell from an average of $500,000 during the 1880s to a little more than $300,000 in 1890. "Consequently," Arrington concluded, "the long-run effect of the Edmunds-Tucker Law was to throw the Church, which had previously enjoyed a creditor status, into a debt of at least half a million dollars."

Other commitments during the 1890s swelled the debt even further. President Woodruff was anxious to complete the construction of the Salt Lake Temple, so a million dollars was spent on this project between 1890 and 1893. Church leaders had also encouraged local units to establish academies to meet the educational needs of the Saints. These schools continued to receive a substantial portion of Church appropriations. Expenditures for welfare also increased during the depression of the mid-1890s. The Church invested funds to develop essential Intermountain industries, but during the business slump they returned no profit. These difficult times led to yet another drop in the Church's tithing income. Thus the Church had to borrow in order to meet its obligations.

When Lorenzo Snow became President of the Church he faced a debt in excess of $1.25 million, most of it owed to "gentile" (or non-Latter-day Saint) creditors.[15] He therefore decided to sell bonds in order to meet the Church's debt. This move had at least three advantages: (1) It gained badly needed time during which a permanent solution could be sought. (2) Interest on the bonds was at a lower and hence more favorable rate than the existing debt. (3) The bonds were sold to the Church's own members. President Snow preferred to borrow "among ourselves" rather than "go into the world." Three issues of a half million dollars each were planned. The first two series were issued in January 1899. Significant new developments, however, would make the third series unnecessary.

President Snow's Revelation on Tithing

During the spring of 1899 President Lorenzo Snow was impressed to go to St. George in southern Utah and to take with him as many of the General Authorities as could be spared at Church headquarters. There he would receive by revelation the key to solving the Church's immediate financial difficulties, providing the solid foundation for the growth that was to occur during the twentieth century. This vital revelation, however, did not come immediately. Upon arrival in St. George, President Snow paced the floor having "the most painful and anxious expression on his face that I had ever seen," his son, LeRoi, later recalled. "Why have I come to St. George? . . ." the President worried aloud. "Why have I come here?"

LeRoi C. Snow described what happened at the special conference on Wednesday, May 17, 1899, in the St. George Tabernacle:

> I was sitting at a table on the stand, reporting the proceedings, when all at once father paused in his discourse. Complete stillness filled the room. I shall never forget the thrill as long as I live. When he commenced to speak again his voice strengthened and the inspiration of God seemed to come over him, as well as over the entire assembly. His eyes seemed to brighten and his countenance to shine. He was filled with unusual power. Then he revealed to the Latter-day Saints the vision that was before him.
>
> God manifested to him there and then not only the purpose of the call to visit the Saints in the South, but also Lorenzo

Snow's special mission, the great work for which God had prepared and preserved him, and he unveiled the vision to the people. He told them that he could see, as he had never realized before, how the law of tithing had been neglected by the people.

The President stressed that faithful compliance with the law would become the means of releasing the Church as well as individual members from the burden of debt. "The word of the Lord is: The time has now come for every Latter-day Saint, who calculates to be prepared for the future and to hold his feet strong upon a proper foundation, to do the will of the Lord and to pay his tithing in full. That is the word of the Lord to you, and it will be the word of the Lord to every settlement throughout the land of Zion."

Referring to the prolonged drought in southern Utah, President Snow assured his listeners that if they would pay an honest tithing they could with faith plant their crops for the coming season. "He promised them, in the name of the Lord," his son reported, "that the clouds would gather, the rains from heaven descend, their lands would be drenched, and the rivers and ditches filled, and they would reap a bounteous harvest that very season."

Later that evening President Snow reflected: "Now I know why I came to St. George. The Lord sent me here, and he has a great work for me to perform. There is no mistake about it. I can see the great future for the Church and I can hardly wait to get back to Salt Lake City to commence the great work. . . ."[16]

On his way back home, President Snow visited various communities, where he repeated his exhortations for the Saints to honor the law of tithing. Upon arriving in Salt Lake City he found the annual conference of the Young Men's and Young Women's Mutual Improvement associations in session. President Snow recognized this gathering as the means of getting the principle of tithing before the youth of the entire Church. At a meeting of the Young Men's officers on May 30, President Snow gave an impressive discourse on tithing that those who were present accepted by formal resolution as "the word of the Lord to them, which they promised to accept and obey themselves, and would do all in their power to get the whole membership of the Church to do likewise." President Snow was visibly affected. He arose and said: "Brethren, the God of our fathers, Abraham, Isaac and Jacob bless you. Every man who is here, who has made this promise, will be saved in the Celestial kingdom. God bless you. Amen."

A solemn assembly of priesthood leaders convened in the Salt Lake Temple on July 2. "The call for this assembly did not originate in his own mind," President Snow's son testified, "but as a command from the Lord who revealed it in vision." All the General Authorities were present, and all forty stakes were represented. During the session, which lasted from 10:00 A.M. to 7:00 P.M., each of the eighteen speakers referred to the renewed tithing revelation, which was again accepted as "the word and will of the Lord through President Snow to the Church."[17]

As a whole, the Saints in southern Utah faithfully accepted President Snow's challenge and gave much more than one-tenth of their income to the Lord's work. After some anxious weeks the rains came and the crops were saved. Similarly, as the Saints all over the Church faithfully complied with the law of tithing, the promised blessings were realized. The burden of debt was overcome. By 1907 Joseph F. Smith, who had succeeded Lorenzo Snow as President of the Church, announced that the increased tithes had enabled the Church to pay all its obligations. Since that time the Church has been able to remain free from debt, and tithing has continued to be the largest source of financial support for many and varied religious programs worldwide.

Worldwide Mission of the Church

At the dawning of the twentieth century, President Lorenzo Snow was impressed with the necessity of taking the gospel message to all the world. To this end, in 1901 he appointed Elder Heber J. Grant of the Quorum of the Twelve to open a new mission in Japan. Elder Grant selected three others to accompany him on this mission. Because of formidable cultural and language barriers, however, the fruits of the Elders'

Elder Heber J. Grant dedicates the land of Japan for the preaching of the gospel on Sunday, September 1, 1901. Accompanying Elder Grant on this wooded hillside just south of Yokohama are (from left) Horace S. Ensign, Alma O. Taylor, and (far right) Louis B. Kelsch. (Utah State Historical Society)

labors were meager. Only after eighteen long months of tedious language study did the first pair of missionaries venture out among the Japanese people. Speaking in general conference upon his return in 1903, Elder Grant admitted, "To be perfectly frank with you, I acknowledge I have accomplished very little indeed." Only three converts had been baptized. "At the same time," he continued, "I have assurance in my heart there will yet be a great and important labor accomplished in that land."[18] These early missionaries had laid a foundation upon which future growth would be built, although the flourishing of the work in that land would not come until after World War II.

President Snow regarded opening the mission in Japan as only a beginning. He also had in mind carrying the gospel to Russia and Austria, as well as to the republics of Latin America.

These desires, however, would not be fulfilled during his lifetime.

Role of the Twelve and the Seventy

President Lorenzo Snow believed that two particular groups of the General Authorities had a special responsibility to take the lead in accomplishing the Church's worldwide mission. In 1901 he declared:

> I want to say, here are the Apostles and the Seventies, their business is to warn the nations of the earth and prepare the world for the coming of the Savior. They have been engaged in this more or less. Now we find ourselves in a compact, gathered condition. . . . It looks to me that our minds ought to extend somewhat, and we get out of the beaten track, and a little change be made. For instance, we have started in this direction by sending Brother Grant over to Japan, but this is only a start. Things seem to be going favorable with him; but whether he will accomplish much or not matters not in one sense; it is for the Apostles to show to the Lord that they are his witnesses to all the nations, and that they are doing the best they can.[19]

During the nineteenth century's era of colonization, Church leaders, particularly the Twelve, had become intimately involved in the administration of local Church affairs. But President Lorenzo Snow now became quite concerned at the amount of time the Twelve Apostles and also the Seventy were spending with auxiliary organizations such as the Young Men's Mutual Improvement Association. In his last public discourse he gave emphasis to this theme:

> . . . It is not for the apostles to look after [local bishops]. The apostles have a work that is in another direction altogether. I want the presidents of stakes hereafter to realize that it is their business, not the business of the Apostles; it is the business of the high priests, the elders, the bishops, priests, teachers, and deacons, to look after these things. Do not lay this duty upon the shoulders of the Apostles. It is not in their line, at least only occasionally. . . .
>
> The apostles and the seventies—it is their business, *by the appointment of the Almighty, to look after the interests of the world.* The seventies and twelve apostles are special witnesses unto the nations of the earth. . . .[20]

This responsibility to carry the gospel to the world was shared by the Church's corps of proselyting missionaries. While at first most missionaries were married men who left home to preach for relatively short periods of time, by the 1890s young unmarried elders were much more common among the missionaries' ranks. In 1898 "lady missionaries" were called for the first time (although wives had sometimes been called to accompany their husbands into the mission field during earlier years). Many of these new missionaries had the benefit of special missionary-preparation courses at the Church's academies. Their work was further strengthened by a new series of tracts, "Rays of Living Light," authored by Elder Charles W. Penrose. These tracts formed the basis of "cottage meeting" discussions on basic gospel topics.

While responsibility for local Church ward activity was being shifted more squarely onto the shoulders of stake presidents and bishops, steps were also being taken to make these units more efficient. Before the turn of the century, some stakes had been very large, having as many as twenty thousand members. The entire Salt Lake Valley, for example, was covered by one single stake. By 1904 this area had been divided into six stakes. Churchwide, the average stake soon had only about five thousand members, a figure which would remain fairly constant throughout the twentieth century.

A New Emphasis on the "Gathering"

Consistent with President Snow's worldwide vision was a new understanding of the Saints' responsibility to "gather." During the nineteenth century, Mormon migration patterns had been dominated by a geographical gathering of converts from the nations of the earth to the centers of Latter-day Saint colonization in America. Early revelations proclaimed the importance of gathering: "Ye are called to bring to pass the gathering of mine elect . . . Wherefore the decree hath gone forth from the Father that they shall be gathered in unto one place . . . and be prepared in all things against the day when tribulation and desolation are sent forth upon the wicked." (D&C 29:7-8.) Another revelation commanded: "Wherefore, prepare ye, prepare ye, O my people; sanctify yourselves;

gather ye together, O ye people of my church, upon the land of Zion. . . . Go ye out of Babylon; gather ye out from among the nations . . ." (D&C 133:4, 7.) Such injunctions held a great appeal for the Saints in the Old World. Many of them lived in grimy industrial cities, while others struggled to earn their living as landless tenant farmers. Most belonged to small, persecuted Mormon branches whose meeting places were often dirty and grossly inadequate rented halls. Thus, during the nineteenth century, thousands of converts left their homes in the Old World, and many more would do so in the new century. While most were leaving unsatisfactory economic conditions behind, many appear to have been motivated primarily by the vision of helping to establish Zion in the promised land.

Revelations given through Joseph Smith also anticipated a second phase of the "gathering" that became more typical of the twentieth century. The time would come when there would no longer be just one gathering place, but "other places" or "stakes" would be appointed for the "strength of Zion." (See D&C 101:20-22.) This phase would be more spiritual than geographical. (See D&C 133:14.) Though remaining in their homelands, Saints would "gather" out of the wicked world and become identified with the Saints.

Church leaders decided to suspend the geographical gathering, at least temporarily, during the 1890s, a decade of particularly severe economic depression. Furthermore, as historian Frederick Jackson Turner noted, 1890 had marked the end of the frontier and of readily available free land in America. Most immigrants congregated in the cities; many failed to find work, became discouraged, and wanted to return home. It was just such conditions the Church wanted to avoid.[21] At about the turn of the century, the General Authorities began emphasizing that the need to gather into one place had passed, and that now the important task was to build up the "other places" around the world.[22]

This advice would be reiterated in a 1921 editorial in the *Millennial Star,* the Church's British magazine:

> The Counsel of The General Authorities to the yet ungathered Saints is not to flock Zionward under existing conditions; but to remain in the countries where they now dwell.

. . . Such as have home and employment especially, should stay and help build up the Lord's work in the various missions and conferences and branches, strengthening the hands of the elders and other missionaries labouring among them.[23]

The Church's counsel would be reinforced by restrictive immigration laws adopted by the United States during the 1920s; although most Latter-day Saint immigrants were from northern Europe, even they found it increasingly difficult to fit within the newly imposed American quotas.

This same counsel has continued to be given during the twentieth century. At the Mexico City area conference in 1972, Elder Bruce R. McConkie explained:

The gathering of Israel consists of joining the true Church, of coming to a knowledge of the true God and of his saving truths, and of worshiping him in the congregations of the Saints in all nations and among all peoples. Any person, therefore, who has accepted the restored gospel, and who now seeks to worship the Lord, in his own tongue, and among his own people, and with the Saints of his own nation has complied with the law of gathering and is entitled to all the blessings promised the Saints in these last days.

As Elder McConkie therefore declared:

The place of gathering for the Mexican Saints is in Mexico; the place of gathering for the Guatemalan Saints is in Guatemala; the place of gathering for the Brazilian Saints is in Brazil; and so it goes throughout the length and breadth of the whole earth. Japan is for the Japanese; Korea is for the Koreans; Australia is for the Australians; every nation is the gathering place for its own people.[24]

Lorenzo Snow presided over the Church for only three years. Nevertheless, his brief administration witnessed developments whose impact would be far-reaching. Not only did his Presidency straddle the turn of the century, but it can be regarded as an era of transition for several other reasons: He was the last President to come from the same generation as the Church's founding prophet, Joseph Smith. He helped define the inspired principles which would continue to guide succession in the Presidency of the Church. Through him, the Lord called for a rededication to tithe paying. President Snow proclaimed the Church's worldwide mission, and took steps to achieve it.

Nevertheless, the transition was not yet complete. Many key developments were to take place during the administration of President Joseph F. Smith, who would see the progress and prosperity that would follow the Church's overcoming its debt through the Saints' faithful payment of tithing. He would see a further reform of priesthood and auxiliary activities. However, he would also witness the resurgence of earlier anti-Mormon agitation. These attacks were at least in part an outgrowth of the "Progressive Era" in American politics that had its roots in the years covered by Lorenzo Snow's administration and would flourish during the opening years of his successor's. These developments are the subject of the following chapters.

2 The Church in the Progressive Era

The opening years of the twentieth century are known in United States history as the Progressive Era. Under the leadership of United States President Theodore Roosevelt, reform legislation sought to remedy such problems as unregulated monopolies, the wasting of natural resources, and unclean conditions in food-packing plants. The press's sensational exposés of slums and a variety of other social evils earned the nicknames "yellow journalism" or "muckraking." This reform era had its roots just before the turn of the century, so it overlapped the administrations of Church Presidents Lorenzo Snow and Joseph F. Smith. It was in this setting that the elections of two General Authorities, Elders B. H. Roberts and Reed Smoot, to the United States Congress sparked a revival of earlier agitation against the Mormons. Nevertheless, the Church took steps to improve its popular image, thus laying the foundation for the public relations efforts that would become increasingly important as the century progressed.

The Saints' Interest in Politics

The events of this period cannot be fully appreciated without an understanding of the background of earlier devel-

1887	Edmunds-Tucker Law provided for confiscation of Church property and barred polygamists from voting or holding office
1890	President Woodruff's Manifesto announced end of plural marriages
1896	Utah admitted as a state of the Union
1898	Lorenzo Snow became President of the Church
1900	Church resumed control of the *Deseret News;* B. H. Roberts excluded from U.S. House of Representatives
1901	Joseph F. Smith became President of the Church
1902	Bureau of Information opened on Temple Square
1904	U.S. Senate committee opened hearing on Elder Reed Smoot's election as a senator; President Joseph F. Smith issued "Second Manifesto" banning all new plural marriages
1905	Thomas Kearns attacked the Church in the Senate and affiliated with the American party in Utah; Elders John W. Taylor and Matthias Cowley resigned from the Quorum because of disagreement with Church leaders over plural marriage
1907	Smoot allowed to retain seat in the Senate; Church issued "Address to the World" to correct misunderstandings
1910	Wave of bitter anti-Mormon articles in national magazines
1917	Saints' support of war effort improved public attitude

opments. As part of the "Compromise of 1850," Utah had become a territory rather than a state. This meant that its key officials were appointed by the president of the United States rather than being elected by the people. Then, in 1852, the Church made the first public announcement of plural marriage. This practice quickly became the focal point of attacks directed against the Latter-day Saints. The federally appointed officials allied themselves with the small non-Mormon or "gentile" minority in Utah to form the Liberal party and to effectively dominate the political scene. In response, the Mormon majority formed the People's party to preserve whatever vestige of local self-government they could. With political issues drawn along these lines during the later nineteenth century, the Church inevitably found itself involved in politics.

A series of antibigamy laws culminated in the Edmunds-Tucker Act of 1887. This harsh law not only punished those convicted of polygamous living but also restricted the Saints' participation in elections, disincorporated the Church as an institution, and provided for the seizure of its assets. In 1889 the United States Supreme Court upheld this law as constitutional. This posed a dilemma for the Latter-day Saints who believed that the practice of plural marriage had been divinely revealed (see D&C Section 132), but who had been instructed to obey "that law of the land which is constitutional" (see D&C 98:5). While praying for guidance, President Wilford Woodruff was shown that the work of the Church would be disrupted by its enemies if the practice of plural marriage continued. Hence in 1890 he issued his inspired Official Declaration or Manifesto declaring: "Inasmuch as laws have been enacted by Congress forbidding plural marriages, which laws have been pronounced constitutional by the court of last resort, I hereby declare my intention to submit to those laws, and . . . publicly declare that my advice to the Latter-day Saints is to refrain from contracting any marriage forbidden by the law of the land." (Read Official Declaration 1 and accompanying statements in the 1981 edition of the Doctrine and Covenants.)

A brief era of good will toward the Mormons followed the termination of plural marriages, and the long-sought-for goal of Utah's statehood now appeared attainable. The People's party was disbanded, and Church leaders urged the Saints to identify themselves with one or another of the national political parties. Utah was finally admitted to the Union as a state in January 1896. Almost from the beginning, the Latter-day Saints had been taught to seek and uphold wise and good men (see D&C 98:10), and with the obtaining of statehood, they looked forward more than ever before to getting involved in the political process. Because the Mormons dominated the population of the new state, there were concerns that the Church would continue to dominate politics. To dispel these fears, and to encourage leading Church officers not to become so involved in political matters that they would neglect their ecclesiastical responsibilities, the General Authorities issued the following "political manifesto" in April of that year:

> We unanimously agree to, and promulgate as a rule, that should always be observed in the church and by every leading official thereof, that before accepting any position, political or otherwise, which would interfere with the proper and complete discharge of his ecclesiastical duties, and before accepting a nomination or entering into engagements to perform new duties, said official should apply to the proper authorities and learn from them whether he can, consistently with the obligations already entered into with the church upon assuming his office, take upon himself the added duties and labors and responsibilities of the new position.[1]

The Roberts Case

It was in this setting that Utah Democrats urged Elder Brigham H. Roberts, a member of the First Council of the Seventy, to run for Congress. Although Utah's constitution provided that new plural marriages should forever be prohibited, there was a general unwritten understanding that men who had already entered into plural marriage prior to the 1890 Manifesto would not be subject to prosecution and would not be required to abandon their plural families as long as they did not marry any additional wives. Elder Roberts had married all three of his wives before 1890, so party leaders were confident that there would be no problem. His nomination in 1898, however, brought the charge of a "reversion to polygamy." Protestant ministers led the attack, accusing the Church of a breach of faith by again attempting to control politics and by renewing the approval of polygamy. Church leaders emphatically denied these charges, and Roberts won the election easily.

His opponents, however, promoted a nationwide campaign against him. When he arrived in Washington, his right to take his seat in Congress was challenged. A "monster" petition claiming over seven million signatures was presented, and the nation's newspapers and magazines were full of articles attacking Roberts and the Mormons. By a ratio of about five to one the House of Representatives voted to exclude Roberts, an action that has been taken extremely rarely in American history. It was evident that the Latter-day Saints had not yet been fully accepted and were still under the necessity of convincing the nation of their good faith.

As Elder Roberts reflected on the nature and motivation of the opposition, he concluded that "the real cause of this anti-Mormon crusade was a fight for the political control of Utah on the part of the crusaders." Although they professed to be interested in "preserving the purity of the American home," Roberts charged that a majority of them were "not exemplars of that chastity [which] they in this struggle affected. . . . Their concern about the alleged evils of polygamy was mere pretense."[2]

The Smoot Case

Elder Reed Smoot was elected to the United States Senate by Utah's Republican legislature in January 1903. Formerly a businessman in Provo and Salt Lake City, he had become a member of the Quorum of the Twelve Apostles three years earlier. Even though he had obtained a "leave of absence" from his ecclesiastical duties, his election immediately revived the old charges of a violation of the proper separation of church and state. As they had done in the case of Elder Roberts four years earlier, Salt Lake City ministers, editors, and others mounted a nationwide campaign, and protests against Reed Smoot poured into the Senate from all parts of the country. However, Elder Smoot was sworn in as a senator and allowed to take his seat. Nevertheless, the Committee on Privileges and Elections was authorized to conduct a thorough investigation of the whole affair and to determine whether or not Smoot was qualified to remain in the Senate.

The committee's chairman was Senator Julius C. Burrows of Michigan. His grandfather had been a member of the Church during the days of the Prophet Joseph Smith and had marched with Zion's Camp in 1834, but was subsequently excommunicated. This family background may have added to Senator Burrows's prejudice against the Latter-day Saints.[3]

The Smoot hearings did not get under way until January 1904. A variety of charges were presented against the Mormon senator. The accusation of polygamy was easily dismissed, as Elder Smoot was a monogamist. Others alleged that Smoot was a member of a "self-perpetuating body of fifteen men" (the First Presidency and the Twelve) who controlled Utah's economy and politics and secretly encouraged the continued practice of plural marriage. He was also accused of having taken a secret oath of disloyalty to the United States. Senator Smoot responded by emphasizing the legality of his election. Numerous and varied witnesses were called by both sides. Even President Joseph F. Smith was required to testify. For three days he frankly admitted that he was still living with his plural wives and answered other prying questions about his personal life and sacred aspects of his religion. He stressed that Latter-day Saints have their agency, that binding doctrines are found in the standard works, and that Church members are not obligated to accept as doctrine the political opinions of those occupying prominent offices. President Smith believed that when his testimony began all the senators except one were unfriendly, but that he had won the respect of several others before he was through.

The committee's hearings dragged on for two and a half years; a report of the proceedings filled more than thirty-four hundred pages in four large volumes. Here again, the press widely reported the hearings, but unfortunately it emphasized only the more sensational aspects of the testimony, and generally that which was less favorable to the Church. Finally, in June 1906, the committee concluded that Reed Smoot was not entitled to serve as the senator from Utah; eight, including Burrows, voted for this majority report. A minority of five other committee members, however, believed that no just grounds had been found to disqualify or expel Smoot.

President William Howard Taft (left) and Senator Reed Smoot share the same car in a parade in Salt Lake City, Utah. (Utah State Historical Society)

    Six months passed before the Senate chose to consider the committee's report. From December 13, 1906, to February 20, 1907, Reed Smoot's fate was debated in the Senate. Boies Penrose, a leader in the Senate, is reported to have quipped: "I don't see why we can't get along just as well with a polygamist who doesn't polyg as we do with a lot of monogamists who don't monog."[4] A two-thirds vote was required to approve the committee's recommendation to oust Smoot. When the vote was taken, twenty-eight, or only 40 percent, voted in favor of the report, forty-two voted against, and twenty abstained. Thus Elder Smoot had received the support of nearly two-thirds of those voting. He went on to a distinguished thirty-year career in the Senate, and earned the respect of his colleagues with his personal integrity and hard work. He played a particularly influential role as chairman of the Senate Finance Committee.

Some Lingering Challenges

Even though Elder Reed Smoot had been allowed to retain his seat in the Senate, the prolonged hearings demonstrated that certain questions continued to trouble many people: Had the Mormons really given up their practice of polygamy? Was the Church attempting to control politics? These concerns sparked the revival of an anti-Mormon political party in Utah and of widespread attacks in the nation's newspapers and magazines.

The Question of Continuing Polygamy

It was only natural that the practice of plural marriage would not be easy to give up. Since it had become so much a part of the belief and personal lives of individual members of the Church, it was not to be expected that everyone involved would suddenly change his feelings, even though the change of practice had been required by the President of the Church.

Mormon polygamy had been a prominent topic in the Smoot hearings, but Church witnesses there emphasized that the practice had been suspended. A Church census revealed only 897 polygamous families in 1902, in contrast to the 2,451 that had existed when the 1890 Manifesto was issued. The Senate committee's investigation, however, disclosed that new polygamous marriages actually had been performed by certain leaders of the Church since the Manifesto. Specifically involved were two Apostles, John W. Taylor and Matthias F. Cowley. Both men believed that the Manifesto applied only to members of the Church living within the United States.

As a result, just a few weeks after his appearance before the Senate committee in Washington, President Smith issued an official statement at the 1904 April conference. Sometimes called the Second Manifesto, the statement reiterated:

> Inasmuch as there are numerous reports in circulation that plural marriages have been entered into contrary to the official declaration of President Woodruff, of September 26, 1890 . . . which forbade any marriages violative of the law of the land; I Joseph F. Smith, president of the Church of Jesus Christ of Latter-day Saints, do hereby affirm and declare that no such marriages have been so solemnized with the sanction, consent,

or knowledge of the Church of Jesus Christ of Latter-day Saints; and I hereby announce that all such marriages are prohibited, and if any officer or member of the Church shall assume to solemnize or enter into any such marriages he will be deemed in transgression against the Church and will be liable to be dealt with, according to the rules and regulations thereof, and excommunicated therefrom.[5]

This new statement clearly stressed that the ban on plural marriage applied worldwide and that no new plural marriages would be authorized anywhere, even in the Mormon colonies of Mexico and Canada. President Smith also directed that the 1890 Manifesto be included in the Doctrine and Covenants; this answered critics who had pointed out that the Doctrine and Covenants included the revelation authorizing plural marriages but did not include the declaration suspending them. The problem remained, however, as some members, including Elders Cowley and Taylor, still refused to accept the new position as binding. In October 1905 the First Presidency took the very unusual step of asking for their resignation. Elder Taylor acknowledged that he was out of harmony with the General Authorities' interpretation of the 1890 Manifesto:

I have always believed that the government of the United States had jurisdiction only within its own boundaries, and that the term, "Laws of the land" in the manifesto meant merely the laws of the United States. I find now that this opinion is different to that expressed by the Church authorities, who have declared that the prohibition against plural marriage extended to every place and to every part of the Church. It is doubtless true that this view of the matter has been given by President Woodruff and others, but I have never taken that as binding upon me or the Church, because it was never presented for adoption by "common consent," as was the manifesto itself, and I have disputed its authority as a law or a rule of the Church.[6]

Several groups continued to insist that plural marriage is an essential doctrine and to perform such marriages. On several subsequent occasions during the twentieth century the First Presidency has denounced these so-called fundamentalists, and the Church's policy has been to excommunicate anyone practicing plural marriage.

Revival of Anti-Mormon Agitation

As has been seen, the elections of Elders Roberts and Smoot to Congress provided the occasion for a revival of attacks directed against the Church and its members. In the spirit of the Progressive Era, "muckraking" journalists dwelled on what they called "the twin relics of Mormonism—polygamy and hierarchy." *Polygamy* of course referred to the alleged continuation of plural marriages, and *hierarchy* to the undue influence Church leaders were accused of exerting over secular affairs, including political and economic concerns. The phrase "twin relics" was borrowed from a plank in the 1856 Republican party platform that promised to eradicate "the twin relics of barbarism—slavery and polygamy."

A leading source of anti-Mormon agitation was Thomas Kearns, a non-Mormon who, along with Reed Smoot, served as a senator from Utah. In 1905, near the close of his term, Kearns delivered a bitter attack in the Senate condemning Mormon leaders as a monarchy that dominated the political, business, and social life in Utah and secretly permitted their favorites to continue taking plural wives. The reason for Kearns's bitterness, the historian B. H. Roberts believed, was President Joseph F. Smith's refusal to help reelect the senator.[7] Ironically, Kearns was now attacking the very political influence that he himself had unsuccessfully attempted to gain from the Church.

Another source of attack was the American party, which had been organized in Utah in 1904. This was actually a revival of the old anti-Mormon Liberal party. Reasons for organizing the new party came from charges in the Reed Smoot hearings of continued polygamy and Church interference in politics. One of the party's chief financial backers was Senator Kearns, who had also purchased the *Salt Lake Tribune.* He named as editor Frank J. Cannon, who had been an influential Mormon but was now an embittered enemy of the Church. Under their leadership, the *Tribune* defamed the Church and specifically President Joseph F. Smith on almost a daily basis. Some commented that the infamous *Nauvoo Expositor* was "holy writ" when compared to the *Tribune.*

Salt Lake City's *Deseret News* was a key medium through which the Church answered these attacks and proclaimed its message. While President Lorenzo Snow had generally desired to sell businesses in which the Church had invested during earlier times, he saw the value of maintaining an active interest in this newspaper. The Church had leased the *News* to a private company in 1892, but resumed direct control January 1, 1899, in the midst of the discussions surrounding Elder Roberts's election to the House of Representatives. Charles W. Penrose, an experienced and capable journalist, was reinstated as the paper's editor. The *Deseret News* came to be recognized as the Church's official newspaper voice, and Penrose (who became a member of the Quorum of the Twelve in 1904) made a substantial contribution in defending the Church.

Many of the charges published in the *Salt Lake Tribune* were picked up by the nation's periodical press. The years 1910 and 1911 brought a revival of anti-Mormon writing in the American press. Four popular magazines particularly involved were *Pearson's, Everybody's Magazine, McClure's,* and *Cosmopolitan.* These sensationalized denunciations of the Church and its leaders displayed little understanding of the spirit and objectives of Mormon society. The depth to which criticism could sink was seen in a particularly negative series of articles in *Cosmopolitan* during 1911. The first article in the series, entitled "The Viper on the Hearth," was headed with an illustration of a huge snake coiled around a defenseless family. The writer asserted that the viper was the Mormon Church preparing for the time when it could inflict a fatal strike on the family structure of America and take over the nation both politically and economically. Another cartoon in the series depicted President Joseph F. Smith as the head of a huge octopus whose tentacles were reaching out to grasp education, industry, the government, and so on.

Being published in nationally circulated magazines, such articles did much to hurt the Church's image. They were often filled with obvious distortions of the facts. For example, the *Cosmopolitan* writer, who claimed to have spent several months among the Mormons researching his articles, asserted that the Saints believed that Thummim and Urim were two "stenographic angels" who aided Joseph Smith with his translation of the Book of Mormon.[8]

President Smith chose not to respond to such charges but rather declared: "I bear no malice toward any of the children of my Father. But there are enemies of the work of the Lord as there were enemies to the Son of God. There are those who speak only evil of the Latter-day Saints. There are those—and they abound largely in our midst—who will shut their eyes to every virtue and to every good thing connected with this latter-day work, and will pour out floods of falsehood and misrepresentation against the people of God. I forgive them for this. I leave them in the hands of the just judge."[9]

Opposition Overseas

Not only in the United States but also in Europe the Church lacked general public acceptance. Negative stories circulated by the clergy and printed in newspapers created suspicion and ill will. Missionaries frequently reported being criticized, driven out of town, and even having stones thrown at them. In 1906, the German government decreed that Mormon teachings were "subversive of morality" and ordered the Church to withdraw from the country. This forced the eight thousand German Saints to conduct the Church activities in Germany themselves. By 1910, however, a few missionaries had returned to various parts of Germany.

A special conference directed by the Apostle Rudger Clawson convened in Berlin on July 21, 1910. "The hall was crowded with Saints and friends, but the occasion was greatly marred by the entrance of several police who unceremoniously and defiant to politeness interrupted President Clawson's speech and closed the meeting." The German members were permitted to leave, but the missionaries, the mission president, and the following day even Elder Clawson were imprisoned and then banished from Prussia.[10]

In Europe as in America, a popular theme in attacks against the Church was the supposed continuation of plural marriages. Reports from the American "muckraking" magazine crusade reached Great Britain at a time when conservatives were speaking out against the erosion of traditional Victorian virtues. British Latter-day Saints shared conservatives' concerns over growing immorality, abortion, and divorce. Ironically, however, certain crusaders made the Mormons the symbol of immoral living, and the evils of polygamy became a central theme of their lectures and rallies. Some novels and movies even followed the plot of an innocent young heroine being rescued from a crafty American missionary. In a few isolated areas emotions ran so high that anti-Mormon rallies turned to violence. Mud and rocks were hurled at chapels in Birkenhead and Nuneaton, a branch president was tarred and feathered, and missionaries were harassed out of town. In the face of such agitation, the level of convert baptisms dropped during the second decade of the twentieth century. Nevertheless, there were some sympathetic newspapers willing to publish the Church's response to such attacks. The *London Evening Times,* for example, carried a statement by the First Presidency explaining the Church's basic teachings and its stand on emigration and plural marriage.[11]

Efforts to Create More Favorable Attitudes

The magazine crusade, together with earlier sensational publicity during the Roberts and Smoot elections, tended to reinforce the negative public attitudes about Mormons and Mormonism that had lingered from the nineteenth century. That had been an era of ignorance and persecution. There had been almost no contact between the main body of the Latter-day Saints and the public as a whole. In such a setting, misrepresentations were accepted as fact because most people had no personal experience with Mormons to suggest otherwise. During the opening years of the twentieth century, however, the Church took steps to remedy the problem, and some improvement resulted.

The First Bureau of Information

At the turn of the century, even those who came to Salt Lake City were not guaranteed to hear the truth about the Latter-day Saints. Hotel operators would send employees with carriages to meet incoming trains and vie for guests. These hack drivers made quite a business of filling visitors with wild

Temple Square in Salt Lake City soon after the Bureau of Information opened in 1902. (Church Archives)

tales about the Mormons. Both community and Church leaders were concerned about the negative image this practice was creating. Discussions among members of the Young Men's Mutual Improvement Association general board and the First Council of the Seventy resulted in the specific recommendation that a "bureau of information" be established on Temple Square to provide correct information to those visiting the city. In 1902 the First Presidency approved this project and assigned the Seventy to take charge of it. The first building was an octagonal structure measuring twenty feet across and costing six hundred dollars. About two dozen volunteers staffed the bureau; during its first year of operation they distributed Articles of Faith cards and other literature to 150,000 visitors. At last visitors to Salt Lake City were learning about the Mormons from the Mormons themselves.

Popularity of the guided tours of Temple Square continued to grow, and in 1906 free organ recitals were added. A new nine-thousand-dollar building was erected in 1904, and as the number of visitors continued to increase, ever more commodious facilities were provided. In later years of the twentieth century, annual visitors to the square would number in the millions.

The "Address to the World"

In April 1907, just a few weeks after the Senate had finally voted to allow Elder Reed Smoot to retain his seat, the Church took another step to present its case. The First Presidency's sixteen-page "Address to the World" was adopted by unanimous vote in general conference. This powerful yet conciliatory statement emphatically denied the charges made against the Church, and clearly set forth its major doctrines, ideals, and aspirations. It upheld the facts that Mormonism respected the sanctity of marriage, that it opposed tyranny, that its tithes were not used for the benefit of the leaders, that the Church believed in and upheld the government of the United States, and that the Church had long since abandoned plural marriage. A group of Utah ministers published a review criticizing the Church's address, but their efforts received little attention and so had minimal effect.[12]

Some Positive Signs

In 1911, at the peak of the "magazine crusade," the Mormon Tabernacle Choir accepted an invitation to sing at the American Land and Irrigation exposition in New York City. During their tour, the choir presented more than four dozen concerts in twenty-five cities, spending ten days at Madison Square Garden in New York City and making an appearance at the White House in Washington, D.C. The choir was well received, and favorable comments by music critics helped contribute to an improving image of the Latter-day Saints.

An important opportunity to present correct information about the Church came when the editors of *Americana* magazine invited Elder B. H. Roberts to respond to some false information published earlier. They were so pleased with his writing that they invited him to prepare a more thorough explanation of the Church's origins and history. When Elder Roberts discussed the scope of the proposed project with the editors, they agreed to expand their magazine from bimonthly publication to a monthly format and to devote most of its space to the Mormon articles. Roberts's history appeared serially from 1909 to 1915 and was later published in book form in connection with the Church's 1930 centennial.[13]

The former president of the United States, Theodore Roosevelt, gave a helping hand to the Church when, on April 15, 1911, he allowed *Collier's* magazine to publish a letter he had written refuting many of the charges made against the Church and its leaders. In the letter he denied allegations that he had made political deals with the Mormons and strongly proclaimed the virtues and high standards of the Mormon people.[14] In Great Britain, an investigation initiated by Home Secretary Winston Churchill had the effect of putting to rest false reports about the Mormons that had been circulating in that land. The interest of such influential individuals as Roosevelt and Churchill augured well for a growing spirit of fairness in dealing with the Church and its members.

Another reflection of the changing situation was the statement made in 1916 by Charles C. Goodwin. Goodwin, who in earlier years as editor of the *Salt Lake Tribune* had been an outspoken enemy of the Church, said: "A more kindly and benevolent man has seldom held an exalted ecclesiastical position in these latter days than President Joseph F. Smith. . . . To his people he is a great spiritual leader. To men at large he is a man of wide sympathies, great business acumen, and a born leader of the great institution of which he is the head."[15]

Thus the opening years of the twentieth century saw the Church of Jesus Christ overcome many problems that had persisted for years. The Church's debt was paid by 1906. The last really bitter attacks in the national press appeared in 1911. That same year marked the end of the anti-Mormon American party's control of Salt Lake City politics. The Church was making headway in answering charges that had been raised by "muckraking" journalists and politicians of the Progressive Era.

But there was much more going on in the Church during these years. Under the leadership of President Joseph F. Smith, the Church expanded its programs, reached out to meet the needs of Saints in other lands, and helped to clarify the members' understanding of key gospel doctrines. In this way foundations were being laid for future progress.

3 Joseph F. Smith: An Era of Transition

President Joseph F. Smith led the Church during most of the first two decades of the twentieth century. His administration as well as his personal life represented important links with the past as well as with the future.

Joseph F. Smith's Earlier Life

Joseph F. Smith was born in Far West, Missouri, on November 13, 1838, in the midst of one of the most bitter periods of anti-Mormon persecution. His parents were Hyrum and Mary Fielding Smith. Within his first year, the Saints had been driven from Missouri and had commenced to build the city of Nauvoo in Illinois. He was only five years old when his father and his uncle, the Prophet Joseph Smith, were martyred in the Carthage Jail. The impression of this personal tragedy would remain with him throughout his life.

In 1848 he helped his widowed mother drive an ox team across the plains to Utah, performing most of the duties of a man. On one occasion their oxen were lost and could not be found despite a diligent search. Suddenly his mother arose and

1838	November 13: Born in Far West, Missouri
1844	Father and uncle, Hyrum and Joseph Smith, martyred at Carthage Jail (age 5)
1852	Became orphan when mother died (13)
1854-57	Mission to Hawaii (15-18)
1859	Called to Salt Lake Stake high council (20)
1860-63	Mission to Great Britain
1864	Special assignment to Hawaii
1865-74	Member of territorial house of representatives
1866	Ordained as Apostle (27)
1874-77	Two terms as president of European Mission
1878	Mission to eastern U.S. to gather Church history information
1880	Became Second Counselor in First Presidency (41)
1884-91	Voluntary exile due to plural marriage persecution
1901	Sustained as President of the Church (63)
1903	Carthage Jail became first of several Church history sites purchased
1904	Testified at Smoot hearings; issued "Second Manifesto"
1905	LDS Hospital opened in Salt Lake City; monument dedicated at Joseph Smith's birthplace in Vermont
1906	Became first to visit Europe as Church President
1909	First Presidency issued statement on "The Origin of Man"
1913	Site dedicated for Alberta Temple
1915	Site dedicated for temple in Hawaii; *Jesus the Christ* by James E. Talmage published
1916	Issued doctrinal exposition on "The Father and the Son"
1917	New Church Administration Building occupied
1918	October 3: Received a vision of the redemption of the dead
	November 19: Died in Salt Lake City (80)

began walking toward a nearby river, even though she had been told that her oxen had been seen earlier in the opposite direction. She found them in a deep gulch by the river bank, perfectly concealed from view. "This circumstance," Joseph later reflected, "was one of the first practical and positive demonstrations of the efficacy of prayer I had ever witnessed. It made an indelible impression upon my mind and has been a source of comfort, assurance and guidance to me throughout my life."[1]

The family settled on a farm just southeast of Salt Lake City. The heavy responsibilities carried by Widow Smith weakened her physically, and she died in 1852, leaving her thirteen-year-old son an orphan.

At the April general conference in 1854, Joseph was one of those whose names were read in a call to fulfill missions to the Hawaiian Islands. As Elder Parley P. Pratt set the fifteen-year-old boy apart, he promised him that he would learn the Hawaiian language "by the gift of God as well as by study."[2] In fulfillment of this blessing, Joseph was able to learn the language in only three months. "My desire to speak was very strong," he later recorded; "it was present with me night and day, and I never permitted an opportunity of talking with the natives to pass without improving it. I also tried to exercise faith before the Lord to obtain the gift of talking and understanding the language." He declared that he could teach the gospel and perform ordinances "with greater ease" in Hawaiian than he could in English.[3] During his three years in Hawaii he had to overcome fatigue, severe and prolonged illness, and material loss by flood and fire. The young missionary healed the sick, cast out devils, and had the opportunity of presiding over several branches of the Church. These trying as well as rewarding experiences helped him to develop an even stronger faith in his Heavenly Father and a lasting love for the Hawaiian people.

By the time Joseph F. Smith was twenty-seven years old, he had served two missions to Hawaii and another to Great Britain. He had married, had gone to work in the Church historian's office, and had been elected to the territorial legislature.

In 1866, at the age of only twenty-seven, Joseph F. Smith was ordained an Apostle by President Brigham Young, and served briefly as one of his special additional counselors. When a vacancy occurred in the Twelve the following year, Elder Smith was sustained as a member of that quorum.

During the next decade and a half, Elder Joseph F. Smith was called to preside over settlements in Utah and Davis counties respectively, to serve twice as president of the European Mission, and to direct the work in the Endowment House. One of his most interesting assignments came in 1878. He was appointed to go east with Elder Orson Pratt "to gather up records and data relative to the early history of the Church." They first went to Missouri, where they visited the temple site in Independence and had several valuable conversations with David Whitmer, one of the Three Witnesses to the Book of Mormon, in nearby Richmond. They visited Elder Smith's birthplace in Far West and stopped at other places in Illinois before going on to Kirtland, Palmyra, the Hill Cumorah, and New York City. On their way back west, they contacted Elder Smith's cousin, Joseph Smith III, the president of the Reorganized Church. This trip heightened Joseph F. Smith's interest in Church history sites, many of which he was later instrumental in purchasing.

When the First Presidency was reorganized in 1880, three years following the death of Brigham Young, George Q. Cannon became the First Counselor and Joseph F. Smith the Second Counselor to President John Taylor. These same two men later served as counselors to Presidents Wilford Woodruff and Lorenzo Snow.

Unfortunately, however, Joseph F. Smith's service in the Presidency was seriously hampered by the persecution of the Saints over their practice of plural marriage. He had married six wives and eventually became the father of forty-three children, plus five more who were adopted. He therefore had to go into "exile" or "retirement" from 1884 to 1891. During this trying period he visited outlying settlements and otherwise served the Church as best he could. In 1888, for example, he was sent to Washington, D.C., to represent the Church there. He was accompanied by Charles W. Penrose, who was the editor of the *Deseret News.* Because of the intense prejudice against the Mormons, the two men had to travel under assumed names— President Smith being known as Jason Mack (the name of his great-uncle) and Brother Penrose as Charles Williams. During an interview, the president of the United States counseled them that if the Mormons would do away with the doctrines of prophets and revelation and abandon the practice of plural marriage, and become like everybody else, all difficulties would disappear. The brethren agreed that the predicted result would follow if they did what the president said, "but to follow such counsel was to destroy the Church and bring to naught the work which the Lord planted in the earth never again to be taken away or destroyed."[4]

Joseph F. Smith did not come out of hiding until the proclamation of amnesty in 1891. At the October general conference the complete First Presidency was seated together on the stand for the first time in seven and a half years. The changing attitude toward the Saints during the 1890s was reflected in the fact that Joseph F. Smith, who had so recently had to spend seven years in exile, was now invited to participate in the convention called to draw up a constitution for the new state of Utah. As has been seen, this decade was only a brief lull in the storm of anti-Mormon persecution that would become one of the challenges facing Joseph F. Smith during his years as President of the Church.

President Lorenzo Snow died on October 10, 1901. Just one week later the Apostles met and sustained Joseph F. Smith as the sixth President of the Church. He and his counselors were sustained at a special conference that convened in the Tabernacle on November 10. His administration would move the Church in a positive direction to reach out and bless the lives of Church members worldwide.

An Era of Prosperity

Being the father of a large family had taught Joseph F. Smith prudent financial practices. This, plus his experience as counselor to three former Church Presidents, helped prepare him to direct the financial affairs of the Church.

Carthage Jail in Illinois, where the Prophet Joseph Smith was martyred. The Church purchased the jail in 1904, the year after this photograph was taken. (Church Archives)

President Smith continued his predecessor's emphasis on tithe paying, and the Saints' faithful response enabled the Church to pay off all its debt by the end of 1906. It was with justifiable pride that President Smith could announce at the April general conference in 1907: "Today The Church of Jesus Christ of Latter-day Saints owes not a dollar that it cannot pay at once. At last we are in a position that we can pay as we go. We do not have to borrow any more, and we won't have to if the Latter-day Saints continue to live their religion and observe the law of tithing. It is the law of revenue of the Church."[5] This ushered in a period of prosperity that enabled the Church to undertake activities not possible when the Saints were saddled with the burden of debt.

Historic Sites Purchased

Joseph F. Smith's personal background undoubtedly heightened his interest in Church history. During his administration the Church for the first time had the funds to begin purchasing sites important in its history. These purchases would help new generations of Latter-day Saints to more fully appreciate their religious heritage and spiritual roots.

The first of these sites to be purchased was the Carthage Jail in Illinois where President Smith's father, Hyrum, and his uncle, the Prophet Joseph Smith, had been martyred. Under his direction two acres were purchased on November 5, 1903, at a cost of four thousand dollars.

The Church also purchased the one hundred acres which constituted the Smith homestead in Manchester township near Palmyra, New York. This property included the Sacred Grove, where the Prophet received the First Vision in 1820. The Smiths' newer home stood near the site of the earlier log structure in which Joseph met the Angel Moroni in 1823.

Through four separate transactions between 1905 and 1907 the Church purchased the homestead of the Mack family (Joseph Smith's maternal ancestors) and some adjoining property, totaling 283 acres. This included the site of the Prophet's birth in 1805. A "memorial cottage" or small visitors' center was constructed on the site. Nearby, an imposing monument of polished Vermont granite was erected to honor the Prophet Joseph Smith. It was dedicated by President Joseph F. Smith on December 23, 1905, the one-hundredth anniversary of the Prophet's birth. The monument stood thirty-eight and one-half feet tall, one foot for each year of the Prophet's life.

Another significant acquisition was in Independence, Jackson County, Missouri, the place identified by revelations as the future site of the latter-day city of Zion. A tract of twenty-five acres was acquired on April 14, 1904. It was part of the original 63 acres purchased for the Saints in 1831, and it lies adjacent to the site which Joseph Smith dedicated for the temple in that year. A chapel and a mission home for the Central States Mission were subsequently erected on this property. The Church also established Zion's Printing and Publishing Company here. From this publishing house countless tracts, pamphlets, books, and other religious literature were furnished to the Latter-day Saint missions of North America. This operation continued until the 1940s, when it was consolidated with the Deseret News Press in Salt Lake City.

President Joseph F. Smith (third from right in back row) and other Church leaders dedicate monument near Sharon, Vermont, in 1905 on centennial anniversary of Joseph Smith's birth. (Church Archives)

A final purchase of property during the first decade of the twentieth century was made at Far West in northern Missouri. Here, under unusually trying circumstances, the Twelve had dedicated a temple site in 1839 in compliance with a revealed command of the Lord.[6]

These sites not only attracted Latter-day Saint visitors, but they also provided opportunities for the Church to share its message with the world. At several of them "bureaus of information" or visitors' centers, patterned after the successful program on Temple Square, were constructed to facilitate sharing the restored gospel.

President Joseph F. Smith also encouraged the work of the Church historian's office. For example, Elder B. H.

Roberts, one of the assistant Church historians, was assigned to edit Joseph Smith's history of the Church for publication in multi-volume form.

Important Building Projects

The Church's building program particularly benefited from the new era of prosperity. New buildings included many local meetinghouses as well as several key structures at or near Church headquarters. In 1905 the Latter-day Saints Hospital opened in Salt Lake City. Construction was financed primarily by general Church funds, to which was added a substantial donation from the estate of Dr. William S. Groves, after whom the hospital was officially named. This facility was the first in what would become a system of Church-operated hospitals during the twentieth century.

To finance such charitable enterprises as the LDS Hospital, as well as the Church's religious programs, President Joseph F. Smith followed the policy of making selected investments. For example, the Church maintained or acquired control of the *Deseret News,* Zion's Savings Bank and Trust Company, Utah-Idaho Sugar, and Beneficial Life Insurance Company. It also purchased about 25 percent of the ZCMI stock. In 1919 the Deseret Sunday School Union Book Store and the Deseret News Book Store combined to form the Church-controlled Deseret Book Company.

One of the Church's largest investments during this period was in the erection of the new Hotel Utah, which opened across the street from Temple Square in 1911. Perhaps no Church building project drew more criticism than did this one. Speaking in general conference, President Smith defended the Church's interest in this venture. He quoted from Doctrine and Covenants section 124, verse 60 and pointed out that the Hotel Utah should fill a function similar to that which the Lord had specified for the Nauvoo House—it should be a place where "the weary traveler" might find a resting place and "contemplate the glory of Zion." Responding to criticism that liquor was sold in the hotel, President Smith explained that the hotel was operated by an independent corporation, and took the

Church Administration Building in Salt Lake City. Completion of this structure in 1917 represented the Church's strength and stability. (Utah State Historical Society)

occasion to urge that the Saints themselves continue to observe the Word of Wisdom faithfully.[7]

In 1910 the Church opened the Deseret Gymnasium on the block just east of Temple Square. This new facility not only served the needs of the Latter-day Saints University located on the block, but provided for the recreational needs of the Saints in general.

One of the most critical needs was for adequate office space. For many years the work of the General Authorities, auxiliaries, and other Church organizations had been conducted from offices scattered around downtown Salt Lake City. The new Bishop's Building, dedicated in 1910 and located directly across the street from the Salt Lake Temple, provided accommodations for the Presiding Bishopric and most of the auxiliary organizations. Seven years later the

Church Administration Building was opened at 47 East South Temple Street. This handsome five-story granite structure featured fine marble and woodwork interiors. Although some people also criticized this building as too extravagant, it provided dignified accommodations for the General Authorities and symbolized the Church's strength and stability. It also provided badly needed space for the Church historian's office and the Genealogical Society.[8]

The Saints in Other Lands

President Joseph F. Smith shared President Lorenzo Snow's understanding of the Church's worldwide mission. As he continued to encourage the Saints to remain and build up the Church in their homelands, Latter-day Saint missions and branches expanded abroad. This expansion was reflected in Joseph F. Smith's becoming the first Church President to visit Europe while serving in that office.

During a period of about two months in 1906, he visited the missions in the Netherlands, Germany, Switzerland, France, and England. President Smith's personal visit did much to promote the growth of Church strength in these lands. Inspirational events confirmed and strengthened the Saints' faith. In Rotterdam, Holland, he was the instrument in restoring full sight to a faithful eleven-year-old boy who had declared that he believed "the prophet has the most power of any missionary on earth" and that if "he will look into my eyes, I believe they will be healed."[9]

President Smith returned to Europe in 1910. He also traveled to the Hawaiian Islands (four times), Canada, Mexico, and to various stakes in the western United States. Many of these travels were occasioned by the need to deal with special problems faced by the Saints in different areas, or by the happier business of preparing for the erection of new temples.

Difficulties in Mexico

President Joseph F. Smith's administration witnessed events that would have a far-reaching impact on the future of the Church in Mexico and in adjoining sections of the United

States. During the last quarter of the nineteenth century Latter-day Saints had established colonies in northern Mexico as they sought a haven from the persecution then raging north of the border. Furthermore, a mission had been established in Mexico City where a few small branches were organized. Nevertheless, because of clerical opposition in Mexico and the Saints' problems at home, the mission had been closed in 1891.

By the turn of the century, conditions seemed right for reopening the mission in Mexico. The Latter-day Saint colonies had become well established and were prospering; their young people, who by this time could speak Spanish fluently and were well acquainted with the Mexican culture, were now available for proselyting duties. In 1901, with the approval of the First Presidency and under the immediate supervision of the Juarez Stake, the mission in Mexico City was reopened.

During the next ten years, the work prospered. The missionary force increased to twenty. President Anthony W. Ivins of the Juarez Stake made frequent visits to the mission, as did a total of six members of the Twelve from Salt Lake City. Local men and women were called and trained as leaders. They received great strength from Rey L. Pratt, who became mission president in 1907 and would preside for nearly a quarter century.

Many new converts were added, so that by 1911, the mission's membership exceeded a thousand. In that year, President Pratt observed that "prospects were never brighter for the spreading of the gospel in this land. . . ."[10] But the whirlwind of revolution had again been unleashed, and within a very short time it would disrupt the Church's progress in Mexico.

As revolutions and counterrevolutions swept the country, missionary work became increasingly difficult. These conditions were complicated by a growing nationalistic, anti-American sentiment. By August 1913 it was necessary to evacuate the missionaries once again.

The Mexican Saints were left alone to take care of themselves. In San Marcos, about fifty miles northwest of Mexico City, for example, Rafael Monroy, a comparatively recent convert, was given the responsibility of serving as branch presi-

Mormon colonists flee their homes in northern Mexico as contending revolutionary armies maraud the area in 1912. (Church Archives)

dent. Just two years after the departure of the missionaries, however, the brutal forces of revolutionary conflict and religious prejudice resulted in the murders of President Monroy and his cousin, Vincente Morales, because they were accused of being members of a rival revolutionary group and because they would not deny their testimony of the gospel.

In 1912 the same forces that had disrupted missionary work also brought trouble to the colonists in northern Mexico. When rebels confiscated the Saints' arms, Mormon leaders ordered an evacuation of women and children by special train to El Paso on July 26. The men followed a few days later, coming out in a mile-long wagon caravan. By February 1913 some began returning to Mexico while others remained permanently in the United States. The revolution raged for several more years, and on repeated occasions the Mormon colonists felt they were protected by divine power.

During later years the colonists' superior education programs and advanced agricultural methods would attract favorable attention for the Church. Furthermore, when the Mexican
government began enforcing laws prohibiting foreign clergy
from functioning, most of the missionaries in Mexico and
almost all of the mission presidents, as well as the leaders in the
Church's growing school system, would come from these
colonists who had become Mexican citizens. In this way, the
Mormon colonies provided the strength that would enable the
Church in later years to grow throughout Mexico and elsewhere in Latin America.

The difficulties in Mexico had a positive by-product even
beyond the borders of that nation: They led to Church expansion in the southwestern United States. Many exiled families
provided new vitality and leadership to Latter-day Saint congregations in Arizona, New Mexico, and Texas. Furthermore,
in 1915 the First Presidency assigned Rey L. Pratt to take
charge of proselyting among the Spanish-speaking peoples in
the United States. This would become an important missionary
field in later years.

Temple Sites

During his first visit to Europe, President Joseph F. Smith
made an important prophetic statement. At a conference in
Bern, Switzerland in 1906, he stretched out his hands and declared: "The time will come when this land [Europe] will be
dotted with temples, where you can go and redeem your
dead." He also explained that "temples would be built in diverse countries of the world."[11] Interestingly, the first Latter-
day Saint temple in Europe would be dedicated nearly a half
century later in the very city where President Smith made his
prophecy.

Although President Joseph F. Smith did not live to see
temples built in Europe, he did inaugurate the construction of
the first two of these sacred edifices away from the traditional
centers of Mormon colonization in Utah. He recognized the
need for temples to bless Church members living in foreign
lands: "They need the same privileges as we do, and that we
enjoy, but these are out of their power. They are poor and

they can't get the means to come up here and be endowed, and sealed for time and eternity for their living and their dead."[12]

One of these new temples was located in Cardston, Alberta, Canada. In 1888, when Elder John W. Taylor had dedicated Cardston as a location for Latter-day Saint colonization, he had declared, "I now speak by the power of prophecy and say that upon this very spot shall be erected a Temple to the name of Israel's God, and nations shall come from far and near and praise His high and holy name." Later, President Joseph F. Smith sent Presiding Bishop Charles W. Nibley to Canada to recommend the best possible sites for a temple. He brought back photographs of four locations. President Smith thoughtfully studied the pictures and, pointing to one of them, said, "I feel strongly impressed that this is the one." He had selected the same site Elder Taylor had dedicated years earlier.[13] President Joseph F. Smith dedicated this site in 1913 and construction commenced on the temple.

He also dedicated a site for a temple in Hawaii, where he had served as a missionary many years before. Following a meeting in honor of President Smith in Laie, June 1, 1915, he invited Elder Reed Smoot and Bishop Charles W. Nibley to join him for an evening walk into the nearby tropical grounds. "I never saw a more beautiful night in all my life," Elder Smoot later recalled. While they were strolling, President Smith unexpectedly confided, "I feel impressed to dedicate this ground for the erection of a Temple to God, for a place where the peoples of the Pacific Isles can come and do their temple work. . . . I think now is the time to dedicate the ground." Elder Smoot continued, "I have heard President Smith pray hundreds of times . . . but never in all my life did I hear such a prayer. The very ground seemed to be sacred, and he seemed as if he were talking face to face with the Father. I cannot and never will forget it if I live a thousand years." Elder Smoot was convinced that nobody could love a person "more than did the natives of the islands love President Joseph F. Smith."[14] President Smith's action was approved by the general conference the following October. Construction on both temples was well under way at the time he died in 1918.

The First Presidency from 1901 to 1910: (from left) Joseph F. Smith, Anthon H. Lund, and John R. Winder. (Utah State Historical Society)

Understanding of Gospel Doctrines Clarified

The early twentieth century was a period of heated debate between religious fundamentalists and liberals or modernists. Many asked where the Mormons stood on the various theological controversies of the time. The Latter-day Saints were fortunate to have the leadership of President Joseph F. Smith, an unusually able and inspired exponent of gospel principles. A compilation of his sermons and writings is found in the volume entitled *Gospel Doctrine,* and Church members still look to his teachings for helpful definitions of basic gospel concepts. President Smith and his counselors in the First Presidency issued several "doctrinal expositions" clarifying the Church's stand on the issues of the day.

Perhaps the most heated and prolonged discussions centered on the creation of the earth and the theory of organic evolution. In their 1909 statement on "The Origin of Man" the First Presidency affirmed:

"God created man in his own image, in the image of God created he him; male and female created he them." In these plain and pointed words the inspired author of the book of Genesis made known to the world the truth concerning the origin of the human family. . . .

All men and women are in the similitude of the universal Father and Mother, and are literally the sons and daughters of Deity.

. . . The doctrine of the pre-existence, revealed so plainly, particularly in latter-days, pours a wonderful flood of light upon the otherwise mysterious problem of man's origin. It shows that man, as a spirit, was begotten and born of heavenly parents, and reared to maturity in the eternal mansions of the Father, prior to coming upon the earth in a temporal body to undergo an experience in mortality. . . .

It is held by some that Adam was not the first man upon this earth, and that the original human being was a development from lower orders of the animal creation. These, however, are the theories of men. The word of the Lord declares that Adam was "the first man of all men" (Moses 1:34), and we are therefore in duty bound to regard him as the primal parent of our race. . . .

Man is the child of God, formed in the divine image and endowed with divine attributes, and even as the infant son of an earthly father and mother is capable in due time of becoming a man, so the undeveloped offspring of celestial parentage is capable, by experience through ages and aeons, of evolving into a God.[15]

Other discussions questioned the traditional concept that the Trinity or Godhead consisted of three persons in one. Some Latter-day Saints also wondered about the relative roles of Elohim (God the Father), Jehovah (or Jesus Christ), and Michael (or Adam). The First Presidency's 1916 exposition, "The Father and the Son," explained that "the term 'Father' as applied to Deity occurs in sacred writ with plainly different meanings" and should be carefully segregated. (1) God is "Father" as the "literal parent" of our spirits. (2) Jesus Christ is the "Father" or creator of this earth. (3) The Savior may also be regarded as the "Father" of those who receive spiritual rebirth through abiding in his gospel. And, (4) Jesus may be called "Father" as he represents Elohim by "divine investiture of authority" here on earth. Concerning the Savior's status as the "Son," the First Presidency explained:

> There is no impropriety . . . in speaking of Jesus Christ as the Elder Brother of the rest of human kind. . . . Let it not be forgotten, however, that He is essentially greater than any and all others, by reason (1) of His seniority as the oldest or first-born; (2) of His unique status in the flesh as the offspring of a mortal mother and of an immortal, or resurrected and glorified Father; (3) of His selection and foreordination as the one and only Redeemer and Savior of the race; and (4) of His transcendent sinlessness. Jesus Christ is not the Father of the spirits who have taken or yet shall take bodies upon the earth, for He is one of them.[16]

President Smith also shed light on a related question. Although the terms *Holy Ghost* and *Light or Spirit of Christ* are often used interchangeably, he explained that "the Holy Ghost is a personage in the Godhead," while the Light of Christ "is the Spirit of God which proceeds through Christ to the world, that lightens every man that comes into the world, and strives with the children of men, and will continue to strive with them, until it brings them to a knowledge of the truth and the possession of the greater light and testimony of the Holy Ghost."[17]

During these years, a further contribution to gospel understanding was made by a group of particularly capable Latter-day Saint scholars. One of these was James E. Talmage, who as a young man had taught science at Brigham Young Academy and later had also served for several years as president of the University of Utah. In 1899 he delivered a very popular series of lectures on the Articles of Faith, and his material was published in book form by direction of the First Presidency. This work has gone through more than fifty editions in English, has been translated into more than a dozen other languages, and continues to be accepted by Church members as an essential exposition of Latter-day Saint theology. Two other important works followed Elder Talmage's call to the Twelve in 1911: *The House of the Lord,* 1912, and *Jesus the Christ,* 1915. Beginning in 1907, a more intense interest in gospel study was being kindled by the *Seventies Course in*

Theology by Elder B. H. Roberts. This work contributed to the establishment of regular weekly priesthood meetings (as will be seen in the next chapter). John A. Widtsoe, an immigrant convert from Norway, drew from his training as a scientist as well as from his personal gospel study in writing *A Rational Theology,* 1915; he became a member of the Twelve six years later. These and other scholarly works of the period have continued to be recognized as key volumes in any Latter-day Saint's library.

A fitting climax to these contributions to gospel understanding resulted from a marvelous experience of President Joseph F. Smith only a few weeks before his death. On October 3, 1918, while President Smith was pondering the atonement of Jesus Christ, he opened his Bible and read in 1 Peter 3:18-20 and 4:6 about the Savior's preaching to the spirits in prison. While he was meditating on these passages, the Spirit of the Lord rested upon him and he saw in vision the "hosts of the dead" who were gathered in the spirit world. He saw the Savior appear among them and preach the gospel to the righteous. He was shown that the Lord commissioned others to continue this work of preaching, and that faithful elders in the present dispensation would also preach to the dead after leaving mortality. In this way, all the dead may be redeemed. This "Vision of the Redemption of the Dead" was presented by President Smith to the First Presidency and the Twelve, who accepted it unanimously. In 1976 this revelation was officially added to the standard works and soon afterwards designated as section 138 in the Doctrine and Covenants.

The Saints and World War I

World War I broke out in Europe in 1914. The United States did not become actively involved until three years later, after Germany had sunk several American vessels in an undeclared submarine war. The United States officially entered the conflict on April 6, 1917.

Members of the Church in America believed the war was being fought for noble purposes. President Wilson had declared that it was a war for the purpose of preserving democracy, liberty, and peace. Since this agreed with long-expressed feelings of the Church, members found no religious conflict in responding quickly to the call to arms.

Since Utah was still the home of most Latter-day Saints, the response of the people of that state was a good reflection of the attitude of the Saints in general to the war. A total of 24,382 enlisted, far exceeding the quota assigned to Utah. Six of President Joseph F. Smith's own sons served in the uniform of their country. The Red Cross asked for $350,000—and received $520,000. When the government began to sell Liberty bonds, Utahns were requested to raise $6,500,000; they purchased $9,400,000 worth.

It was the custom for each state to raise a volunteer military unit. Utah provided the 145th Field Artillery Regiment. An overwhelming majority of its approximately fifteen hundred officers and men were members of the Church. The unit's chaplain was Elder B. H. Roberts of the First Council of the Seventy. Six hundred of this modern "Mormon Battalion" saw duty overseas.

The Church, as an institution, participated officially in the war by purchasing $850,000 in Liberty Bonds. In addition, auxiliary organizations purchased bonds with their own funds, amounting to nearly $600,000, and women of the Relief Society actively participated with the Red Cross.

The Church of Jesus Christ of Latter-day Saints was uniquely prepared to help provide food for the starving peoples of war-torn Europe. For years the Relief Society had been storing wheat in preparation for just such an emergency, so it was able to sell over two hundred thousand bushels to the United States government. The sisters put this money into a special wheat fund for future charitable purposes.

The prompt response of the Church and its members to the war emergency was effective evidence of the Saints' loyalty and patriotism. The American press praised their actions, fairly well canceling any negative impressions that may have lingered from the anti-Mormon magazine crusade of earlier years.

Overseas Saints also responded patriotically to the calls of their own countries. In England, the *Pudsey News* reported:

> Patriotic Latter-day Saints at Pudsey.—The Church of Jesus Christ of Latter-day Saints, Pudsey branch, has (writes a

correspondent) a record of patriotism which will be hard to beat, as every man of military age, with the exception of those engaged in government and munitions work, has enlisted. Whatever we may say about the so-called "Mormons," we must admit that they are certainly "very patriotic at Pudsey."[18]

Even in Germany, Latter-day Saints fought for their fatherland; about seventy-five gave their lives in the conflict.

The Church's April general conference was in session when the United States officially entered the war in 1917. The attitude of the Church toward war was well expressed in President Joseph F. Smith's opening address. He reminded the Saints that even in the face of conflict, the spirit of the gospel must be maintained. He declared that even in war the people should maintain the spirit of humanity, of love, and of peacemaking. He instructed prospective soldiers to remember that they were "ministers of life and not of death," and that they should "go forth in the spirit of defending liberties of mankind rather than for the purpose of destroying the enemy."[19]

Links with the Future

President Joseph F. Smith died on November 19, 1918, just one week after the armistice was signed ending World War I. While President Smith's personal life represented important links with the past, inspired developments during his presidency formed key links with the future. An improved popular attitude toward the Latter-day Saints, financial stability, key Church buildings, and clarification of doctrinal understanding were only some of the lasting contributions of President Smith's administration.

The opening decades of the twentieth century had seen a new generation of Church leaders assuming responsibility. While Lorenzo Snow had been a personal associate of the Prophet Joseph Smith, Joseph F. Smith was the son of the Prophet's brother and hence represented a younger generation. Furthermore, President Smith was instrumental in calling to the Quorum of the Twelve a group of men whose contributions would have a major impact during the new century. Elders Charles W. Penrose, Orson F. Whitney, James E.

General Authorities in April 1918: (standing, from left) Orrin P. Miller, Anthony W. Ivins, Charles Hart, Orson F. Whitney, David O. McKay, Rulon S. Wells, Joseph Fielding Smith, J. Golden Kimball, James E. Talmage, Stephen L Richards, Joseph F. McMurrin, Hyrum G. Smith, Richard R. Lyman, Levi Edgar Young, David A. Smith; (seated, from left) Rudger Clawson, Heber J. Grant, Anthon H. Lund, Joseph F. Smith, Charles W. Penrose, George Albert Smith, Charles W. Nibley. (Church Archives)

Talmage, and Joseph Fielding Smith all made substantial additions to the body of Latter-day Saint doctrinal and historical literature. A group of relatively young appointees would carry important leadership responsibilities in coming years: George Albert Smith, George F. Richards, David O. McKay, Joseph Fielding Smith (a son of President Smith), and Stephen L Richards. Three of these would later serve as Presidents of the Church.

Yet other contributions of President Joseph F. Smith's administration would bless the Saints directly. Under his leadership, the Church made significant refinements in its priesthood and auxiliary programs, and launched several important publications. These inspired developments are the subject of the following chapter.

4 Priesthood and Auxiliary Expansion

President Joseph F. Smith's administration witnessed a major expansion and "reform" in both priesthood and auxiliary programs. During these years the Church also standardized the schedule of basic local meetings which would be followed for most of the twentieth century.

The Church of Jesus Christ with its varied programs had been established with the goal of helping to perfect the Saints (see Ephesians 4:11-13). Some have supposed that the full Church organization was restored on April 6, 1830. This, however, was not the case. Of the nine priesthood offices, duties for only four—elders, priests, teachers, and deacons—were explained in Doctrine and Covenants section 20, the revelation that directed the original organization of the Church. Other offices—bishops, high priests, patriarchs, Apostles, and seventies—were added during the next five years. In 1835 Doctrine and Covenants section 107 outlined the structure and functions of quorums related to these priesthood offices. The first stake was established at Kirtland, Ohio, in 1834, but the first wards were not created until five years later in Nauvoo, Illinois.

The auxiliary organizations came even later. Most developed during the time when Brigham Young presided

over the Church. The first Relief Society had been organized at
Nauvoo in 1842 with the object of caring for the needy and
strengthening community morals. Latter-day Saint Sunday
Schools had also met irregularly in both Kirtland and Nauvoo.
Richard Ballantyne organized the first Sunday School in the
Rocky Mountains in 1849. Neither the Relief Society nor the
Sunday School, however, was formally established Church-
wide until the 1860s. At that time President Brigham Young
directed Eliza R. Snow to promote the establishment of Relief
Societies in every branch of the Church, and Elder George Q.
Cannon headed the first union organization of the formerly
independent local Sunday Schools. President Young personally organized the forerunner of the Young Woman's Mutual
Improvement Association in 1869 and a similar association for
the Young Men in 1875. These programs helped the young
people to live the gospel more fully and provided them with
intellectual and cultural development. Finally, Aurelia Spencer
Rogers started the first Primary in 1878, the year following
Brigham Young's death. This organization provided weekday
religious training for Latter-day Saint boys and girls.

In 1890, when a Utah territorial law prohibited all
religious instruction in public schools, Church leaders recognized the continuing necessity of more thorough practical
training of the children of the Latter-day Saints in the requirements of the gospel and therefore established Religion Classes
throughout the Church. Like the Primary, the new classes met
in a Church building after school hours, generally one afternoon each week. The Religion Classes emphasized religious
instruction, while the Primary featured religious activities.
These two organizations would function side by side until
finally being merged in 1929.

Even though priesthood quorums and auxiliary associations were established during the nineteenth century, the programs sponsored by these organizations underwent substantial
development and expansion during the years immediately preceding and following the beginning of the twentieth century. A
person who had been active in the Church prior to 1890 might
scarcely be able to recognize the programs that developed

1842	Relief Society organized in Nauvoo
1849	First Sunday School in the Rocky Mountains
1866	*Juvenile Instructor* published by George Q. Cannon
1869	Cooperative Retrenchment Association, forerunner of YWMIA
1875	Young Men's Mutual Improvement Association founded
1878	Primary Association started
1890	Religion Classes organized
1894	Communitywide sacrament meetings discontinued
1896	Fast day shifted from Thursday to Sunday
1897	Conference Reports and *Improvement Era* inaugurated
1901	*Juvenile Instructor* became official organ of the Sunday School
1902	New edition of the Pearl of Great Price approved; *Children's Friend* published by the Primary; Mothers' Classes added to the Relief Society
1904	Society for the Aid of the Sightless organized
1906	Sunday School conducted first class for adults; President Joseph F. Smith anticipated emphasis on priesthood
1907	Committee on Adjustments recommended consolidations
1908	General Priesthood Committee called
1909	Weekly ward priesthood meetings commenced
1910	*Utah Genealogical and Historical Magazine* inaugurated
1911	YMMIA adopted Boy Scouts program
1915	*Relief Society Magazine* instituted
1920-21	Improved editions of standard works published
1929	*Improvement Era* and *Young Woman's Journal* amalgamated
1931	Weekly *Church Section* launched by Salt Lake's *Deseret News*

during the following two or three decades. These changes not only affected the work of the priesthood and the auxiliaries but had an impact on the Saints' basic meeting pattern as well.

Developments in Basic Meetings

Significant modifications in the pattern of sacrament and fast meetings occurred during the 1890s. Changes in two other important Sunday meetings—Sunday School and priesthood meetings—followed during the next decade and will be considered in later sections of this chapter.

Sacrament Meetings

The scriptures have directed that members of the Church meet together often to instruct and strengthen one another and to partake of the sacrament (see D&C 20:45, 75; 43:8). Although the basic objectives have remained constant, the pattern of these meetings has changed over the years to meet varying needs and conditions.

The schedule the early pioneers were to follow was outlined at the April general conference in 1852:

> President Young then gave notice that from henceforth we should hold meetings regularly each Sabbath at 10 A.M., and 2 P.M., and in the evening, the several quorums of the priesthood would assemble to receive instructions. On Thursdays the brethren and sisters would come together at 2 P.M. for prayer and supplication; and on the first Thursday in each month, at 10 A.M., for the purpose of fasting and prayer, calling on the saints to observe that day.[1]

In some of the larger centers, such as Salt Lake City and Provo, it became customary to hold just one worship service at a central location on Sunday afternoons, and the sacrament was administered in these meetings rather than in the separate wards. In 1894, however, Church leaders directed that the administration of the sacrament should be moved to the regular Sunday evening services held in each ward.[2] Thus, the ward sacrament meeting became a Churchwide practice.

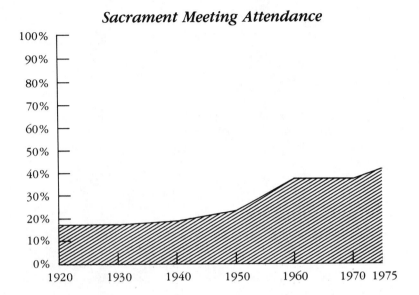

Sacrament Meeting Attendance

Fast Day

The familiar pattern for fast meetings developed in very early times. By 1896, however, new patterns of life made a shift in the fast day advisable. In an official statement, the First Presidency explained the reasons for the change:

> Shortly after the arrival of the people in the valley of the Great Salt Lake, the first Thursday in each month was set apart as a day of fasting and prayer. The members of the Church were enjoined to bring on that day their contributions for the relief and sustenance of the poor, and hand them to the Bishop of the ward.
>
> At the time of the adoption of this regulation it was very convenient for the people generally to meet together in their places of worship on that day. The conditions were such that they, being of one faith, employers and employed, could leave their labor and devote a few hours to the Lord. . . .
>
> As the years rolled by, conditions changed, and it became more difficult for the people generally, and especially those in steady employment, to attend these meetings, until at the pres-

ent time they have dwindled to such an extent that comparatively few have the opportunity of attending them. Thursday as a day of fasting and prayer in the Church no longer serves the object for which it was intended.

Our attention has been called to this subject, and after mature deliberation, it has been decided to change the day that has heretofore been devoted to this purpose. Instead of the customary assemblages in the various wards throughout Zion on the first Thursday in each month, we have concluded to set apart the first Sunday in every month as the day for the regular fast meetings.

Hereafter, therefore, we desire the Latter-day Saints, under the direction of the Presidents of Stakes and the Bishops, to meet in their several places of worship on the afternoon of the first Sunday in each month, whenever it can be done conveniently, and devote the meeting to the administration of the Sacrament, to the bearing of testimony by the members of the Church, to the blessing of children and the confirming of members in the Church, and to such other services as have usually been attended to at such meetings.[3]

Auxiliary Expansion

The Church's auxiliary organizations were most greatly affected by the developments during the opening years of the twentieth century. Although specific changes varied from one organization to another, they generally involved an improvement in teaching methods and materials directed to specific age groups, a greater emphasis on the scriptures rather than on secular materials, and a greater role for each organization's general leaders.

Opportunities for Learning

During the nineteenth century the Latter-day Saints had been in the forefront of educational development. The School of the Prophets in the 1830s, for example, had been one of the nation's first adult education programs. At the dawning of the twentieth century the Saints were again in the lead as several of the Church's organization's commenced new instructional programs especially for adults.

During the nineteenth century the Relief Society had stressed "compassionate service" and had emphasized sewing

Relief Society general board in 1916, at a time when this organization was unfolding its educational programs and launching its own magazine. (Utah State Historical Society)

or other projects directly related to assisting the needy. In 1902, however, the Society inaugurated a greater emphasis on education. Special eight-month nursing courses taught care for the sick. Mothers' Classes, launched Churchwide that same year, became the forerunners of a much broader uniform curriculum that would be introduced a few years later. At first local Relief Societies provided their own study materials, but in 1914 the general board began providing uniform lessons for these weekly classes. The pattern soon developed to feature theology the first week, and then studies of homemaking, literature, and social science, respectively, during the other weeks of the month.

Even after the turn of the century the Sunday School still remained an organization only for children. The first class for adults, the Parents' Class, was not inaugurated Churchwide until 1906, just four years after the Relief Society had instituted its Mothers' Class. At this time, David O. McKay had a profound impact on Sunday School development. As a young returned missionary at the turn of the century, he was called to be a member of the Weber Stake Sunday School superintendency and to give particular attention to instruction. He introduced refinements in teaching methods, such as defining lesson goals, outlining materials, using teaching aids, and making practical application of lessons to daily life. Students were "graded" according to age, and a specific course was developed for each age group, to be used throughout the stake. In 1906 Elder McKay was called to the Council of the Twelve and also became a member of the Sunday School general superintendency; in this position he was able to promote these improvements throughout the Church. During the following years a thorough departmentalization of Sunday School work was accompanied by an improvement of published lesson materials.

Priesthood quorums also commenced regular lesson work, as will be seen below. Furthermore, the opening years of the twentieth century saw the addition of college-level classes to several of the Church's schools and the inauguration of seminaries for high school students.

Improved Activities

During the nineteenth century the Young Men's and Young Ladies' Mutual Improvement Associations had followed similar but separate patterns of development. Originally the two MIAs met separately, consistent with the wishes of Brigham Young, who did not want the sessions to degenerate into "courting meetings." Following the turn of the century, the move to unite the two associations gained impetus, and by 1914 joint meetings had become a rule. At first, MIA meetings had consisted of lectures on theology, science, history, and literature—the four designated areas of emphasis. Formal classwork was introduced about 1890, but until after the turn of the century just one large class was held for all ages. Several local

Relief Society Activity

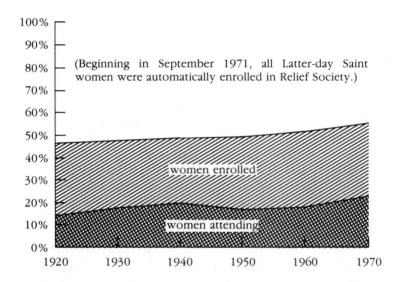

(Beginning in September 1971, all Latter-day Saint women were automatically enrolled in Relief Society.)

women enrolled

women attending

groups, however, felt the need to separate the younger and older members. By 1903 the practice of conducting separate junior and senior groups had been implemented Churchwide. In 1911 the Young Men's organization adopted the growing Boy Scout program, and the Church eventually became one of the largest sponsors of this international movement. In 1913 the Young Ladies adopted the Campfire Girls summer program, but they replaced it the following year with the Church's own year-round Beehive Girls program. Later years saw the formation of still other age-group programs to better serve the needs of the youth. As the Sunday Schools, and especially the priesthood quorums, expanded their theological study, this was dropped from MIA activity. As more and more Latter-day Saints moved into the cities, Church leaders became concerned that the new environment and increased leisure would erode traditional virtues and family life. They therefore placed increasing emphasis on modesty, chastity, and marriage within the Church. Leaders encouraged the youth to avoid pool halls, card games, non-LDS dances, and Sunday sports. The wards, which were at the center of Mormon community life, sponsored more picnics, excursions, and other well-supervised recreational activities. The MIAs also expanded their music, dance, speech, drama, and sports activities.

Similarly, the Primary Association enhanced its educational and activity programs for children. Special class names and emblems were introduced to increase interest: boys became known as "Trail Builders" and girls as "Home Builders." The Primary even opened its own children's hospital in 1922. A few years earlier, Louie B. Felt, president of the Primary, and May Anderson, one of her counselors, had seen a crippled child and felt impressed that their organization should do something for such children. They studied the latest methods used in children's hospitals in the eastern United States before going ahead with this project.

Following the lead of the Sunday School, the other auxiliary organizations began "grading" their classes for specific age groups. They increasingly adopted centrally prepared uniform lessons. The opening years of the twentieth century also brought a greater emphasis on regional conventions and general auxiliary conferences for the training and motivation of local workers. All these developments tended to strengthen the role of the auxiliaries' general boards.

The Priesthood Reform Movement

At the height of this rapid auxiliary expansion, President Joseph F. Smith looked forward to a time when the priesthood would again occupy a position of preeminence. At the April general conference in 1906 he declared:

> We expect to see the day, if we live long enough (and if some of us do not live long enough to see it, there are others who will), when every council of the Priesthood in the Church of Jesus Christ of Latter-day Saints will understand its duty; will assume its own responsibility, will magnify its calling, and fill its place in the Church, to the uttermost, according to the intelli-

gence and ability possessed by it. When that day shall come, there will not be so much necessity for work that is now being done by the auxiliary organizations, because it will be done by the regular quorums of the Priesthood. The Lord designed and comprehended it from the beginning, and he has made provision in the Church whereby every need may be met and satisfied through the regular organizations of the Priesthood. It has truly been said that the Church is perfectly organized. The only trouble is that these organizations are not fully alive to the obligations that rest upon them. When they become thoroughly awakened to the requirements made of them, they will fulfill their duties more faithfully, and the work of the Lord will be all the stronger and more powerful and influential in the world.[4]

Speaking at the same conference, Elder J. Golden Kimball of the First Council of the Seventy assessed even more bluntly the need for a revival of priesthood activity:

> The auxiliaries have been urged forward with great enthusiasm . . . [and] these organizations are to the front. The priesthood quorums are apparently weary in well doing. . . . They have become lax in their work and let loose their hold. While the auxiliary organizations have taken the right of way, the priesthood quorums stand by looking on awe-struck. . . . So the auxiliary organizations are going way up the hill and we, the priesthood quorums, stand down in the valley and look on.[5]

Records indicate that during the later nineteenth century, priesthood meetings were held at varying intervals. Most quorums met only monthly. Customarily these gatherings were held on various week nights rather than on Sunday, and all the quorums within a given ward did not usually meet at the same time. With such infrequent and often irregular meetings, the priesthood quorums' effectiveness declined. By the beginning of the twentieth century, Church leaders lamented that less than half of Latter-day Saint men were active in their priesthood quorums. The leaders suspected that one problem was the growing popularity of fraternal lodges. They believed that all needs—spiritual and temporal—should be met by the Church, and that the priesthood quorums themselves should provide true brotherhood.

The revival of priesthood activity appears to have started among the seventies. In 1907 President Joseph F. Smith reminded them of their responsibility to be prepared for missionary service. They should not depend on the auxiliaries or Church schools for their knowledge of the gospel, but, he exhorted, make their own quorums "schools of learning and instruction wherein they may qualify themselves for every labor that may be required at their hands." In November of that same year, Elder B. H. Roberts of the First Council of the Seventy announced the "New Movement" among the seventies. It would include study of *The Seventies Course in Theology* each Sunday morning. "To become a seventy," he declared, "means mental activity, intellectual development, and the attainment of spiritual power." The *Improvement Era* became the official vehicle through which monthly instructions were received by these priesthood quorums.[6] The success of these efforts among the seventies attracted admiration and led to a broadening of the reform movement.

Weekly Ward Priesthood Meetings

In 1908, to give direction to the revitalization of the priesthood and specifically to provide lesson materials for Aaronic and Melchizedek Priesthood quorums, the First Presidency appointed a General Priesthood Committee. David O. McKay became committee chairman, and other General Authorities served as members. One of the committee's most far-reaching recommendations was for the inauguration of weekly ward priesthood meetings.

In 1909 the First Presidency explained the advantages of implementing this new plan:

> Special attention is called to the weekly meetings of the priesthood quorums in all wards. We believe this movement will not only increase the proficiency of the priesthood by reason of its educative features, but by bringing all the brethren together once a week they will acquire the habit of regular activity as servants of the Lord. It has the additional advantage of putting the bishop in communication with every home once a week. We like the idea of these weekly reunions of the fathers of the ward with their sons and associates.[7]

Melchizedek Priesthood Activity

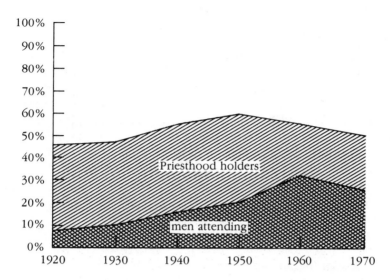

At first these ward priesthood meetings were scheduled for Monday evenings. This time, however, interfered with evening chores, especially in farming areas, so Sunday morning gradually became the preferred time.

The General Priesthood Committee increased the effectiveness of these ward meetings by providing uniform courses of study to be used throughout the Church. This committee continued preparing these lessons for the quorums until it was released in 1923. After that time, responsibility for the Melchizedek Priesthood was assigned directly to the Council of the Twelve, and for the Aaronic Priesthood to the Presiding Bishopric.

Aaronic Priesthood Age Groupings

Another important accomplishment of the priesthood reform movement was systematizing ordinations to offices in the Aaronic Priesthood at specified ages. As early as 1877, the First Presidency had endorsed the practice of ordaining young men to the lesser priesthood to give them needed experience before they received the higher or Melchizedek Priesthood. Although it became typical to ordain boys to the office of deacon at age twelve, no ages were fixed for ordination to subsequent offices. In 1908 the General Priesthood Committee recommended that deacons be ordained at twelve, teachers at fifteen, priests at eighteen, and elders at twenty-one, thus giving young men three years' experience in each Aaronic Priesthood office. Standardizing the ages of ordination enabled the committee to more effectively plan the program for each priesthood group. The concept of set ages for ordination has continued even though some of the ages have been modified.

Key Developments in Church Publications

From the time that Joseph Smith read in the Bible James's exhortation "to ask of God," the printed word has played a key role in the unfolding of the Lord's work on earth. As Elder Mark E. Petersen declared: "I feel that our publications and communication system are positively essential, vital, and basic to the life blood of the Church."[8] The early years of the twentieth century brought a variety of important developments in Church literature. With the rapid expansion of priesthood and auxiliary programs, new lesson outlines and other instructions were published. Church organizations either inaugurated magazines or made greater use of existing ones to help promote their programs. These years brought important improvements even to the published editions of scriptural works.

Developments in Periodicals

While the Latter-day Saints had been active in publishing newspapers and magazines since as early as 1831, most of the publications that became best known during the twentieth century date from the years immediately preceding or following the turn of the century. Many of the nineteenth-century publications had been sponsored by private individuals or groups. Those dating from the early twentieth century, on the other hand, were all published under the auspices of individual Church organizations, particularly the auxiliaries.

When the *Juvenile Instructor* was inaugurated in 1866, it had been a personal project of Elder George Q. Cannon, who saw the magazine as a means of teaching the gospel to the youth of the Church. This semimonthly publication is credited as being the first magazine for children published between the Mississippi River and the Pacific Coast. Following Elder Cannon's death in 1901, the Deseret Sunday School Union purchased the magazine from the Cannon family and made it the Sunday School's official organ. In 1908 it became a monthly publication, and during the first decades of the twentieth century it carried Sunday School lesson materials. Just as the Sunday School added adult classes, so also was the field of the magazine enlarged. The periodical's broadened scope was reflected in 1930 when the word *Juvenile* was dropped from the title.

In 1897 the Young Men's Mutual Improvement Association replaced its *Contributor* with a new periodical entitled *The Improvement Era*. Joseph F. Smith of the First Presidency and B. H. Roberts of the First Council of the Seventy were editors, and Elder Heber J. Grant of the Twelve was the business manager. In 1929 this magazine was merged with the *Young Woman's Journal,* which had been published since 1889 by the Young Ladies' MIA. Gradually the enlarged *Improvement Era* came to be recognized as the basic Church magazine for adults.

Beginning in 1872, a group of women, some of whom were members of the Relief Society general board, began publishing the *Woman's Exponent.* When the Relief Society began supplying lesson materials to be taught in its weekly meetings Churchwide, this provided the basis for launching its own official magazine in 1915.

Two other organizations launched periodicals during the first decade of the twentieth century. These were the *Children's Friend,* started by the Primary Association in 1902, and the *Utah Genealogical and Historical Magazine,* a quarterly published by the Genealogical Society beginning in 1910.

Development of Church Magazines

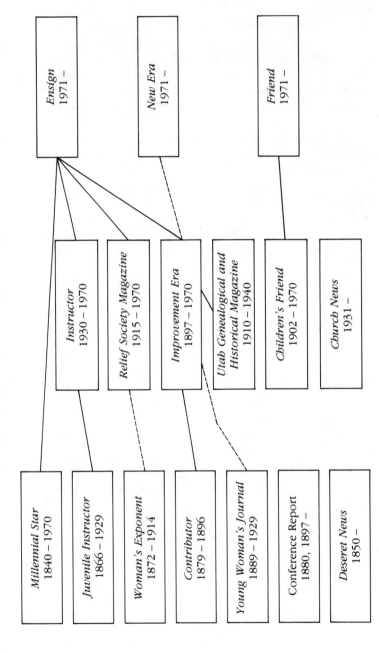

Ensign 1971 –

New Era 1971 –

Friend 1971 –

Instructor 1930 – 1970

Relief Society Magazine 1915 – 1970

Improvement Era 1897 – 1970

Utah Genealogical and Historical Magazine 1910 – 1940

Children's Friend 1902 – 1970

Church News 1931 –

Millennial Star 1840 – 1970

Juvenile Instructor 1866 – 1929

Woman's Exponent 1872 – 1914

Contributor 1879 – 1896

Young Woman's Journal 1889 – 1929

Conference Report 1880, 1897 –

Deseret News 1850 –

Albert Talmage published a braille magazine and directed the Church's programs for the blind during the opening decades of the twentieth century. Here, aided by his sister, he prints an issue of the monthly *Messenger to the Sightless.* (*Improvement Era* photo)

Literature for the Blind

Since the beginning of the twentieth century, the Church has provided religious literature to a special group of members. In 1904 the Society for the Aid of the Sightless was created under the direction of President Joseph F. Smith. It was charged with the responsibility of publishing literature for the blind, "aiding in their education, endeavoring to improve their condition, becoming interested in all that pertains to their welfare," and cooperating with others as opportunity came to work for these ends through education and legislation.[9]

The lack of such literature as braille scriptures, hymns, or lesson materials was a substantial obstacle to blind Latter-day Saints' becoming fully involved in the mainstream of Church activity. Largely through the efforts of Albert M. Talmage (a blind brother of the Apostle) and his wife, Sarah, the society worked to fill this void. Beginning in 1912, a monthly braille periodical, *The Messenger to the Sightless,* published materials of religious and general interest.

Publishing the Book of Mormon in braille was an important project for Albert and Sarah Talmage. They had to prepare the metal printing plates by hand. The special braille paper had to be moistened thoroughly before the dots could be embossed by means of a hand-powered press. Completed pages were then hung up to dry on clotheslines that had been strung all around the Talmages' home. As the embossed braille pages became available, they were distributed piecemeal to eagerly waiting readers. By the early 1930s, however, only the first half of the book had been brailled. At this point the Church decided to have the entire book embossed by a national braille publisher and in 1936 the book appeared in seven large braille volumes. Copies were made available to individuals and were also sent to Latter-day Saint missions around the world.[10] Since then the Doctrine and Covenants, the Pearl of Great Price, and a few other Church books have also been released in braille.

During the second half of the twentieth century the programs launched by Albert and Sarah Talmage would undergo substantial expansion. In 1953 the braille magazine was expanded greatly and renamed *The New Messenger*. Five years later a significant step was taken, in the inauguration of a magazine in recorded form. Lesson manuals for adults, as well as several other Church works, have also been released on "talking book" records. All these materials were made available free of charge to libraries and to blind individuals free or at a nominal cost.

The Standard Works

Latter-day Saints accept four volumes as the standard works, or canonized scriptures, of the Church. Faith in the Bible is shared with other Christians, but the Book of Mormon, the Doctrine and Covenants, and the Pearl of Great Price are unique to the restored gospel. The original publication of all three of these volumes of scripture took place during the nineteenth century.

Translation of the Book of Mormon was completed in June 1829, and the first edition was published in March 1830, just prior to the organization of the Church. In 1831 a special conference directed that a compilation of revelations given through Joseph Smith be published. This became known as the Doctrine and Covenants. The Pearl of Great Price, "a selection from the revelations, translations, and narrations of Joseph Smith," as compiled by Elder Franklin D. Richards of the Council of the Twelve and president of the British Mission, was first published in England in 1851.

The present verse divisions, together with improved historical notes and cross-references prepared by Elder Orson Pratt, were features of new editions of the Doctrine and Covenants in 1876 and of the Book of Mormon in 1879. A similar new edition of the Pearl of Great Price was prepared under the supervision of Elder James E. Talmage in 1902.

The general conference assembled on October 10, 1880, voted to accept the Doctrine and Covenants and the Pearl of Great Price as revelations of God to the Church and to the world.

A new edition of the Book of Mormon appeared in 1920, and new editions of the Doctrine and Covenants and the Pearl of Great Price in 1921. Improvements in these new editions included printing the text in two columns to make reading easier, adding headings or superscriptions to introduce and summarize the contents of each chapter or section, amplifying footnotes, and adding an index to each of these three scriptural works. The new edition of the Book of Mormon also included an account of its origin, an analysis of the various sets of plates from which it was translated, a chronology, and a new pronouncing vocabulary. Useful additions to the Doctrine and Covenants included a brief history of its beginnings, together with a chronological summary of its contents. The 1921 edition of the Doctrine and Covenants also omitted the "Lectures on Faith," which formerly had been published along with the revelations; these lectures never had been accepted formally by the Church as anything more than theological lessons.

Future Developments Anticipated

While the opening years of the twentieth century witnessed many substantial developments in priesthood and auxiliary activity, still others were considered but would not be achieved until later. In 1906 President Joseph F. Smith anticipated a time when the priesthood quorums would more fully assume their proper role in Church government and activity. Many Church leaders have referred to the unfolding of "priesthood correlation" during the 1960s as a fulfillment of President Smith's prophecy. Then in 1907 a Committee on Adjustments and Correlation recommended that the Primary and the similar Religion Class programs be merged; this was achieved in 1929. The committee also suggested that all of the Church's magazines for adults be consolidated. Important steps in this direction were taken when the *Improvement Era* absorbed the formerly separate *Young Woman's Journal* in 1929, the *Utah Genealogical and Historical Magazine* in 1940, and the *Liahona-Elder's Journal* in 1945. The goal was fully realized when in 1971 the *Ensign* replaced all other LDS magazines in English for adults. The 1907 committee also proposed that focus be placed on the home as the prime place for teaching the gospel. This recommendation was echoed in President Smith's 1915 call for regular home evenings Churchwide. The formal family home evening program was instituted fifty years later. All of these developments will be treated in later chapters.

5 Heber J. Grant Begins His Administration

The year 1918 marked a major milestone or turning point in the course of world and Church events. In the world, it brought the end of hostilities and a turning to peace. Then, within two weeks of the November 11 armistice, President Joseph F. Smith died and Heber J. Grant became the new leader of The Church of Jesus Christ of Latter-day Saints. Not only did the Church get a new President, but as Heber J. Grant began his administration new patterns could also be seen in several aspects of Saints' activities. While the nineteenth century had been an era of gathering, the 1920s saw the first substantial outward migration from the centers of Mormon settlement in the Intermountain states. A world tour of missions by Elder David O. McKay further reflected the Church's outward reach. During this decade the Saints also commemorated important events that had occurred just a hundred years earlier. Thus the Saints' appreciation of their historical heritage was being strengthened at the same time as they were moving out into new spheres of activity. Many facets of this heritage and of the Church's experience were reflected in the personal life of President Heber J. Grant.

1856	November 22: Born in Salt Lake City; father died nine days later
1875	Member of first local YMMIA superintendency (18)
1880	Called to serve as president of Tooele Stake (23)
1882	Filled vacancy in the Quorum of the Twelve (25)
1897	Member of general YMMIA superintendency
1901	Appointed to open new mission in Japan (45)
1904-6	Presided over European Mission
1918	Became President of the Church (62)
1919	Dedicated Hawaii Temple; Church membership reached half a million
1923	Dedicated Alberta Temple
1927	Arizona Temple dedicated
1928	Purchase of Hill Cumorah completed
1930	Church celebrated its centennial
1933	Prohibition of alcohol repealed
1936	Churchwide Welfare Plan organized
1937	Visited missions in Europe
1939	Missionaries withdrawn from Europe as World War II began
1941	Assistants to the Twelve appointed
1945	May 14: Died in Salt Lake City (88)

Heber J. Grant's Earlier Life

Heber J. Grant represented a personal link with the early leaders of the Restoration. He was the son of Jedediah M. Grant, a New York convert, who became the first mayor of Salt Lake City and a counselor to President Brigham Young. Heber's mother, Rachel Ivins, however, had been sealed to Joseph Smith after his death and before her marriage to Jedediah. Thus, in terms of eternal family relationships, Heber J. Grant considered himself a son of the Church's first prophet, a heritage which he valued highly.[1] He was the first Church President to be born after the Saints' exodus to the Rocky Mountains, being born in Salt Lake City in 1856, just nine years after the Mormon pioneers had arrived there. As a boy, Heber was very close to Brigham Young's family and became well acquainted with the great colonizer.

Heber was not to enjoy the companionship or counsel of his earthly father. Jedediah died suddenly at the age of forty, only nine days after Heber's birth. A talented, faithful, and persistent mother would be the major guiding light of Heber's childhood and youth. Rachel supported herself and her son by sewing and taking in boarders. Sometimes she worked at her foot-powered sewing machine for so many hours that her legs gave out, and she would have Heber help by working the treadle with his hands. Through such experiences young Heber learned lessons of thrift and industry, which would be important virtues to teach the Saints during the Great Depression of the 1930s.

His mother was convinced that Heber was a child of destiny. She cherished promises made to him during his childhood and had faith they would be fulfilled, if, and only if, he lived to be worthy of them. To this end she admonished him: "Behave yourself, Heber, and some day you will be an Apostle." After he was called to the Council of the Twelve, she reminded him of occasions when Heber C. Kimball and also Eliza R. Snow had prophesied that he would "become an Apostle of the Lord Jesus Christ." Elder Kimball, who like Jedediah was a counselor to Brigham Young in the First Presidency, had further prophesied that young Heber would "become a greater man in the Church" than his own father. His mother then added: "That is why I told you to behave yourself."[2]

Overcoming Difficulties

At the youthful age of seventeen, Heber J. Grant outlined what he hoped to accomplish in his life, and then he persisted until he had achieved his goals. Ralph Waldo Emerson's words became a favorite motto: "What we persist in doing becomes easy to do, not that the nature of the task has changed, but that our capacity to do has increased." This principle was carried out repeatedly in the life of Heber J. Grant. For instance, he overcame physical frailty to develop his skill as a baseball player. When he joined a baseball club, he was permitted to play only with much younger boys, but he determined that one day he would play on the team that would win the territorial championship. He later recalled how he reached this goal:

> My mother was keeping boarders . . . and I shined their boots until I saved a dollar which I invested in a baseball. I spent hours and hours throwing the ball against Bishop Edwin D. Woolley's barn, which caused him to refer to me as the laziest boy in the Thirteenth Ward. Often my arm would ache so that I could scarcely go to sleep at night. But I kept on practicing. . . .

Through these efforts Heber eventually succeeded in playing with the team that took the championship of Utah Territory and defeated champion teams from neighboring areas.[3] He also overcame the problem of poor handwriting, winning prizes at fairs and obtaining a coveted position as a bookkeeper because of his excellent penmanship.

Being tone-deaf, he was challenged by his inability to sing. Nevertheless, he was determined to practice. After becoming a member of the Twelve, he humorously admitted: "Upon my recent trip to Arizona, I asked Elders Rudger Clawson and J. Golden Kimball if they had any objections to my singing one hundred hymns that day. They took it as a joke and assured me that they would be delighted. . . . After I had sung about forty times, they assured me that if I sang the remaining sixty they would have nervous prostration. I paid no attention whatever to their appeal but held them to their bargain and sang the full one hundred."[4] Many years later he must have derived some personal satisfaction when he learned that because he had been seated close to the microphone during a radio broadcast from the Tabernacle, listeners seemed to hear him singing a solo accompanied by the choir and organ.[5]

Important Church responsibilities came to Heber at a young age. When the first Mutual Improvement Association was organized in the Salt Lake Thirteenth Ward in 1875, eighteen-year-old Heber J. Grant was a member of its superintendency. He subsequently helped pioneer this movement throughout the Church. At age twenty-three he was called to be president of the Tooele Stake in western Utah; he accepted this call even though it required him to move away from Salt Lake City at just the time he was getting established in his business career. Then, two years later, he was called to fill a vacancy in the Council of the Twelve Apostles.

Call to the Apostleship

President Grant later recalled the circumstances of his call to be a General Authority:

> I met the late Elder George Teasdale at the south gate of the Tabernacle grounds. He shook hands with me and said: "Brother Grant, I am delighted to see you. You and I are going to be—" and he stopped suddenly and his face turned red. But the Lord gave me the balance of the sentence. The balance of Brother Teasdale's sentence was—"sustained this afternoon as apostles of the Lord Jesus Christ to fill the vacancies in the Quorum." And that went through me like a shock of electricity. Those of you who were at that conference remember that it adjourned without filling those vacancies. I do not believe any mortal man ever more humbly supplicated God during the next few days to forgive him for his egotism than I did for thinking I was to be chosen an apostle.[6]

Within a week, President John Taylor published a revelation which read in part: "Thus said the Lord to the Twelve, and to the Priesthood and people of my Church: Let my servants George Teasdale and Heber J. Grant be appointed to fill the vacancies in the Twelve, that you may be fully organized and prepared for the labors devolving upon you, for you have a great work to perform. . . ."[7]

Even though this call was preceded by a spiritual premonition and came in the form of a written revelation, still Elder Grant did not feel comfortable in his new position. He later wrote:

> I felt that the honor was beyond anything that ought to have come to me, that I was too young, too inexperienced and really unworthy of such a great honor. The adversary tried to convince me that I should resign. On more than one occasion when I would testify of my knowledge that Jesus is the Savior it

seemed—although I did not hear a voice—as though I was told: "You lie. You have never seen the Savior, and you have no right to testify of him." On more than one occasion I woke up in the night with a strong feeling: You ought to resign; you ought to resign as an apostle.

I was riding through the Navajo Indian reservation in Arizona. . . . I was feeling very, very depressed. All at once I stopped the mule on which I was riding, and, in the language of Nephi, "I seemed to see," I didn't see but I seemed to see a council in heaven, where they were discussing the fact that the general conference of the Church had adjourned and that no choice had been made to fill the two vacancies in the quorum of the Apostles. A general discussion ensued, and the Prophet and my father favored sending a revelation that I should be one of the two persons chosen to fill those vacancies. I had with me a copy of the revelation to John Taylor calling George Teasdale and myself to the apostleship, and I took it out of my pocket and sat there and wept for joy to think that it had been manifested to me that the Prophet Joseph and my father had interceded in my behalf.[8]

In 1877 Heber J. Grant had married Lucy Stringham, and in 1884 he married Emily Wells and Augusta Winters. This thrust him into the midst of the difficulties caused by the anti-plural marriage persecution of the late nineteenth century. By the time he became President of the Church, however, only Augusta was still living. Despite the many demands placed on his time as a General Authority, Heber J. Grant consistently was a considerate husband and devoted father. His ten daughters and their families always had an important place in his life.

Elder Grant's mission to Japan was one of the most challenging assignments he ever received. The ability to converse in Japanese did not come easily to him but required much tedious effort. After about two years Elder Grant went out into a woods and prayed, saying that when his work was finished in Japan, he would "appreciate it" if he were called to the British Isles. Two or three days after uttering that prayer he received a cable to come home on the first vessel.[9] Soon after his return from Japan his prayer was answered; he was sent to preside over the British Mission for three years. These experiences did much to round out his personal understanding of the opportunities as well as the challenges facing the Church worldwide.

President Grant's Character and Teachings

Following the death of President Joseph F. Smith in November 1918, Heber J. Grant became the seventh prophet and President of The Church of Jesus Christ of Latter-day Saints. He was not sustained publicly for several months, however. Because of the serious flu epidemic, the general conference normally held in April was not convened until June 1, 1919. On that occasion President Grant was sustained in a solemn assembly, the vote being cast by individual priesthood groups. He would preside longer than any other president except Brigham Young. His twenty-seven-year administration stretched from the conclusion of World War I to the end of World War II.

President Grant delegated much of the detailed administrative responsibility for ecclesiastical programs to his capable counselors, leaving him more time to make important contributions in the realms of business affairs and personal relations. Heber J. Grant was at home with the financial leaders and chief executives of many of the nation's largest corporations. They were his personal friends who "welcomed him warmly" and listened as he related faith-promoting experiences or spoke of the Saints' aspirations. These businessmen "found in President Grant a man of simple faith, one whose utter frankness bespoke an honesty that could be relied upon implicitly. . . ."[10] These contacts were not only an important force in developing a more favorable attitude toward the Church and its members but were also vital in securing aid during periods of financial difficulty. On several occasions he was instrumental in arranging necessary financing for Church-related enterprises.

Heber J. Grant's ability to make friends, to deal with people both great and small, and to show concern for the individual were important qualities of his life. A close associate observed that "he had no particular interest in the accumulation of money except for the good he could do with it." For example, "no one will ever know how many mortgages on homes of widows he paid out of his own funds."[11] He loved to present good books to his associates or even to casual acquaintances, each year distributing scores, or probably hundreds, of volumes in this way.

President Grant was a particularly powerful advocate of the need to obey God's commandments. He often reflected a strong personal commitment to the principles of tithing and to abstinence from liquor and tobacco as taught in the Word of Wisdom. Concerning tithing he declared:

> Now, I believe that people are blessed in proportion to their liberality. I am not saying that they always make more dollars, perhaps, than the other man, but so far as an increase in the faith and in the testimony and the knowledge of the divinity of the work in which we are engaged, men that are honest with the Lord in the payment of their tithing grow as men never grow that are not honest; there is no question in my mind. . . . I believe that to those who are liberal the Lord gives ideas, and they grow in capacity and ability more rapidly than those that are stingy. I have that faith, and I have had it from the time I was a boy.[12]

On the subject of the Word of Wisdom he testified: "There is absolutely no benefit to any human being derived from breaking the Word of Wisdom, but there is everything for his benefit, morally, intellectually, physically, and spiritually, in obeying it."[13] In 1931 President Grant and his counselors lamented: "Never before have the emissaries of the tobacco interests been so active as now in the endeavor to fasten the cigarette habit upon our boys and girls." They believed this was a fulfillment of the Lord's warning against the "evils and designs which do and will exist in the hearts of conspiring men in the last days." "In view of the present conditions," the First Presidency concluded, "we feel constrained to call upon all Saints to be faithful in observing the warning contained in this revelation [the Word of Wisdom], that they may enjoy the wonderful promises made by the Lord to those who walk in obedience to his commandments."[14] President Grant increasingly emphasized observance of the Word of Wisdom as an appropriate measure of worthiness for baptism, priesthood advancement, or temple privileges.

"Keep the commandments" was an oft-repeated admonition by President Heber J. Grant. In his first sermon as President of the Church he anticipated this emphasis:

President Heber J. Grant, a physical-fitness enthusiast, often transacted Church business while golfing with ecclesiastical and business associates. Shown here are (from left) Stephen H. Love, James H. Wattis, President Grant, President Charles W. Nibley, and Elder Reed Smoot. (Church Archives)

I will ask no man to be more liberal with his means than I am with mine in proportion to what he possesses, for the advancement of God's kingdom. I will ask no man to observe the Word of Wisdom any more closely than I observe it. I will ask no man to be more conscientious and prompt in the payment of his tithes and his offerings than I will be. I will ask no man to be more ready and willing to come early and to go late and to labor with full power of mind and body than I will labor, always in humility.[15]

Related to President Grant's emphasis on the Word of Wisdom was his keen interest in personal fitness. "I have excellent health," he wrote during his mature years, "and attribute part of it to the fact that for several years past I have seldom missed a day without taking exercise unless I had the privilege of playing a game of golf." President Grant often combined business with pleasure, discussing important ecclesiastical or financial matters with his golfing companions. Another feature of his regimen was a one- or two-hour nap taken each afternoon in his office.[16]

Still, Heber J. Grant did not waste time. President Grant's personal secretary, Joseph Anderson, concluded: "I am convinced that one of the qualities most responsible for his prodigious achievements was his love of work." For example, thousands of Latter-day Saints or business associates received long letters dictated by President Grant when he could not sleep at night. In later years these would provide a valuable insight into his thinking and activities. Furthermore, in hotel rooms or when traveling by train he was often at work with Brother Anderson by six or seven in the morning taking care of necessary business.[17]

President Grant did not depend on his resources alone. Another important quality of his character was his deep spirituality and faith in God. His dependence on divine guidance was illustrated in an experience he had just after becoming President of the Church. For two months he pondered who should fill the vacancy he had left in the Quorum of the Twelve. As he considered those whom he regarded as worthy and qualified, he returned again and again to the name of Richard W. Young, a lifelong friend who had served as a general in the army, lawyer, successful businessman, and stake president. Finally, with the approval of his counselors, President Grant wrote the name Richard W. Young on a slip of paper, intending to present this nomination at the regular weekly meeting of the First Presidency and the Twelve in the temple. "President Grant removed the paper with the name written on it, fully intending to present him to the council for approval. But for a reason he could never fully explain, he was unable to do so; instead, he presented the name of Melvin J. Ballard, president of the Northwestern States Mission, a man with whom he had had very little personal contact."[18] This was a valuable lesson to President Grant, and confirmed the counsel he had received from President Joseph F. Smith just before that prophet's death: "The Lord bless you, my boy, the Lord bless you: you have got a great responsibility. Always remember that this is the Lord's work and not man's. The Lord is greater than any man. He knows whom he wants to lead his Church, and never makes any mistake."[19]

Not only did President Heber J. Grant represent a personal link with nineteenth-century beginnings but he was also well qualified to lead the Church in the twentieth century. His spiritual experiences, his example of overcoming difficulties through persistent effort, his business acumen, and his love for people, all combined to prepare him to meet the challenges that would face the Church and its members.

Geographical Expansion

Within the first few months of President Heber J. Grant's administration, Church membership passed five hundred thousand. Three-fourths of these Saints still lived in the essentially rural Intermountain area in western America. The next few years, however, would bring a definite geographical expansion of the Church's membership. Evidences of this trend included the growing number of Latter-day Saints in major cities, the dedication of new temples, and the increased personal involvement of General Authorities in supervising and directing the Church's progress worldwide.

Exodus from the Intermountain Area

Following the close of World War I, thousands of Latter-day Saints left the traditional centers of Mormon colonization in Utah and Idaho. The basically agricultural economy of the semi-arid Intermountain West did not share in the general prosperity of the 1920s. Furthermore, the coming of the tractor and other machinery reduced the need for manpower, thus lessening the number of jobs available on the farm. This resulted in the exodus, especially of younger people, from these areas to seek improved economic opportunites in major metropolitan centers, particularly in southern California. This outward flow was increased during the 1930s by the unusually severe impact of the Great Depression in the Mountain West.

The Latter-day Saints therefore were part of the continuing westward movement and the prevailing rural-urban shift of the general population. Church activity came to play a new and important role in the lives of these transplanted Saints. Though living in large cities, they found through their branches or wards the close friendships and associations they had enjoyed in the small towns left behind.

In 1920 there were 3,967 Church members in California; during the next ten years this number soared to 20,599, and by 1940 the total reached 44,784. During these same twenty years, the portion of all Latter-day Saints living in the Pacific Coast states increased from 2.8 percent to 10.9 percent.

While most nineteenth-century migrations of the Saints had been encouraged or even sponsored by the Church, the movements during the twentieth century were the results of individual decisions. At least some of the Saints leaving the Intermountain area wondered if they were doing the right thing. A group in Santa Monica, California, for example, asked President Heber J. Grant in 1921 if they were out of harmony with Church policy by living there. President Grant answered their letter in person during one of his frequent visits to the Golden State. He assured them that "at the present time the idea of a permanent Mormon settlement at Santa Monica was in full accordance with Church policies."[20]

The formation of new stakes was clear evidence of Latter-day Saint growth in widely scattered urban centers. In 1844 Joseph Smith had declared: "I have received instructions from the Lord that from henceforth wherever the Elders of Israel shall build up churches . . . there shall be a stake of Zion. In the great cities, as Boston, New York, etc., there shall be stakes."[21] In 1923 and 1927 stakes were established in Los Angeles and San Francisco, respectively, and during the 1930s stakes were organized in several other prominent United States cities.

The first stake east of the Intermountain area in modern times was formed in New York City in 1934. Mission President James H. Moyle had helped prepare the mission district to become a stake by setting up a stake organization in every detail.

The Washington D. C. Chapel (above) and the Hollywood (now Los Angeles) Stake Center symbolize the strength of the Church's growth in areas outside the Intermountain West. (Church Archives)

A series of other "firsts" followed: The Oahu Stake was formed in Hawaii in 1935. In 1936 the Chicago Stake became the first in the Midwest. The first stakes in the Pacific Northwest were organized two years later at Portland and Seattle. In 1940 the Denver and Washington stakes became the first along the east front of the Rockies and in the nation's capital, respectively. The construction of substantial chapels also was evidence of Latter-day Saint growth in these urban centers. Examples included the beautiful Hollywood (or Los Angeles) Stake Center and the Washington D.C. Chapel, dedicated in 1929 and 1933 respectively. Not only did these buildings provide adequate facilities for Church activities, but they were attractive places where the Saints could bring their nonmember friends.

Not all Church members leaving the Intermountain area went to large cities. Many joined the thousands already scattered throughout the United States and Canada. Organization of the Church's first branch in Alaska during 1938 was symbolic of this diffusion. In some areas nearly half of the members lived too far from the nearest chapel to participate in any group programs. Providing meaningful activity for these scattered Saints was a challenge. To relieve this problem, several missions had sponsored regional colonies where the scattered Saints might gather. Kelsey in northeast Texas, for example, flourished as a Mormon colony during the first several decades of the twentieth century.

The dispersion of Church membership was reflected by the location of the first three temples dedicated during the twentieth century. In contrast to the previous four temples, all located in Utah, these new structures all were located far from the headquarters of the Church. Construction of the Hawaii and Alberta temples had begun under the leadership of President Joseph F. Smith, but they were dedicated in 1919 and 1923, respectively, by President Heber J. Grant. In 1921 President Grant selected the site for a temple in Mesa, Arizona; he dedicated that beautiful structure six years later. These three imposing buildings attracted much favorable comment and symbolized the Church's commitment to continued activity and growth in Hawaii, western Canada, and Arizona.

Developments Abroad

As missionary work began to revive following the close of World War I, the General Authorities felt the need to have at least one of their number become personally acquainted with conditions in all parts of the world. President Grant therefore assigned Elder David O. McKay of the Quorum of the Twelve to undertake a personal inspection tour of the Church's far-flung missions and schools. At the time of this appointment, Elder McKay was serving as head of the Church's educational system, as General Superintendent of the Sunday School, and as chairman of the committee assigned to correlate priesthood and auxiliary activities. This broad experience would enable him to be an effective observer of Church activities around the globe. Assigned to be his companion was Hugh J. Cannon, editor of the *Improvement Era,* who had served a mission to Germany and as president of the Liberty Stake in Salt Lake City. Elders McKay and Cannon were set apart for their tour by President Heber J. Grant on December 2, 1920, and departed almost immediately.

During the next thirteen months the two men traveled approximately fifty-six thousand miles by sea and by land. They visited the Church's missions on the islands of the Pacific, dedicated China for the preaching of the gospel, experienced the unique challenges in the non-Christian lands of southeast Asia, witnessed firsthand the Jewish-Arab tensions in the Holy Land, and finally toured the missions of Europe before returning home.

Their report gave the General Authorities an unprecedented worldwide vision of the Church's challenges and opportunities. More than ever before, Church leaders were now in a position to weigh the needs of one area against those of another. This perspective undoubtedly influenced developments in many parts of the world.

By 1924 the outlook for missionary work in Japan had become quite bleak. Since the mission had opened in 1901, only 174 converts had been baptized. Linguistic and cultural differences were now compounded by a growing sense of

Japanese nationalism. The 1924 United States immigration law greatly restricted the number of Orientals who could enter the country and was very offensive to the Japanese. These and other conditions led President Heber J. Grant, who had opened the mission twenty-three years earlier, to order the temporary removal of all Latter-day Saint missionaries from Japan. Although the accomplishments of the mission may have appeared meager, there were some lasting contributions. The Book of Mormon and other Church literature had been translated into Japanese. There were a few active Saints who worked to keep the Church organization functioning and who remained faithful during the dark years that would follow. Some of them would be present to help the Church get reestablished in Japan following World War II.

While proselyting was being closed in Asia, missionary work in South America was about to begin. The first gospel seeds were sown not by missionaries from North America but by immigrants from Europe, and not among South America's Spanish-speaking majority but among a German-speaking minority. Following the close of World War I, a large number of Germans left Europe in quest of a better future in South America, particularly in Argentina and southern Brazil. Wilhelm Friedrichs, a Latter-day Saint convert, and his family arrived in 1923. Emil Hoppe, whom Friedrichs had helped convert in Germany, followed soon afterwards. Friedrichs and Hoppe eagerly shared the gospel with other German immigrants, and soon several families were interested. Friedrichs reported his activities to the First Presidency and requested that missionaries be sent to Argentina.

In the fall of 1925 Church leaders sent Elder Melvin J. Ballard of the Quorum of the Twelve to South America to open a mission there. He was accompanied by two members of the First Council of the Seventy—Elder Rulon S. Wells, who spoke fluent German, and Elder Rey L. Pratt (then serving as president of the Mexican Mission), whose knowledge of Spanish and of Latin American culture would prove essential. Upon their arrival in Buenos Aires, they were greeted by the Friedrichs and Hoppe families with tears of gratitude. Early on Christmas morning 1925, Elder Ballard and his companions

On Christmas Day of 1925, Elder Melvin J. Ballard (center) dedicated the continent of South America for the preaching of the gospel. (Church Archives)

went to a secluded grove of weeping willows near the banks of the La Plata. On this beautiful summer morning the group knelt and Elder Ballard offered a prayer dedicating South America for the proclamation of the gospel. He especially petitioned that promises made to the descendants of Lehi might soon be fulfilled. Just before returning home a few months later, Elder Ballard prophesied that the work would grow slowly at first, but that eventually thousands would be baptized. Within a few years, missionary work had spread into southern Brazil, but the full realization of Elder Ballard's prophecies would not come until after World War II.[22]

Church leaders continued to counsel European Saints to remain in their homelands and build up the Church there. Despite this counsel, however, many remembered the earlier ideal of "gathering to Zion" and believed that they could escape from poverty by emigrating to America. Therefore the

years 1923 to 1930 witnessed the heaviest emigration the German Mission had ever experienced up to that time. Consequently, Church membership in Europe grew very slowly, increasing from 25,500 in 1920 to only 28,000 a decade later.
There was, however, at least one new area into which the
gospel was introduced during these years; Czechoslovakia was
opened to missionary work in 1929.

The Church's Centennial

The decade of the 1920s witnessed a series of centennial
observances. At the April general conference in 1920, Church
leaders marked the one-hundredth anniversary of Joseph
Smith's vision of the Father and the Son by stressing the
authenticity of his testimony and by paying tribute to his
work. A cantata entitled "The Vision," especially prepared for
the occasion by Evan Stephens, was also presented. In 1923
and 1927 Saints and missionaries from the eastern states
gathered at the Hill Cumorah and the Sacred Grove near Palmyra, New York, to commemorate respectively the first visit of
the Angel Moroni and Joseph Smith's receiving the gold plates
of the Book of Mormon one hundred years earlier. In 1928 the
Church completed the purchase of 283 acres that included the
entire Hill Cumorah. Two years earlier, the Church had also
purchased the Peter Whitmer farm near Fayette, New York,
where the Church was organized in 1830. In 1937 the Church
would purchase a portion of the Martin Harris farm near Palmyra, and would also begin to acquire property in Nauvoo,
Illinois, including the former temple site. All these celebrations
reached a climax with the centennial of the Church's organization. A group of General Authorities were assigned to plan the
1930 observance. George Albert Smith, a member of the
Twelve deeply interested in Church history, was chairman.
The appointment of these key leaders reflected the importance
the Church gave its centennial observance.

As the time of the centennial conference drew near, Saints
began pouring into Salt Lake City from all parts of the Church.
To accommodate the huge crowds desiring to attend one of
the sessions in the Tabernacle, Church leaders added a fourth

day to the usual three-day conference format. The opening day, Sunday, April 6, the one-hundredth anniversary of the Church's organization, was the highlight.

Special services were outlined for the opening session Sunday morning. President Heber J. Grant read the First Presidency's centennial message to the peoples of the world. It bore witness to the divine mission of the Savior and to the latter-day restoration of his Church through the Prophet Joseph Smith. The message called on Church members around the world "to rededicate their lives to the service of the Master and the establishment of His kingdom upon the earth."[23]

Church leaders were sustained by the vote of the various orders of the priesthood separately and then by the entire congregation. Each priesthood group sat in an assigned area on the main floor in the Tabernacle and stood as a body to vote when its turn came. Normally this procedure is reserved for "solemn assemblies" at which a new president of the Church is being installed. When the voting was concluded, the entire congregation stood and rendered the hallowed "Hosanna Shout" by waving white handkerchiefs as they shouted in unison: "Hosanna, Hosanna, Hosanna to God and the Lamb; Amen, Amen, and Amen." Because the Saints identified it with such special events as temple dedications, the shout, like the special manner of voting, added impressively to the spirit and solemnity of the conference.

The Church's seven temples were illuminated for the first time during conference week "to indicate the joy of the people that the work of the Lord had successfully completed its first century of existence."[24] A centennial pageant, "The Message of the Ages," opened in the Tabernacle on Sunday evening, April 6. A working force of fifteen hundred persons included the cast, the Tabernacle Choir, and an orchestra. The pageant reviewed how the gospel, known to ancient prophets, was again restored in the latter days.

The centennial observances reinforced the Latter-day Saints' interest in Church history. During the Sunday afternoon session of conference, Elder B. H. Roberts presented the several large volumes of his *Comprehensive History of the Church,* which was being published as an official part of the centennial. He indicated that this work contained the sermon he would like to preach and the testimony he would like to bear on the occasion of the Church's centennial. The six volumes represented a publication in book form of the history originally written by Elder Roberts for *Americana* magazine between 1909 and 1915. Two of Elder Roberts's associates in the Church historian's office were also making significant contributions: Elder Joseph Fielding Smith's *Essentials in Church History,* which had been published in 1921 as a lesson manual for the Melchizedek Priesthood quorums, would continue to be the most popular single-volume Church history for more than half a century. Andrew Jenson had compiled eight hundred large manuscript volumes, about half giving histories of specific local units and the remainder being the day-by-day "Journal History of the Church." At the time of the Church's centennial, Jenson was completing publication of his multi-volume *Latter-day Saint Biographical Encyclopedia* and was condensing his histories of Church units for publication in a single reference volume to be known as the *Encyclopedic History of the Church.*

The opening years of Heber J. Grant's administration, then, saw a substantial geographical expansion in Church membership at the same time as the series of centennial observances was focusing the Saints' attention on their heritage. But there were other important developments occurring during these same years. One of the most important of these was a redefinition of emphasis in the Church's educational program, which is discussed in the next chapter.

6 Charting the Course in Education

L atter-day Saints have always been interested in education, believing that knowledge has eternal significance. During President Heber J. Grant's administration, however, serious questions were raised concerning the nature of the Church's educational program and what direction it should take. These concerns arose because of the economic burden of operating a system of schools and because of worries of the possible adverse effect of purely secular scholarship on the faith of young Latter-day Saints.

The Saints have turned to revelations received through the Prophet Joseph Smith in order to support their commitment to education. Frequently cited passages include: "The glory of God is intelligence, or in other words, light and truth." "It is impossible for a man to be saved in ignorance." (D&C 93:36; 131:6; see also 130:18-19.) Although the foregoing passages refer primarily to spiritual knowledge and attainment, the following injunction refers more clearly to the importance of gaining a broad education: "And I give unto you a commandment that you shall teach one another the doctrine of the kingdom. . . . [And] of things both in heaven and in the earth, and under the earth; things which have been, things which are, things which must shortly come to pass; things

1888	Church Board of Education organized
1890	Religion Classes founded for elementary school students
1912	First seminary established near Salt Lake City
1920	Church decided to close its academies
1926	First Institute of Religion at University of Idaho
1931-33	Church's junior colleges, except Ricks, closed
1932	Deseret Club organized in Los Angeles
1938	President J. Reuben Clark, Jr., delivered address on "The Charted Course of the Church in Education"; boards of Church schools consolidated

which are at home, things which are abroad; the wars and the perplexities of the nations, and the judgments which are on the land; and a knowledge also of countries and of kingdoms. . . . Yea, seek ye out of the best books words of wisdom; seek learning, even by study and also by faith." (D&C 88:77, 79, 118; see also 90:15 and 93:53.)

Consequently the Saints organized the School of the Prophets in Kirtland, one of the earliest programs for adult education in the United States. Upon arriving in the Great Basin they quickly established local elementary schools and a territorial university. In the 1870s Brigham Young inaugurated a system of "academies" or Church high schools, which grew to more than two dozen schools from Canada to Mexico during the following decade. To promote and give direction to these schools, the Church organized its board of education in 1888.

By the end of the nineteenth century, forces were at work that would drastically change the character of the Latter-day Saints' educational system. The increasing number of non-Mormons in Utah led in 1890 to the passage of a territorial law forbidding religious instruction in public schools and providing for the establishment of public high schools. Therefore, during that same year the Church founded Religion Classes to provide weekday religious instruction that would supplement the secular learning children were receiving in public elementary schools. These classes convened in ward buildings after school, generally one afternoon each week. Thus, this new auxiliary functioned side by side with the Primary, which had been organized twelve years earlier. While the Primary emphasized religious activity, the Religion Class concentrated on instruction. Then, as religious instruction was eliminated from the University of Deseret (which was renamed the University of Utah in 1892), several of the Church's academies began to add college-level courses, particularly in the field of teacher education.

With the growth of the free tax-supported high schools, enrollment declined in the LDS academies, where students were required to pay tuition. President Joseph F. Smith was quite concerned over this trend. He explained why the Church continued to spend a substantial share of its tithing funds to support the academies:

> The object, I may say, almost the only purpose, for the maintenance of church schools is that true religion undefiled before God the Father may be inculcated in the minds and hearts of our children while they are getting an education, to enable the heart, the soul, and the spirit of our children to develop with proper teaching in connection with the secular training that they receive in schools.[1]

Nevertheless, the trend continued, and by 1911 there were more Latter-day Saint youth attending the public than the Church schools. The Church therefore inaugurated a part-time religious education program similar to the Religion Classes, but for high school students. The first of these "seminaries" was opened in 1912 at Granite High School near Salt Lake City. This was done on recommendation by the Granite Stake Presidency. The new program quickly proved to be an effective way to supplement the secular education students were receiving in public high schools, and within a few years several more seminaries were opened, primarily in Utah. Thus, in the early twentieth century, the Church was conducting two distinct types of educational programs: (1) full-time schools providing secular as well as religious instruction; and (2) part-time religious education, the Religion Classes and seminaries, which supplemented secular instruction in public schools.

A Decade of Decision

The Church needed to decide whether to emphasize its full-time schools or its part-time religious education programs. In 1919 three members of the Twelve were called to give direction to the education work. Elder David O. McKay, formerly principal of one of the Church's academies, and recently appointed general superintendent of the Sunday School, became commissioner; Elders Stephen L Richards and Richard R. Lyman became assistant commissioners. Adam S. Bennion became the new superintendent of Church schools the same year.

The first step toward the Church's discontinuing its full-time schools came in 1920. The Board of Education adopted the following recommendations of Commissioner McKay: (1) Most of the academies should be closed because they were supported by funds from all over the Church while benefiting a relatively limited area. (2) A few of the academies, where college-level courses had already been incorporated—Dixie Academy in St. George, Brigham Young College in Logan, Weber Academy in Ogden, Snow Academy in Ephraim, all in Utah; and Ricks Academy in Rexburg, Idaho—would become Church junior colleges stressing "normal" or teacher-education programs. (3) Courses leading to a four-year degree would be concentrated at Brigham Young University.[2] By 1923 nine academies had been closed and their buildings made available to the state at nominal cost. High school courses were also eliminated from the junior colleges.

The next major step in reshaping the Church's educational program came following a series of key Board of Education meetings during February and March 1926. President Heber J. Grant identified the underlying cause for this reappraisal of the Church's activities in education when he declared: "I am free to confess that nothing has worried me more since I became president than the expansion of the appropriation for the Church School system. With the idea of cutting down the expense, we appointed three of the Apostles as Commissioners; but instead of cutting down, we have increased and increased. . . ." In 1925 the Church had spent $958,440.67 for education, which amounted to 25.9 percent of its total tithing expenditures.[3]

To guide the board in its deliberations, Superintendent Adam S. Bennion in 1926 formulated some specific questions (some of which are still being asked a half-century later): "1. Does the Church receive benefit in return from an eight to one investment in Church schools as against Seminaries? 2. Do these returns equal the returns possible in other fields from the same investment? 3. Does there lie ahead in the field of the Junior College the same competition with State institutions that has been encountered in the high school field? 4. Can the Church afford to operate a university which will be able creditably to carry on against the richly endowed universities of our land?"

At the conclusion of these discussions the board decided to continue establishing seminaries wherever they were needed and wanted, and to "withdraw from the field of the junior colleges" as the state made provisions to operate its own schools. Brigham Young University was to concentrate on upper division work, especially the preparation of teachers, and to work toward becoming a superior, though not necessarily large, Church university.[4]

The first school to be closed was the Latter-day Saints College in Salt Lake City. After 1931 only two departments continued, as the LDS Business College and the McCune School of Music. The college's campus, located just behind the Hotel Utah on the block east of Temple Square, provided badly needed space for the Genealogical Society library and for administrative offices of the auxiliaries and other Church organizations.

The board offered the facilities of other Church junior colleges to the respective local governments at nominal cost, with the understanding that these schools would be kept open. Under such an agreement Snow College in Ephraim was transferred to the state of Utah in 1932, as were Weber College in Ogden and Dixie College in St. George the following year.

Gila College in Thatcher, Arizona, was transferred to the county in 1933. When Ricks College property was offered to Idaho, however, the state declined to assume this added economic burden. The Church therefore appropriated its own funds to keep Ricks College going.[5]

The board decided to retain Brigham Young University as part of the Church's educational program. Commissioner Joseph F. Merrill explained three reasons for this decision:

> 1. . . . a university [is] an essential unit in our seminary system. For our seminary teachers must be specially trained for their work. The Brigham Young University is our training school.
> 2. We are living in a "scientific age," many are pleased to call it an age in which the methods of science have permeated to a greater or lesser extent into all the activities of the human mind. And do we not need in the Church a group of scholars, learned in history, science and philosophy, scholars of standing and ability who can interpret for us and make plain to us the results of research and the reasoning of the human mind? When men find that we are learned in their science and philosophy they have respect for us, one that ignorance could never command. How can we be assured a group of scholars, familiar and sympathetic with our doctrines and ideals, scholars able and ready to be our advocates and defenders, unless we have a university?
> 3. I offer as a third reason why we need a university the fact that Latter-day Saint ideals are in many respects different from, and higher than, those of the average non-Latter-day Saint. Do we not need a university that shall hold up Latter-day Saint ideals so high in the educational world that all students in all schools of all grades may see the beauty thereof, and perhaps be influenced by them?[6]

Thus by 1930 the Church had definitely placed its emphasis on part-time religious education. Only a few Church schools remained. These included Brigham Young University, Ricks College, LDS Business College, and McCune School of Music. The Church continued to operate the Juarez Academy and elementary schools in its northern Mexican colonies. Missions also operated several small schools in the South Pacific; one of the largest of these, the Maori Agricultural College in

Payson, Utah, Seminary in 1926, at a time when the Church was expanding its part-time programs for religious education. (Church Archives)

New Zealand, however, closed following a disastrous earthquake in 1931.

Emphasis on Seminaries and Institutes

While the Church was taking steps to close most of its full-time schools, its part-time programs of religious instruction were expanding. For example, seminary enrollment grew from about five thousand in 1922 to nearly thirty thousand a decade later. The relative economy of these part-time programs would become increasingly attractive as the Great Depression of the 1930s tightened restrictions on Church funds. By 1938 seminary enrollment had reached 38,939. Typically these classes were offered in Latter-day Saint communities, mostly in Utah and southern Idaho, but a few scattered classes were also offered in Colorado, Nevada, and Wyoming.[7]

Seminary classes were conducted on a "released-time" basis. This meant that students would take seminary instruction much the same as any other class during their regular

Development of Latter-day Saint Education

Elementary Education	Secondary Education	Higher Education
Schools founded in Ohio, Missouri and Illinois	Provided in Ohio, Missouri and Illinois beginning with the School of the Prophets in 1833	University of Nauvoo chartered 1840
Sunday School founded in 1849 Tax-supported schools established immediately in pioneer settlements in the Rocky Mts.	Gap existed between elementary and secondary education	University of Deseret chartered 1850
Primary Association organized in 1878	Protestant groups founded schools in Utah to convert the Mormons	
Increasing non-Mormon population lessened Church influence over schools	Brigham Young Academy founded in 1875—first of 22 Church academies	Increasing non-Mormon population lessened L.D.S. influence
	Church Board of Education founded 1888	
Public School Law 1890 prohibited religious instruction in the public school	First public high school—1890	University of Deseret became University of Utah 1892
Religion Classes established 1890		

Church stressed "normal" work to provide public school teachers

B.Y. Academy added college level courses and name changed to Brigham Young University 1903

B.Y. College, Logan, Weber, Dixie, Gila, Snow and Ricks became Church junior colleges 1920s

First Institute of Religion at University of Idaho 1926

Church junior colleges (except Ricks) transferred to states 1930s

In 1911 public high schools exceeded declining academies' enrollment

First Seminary established at Granite High School in S.L.C. 1912

Church academies abandoned (except Juarez) 1920s—some became junior colleges, others became public high schools

Junior Seminaries established 1929

Religion Classes merged into Primary 1929

Church has expanded school systems in the Southern Pacific and in Latin America

Early-morning seminaries expand during 1950s

Unified Church School System Organized 1953

Church College of Hawaii opened 1955

Home Study Seminary 1967

Church Commissioner Appointed 1970

CCH became BYU Hawaii Campus 1974

school day. Over the years there have been several inconclu-
sive challenges to this system. One of these came in 1930 when
the state high school inspector charged that the principle of
separation between church and state was being violated because high school credit was granted for religion classes and
because public funds helped bus students who spent one hour
of their day in seminary. In response, Commissioner Joseph F.
Merrill pointed out that giving credit for Bible courses taught in
private schools was an accepted practice, and that seminaries
actually reduced public educational costs by providing classes
for many students one hour each day.

Finally, the state board of education ordered the seminaries be operated as completely separate units but approved
granting high school credit for some seminary classes.[8] Most
local school boards supported the LDS seminary program.
Ironically, only in Salt Lake City did the board reject the released-time concept, resulting in seminary classes being held
early in the morning before school hours. Consequently,
seminary enrollment was only 10 percent in Salt Lake City,
while the average in released-time areas was 70 percent.

A similar part-time religious education program, originally
called Collegiate Seminary, had developed on the university
level. It began in 1926 when the First Presidency personally
appointed J. Wylie Sessions to go to the University of Idaho in
Moscow "to take care of our boys and girls" there, and "to see
what the Church ought to do for our students attending state
universities." Sessions, who had a background in education
but not in religious instruction, analyzed any information he
could find about what other groups were doing to get religion
onto college campuses. He particularly patterned his program
after the religious "foundations" at the University of Illinois.
The name "Institute of Religion" was suggested by a non-
Mormon friend in Idaho. Sessions believed that classes with
solid academic content, along with well-planned social activities and an attractive, well-equipped building, were all essential
to his program for competing successfully for the students'
time.[9]

By 1929 similar programs had been established on two
other campuses, and during the 1930s institutes spread to a

total of seventeen locations, including all major schools in the Intermountain states as well as the University of Wyoming and several locations in California. Sessions personally supervised the inauguration of the program and the erection of facilities at several of these locations.

Unusual circumstances led to the establishing of institutes in southern California. In 1935 the University of Southern California invited the Church to send a representative to instruct academic classes on Mormonism in its school of religion. Elder John A. Widtsoe of the Council of the Twelve, a former university president, received this assignment. Following the 1935-36 school year, G. Byron Done was appointed to succeed Elder Widtsoe and to become director of the institute in Los Angeles. In order to promote the institute programs and to provide additional social contacts for students, Done inaugurated "fireside chats," informal gatherings on Sunday evenings that treated topics of current interest.

The institutes provided an opportunity to integrate religious instruction with the secular university studies. By 1938 there were approximately four thousand students enrolled.

A companion program, the Deseret Club, had its beginning in southern California. A group of leading Latter-day Saints felt the need to bring students together for intellectual and social activities within the influence of Latter-day Saint ideals and standards. The Deseret Club was formally organized in 1932 at the campus of the University of California at Los Angeles (UCLA). The clubs soon spread to other Los Angeles college campuses. When Elder Widtsoe was in the area, he recognized the value of the Deseret Club activity in the lives of LDS students, and in 1936 he was instrumental in bringing it under the official sponsorship of the Church Board of Education. Eventually, Deseret clubs came to be organized on campuses where there were not enough Latter-day Saint students to justify establishing an institute of religion.[10]

Worldly Scholarship and the Gospel

LDS educational leaders during the twentieth century have stressed the importance of scholarly preparation for faculty members, especially in the Church's schools. This training, however, made some Church authorities and even members fear that the classes of certain teachers were becoming increasingly tainted by the false notions of the world.

President George H. Brimhall of Brigham Young University was eager to strengthen the school's faculty and to expand its curriculum. Between 1907 and 1909, therefore, he hired four new teachers who had advanced degrees from leading universities of the nation; one of these was the first Ph.D. to teach at BYU. These teachers, however, enthusiastically presented their speculative theories as the product of the most current scientific research. Students were confused when these ideas came into conflict with traditional gospel teachings. Following a careful investigation, the Church's superintendent of schools concluded that these professors treated the Bible as only "a collection of myths [and] folklore" with "some inspiration," that they rejected the idea of miracles, and presented "the theory of evolution . . . as demonstrated law."[11] Just two years earlier, the First Presidency had affirmed that Adam was "the primal parent of our race" who "began life as a human being, in the likeness of our heavenly Father," and that the notion that "the original human being was a development from lower forms of the animal creation" is just one of "the theories of men."[12] When these teachers were dismissed in 1911, many predicted that this action would lead to the demise of BYU. In response, President Brimhall asserted, ". . . if the life of the college depends on any number of men out of harmony with the brethren who preside over the Church, then it is time for the college to die." He believed that he could have sided with the professors and received much popular acclaim, but added, "I would rather be a Moses on the Mount with all of Israel against me, than Aaron at the altar of the golden calf with all of Israel dancing around and praising me."[13]

President Joseph F. Smith was concerned that inexperienced students were not always equipped to determine whether or not a given theory was true, and that discussions of such topics only leave the young people "in an unsettled frame of mind." He explained that "the conclusion that evolution would be best left out of discussion in our Church schools" was not any indication of how much of this theory may be true or false. While the Lord has not revealed the "modus operandi" employed in creating the world, President Smith declared, he has revealed the "simple way we may serve him" and there need be no speculation about this. President Smith was concerned that speculation on modern theories would only lead to the formation of a "scholarly aristocracy" which would undermine the unity that should exist among members of the Church.[14]

Academic scholarship, particularly in the field of religion, received increasing emphasis in the later 1920s and 1930s. With the expansion of the seminaries and the inauguration of the institutes, Church educational leaders felt the need to provide more adequate training and curriculum materials for the teachers in these programs. Instruction in theology was expanded at Brigham Young University. In 1930 Guy C. Wilson, who had opened the first seminary nearly two decades earlier, now became the first full-time religion teacher at BYU. Special summer courses were offered for seminary and institute teachers, and from 1930 to 1933 noted scholars in biblical and religious studies came to BYU as guest lecturers. At the same time, several promising graduate students were encouraged to seek advanced degrees at such noted centers as the Chicago Divinity School. By the mid-1930s, however, an increasing number of Church members and leaders were concerned over teachers of religion being trained by non-Latter-day Saint scholars, and were worried that "higher criticism of the scriptures" and other "humanistic" ideas were creeping into what was being taught. These concerns led the General Authorities to give much closer supervision to the Church's educational system, especially to religious instruction. Two members of the Twelve were assigned to interview all faculty members at Brigham Young University to determine their loyalty to the Church and its teachings. As a result of this attention, several teachers felt uncomfortable and left BYU to accept positions elsewhere.[15]

Two new counselors called to the First Presidency during the 1930s played a key role in giving important direction to education as well as to other Church programs. J. Reuben

The First Presidency from
1934 to 1945: (from left) J.
Reuben Clark, Jr., Heber J.
Grant, and David O. McKay.
(Utah State Historical Society)

Clark, Jr., and David O. McKay became counselors to President
Heber J. Grant in 1933 and 1934 respectively. Following a
quarter-century's distinguished diplomatic career, President
Clark had become under-secretary of state and was serving as
the United States ambassador to Mexico at the time of his call
to the First Presidency. Perhaps none have come into the Presidency with a richer background in Church service than did
David O. McKay; his name has appeared in earlier pages of this
work in connection with his significant priesthood, Sunday
School, correlation, education, and missionary assignments.

In 1938 President Clark was assigned to set forth the mission of the Church's education program and to outline the
duties of those employed to teach in the Church's schools,
institutes, and seminaries. His address, "The Charted Course
for the Church in Education," was delivered at a special
summer gathering of teachers at Aspen Grove in Provo
Canyon near the BYU campus and has become an oft-quoted
classic. President Clark began by citing "some of the more outstanding and essential fundamentals underlying our Church
school education":

The following are to me those fundamentals.

The Church is the organized Priesthood of God, the priesthood can exist without the Church, but the Church cannot exist without the Priesthood. The mission of the Church is . . . to teach, encourage, assist, and protect the individual member [and] the membership as a group in its living of the Gospel. . . . The Church is militantly to proclaim the truth, calling upon all men to repent, and to live in obedience to the Gospel, "for every knee must bow and every tongue confess."

In all this there are for the Church and for each and all of its members, two prime things which may not be overlooked, forgotten, blinked, shaded, or discarded:

First: That Jesus Christ is the Son of God, the Only Begotten of the Father in the flesh, the Creator of the world, the Lamb of God, the sacrifice for the sins of the world, the atoner for Adam's transgression; that He was crucified, that His spirit left His body, that he died; that He was laid away in the tomb; that on the third day His spirit was reunited with His body, which again became a living being; that He was raised from the tomb a resurrected being, a perfect being, the First Fruits of the Resurrection; that He later ascended to the Father; and that because of His death and by and through His resurrection every man born into the world since the beginning will be likewise literally resurrected.

These positive facts, and all other facts necessarily implied therein, must all be honestly believed in full faith, by every member of the Church.

The second of the two things to which we must all give full faith is: That the Father and the Son actually and in truth and very deed appeared to the Prophet Joseph in a vision in the woods; that other heavenly visions followed to Joseph and to others; that the Gospel and the holy Priesthood after the Order of the Son of God were in truth and fact restored to the earth from which they were lost by the apostasy of the Primitive Church; that the Lord again set up His Church, through the agency of Joseph Smith; that the Book of Mormon is just what it professes to be; that to the Prophet came numerous revelations for the guidance, upbuilding, organization, and encouragement of the Church and its members; that the Prophet's successors, likewise called of God, have received revelations as the needs of the Church have required and that they will continue to receive revelations as the Church and its members, living the truth they already have, shall stand in need of more; that this is in truth The Church of Jesus Christ of Latter-day Saints; and that its foundation beliefs are the laws and principles laid down in the Articles of Faith. These facts also, and each of them, together with all things necessarily implied therein or flowing therefrom, must stand, unchanged, unmodified, without dilution, excuse, apology, or avoidance; they may not be explained away or submerged. Without these two great beliefs the Church would cease to be the Church.

Any individual who does not accept the fulness of these doctrines as to Jesus of Nazareth or as to the restoration of the Gospel and Holy Priesthood, is not a Latter-day Saint; the hundreds of thousands of faithful, God-fearing men and women who compose the great body of the Church membership do believe these things fully and completely; and they support the Church and its institutions because of this belief.

Then, speaking more directly to teachers, President Clark continued:

The youth of the Church, your students, are in great majority sound in thought and in spirit. The problem primarily is to keep them sound, not to convert them.

The youth of the Church are hungry for things of the spirit; they are eager to learn the Gospel, and they want it straight, undiluted. . . . Doubt must not be planted in their hearts. Great is the burden and the condemnation of any teacher who sows doubt in a trusting soul. . . .

May I not say now a few words to you teachers?

In the first place, there is neither reason nor is there excuse for our Church religious teaching and training facilities and institutions, unless the youth are to be taught and trained in the principles of the Gospel, embracing therein the two great elements that Jesus is the Christ and that Joseph was God's prophet. The teaching of a system of ethics to the students is not a sufficient reason for running our seminaries and institutes. The great public school system teaches ethics. . . .

The first requisite of a teacher for teaching these principles is a personal testimony of their truthfulness. No amount of learning, no amount of study, and no number of scholastic degrees, can take the place of this testimony, which is the *sine qua non* of the teacher in our Church school system. No teacher who does not have a real testimony of the truthfulness of the Gospel as revealed to and believed by the Latter-day Saints, and a testimony of the Sonship and Messiahship of Jesus, and of the divine mission of Joseph Smith—including in all its reality the First Vision—has any place in the Church system. . . .

You do have an interest in matters purely cultural and in matters of purely secular knowledge; but, I repeat again for emphasis, your chief interest, your essential and all but sole duty, is to teach the Gospel of the Lord Jesus Christ as that has been revealed in these latter days. You are to teach this Gospel using as your sources and authorities the Standard Works of the Church, and the words of those whom God has called to lead His people in these last days. You are not, whether high or low, to intrude into your work your own peculiar philosophy, no matter what its source or how pleasing or rational it seems to you to be. To do so would be to have as many different churches as we have seminaries—and that is chaos.[16]

Organizational developments also reflected the General Authorities' continuing interest in education and their desire to have more direct supervision of Church schools. Brigham Young University, Ricks College, and the LDS Business College each had been under a separate board of trustees. To achieve "a more centralized control," these local boards were released in 1938, and all units were brought under the direct supervision of the General Church Board of Education. This board consisted of General Authorities and a few others.[17] This increased supervision helped keep the educational system a powerful spiritual force in the Church. Unlike many other universities that started as church-related schools but gradually became merely secular institutions, Brigham Young University continued to relate the learning of the world to the revealed truths of the gospel.

A tangible vote of confidence in Brigham Young University's future came in the Church's decision to erect the Joseph Smith Building. Construction commenced in 1939 and became a project of the Church's welfare plan, local wards helping to supply needed labor. The new building would house Church, social, and cultural activities, as well as classes in religious instruction. As he dedicated the Joseph Smith Building in 1941,

Joseph Smith Memorial Building, dedicated in 1941, represented the Church's continuing commitment to Brigham Young University. (Harold B. Lee Library, BYU)

President David O. McKay described the edifice as "a place of worship, a temple of learning, and a place of spiritual communion" which stood for the "complete education of youth— the truest and the best in life."[18]

Attainments in Education

Latter-day Saints understandably pointed with pride to their educational attainments. Census data in 1940 indicated that Utah, where the majority of the population were Church members, had the highest level of educational attainment of any state in the Union: young adults in Utah had completed an average of 11.7 years of school compared to 11.3 in the next two highest states and a national median of 10.3 years.[19] The *Improvement Era* reported with interest the results of studies conducted by E. L. Thorndike of Columbia University. He found that Utah had the highest proportionate number of persons listed in *Who's Who* and *American Men of Science*. Thorndike concluded that "the production of superior men is surely not an accident, but is closely related to the kind of persons living in the area."[20]

7 Temporal Concerns and Current Issues

Latter-day Saints regard their religion as embracing a total way of life. They accept the President of the Church as prophet not only to the Saints but to the whole world. Hence there is no hard line between that which is spiritual and that which is temporal, or between that which is religious and that which is secular. In an early revelation, the Lord had stated that "all things unto me are spiritual, and not at any time have I given unto you a law which was temporal" (D&C 29:34). Furthermore, as President Joseph F. Smith had declared: "It is the purpose of God in restoring the Gospel and the holy priesthood, not only to benefit mankind spiritually, but also to benefit them temporally."[1]

It is no wonder, then, to find the Church involved in what may be regarded as temporal or secular matters. During President Heber J. Grant's administration, for example, the Church launched several programs for the temporal benefit of the Saints, and its leaders found it necessary to speak out on a variety of current issues including gambling, prohibition of liquor, and communism.

Three new Church agencies were particularly interested in seeking remedies for some rather diverse social problems. In 1916 the First Presidency had appointed the Social-Advisory

Committee to coordinate the work of the auxiliary general boards in supporting higher community standards. This committee, plus Social-Advisory committees at the stake and ward levels, promoted "moral retrenchment," including more wholesome conditions at dances, sought to curb immorality, advocated professional standards in social work, and led anti-tobacco campaigns.[2] In 1919 the Relief Society organized its Social Service Department to promote maternal health and child welfare, working in cooperation with public social welfare agencies. This department would play a key role in supervising the adoption of children. The Relief Society's general board conducted a special summer course at Brigham Young University in 1920 followed by 126 local institutes to teach "scientific methods in family welfare work." Then, in 1922, the Primary Association opened its children's hospital in Salt Lake City. The Church remodeled and equipped a large home on North Temple Street across from Temple Square for this purpose. The hospital resulted from the desire to help crippled children on the part of Primary President Louie B. Felt and her counselor May Anderson.

Government and Politics

Throughout the twentieth century, Church leaders have urged the Saints to fulfill their responsibilities as good citizens by prayerfully considering and supporting worthy candidates and issues, and by getting involved in the political party of their choice. Over the years Church authorities have suggested guidelines for members' political involvement, explaining that the Church as such also has a responsibility to let its voice be heard on some, but not all, issues. "While strictly political matters should properly be left in the field of politics where they rightfully belong," the First Presidency has affirmed, "on moral issues the Church and its members should take a positive stand."[3] The Presidency has given this admonition and caution concerning Church members' responsibility:

> We encourage all members, as citizens of the nation, to be actively involved in the political process, and to support those measures which will strengthen the community, state, and

nation—morally, economically, and culturally. We urge Latter-day Saints everywhere to become actively engaged in worthy causes to improve our communities and to make them more wholesome places in which to live and to rear families.

The many and varied circumstances in which our Church members live, however, make it inadvisable for the Church to involve itself institutionally in every local community issue. These challenges are best responded to by members as they meet their obligations as citizens—preferably in concert with other like-minded individuals. Only the First Presidency and Twelve can declare a particular issue to be a moral issue worthy of full institutional involvement. . . .

Again we emphasize the long-stated policy of the Church of not endorsing political candidates or parties in elections and of not using Church facilities for political purposes.[4]

Nevertheless, Church leaders have urged the Saints to protect their spirit of unity despite differences in political persuasions. Speaking for the First Presidency, Stephen L Richards declared:

A threat to our unity derives from unseemly personal antagonisms developed in partisan political controversy. . . .

It is reasonable to assume that men may entertain honest differences of opinions with reference to governmental policy. . . . I hope with all my heart that men of the priesthood, of the same quorum perhaps, and women of the sisterhood of the Church will not permit themselves to be estranged in any degree by these considerations, and that they will always subordinate such differences and their own personal ambitions to the achievement of the lofty and exalted goal to which they have pledged their eternal allegiance—the building of the kingdom of God.[5]

President Heber J. Grant, for example, had been very active in Democratic party politics during his earlier life. He therefore had strong opinions on most political issues. As President of the Church, however, he was very cautious in expressing his personal feelings. He respected the principle of the separation of church and state, and he did not want to offend faithful Church members who might hold views opposite to his own. Nevertheless, as will be seen in this chapter, there were many issues on which the Church felt compelled to take a stand, although it refrained from declaring a position on others.

An issue on which the Church did not take a stand was the question of America's joining the League of Nations following the close of World War I. During 1919 United States President Woodrow Wilson was urging the importance of joining the league as the only effective means of preserving the peace so recently won. President Wilson had the support of the members of his Democratic party in the Senate, but most Republican senators favored entry into the league only if there were certain "reservations" or amendments made which they believed were necessary to protect America's sovereignty. Elder Reed Smoot was one of these "Reservationists" and spoke out in opposition. A large group of Church leaders, notably Elder B. H. Roberts, on the other hand, were open in their support of the league. Both sides recited passages from the Book of Mormon to support their respective positions. Speaking at a stake conference on September 21, 1919, President Grant acknowledged that he favored joining the league, but clearly stated that this was his personal belief and not the official stand of the Church. "I regret exceedingly," he declared, "that the standard works of the Church have been brought into this controversy." President Grant had his remarks published with the report of the general conference which convened two weeks later.[6] Soon afterward the Senate defeated the treaty that would have involved the United States in the League of Nations and this question faded as a topic for debate. That Heber J. Grant did not allow differences on this issue to divide him from his brethren is reflected in the fact that he subsequently called as counselors three men—Charles W. Nibley, J. Reuben Clark, Jr., and David O. McKay—who had questioned the wisdom of joining the league.[7] In coming years there were other issues on which the Church did declare an official position.

Protecting Moral Virtues

Over the years, Church leaders have taken positive stands on a variety of issues affecting the Saints' basic way of life. For example, the First Presidency has exhorted:

We urge our members and people of good will everywhere to unite to protect and honor the spiritual and religious
heritage of our nation and to resist the forces that would transform the public position of the United States from the constitutional position of neutrality to a position of hostility toward
religion.[8]

Community Standards

During the 1920s, President Grant and his counselors had
the occasion to speak out on a number of matters affecting the
moral standards of the community. For example, in 1925
when the demand arose to legalize betting on horse races, the
Presidency declared:

. . . The Church has been and now is unalterably opposed
to gambling in any form whatever. It is opposed to any game of
chance, occupation, or so-called business, which takes money
from the person who may be possessed of it without giving
value received in return. It is opposed to all practices the ten-
dency of which is to encourage the spirit of reckless speculation, and particularly to that which tends to degrade or weaken
the high moral standard which the members of the Church, and
our community at large, have always maintained. . . .[9]

The following year Church leaders also condemned card
playing as a waste of time which "brings no good, bodily,
intellectually, or in any way," and may lead children to take up
gambling as they become expert card players.[10]

In many parts of the nation the 1920s were a decade of
expanding prosperity. A spirit of speculation was engendered
as stock prices spiraled upward, and many people borrowed
heavily to invest in securities which they were sure would continue to increase in value. Others went into debt to buy luxury
goods they really didn't need. In the spirit of the foregoing
counsel against gambling, Church leaders urged the Saints to
resist the lure of quick profits, and never to risk funds they
could not afford to lose. The pioneer virtues of industry and
thrift were advocated as more sure means to financial prosperity.

The wider availability of automobiles during the 1920s
created new pressures on proper Sabbath observance. In 1928
the First Presidency counseled:

The Lord's day is a holy day—not a holiday. It has been set apart as a day of rest and worship. A sacred Sabbath begets reverence for God. It is not pleasing in His sight that the day be given over to pleasure seeking in places of amusement or elsewhere.

Sunday Schools and meetings have been so arranged as to meet the convenience of the people and leave a considerable portion of the Sabbath day without Church appointments. We earnestly appeal to the people to keep their meeting appointments faithfully and to utilize that portion of Sunday not appointed for meetings in promoting family association in the home, with the purpose of stimulating and establishing greater home fealty, a closer companionship among parents and children, and more intimate relations among all kindred.

We believe that it is unnecessary for families to go beyond their own homes or those of their kindred for the relaxation and association which are proper for the Sabbath day, and we therefore discourage more traveling than is necessary for this purpose and attendance upon appointed meetings.

Let all unnecessary labor be suspended and let no encouragement be given by the attendance of members of the Church at places of amusement and recreation on the Sabbath day. If Sunday is spent in our meetings and in our homes greater blessings will come to our families and communities.[11]

"Latter-day Saints with a testimony of the Gospel and a knowledge of the spiritual blessings that come from keeping the sabbath," a later First Presidency statement asserted, "will never permit themselves to make it a shopping day, an activity that has no place in a proper observance of the Holy Day of the Lord. . . ."[12]

The Repeal of Prohibition

Perhaps no other political issue of the early twentieth century touched the standards and beliefs of Mormonism more than did the question of prohibition. Latter-day Saints accept as revelation from God the Word of Wisdom, which declares: "Inasmuch as any man drinketh wine or strong drink among you, behold it is not good. . . . And again, tobacco is not . . . good for man. . . ." (D&C 89:5, 8.)

The question of prohibiting the manufacture or sale of alcoholic beverages had become a hot political issue in Utah as early as 1908. A senator and Apostle, Elder Reed Smoot, advocated local option, the position of the national Republican party, which held that each locality should be free to decide whether or not to outlaw liquor. Most Latter-day Saints favored total national prohibition. Perhaps the most vocal spokesman for this point of view was Elder Heber J. Grant of the Council of the Twelve. His position was based on strong personal convictions. Two of his close friends died in early manhood after taking up the tobacco and alcohol habits. "As I stood at their graves," Heber J. Grant later emphasized, "I made a solemn pledge to give the best that was in me to fight the cigarette and liquor habits."[13] The Church, however, did not officially endorse either local option or outright prohibition at that time. President Joseph F. Smith declared: "We endorse any movement looking to temperance. . . ."[14] In 1917 the Utah legislature approved prohibition for the state, and by 1920 the Eighteenth Amendment to the United States Constitution made it the law of the land nationwide.

The benefits of prohibition were accompanied by some problems. Bootleggers illegally produced and sold alcoholic beverages, and much of this traffic came to be dominated by criminal gangs. As the 1920s progressed, the demand for repealing the prohibition amendment increased. President Heber J. Grant rejected these demands. The Eighteenth Amendment, he argued, was "one of the greatest benefits that has come to the people of the United States." He countered arguments of increased crime with the statement that one should not give equal weight to the few who break the law as to the millions who benefit from it. He believed there had been a dozen times as much drinking before prohibition went into effect. Millions of homes were thus being spared from being wrecked through drunkenness.[15]

During the early 1930s, various Church organizations gave renewed emphasis to living the Word of Wisdom. Each week during the 1931-32 season, the young people of the Church recited the following slogan in their Mutual Improvement Association meetings: "We stand for Physical, Mental and Spiritual Health through Observance of the Word of Wisdom." Observing the Word of Wisdom's centennial, February 27, 1933, helped focus still more attention on this principle.

Throughout the Church this revelation had been the theme of all meetings of the previous Sunday.

Thus the anti-prohibition planks in the 1932 platforms of both major political parties were diametrically opposed to the stand being taken by the Church. Although both parties opposed a "return of the saloon," the Republicans advocated states' rights in dealing with the problem. The Democrats more specifically declared: "We advocate the repeal of the Eighteenth Amendment."[16]

The Church had declared its opposition to repeal as the 1932 election drew near. This issue, the First Presidency declared, "concerns very intimately the personal moral welfare of the men and women and youth of the Nation and of the Church in the Nation." The Presidency emphasized that the prohibition of alcohol was still part of the United States Constitution, and that strict enforcement was the only way to test ultimate worth of this law. "The Church is so firmly committed to the maintenance and support of the governments in which its members have citizenship, that it must regard violations of the law of the land as serious infractions of its own discipline and principles of Church government."

While the Church had "complete sympathy" with prohibition's objective of promoting "the cause of temperance," the First Presidency insisted that it was not their desire to get involved in partisan controversies. "It is our earnest hope," the Presidency concluded, "that the members of the Church may be foremost among the citizens of the Country in living and otherwise encouraging and fortifying the maintenance of our laws under the Constitution of the Nation."[17]

The heavy Democratic victories (including Utah) were at least in part a vote for the repeal of prohibition. After the election, the campaign against prohibition accelerated. By February 1933 the Twenty-first Amendment, which would repeal the Eighteenth, had passed both houses of Congress. By the fall of that year, thirty-three of the necessary thirty-six states had ratified the new amendment. A special election was called for November to elect delegates (whose stand for or against repeal would be known) to conventions that would decide whether or not Utah and some other states would ratify the

Twenty-first Amendment. As the election drew closer, the pace of the campaign quickened. Numerous articles appeared in the Church's *Deseret News* and monthly magazines. At the October general conference, President Heber J. Grant warned:

> Let me promise you right here and now that if you vote for the repeal of the Eighteenth Amendment, there will be a great many more professing Latter-day Saints who will be drunkards than there have been while the Eighteenth Amendment has been in force.
>
> By the way, I received a postal card—the man who sent it did not have the courage to sign his name—asking me not to talk on the Word of Wisdom at this conference.
>
> I request each and every Latter-day Saint within the sound of my voice to read what I said about the Word of Wisdom just six months ago. Every word that I said I meant, and among other things I said I hoped and prayed that we as a people would not vote for the repeal of the Eighteenth Amendment. Really, I was almost tempted this morning to read my whole sermon over again, and let it go at that. . . .[18]

The election returns clearly indicated that many of the Saints did not follow their Church President's counsel. Salt Lake City, for example, defeated prohibition by a margin of better than three to one. These facts were reported widely in the press. On December 5 conventions met in three states. The group in Utah prolonged its proceedings to allow Pennsylvania and Ohio to vote first. Thus Utah, a majority of whose population were Latter-day Saints, deliberately gained the distinction of being the final state needed to ratify the Twenty-first Amendment repealing prohibition. Upon receiving word of the vote in Utah, the pro-liquor forces in New York City staged a parade featuring a banner proclaiming "Thank God for Utah!"

The defeat of prohibition was a keen disappointment to Church leaders and was a recurring theme in their talks for at least a decade. Elder George F. Richards of the Council of the Twelve expressed these sentiments: "When the President of the Church . . . who I believe expressed the mind and will of God unto this people . . . stands up in general conference and declares in favor of prohibition, it has been a source of great regret to me that prominent, leading, faithful men in this

Church have felt justified in voting in favor of the return of liquor."[19] As late as 1941, President Grant lamented that the Saints' love did not extend far enough for them to pay any attention to his counsel. He wrote: "Many of them have such a bad case of politics that they ought to have a provision attached to their singing of 'We Thank Thee, O God, for a Prophet'—provided he keeps his mouth shut politically."[20] The following year he declared in conference: ". . . may I never live long enough that when I am in favor of a thing and all the Brethren are in favor of it, such as was the case when we were opposed to bringing whiskey back, that Utah and the Mormons will be in opposition to us."[21] In 1943 Elder George Albert Smith recalled: "From this very stand he [President Grant] pleaded with us not to repeal the Eighteenth Amendment to the Constitution of the United States. He didn't speak as Heber J. Grant, the man. He spoke as the President of the Church and the representative of our Heavenly Father. And yet in a state where we could have retained what we had, there were enough Latter-day Saints, so called, . . . who paid no attention to what the Lord wanted, ignored what He had said through his prophet, and what is the result? Such delinquency as we have never known in our community today, and the sons and daughters and grandchildren, and in many cases the fathers and mothers, who defied the advice of our Heavenly Father and said 'we will do as we please,' are paying the penalty and will continue to do so until they turn away from their foolishness and desire with all their hearts to do what our Heavenly Father desires us to do."[22]

The repeal of prohibition in 1933 did not end the Church's involvement with the liquor question. Utah and several other states chose to have liquor sold only in state-operated stores. Over the years various business interests advocated making alcoholic beverages available in restaurants. In 1969 the First Presidency would oppose such a "liquor by the drink" proposal, as they believed it would only make alcohol more readily available.[23] In opposing such measures the Saints were not alone, but were able to cooperate with several non-Mormon groups having similar ideals.

The Great Depression and the New Deal

Few external forces had a greater impact on the course of Church history in the twentieth century than did the Great Depression of the 1930s. The seeds of this economic calamity were actually sown during the 1920s as the wave of speculative buying drove prices and production to ever-new heights. During the autumn of 1929, however, this optimism cooled. A wave of selling then drove stock prices downward, and, on October 29, known as "black Tuesday," the bottom fell out of the market and millions of investors were ruined. People stopped buying unnecessary goods, and many businesses failed. The impact of the Great Depression was particularly severe in the semi-arid Mountain West, the home of most Latter-day Saints, where mining and agriculture were particularly hard hit. In 1932 unemployment in Utah reached 35 percent, compared to a national peak of 24.9 percent. During these years, average personal income in the Beehive State fell by 48.6 percent.[24]

Along with its members, the Church as an institution felt the brunt of the depression, although the Latter-day Saints did not share in the slump in religious activity experienced by most other denominations. A serious problem, however, was the decline in tithes, the Church's major source of income. Even though the amount of tithes dropped substantially, the number of those paying their tithing decreased only slightly; the Saints' continued faithfulness was gratifying to Church leaders. Nevertheless, expenditures from tithes dropped from $4 million in 1927 to only $2.4 million in 1933, expenditures for building dropping most sharply.[25]

As the General Authorities urged economizing throughout all departments, the Church was able to preserve its financial solvency. Nevertheless, this was accomplished only through curtailing worthwhile activities, such as local congregations postponing or having to forget about building badly needed chapels. Many members also had to put off the blessing of serving a mission.

In the midst of these difficulties, the 1932 United States

elections were of special interest to the leaders and members
of the Church. Elder Reed Smoot, whom President Grant
regarded as a staunch defender of prohibition, was up for re-
election to the Senate. In the presidential race, the Republicans
praised Herbert Hoover's handling of the depression crisis,
while the Democrats and their candidate Franklin D. Roosevelt
promised a "new deal" for the "forgotten man." The result
was a landslide victory for the Democrats that swept most
Republicans, including Senator Smoot, out of office. During
the "one hundred days" following Roosevelt's inauguration in
1933 the Congress enacted a series of sweeping measures
giving the federal government power to combat the depression. These "New Deal" programs included the Agricultural
Adjustment Administration, which subsidized and regulated
farm production; the Tennessee Valley Authority, which constructed dams and hydroelectric generating plants; the Civilian
Conservation Corps, which put more than 1.6 million youth to
work at camps across the country; the Federal Emergency
Relief Administration, which provided aid to the needy; and
the National Recovery Administration, which curbed unfair
competition and regulated wages and hours. As these programs got under way, they had the general support of most
Latter-day Saints, and Church leaders encouraged cooperation
with the government's efforts to relieve suffering. Elder
Stephen L Richards called on the Latter-day Saints to support
the government's policies. "It is true that we may entertain
some different views, and we have the right to our opinion,"
he conceded, "but in an emergency an army follows its com-
mander. . . ." He urged the Latter-day Saints to support, "not
only the form of government under which they live, but [also]
those who preside over them. . . ."[26]

Although Church leaders generally approved of the New
Deal during its first years, they did, nevertheless, voice some
reservations. Perhaps the greatest worry to Church leaders was
that some of the Saints could possibly succumb to a "dole
mentality." President Grant sadly acknowledged that many
were saying: "Well, others are getting some government relief,
so why should not I get some of it?" "I believe that there is a
growing disposition among the people," he said, "to try to get

something from the government . . . with little hope of ever paying it back. I think this is all wrong."[27] "The practice of 'sponging' off the government," Elder Stephen L Richards lamented, "is perverting the finest virtues of American citizenship—self-respect, self-reliance, and integrity. Furthermore, I cannot but conclude that this distortion to the morale of our people makes fertile ground for the seeds of disloyalty and anarchy which those inimical to our form of government are ever seeking to sow."[28] Another concern was the government's going into debt in order to finance relief programs. The United States national debt, which had peaked at $25.5 billion at the end of World War I, had dropped to $16 billion by 1930. As New Deal programs multiplied, however, the debt doubled by 1936, reaching $33.8 billion. This expansion of the federal government's role raised yet other concerns. President J. Reuben Clark, Jr., stressed that the United States Constitution had been framed by inspired men, quoting the Lord's declaration that it had been established "by the hands of wise men whom I raised up unto this very purpose" (D&C 101:80). He believed that the inspired Constitution's greatest contribution was the separation of powers by which the executive, legislative, and judicial branches of government checked one another and yet worked harmoniously together. He feared that the New Deal was upsetting this balance as well as the proper division of power between the national government and the states.[29] The First Presidency would raise a similar concern a quarter of a century later in relation to the question of federal aid to education:

> We are frankly gravely concerned over the increasing tendency of the Federal Government to assume more responsibilities with an ever-increasing indebtedness. . . . In our judgment, the tendency of the Federal Government more and more to control the revenue of the country should be reversed, not increased.[30]

During the depression decade the First Presidency declared the Church's position on two other issues relative to political and social philosophy.

Communism

Russia and communism became a frequently discussed point of controversy following the Bolshevik Revolution of 1917. Throughout the United States, congregations of Catholics, Protestants, and Jews joined on Sunday, March 23, 1930, to protest religious intolerance in the Soviet Union. In Salt Lake City the First Presidency personally presided over and participated in the service held for that purpose in the Tabernacle. The official recognition of the Soviet Union by the United States government under President Franklin D. Roosevelt in November 1933 sparked further debate. Finally, during the depression of the 1930s a few Latter-day Saints advocated communism as the means of solving the world's economic problems and of reestablishing the Law of Consecration or United Order. In the light of all these developments the First Presidency in 1936 wrote:

> To our Church members we say: Communism is not the United Order, and bears only the most superficial resemblance thereto; Communism is based upon intolerance and force, the United Order upon love and freedom of conscience and action; Communism involves forceful despoliation and confiscation, the United Order voluntary consecration and sacrifice. Communists cannot establish the United Order, nor will Communism bring it about. The United Order will be established by the Lord in His own due time and in accordance with the regular prescribed order of the Church.
>
> Furthermore, it is charged by universal report, which is not successfully contradicted or disproved, that Communism undertakes to control, if not indeed to proscribe the religious life of the people living within its jurisdiction, and that it even reaches its hand into the sanctity of the family circle itself, disrupting the normal relationship of parent and child, all in a manner unknown and unsanctioned under the Constitutional guarantees under which we in America live. Such interference would be contrary to the fundamental precepts of the Gospel and to the teachings and order of the Church.[31]

Labor Unions and the Right to Work

The growing labor movement during the 1930s provided still another issue on which the Church leaders took a stand. Widespread difficulties accompanied attempts by the Congress of Industrial Organizations (CIO) to apply collective bargaining to entire industries for the first time. The Church's labor philosophy was influenced by the traditional pioneer virtues of industry, freedom, and self-reliance on one hand, and of cooperation and love and concern for one's fellows on the other. In 1934 President Heber J. Grant wrote: "We have never at any time advised our people that they should not join labor unions, neither have we recommended that they should do so." Church leaders, however, clearly regarded one of the unions' weapons, the "closed shop," as a violation of free agency. As early as 1919, President Grant had approved men banding together in labor unions to protect their rights as long as they did not infringe on the rights of others. He described the practice of using strikes or boycotts to protest a nonunion man being on the job as being "in direct opposition to the law of God."[32]

Unfortunately, violence sometimes accompanied strikes during the later 1930s. In 1941 the First Presidency endorsed a *Deseret News* editorial that declared:

> No one at all conversant with industrial history and practices can deny that in many places and under adverse conditions labor must have organization in order to protect its members against exploitation. Furthermore, labor is entitled to a fair return for its work. . . . As President McKay once said: "The right to work is a divine right.". . . The worker must be left free to work when he will, be idle when he will, and to work for what he wishes, when he wishes, and where he wishes . . . there must be no "closed shop" because this means the denial of the divine right to work. . . .
>
> Where there are Latter-day Saints in unions they should assume a conservative attitude and never arouse men's prejudices by inflaming their passions. There can be no objections to a firm and persistent contention for the right of labor, if the contention is maintained in the spirit of reason and fairness.[33]

Thus, during the 1920s and 1930s the Church took a stand on a variety of contemporary issues. Many were related directly or indirectly to the Great Depression, which profoundly affected the Church and its members. This crisis became the setting for the Church's launching of its Welfare Plan during the mid-1930s.

8 The Welfare Plan

As the Great Depression of the 1930s spread economic suffering throughout the world, Latter-day Saint leaders were not left without guidance as to how they should respond to the crisis. From the beginning the Lord had commanded, "Thou shalt love thy neighbor as thyself," a principle which the Apostle James designated "the royal law" (see Leviticus 19:18; Matthew 22:36-40; James 2:8). When the Lord gave this commandment to the children of Israel he also instructed them to provide for the poor (see Leviticus 19:10). During his earthly ministry the Savior linked helping the poor with becoming perfect (see Matthew 19:21). In the present dispensation the Lord again commanded his Saints to remember, visit, and administer to those in need (see D&C 44:6; 52:40). He has vigorously condemned those who are able to but refuse to help their less fortunate brethren (see, for example, Mosiah 4:16-18; D&C 56:16; 104:18).

In 1834 the Lord declared that it was his purpose to care for his Saints, but cautioned, "it must needs be done in mine own way" (D&C 104:15-16). Three years earlier he had revealed his "own way." The Saints had been commanded to consecrate their property to the bishop (the Lord's earthly representative in temporal matters) for the care of the poor.

1929	Stock market crash led to Great Depression
1930	Presiding Bishop urged Church to care for the needy; local projects begin in various areas
1932	Pioneer Stake storehouse established by Harold B. Lee
1933	First Presidency outlined basic principles for aiding those in need
1935	Harold B. Lee called to formulate Churchwide welfare program
1936	Churchwide organization launched at April general conference; general welfare committee and regions formed
1937	President J. Reuben Clark, Jr., challenged Church members to store a year's supply of food, clothing, and other supplies; Cooperative Securities Corporation organized to hold title to and coordinate welfare projects
1938	Deseret Industries created

Each individual then received a stewardship based not only on his or her family's needs but also on their circumstances (such as abilities or talents) and on their "just" wants (see D&C 42:30; 51:3; 82:17). Each person was then expected to work to the extent of his ability for what he would receive (see D&C 42:42; 68:30-31; 75:29). The individual then felt not only the usual economic pressures but also a religious or spiritual obligation to develop or magnify his stewardship for the benefit of others. Any surplus beyond his family's wants and needs was transferred to the bishop's storehouse for the good of the whole group. Latter-day Saints often refer to living this law of consecration as the united order.

As Church leaders contemplated the needs of the Saints during the depression they could also look back at the examples of at least two groups who had lived the united order— Enoch's city of Zion, and the Book of Mormon people following the Savior's visit to America (read Moses 7:13-19, esp. verse

18; 4 Nephi 1:2-5; 15-17, esp. verse 3). The New Testament suggests that early Christians may also have lived this principle (see Acts 4:32-35).

Even before the depression decade, the Church had an ongoing welfare program. During the 1920s the Presiding Bishopric and the Relief Society general board were especially active in finding employment, maintaining a storehouse, and in other ways aiding the needy. As economic conditions grew worse, therefore, the Church was able to build on already existing foundations. In 1930 Presiding Bishop Sylvester Q. Cannon declared that "it is our business . . . to see to it that none of the active members of the Church suffer for the necessities of life." He explained that the object was to "help the people to help themselves," aiding them to become independent rather than having to depend on the Church for assistance.[1]

Local leaders were quite innovative as they sought solutions to the economic distress of their members. The Granite Stake in Salt Lake City put the unemployed to work on various stake projects, operated a sewing shop where donated clothing was renovated, and helped secure food for the needy through cooperative arrangements with nearby farmers. The Pioneer Stake, also in Salt Lake City, was probably hardest hit by the depression. Under the leadership of Stake President Harold B. Lee, a stake storehouse was established for the benefit of the poor. It was stocked with goods produced on a variety of stake projects or donated by Church members.

A Churchwide Effort

The General Authorities were extremely concerned about the suffering caused by the depression. They therefore gave encouragement, counsel, and support to efforts by local Church units to meet the emergency.

First Presidency's Instructions, 1933

An especially important document in the history of the welfare program was the First Presidency's circular letter issued in July 1933. J. Reuben Clark, Jr., President Grant's newly appointed counselor, had a significant role in formulating these instructions. It not only set forth basic governing principles, but for the first time it outlined activities and practices that were to be implemented Churchwide. "While it seems that our people may properly look, as heretofore, for relief assistance from governmental and perhaps other sources," the Presidency acknowledged, "reported conditions in the state and nation suggest that a considerable burden may rest upon our Church relief activities in the near future." The Church had a particular responsibility to care for those who had faithfully paid their tithes and offerings before losing their jobs. The First Presidency believed that the regular Church organization, "if properly coordinated by the bishops and presidents of stakes," would be capable of meeting the emergency. "The spiritual condition and faith of the members of any ward or stake may be gauged by their response to this urgent call of the unfortunate for help." Nevertheless, the Presidency cautioned:

> Our faithful Church members are independent, self-respecting, and self-reliant; they do not desire charity. Our able-bodied members must not, except as a last resort, be put under the embarrassment of accepting something for nothing. In recognition of this wholly praiseworthy and admirable attitude of mind, Church officials administering relief must devise ways and means by which all able-bodied Church members who are in need, may make compensation for aid given them by rendering some sort of service.

Local leaders were assured that the Church stood "ready to assist the wards in this relief work to the utmost of its ability," but the first Presidency reminded them that the plan's success depended on "a most generous, free giving by the people of all materials needed for relief purposes." Individual wards were to be not only prepared to meet the needs of their own members but also ready to help other units that might require extra assistance.

The Presidency specifically called for a "detailed and exhaustive study of the actual condition of every ward." Careful yet prompt response by bishops and stake presidents was imperative so that plans for the coming winter might be completed in time.

The Presidency concluded its message by urging upon the members "the paramount necessity of living righteously, of avoiding extravagance, of cultivating habits of thrift, economy, and industry, of living strictly within their incomes, and of laying aside something, however small the amount may be, for the times of greater stress that may come to us. By no other course will our people place themselves in that position of helpful usefulness to the world which the Lord intends we shall take."² This important message anticipated many of the points that would be stressed when the Church more fully organized its welfare program three years later.

Ninety-five of the 104 stake presidents responded. Of these, only ten knew of members who needed direct relief who were not receiving it, and nine were aware of members receiving help who didn't need it. All but eleven presidents reported that they had coordinated efforts with governmental agencies in providing relief or employment to needy members.

Harold B. Lee's Call, 1935

A most significant step and perhaps the key turning point in developing the Church's welfare program occurred on April 20, 1935, when the First Presidency consulted with Stake President Harold B. Lee. The Presidency was familiar with his experience in the Pioneer Stake and had previously asked him to make a study of stake statistics respecting the welfare of the Saints. "I was astounded to learn," President Lee later recalled, "that for years there had been before them, as a result of their thinking and planning and as the result of the inspiration of Almighty God, the genius of the very plan that is being carried out and was in waiting and preparation for a time when in their judgment the faith of the Latter-day Saints was such that they were willing to follow the counsel of the men who lead and preside in this Church." The Presidency informed Harold B. Lee that he was to have a part in educating the people and introducing the new welfare program Churchwide. They would release him as stake president and wished him to resign from the city commission so he could give full time to this assignment. This important interview took place on a Saturday morning when Presidents Grant and McKay did not have other commitments so they could spend the entire forenoon with President Lee. "I had thought I was overstaying their hospitality," he later reflected, "but they were instructing, encouraging, and outlining what I was supposed to do."

At the conclusion of this meeting, Harold B. Lee drove his car up to the head of nearby City Creek Canyon and walked up into the trees where he could be alone.

> I prayed most earnestly. I had started out with the thought that there would have to be some new kind of organization set up to carry forward the Welfare Program. . . . My spiritual understanding was opened, and I was given a comprehension of the grandeur of the organization of the Church and the Kingdom of God, the likes of which I had never contemplated before. The significant truth which was impressed upon me was that there was no need for any new organization to do what the Presidency had counseled us to do. It was as though the Lord was saying: "All in the world that you have to do is to put to work the organization which I have already given."[3]

Launching the Welfare Program, 1936

On Monday afternoon, April 6, 1936, following the close of the final regular general conference session, a special priesthood meeting for stake presidencies and ward bishoprics convened in the Assembly Hall on Temple Square. The First Presidency reviewed the results of the 1935 survey, pointing out the distressing fact that nearly one-sixth of all Church members were being supported by public relief, and many of them were not being required to work for what they received. The Presidency appealed to the local leaders "to build again within the ranks of the Latter-day Saints a feeling of financial independence and social security." Church leaders counseled that "for the time being" Latter-day Saints employed on such government work projects as the Works Progress Administration "should endeavor to retain their positions, being scrupulously careful to do an honest day's work for a day's pay." Church authorities estimated that approximately $842,000 would be required annually for the Church to assume responsibility for

those "actually needing relief and without means of self-help."
Nevertheless, the First Presidency concluded, "the curtailment
of Federal aid which is now forecast, makes it imperative that
the Church shall, so far as it is able, meet this emergency." The
First Presidency declared: "The Lord has given us, within our
Church, the government, organization and leadership to accomplish this great purpose, and if we fail we stand condemned."

President David O. McKay read a lengthy document
(which would be issued the following day as a circular letter of
the First Presidency) setting forth basic principles and specific
guidelines for the Church's new program. An immediate goal
was to provide sufficient food and clothing for all the needy in
the Church by October 1, 1936. This was to be accomplished
largely through the existing organization. "Ward teachers,"
who for decades had been assigned to visit the homes of all
Church members monthly, were to work closely with the Relief Society, the women's service organization, in "discovering
and appraising the wants of the needy in the ward." While
"the bishop is the father of his ward," President J. Reuben
Clark later observed, "the Relief Society is the mother. The
Church Welfare Plan could not be carried on without them.
. . ." While tithing in cash was still preferred, "tithing in kind"
(commodities) could be paid. The Saints were also challenged
to increase their per capita annual fast offerings to one dollar
(the figure at the time was less than one-fourth that amount).
Available funds were to be spent first for relief in the ward
where they were donated. Surpluses, if any, could be shared
with other wards within the stake or with other stakes in the
Church. The First Presidency's message concluded with the
admonition that the program's success depended on the faithfulness of the Saints themselves.[4]

The First Presidency reaffirmed the Presiding Bishopric's
prime responsibility in directing the welfare program. The
Presidency appointed a Church Relief Committee to aid the
Bishopric with the details of administration. Elder Melvin J.
Ballard of the Council of the Twelve was named chairman of
the committee and Harold B. Lee and Mark Austin as members.

The Church Security (Welfare) Committee in April 1938: (from left) Ted De Bry, J. Frank Ward, Mark Austin, Stringham A. Stevens, Campbell M. Brown, Harold B. Lee, J. Reuben Clark, Jr., Heber J. Grant, David O. McKay, Melvin J. Ballard, John A. Widtsoe, Albert E. Bowen, Sylvester Q. Cannon, Henry D. Moyle, and Robert L. Judd. (Church Archives)

Their assignment was to motivate and coordinate the welfare activities of local Church units.

A new level of Church administration, the region, was created to coordinate the functioning of the welfare program. A quarter of a century later the functions of these regions would be expanded to include the correlation of other Church activities besides welfare, and in 1967 Regional Representatives would be called to play a key role in training and supervising stake leaders.

The original fourteen welfare regions were set up at a series of meetings beginning April 21, 1936, in Ogden, Utah, and continuing at other points in the western United States and Canada through May 8. Each region, consisting of four to sixteen stakes, was to have a storehouse where surpluses from its own stakes or from other regions could be exchanged.

Fundamental Principles Reemphasized

At the October 1936 general conference, the First Presidency reviewed the welfare program's accomplishments during the past six months. An immediate objective had been to provide for the estimated fifteen thousand Church members receiving direct public relief rather than being involved in work programs. The Presidency, however, reminded the Church that there had been a more fundamental objective:

> Our primary purpose was to set up, insofar as it might be possible, a system under which the curse of idleness would be done away with, the evils of a dole abolished, and independence, industry, thrift and self-respect be once more established amongst our people. The aim of the Church is to help the people help themselves. Work is to be re-enthroned as the ruling principle of the lives of our Church membership.
>
> Our great leader, Brigham Young, under similar conditions, said: "Set the poor to work—setting out orchards, splitting rails, digging ditches, making fences, or anything useful, and so enable them to buy meal and flour and the necessities of life."
>
> This admonition is as timely today as when Brigham Young made it.[5]

The First Presidency in outlining the program had cautioned: "Relief is not to be normally given as charity; it is to be distributed for work or service rendered."

Expanding on this idea, President David O. McKay declared:

> It is something to supply clothing to the scantily clad, to furnish ample food to those whose table is thinly spread, to give activity to those who are fighting desperately the despair that comes from enforced idleness, but after all is said and done, the greatest blessings that will accrue from the Church Security Plan are spiritual. Outwardly, every act seems to be directed toward the physical: re-making of dresses and suits of clothes, canning fruits and vegetables, storing foodstuffs, choosing of fertile fields for settlement—all seem strictly temporal, but permeating all these acts, inspiring and sanctifying them, is the element of spirituality.[6]

In a key general conference address in 1937, President J. Reuben Clark focused on the responsibilities of individuals and families. He exhorted:

> Let us avoid debt as we would avoid a plague; where we are now in debt let us get out of debt; if not today, then tomorrow.
>
> Let us straitly and strictly live within out incomes, and save a little.
>
> Let every head of every household see to it that he has on hand enough food and clothing, and, where possible, fuel also, for at least a year ahead. You of small means put your money in food stuffs and wearing apparel, not in stocks and bonds; you of large means will think you know how to care for yourselves, but I may venture to suggest that you do not speculate. Let every head of every household aim to own his own home, free from mortgage. Let every man who has a garden spot, garden it; every man who owns a farm, farm it.
>
> Let us again clothe ourselves with these proved and sterling virtues—honesty, truthfulness, chastity, sobriety, temperance, industry and thrift; let us discard all covetousness and greed.[7]

A most comprehensive exposition of the philosophy underlying the welfare program was presented by President J.

Reuben Clark, Jr., in 1939 at a citizens conference in Estes Park, Colorado. President Clark explained:

> While . . . the first task of the Church Welfare Plan is to supply food, clothing and shelter, it was recognized from the outset that the measures taken to meet this task would not be cures but palliatives, would be treating the symptoms and not the disease, and that as rapidly as possible treatments must be developed to meet the financial disorders of the social and economic body. Many of these disorders appeared so clearly discernible and so urgent that a tendency to broaden the scope of our operations to include them all has had to be constantly and consciously restrained.
>
> The general economic principle behind the Church Plan is to build up, develop, and establish individual security which promotes and preserves religious free agency and civic freedom and liberty, as against the presently touted tendencies to set up an alleged mass security which destroys all three.

President Clark believed that all able-bodied individuals were entitled to the opportunity of earning "the necessaries and the essential comforts of life, which embrace food, clothing, shelter, hospitalization, education, amusement and cultural activities, and above all, opportunity for spiritual growth and joy." Yet everyone's needs are not the same. Instead of handing out a standardized cash allotment to all, "the Church Plan aims to give wisely in kind and amount . . . the exact help which each individual needs." President Clark was convinced that seeking absolute economic equality has generally meant "a leveling downward not upward."

"Not all Church members believe in the plan," President Clark regretted. "It is hard to persuade some people who can get something for little or nothing that they should labor for what they get. . . ." But, President Clark gratefully recognized, "the bulk of the Church has been devotedly loyal to the Plan, else it would not have worked at all."

President Clark contrasted the Church's plan with the large bureaucratic agencies of government that are often quite impersonal. The Church's program helps Latter-day Saints keep the commandment to love their neighbors. The sack of flour given across the back fence "hallows the giver, and raises and inspirits with the human love and sympathy behind it, him who thankfully eats it. . . ." President Clark further pointed out that only a handful of administrators at the general level received a salary, a modest one, while some fourteen thousand supervisors at the regional or local levels served without any material compensation.

Finally, President J. Reuben Clark insisted, the Church Welfare Program was not designed to set up any collectivism nor to compete with private enterprise. "The Church does not aim to destroy but to promote individualism."[8]

Expansion of the Welfare Program

Statistics during the later 1930s reflect a quickening of the pace in providing relief for the economically distressed. Reported Church expenditures for welfare increased by more than one-third between 1935 and 1936. The output of welfare projects in the latter year included 37,661 bottles of fruit, 175,621 cans of fruit or vegetables, 134,425 pounds of fresh vegetables, 105,000 pounds of flour, 1,393 quilts, and 363,640 items of clothing. Fast offerings, a major source of cash within the welfare program, continued to receive emphasis. Consequently, there were substantial gains in both the number paying and in the size of the offerings. Furthermore, wards and stakes continued to acquire farms, canneries, and other projects to produce food, clothing, or other items required to help those in need.

The Co-operative Securities Corporation was created in 1937 to hold title to welfare program properties and to coordinate its finances. This corporation also made loans to individuals who could not borrow from banks or through other ordinary channels.

From the beginning, an objective of the welfare program had been to inculcate the virtue of productive work and self-reliance. Many Latter-day Saints who wanted to work, however, could not find jobs because of age or because of physical, mental, or emotional handicap. Consequently, in 1938 Church leaders decided to launch a new program which they named "Deseret Industries." The new venture was pat-

Deseret Industries, established in 1938, provides jobs for the elderly, the handicapped, and others who cannot obtain employment. Early administrative offices were located in an old warehouse in Salt Lake City. (Church Archives)

The first Deseret Industries truck. (Church Archives)

terned after the Good Will Industries sponsored by a group of Protestant churches in southern California. Members would donate clothing, furniture, appliances, newspapers, magazines or other items they no longer needed. Employees would sort, clean, and repair these materials, which could then be sold at thrifty prices in the Deseret Industries' own retail stores. Proceeds from these sales would pay the employees' wages and cover other operating expenses. The modest salary could be supplemented with help from the bishops' storehouse if necessary. The important thing was that these members were doing worthwhile work, and had proven to themselves and to the world that they could earn their own way.

The Relief Society continued to play a vital role in helping families to help themselves. With the encouragement of the First Presidency, the Relief Society in 1937 sponsored courses in such homemaking skills as sewing, baking, food preserving, etc. Individual instruction was provided in the home, and group classes convened at welfare program canning or sewing centers.

Welfare Plan in Perspective

Even though the welfare plan followed already well-known principles, Latter-day Saints often refer to it as an example of the Church being guided by divine revelation. As early as 1933, President J. Reuben Clark referred to President Heber J. Grant's having received a revelation directing him to prepare a plan from out of the Doctrine and Covenants.[9] Harold B. Lee's testimony of divine guidance in 1935 has already been cited above. William E. Berrett, a well-known Latter-day Saint historian, described the process by which the welfare program was then developed by 1936. "President Grant related that individuals had asked him whether he had been talking to heavenly beings, whether the Lord had given him a vision. His answer was, 'No, I have not talked to angels; I have not had a vision.' And he recounted that the word of the Lord . . . was already given. A plan was worked out in accordance to earlier revelations." On another occasion Berrett recalled that President Grant had stated: "We have been meeting morning after morning for months. . . . After we had evolved a plan I went especially in prayer to the Lord and prayed with all earnestness to know whether or not this plan met with his approval. In response there came over me, from the crown of my head to the soles of my feet such a sweet spirit and a burning within, that I knew God approved." Berrett concluded that this revelation was in the form of a divine confirmation of what had been developed through the exercise of free agency by the Lord's servants.[10]

Elder Harold B. Lee regarded the welfare program of the 1930s as a fulfillment of prophecy:

> . . . the voice of the Lord was declared back in 1894, in October of that year, by that man whom we sustained then as the prophet, seer, and revelator unto this Church. He said:
> "So far as temporal matters are concerned we must go to work to provide for ourselves. The day will come, as we have all been told, that we shall see the necessity of making our own shoes and our own clothing, and providing our own foodstuffs, and uniting together to carry out the purposes of the Lord. We will be preserved in the mountains of Israel in the days of God's judgments. I therefore say unto you, my brethren and sisters, prepare for that which is to come."
> The voice of the Lord was again heard in 1936, when again we were told by our leaders that there should be a production of all the things needed by those who would otherwise be unable to provide for themselves.[11]

Did the welfare program have any significance beyond relieving economic distress during the depression? Elder Lee recalled that in 1936 some stake presidents were critical of the Church's efforts, believing that the effort of reacquiring projects like the old tithing yards was not worthwhile.

> It was in August [1936] . . . there was an upturn in business, so much that some were questioning the wisdom of this kind of activity, and why hadn't the Church done it before now? There came to me . . . a distinct impression that was as real as though someone had spoken audibly, and this was the impression that came, and has stayed with me through these years: There is no individual in the Church that knows the real purpose for which the program then launched had been intended, but hardly before the Church has made sufficient

preparation, that reason would be made manifest, and when it comes it will challenge every resource of the Church to meet it.[12]

What is this purpose? Elder Lee recalled that in 1936 Elder Melvin J. Ballard was repeatedly asked, "Is this the beginning of the United Order?" He consistently replied in the negative and added: ". . . but it may be that in this movement the Lord may be giving his people an examination to see how far they have come toward a condition where they might live as one."

The role of the welfare program as a "schoolmaster" was clearly set forth in an oft-quoted statement by President Clark:

> We have all said that the Welfare Plan is not the United Order and was not intended to be. However, I should like to suggest to you that perhaps, after all, when the Welfare Plan gets thoroughly into operation—it is not so yet—we shall not be so very far from carrying out the great fundamentals of the United Order.[13]

9 New Strides in Church Activity 1928-1941

The second decade of Heber J. Grant's administration not only brought the formation of the Church's welfare plan but also witnessed a series of rather extensive restructurings of other basic program and activity patterns. Church leaders were seeking the optimum method of accomplishing the weighty assignment of perfecting the Saints and sharing the gospel with the world.

The Priesthood-Auxiliary Movement, 1928-1937

Efforts to enhance the effectiveness of Church programs by consolidating activities sponsored by the priesthood quorums and auxiliary organizations came to be known as the Priesthood-Auxiliary Movement. There were two important guiding principles:

(1) The priesthood was to assume its proper place at the center and core of all Church activity. Declared the Presiding Bishopric: "The priesthood is the very foundation upon which the Church is built, as also the framework which supports the structure. It is the most potent means of real service. Unless the quorums of the Priesthood generally are trained and active in the performance of their duties, there cannot be the progress

1928	Priesthood-Auxiliary Movement launched
1929	Tabernacle Choir network broadcasts began
	MIA magazines merged; Primary and Religion
	Classes combined
1931	Aaronic Priesthood youth correlation program
	outlined
1933	Churchwide program launched to reactivate Aaronic
	Priesthood adults
1935	General Authorities released from auxiliary presi-
	dencies and boards
1936	Welfare plan, stake missions, and youth award
	programs instituted
1937	President Heber J. Grant visited missions in Europe
1938	LeGrand Richards, new Presiding Bishop,
	emphasized youth work
1940	First Presidency declared Church organizations exist
	to strengthen the home; formerly separate
	genealogy meetings became class in Sunday School
1941	Assistants to the Twelve appointed

that there should be."[1] Official publications made frequent reference to President Joseph F. Smith's 1906 prophecy of a time ". . . when every council of the Priesthood . . . will understand its duty; will assume its own responsibility, will magnify its calling, and fill its place in the Church. . . . When that time shall come, there will not be so much necessity for work that is now being done by the auxiliary organizations, because it will be done by the regular quorums of the Priesthood."[2]

(2) Church programs needed to be simplified. Because all Church organizations served the same group of members, Elder Melvin J. Ballard asserted that "There must be one unified, simplified program for this work. No one organization in the Church can do everything for the entire group. There has been delegated to each organization its specific field." He was concerned about the frequent duplication in the lessons and

activities of the priesthood quorums and auxiliary organizations and explained that the priesthood-auxiliary plan should remedy "this competition and rivalry and multiplicity of meetings."[3] These same two objectives would also be at the heart of the priesthood correlation developments of the 1960s.

Church leaders announced that beginning in 1928 formal theological study would be shifted from the weekly priesthood meetings into the Church Sunday School, which was to be lengthened to a full two hours.[4] Lessons for adults were to be prepared under the direction of the Council of the Twelve. Changing the name "Parents' Class" to "Gospel Doctrine Class" reflected this course's heightened status as the official gospel study period for the priesthood and adult women of the Church. Sunday School Superintendent David O. McKay regarded these developments as a "distinct epoch" in the seventy-nine-year history of Sunday School.[5]

Church leaders also announced that the quorum business instruction in basic duties could be conducted in brief priesthood activity meetings held in conjunction with MIA on Tuesday nights. This made a separate weekly priesthood meeting unnecessary.[6] MIA officials anticipated that this combination would lend impetus to the association's activities. By the early 1930s, however, most wards and stakes had found greater success in scheduling the priesthood activity meetings on Sunday mornings before, during, or following Sunday School. Numerous reports from the field indicated that Church members found the resulting schedule changes to be confusing; therefore the attempt to combine priesthood and Sunday School meetings was dropped.

Even though the familiar pattern of a separate Sunday morning priesthood meeting was restored in 1938, the priesthood-auxiliary movement had more firmly established some important principles: (1) The auxiliaries were truly "aids to the priesthood." For example, the concepts of the MIA as the "activity arm of the priesthood" and of the Gospel Doctrine class as the prime occasion for formal scripture study continued to influence the direction of Church programs in later decades. (2) Emphasis on the primacy of the priesthood led to new efforts at strengthening the quorums and making their activity more effective in the lives of Church members.[7]

Consolidating Activities

The effort to simplify Church meetings and programs resulted in the consolidation of formerly separate activities in several areas. Since 1889 the *Young Woman's Journal* had served the Young Ladies' Mutual Improvement Association as its official organ. In 1897 the *Improvement Era* replaced the *Contributor* as the official publication of the Young Men's association. As the work of the two MIAs came more and more to be united, the idea of consolidating these two magazines gained popularity. In fact, as early as 1907 the auxiliary organizations' Committee on Adjustments proposed a unification of all adult Church periodicals.

As part of the priesthood-auxiliary movement's spirit of simplifying Church programs, the decision was made in 1929 to combine the two MIA-sponsored magazines. At the June conference during that year, a "storybook wedding" dramatized the union of the two publications. The name *Improvement Era* was retained because it fit the two associations equally. The first of the combined issues appeared in November 1929. Not only had it been enlarged, but other improvements in format were made as well. The editorial board included representatives from both former magazines.

Beginning in 1878 the Primary Association had provided religious training for boys and girls one afternoon each week. Another program had resulted when in 1890 the Utah Territory prohibited the teaching of religion in public schools. In October of that same year the Church Board of Education organized the Religion Class program to provide religious instruction for children, supplementing the secular training they received in the elementary schools.

Among the 1907 recommendations of the Committee on Adjustment was the proposal that the similar programs of the Primary Association and the Religion Class be merged. This was accomplished in 1929 when the activities sponsored by Religion Class were absorbed into those of the Primary.[7] This step was consistent with the desire to consolidate and simplify Church programs which characterized the priesthood-auxiliary movement.

Strengthening Melchizedek Priesthood Quorums

"For over a hundred years the Lord has had in his Church . . . a force for good," Church leaders asserted, "but until recently part of this force (the quorums of the priesthood) has been left unused. The quorums are a mighty potential power for good. The clarion call for the present is to turn this potentiality into actuality."[8] To this end in 1928, the first year of the priesthood-auxiliary movement, the Church issued *A Guide for Quorums of the Melchizedek Priesthood.* After considering the nature and authority of the priesthood, this manual then devoted most of its space to the work of the quorum. In his preface, Elder Rudger Clawson, President of the Council of the Twelve, wrote: ". . . by a simple but definite organization for quorum activity, the miscellaneous and scattered undertakings of the Priesthood may be concentrated and made more effective for the good of the Priesthood and the Church."[9] The *Guide* called for the organization of standing committees to supervise such concerns as personal welfare—spiritual, intellectual, financial, and physical; class instruction; encouragement of Church service and instruction in performing ordinances; and the sponsoring of social or athletic events. This committee system of administering quorums, though modified somewhat from time to time, has continued.

The *Guide* may well be regarded as the Church's first Melchizedek Priesthood handbook. Its material was quoted repeatedly and extensively in subsequent instructions, and it became the foundation for later handbooks. When Elder John A. Widtsoe compiled his *Priesthood and Church Government* a decade later, he drew heavily from this work in his chapters dealing with the priesthood quorums.

Aaronic Priesthood Youth Correlation Plan

Church leaders devoted considerable thought to how the Aaronic Priesthood should be strengthened. Their attention focused on qualifications for missionary service and on the various Church organizations working with the youth. They realized that "there should be, and necessarily must be, correlation of the work of these various agencies . . . in preparing the young men for missions."[10]

After extensive preparation, the Aaronic Priesthood Correlation Plan was introduced at a special meeting held April 4, 1931, in conjunction with the general conference. A pamphlet outlined how various Church programs were to be correlated in working with the young men of Aaronic Priesthood age: Quorums would train members in priesthood responsibilities, promote worthiness and Church activity, and provide for social or fraternal needs. The Sunday School would teach gospel principles and ordinances, Church history, and doctrine. The Young Men's Mutual Improvement Association would provide a practical application of gospel principles in the physical, moral, social, recreational, cultural, as well as spiritual dimensions of life. The overall objective was "to prepare young men for missionary activity, for other Church service, and for life."[11]

It can be seen that the above assignments did not represent a redefinition of the roles of these Church organizations. The new plan's contribution was that the work of these agencies was to be correlated more completely than ever before.

Achieving this objective was facilitated in monthly ward "correlation meetings." Under the personal direction of the bishopric, executives and teachers working with the boys in Aaronic Priesthood quorums, Sunday School, and YMMIA would meet "to correlate activities and cooperate in the welfare of the young men"; special attention was to be given to leadership training and to involving the youth in planning and directing their own activities. Similar meetings would be held at the stake and all-Church levels to coordinate programs and instructions.[12] A special survey revealed that many boys had not yet been reached by Church programs, and through the Aaronic Priesthood Correlation Plan positive steps were taken to reclaim these youth. The Presiding Bishopric announced a goal of having one million priesthood assignments performed during 1935, and that every boy ought to perform at least one assignment. The following year they introduced certificates of award for those quorums meeting specified minimum standards. When LeGrand Richards became Presiding Bishop in 1938, the Aaronic Priesthood received further stimulus and made even greater progress.

Reactivating Aaronic Priesthood Adults

During the 1920s and especially during the 1930s, Church members began moving from the Intermountain area to seek better economic opportunities. At the same time, more non-Mormons began moving into Latter-day Saint communities. This meant that an increasing number of Church members were living in non-Mormon environments. One result of this influence was a larger number of young men becoming inactive and growing to adulthood without receiving the Melchizedek Priesthood. Even before the 1920s, however, the Church had been concerned about adult bearers of the Aaronic Priesthood.

As early as 1911 the General Priesthood Committee considered what should be done for these men. Because there was a campaign to have everyone enrolled in his proper quorum, the Committee wondered if inactive men should now associate with the younger members of their respective Aaronic Priesthood quorums. President Joseph F. Smith answered that question: "It is not a good idea to mix up the old men with bad habits with young boys. If they are not worthy to meet with their quorums," he instructed, "they should be labored with and that to get them to reform."[13]

In 1926 the Presiding Bishopric emphasized that these "overgrown members" of Aaronic Priesthood quorums cannot be dropped, but should be invited to attend whatever priesthood class was closest to their age and interests.[14]

Much of the credit for pioneering a successful program belongs to A. P. A. Glad, bishop of the Salt Lake Twenty-eighth Ward. At first he invited senior members of the Aaronic Priesthood to attend the elders quorum, but he soon discovered these men did not feel at home. "The elders are so far advanced," the inactive men explained. "We would like to attend but feel out of place."

Guide for Stake and Ward Leaders
of
Adult Members of Aaronic Priesthood

Through the Adult Aaronic Priesthood program, instituted in the 1930s, the Church reached out to reclaim those who had fallen into inactivity. This cartoon appeared on the cover of a guide for program leaders. (Harold B. Lee Library, BYU)

The bishop realized that these men needed a separate class they could feel was their own. He called a distinct group of enthusiastic and devoted men to give their full attention to this program. The first session of the class convened September 18, 1932. Group members were involved in planning their own activities; one of Bishop Glad's slogans was "We learn to do by doing."[15] After eight months of persistent effort and consistent missionary labor, forty men had been brought into activity. M. Main Stauffer, a member of the original group, recalled how Bishop Glad rousted him out of bed to get him to attend the class. For him this began a pattern of regular Church activity, which led to his receiving the Melchizedek Priesthood. He went on to serve as high priests group leader, bishop, and high councilor.[16] Bishop Glad's work became the basis of the program introduced Churchwide during the fall of 1933.

Missionary Work During the Depression Decade

While the Church was taking steps to reactivate those who were already members, it was also reaching out to those who had not yet heard the gospel. The Church continued to place emphasis on missionary work despite the problems caused by the Great Depression. Unusual missionary service characterized the lives of the General Authorities who presided over the Church in the 1930s. Almost all had served personally as missionaries, many for periods far longer than the two years normally given by faithful Latter-day Saints. President David O. McKay had made a yearlong around-the-world tour of the Church's missions in 1921. In addition, he and several other members of the Twelve had taken their turns presiding over the European Mission. Almost all who served in the First Council of the Seventy had acted as mission presidents, either before or following their calls as General Authorities, some for prolonged periods of time. Charles A. Callis had presided over the Southern States Mission from 1908 until 1934, when he became a member of the Twelve. Rey L. Pratt of the First Council of the Seventy had been president of the Mexican Mission from 1907 until his death in 1931. Samuel O. Bennion, who was called to the First Council of Seventy in 1933, presided over the Central States Mission and directed Church publishing activities in Independence, Missouri, from 1906 until 1935. Elder Joseph W. McMurrin, also a President of the Seventy, had served fifteen years as a short-term or local missionary, plus nearly twenty-five years as a full-time missionary; he acted as a counselor to the European Mission president just before the turn of the century, and presided over the California Mission for more than a decade, 1919-31. With such a background, these leaders enthusiastically gave impetus to the Church's missionary efforts.

Economic hardships of the early 1930s, however, curtailed many missionary activities, and reduced the number of missionaries. Because of the depression, many families felt that they needed their sons to work at home, and therefore could not afford a mission experience. Consequently the number of missionaries entering the field fell sharply as the effects of the depression spread throughout the country. During the 1920s eight hundred to thirteen hundred were called by the First Presidency as missionaries each year; this represented from 13 percent to 20 percent of the total young men of missionary age. In 1932, on the other hand, only 399 were able to respond, or only 5 percent of the potential. The shortage of missionaries was compounded by the fact that many had to be released early because of economic difficulties at home.

Mission presidents from all over the world reported that the work was being handicapped severely because of the lack of missionaries, and urgently requested that more be sent. In France, for example, all but four branches had to be closed to missionary work; the scattered members were organized into a "branch at large" and could be contacted only by letter. The decision to begin proselyting in Italy was delayed, not because of possible religious opposition but because of depression-caused missionary shortage.[17] However, the consequences of the missionary shortage were not all negative.

To compensate for reduced numbers, the remaining missionaries were determined to work harder and more systematically in order to maintain productivity. Ideas on effective methods of contacting and teaching were incorporated in *The Missionary's Handbook,* published in 1937. In that same year, President LeGrand Richards of the Southern States Mission first issued "The Message of Mormonism," outlining twenty-four weekly presentations of basic gospel topics. Missionaries also employed more innovative techniques to find interested persons to teach: A missionary chorus attracted favorable note in England and Ireland. Athletics were especially useful; a missionary basketball team made friends in Czechoslovakia, and in Germany four Elders were recruited as basketball judges for the 1936 Berlin Olympics. Lectures featuring colored slides of ancient America were particularly productive in making contacts. The Church Radio, Publicity, and Mission Literature Committee was organized in 1935 to supply materials for these illustrated lectures. With Gordon B. Hinckley (recently returned from a mission to Britain) as executive secretary, the committee directed the preparation of tracts and other mission literature and prepared scripts for special radio programs.

One beneficial by-product of the Great Depression was a greater involvement of local members in missionary work. In California, members' having missionaries stay in their homes to cut expenses proved to be a blessing to both the members and the missionaries. Alabama Saints traveled long distances in order to take investigators to dictrict conferences. In many areas members provided referrals, enabling missionaries to phase out less productive door-to-door tracting. The missionary corps around the world was expanded as local members donated several hours a week to go out with the full-time missionaries or accepted special short-term mission calls. Church members became involved in yet another way. In many areas, congregations had been led by missionaries rather than by local officers. But as the Great Depression cut the number of Elders, the Saints had to assume more responsibility for their own affairs. This not only freed the missionaries' time for proselyting, but it also enabled the local Saints to take greater pride in their own branches. The shortage of missionaries "has probably been a blessing in disguise," President Heber J. Grant concluded, "because it has forced us to make greater use of the local Saints."[18] The depression decade also witnessed a new missionary thrust within the stakes.

Stake Missions

Stake missions were implemented Churchwide during the 1930s. Latter-day Saints began to move into areas of predominantly non-Mormon population, such as California and the Pacific Northwest, and as non-Mormons began to move into the predominantly Mormon Intermountain region, many stake leaders began to organize efforts to preach the gospel to their new nonmember neighbors.

In 1932 J. Golden Kimball, a member of the First Council of the Seventy, reported that hundreds had been converted to the Church as result of missionary efforts in Los Angeles, Maricopa, Liberty, Salt Lake, Grant, East Jordan, and other stakes. This work was going forward under the direction of the several stake presidents. Elder Kimball emphasized that all who held the office of seventy had the particular duty of preaching the gospel and, therefore, admonished them to be willing to serve as stake missionaries. He wrote: "We know of no more promising field for missionary activity than right here at home where, who knows, precious souls are brought to us or we to them for the express purpose that they might hear the gospel sound."[19]

At the general conference in April 1936, Church leaders announced that supervision of these stake missions was being assigned to the First Council of the Seventy and that a mission was to be organized immediately in each stake. The Twelve and the Seventy anticipated that the new stake missionary work "can be made to rival in importance" the accomplishments of the full-time missionary work "for which the Church is so universally noted."[20]

Statistics for the first full year of operation of the expanded stake missionary program revealed its effectiveness. By the end of 1937, some 105 of the 118 stakes had organized missions. A total of 2,030 missionaries were instrumental in the baptism of 1,757 converts. In addition, 2,756 members of the Church had been brought back into activity. One ward reported that as a result of stake missionary efforts there had been a 50 percent increase in overall activity among its members.[21]

Reaching the Public

During the Great Depression the Church employed a variety of methods to supplement the work being done by its increasingly scarce proselyting missionaries. These methods, developed during the 1930s, would become even more important in later decades.

The new medium of radio broadcasting emerged during the 1920s, and the Church was involved almost from the beginning. In 1924 the Church purchased a radio station whose call letters soon were changed to the familiar KSL. The Tabernacle Choir began its weekly nationwide broadcasts in 1929. At first the announcer had to climb a tall ladder to reach the only microphone available. The series was planned for only three months, but favorable response from throughout the United States and from Europe prompted the network to continue the program indefinitely. During its first three years the broadcasts were on Monday afternoons. An average of two hundred choir members donated their time without compensation, and Salt Lake area employers cooperated by giving singers time off from the job. The choir program proved to be a very productive source of goodwill toward the Church and fifty years later would be acclaimed as the oldest continuous program in the history of American network radio. Several local Latter-day Saint groups also originated radio programs of their own. Elders in the Eastern States Mission were especially successful in broadcasting their messages over the air. The Church early showed an interest in international shortwave radio, and a portion of general conference was broadcast to Europe via this medium on April 5, 1936. Later that same year the Church applied for a license to operate its own shortwave station, but was not able to obtain its own shortwave transmitters until 1962.

Partly as a result of the Tabernacle Choir's increasing popularity, Temple Square continued to be an effective missionary tool. Many visitors went miles out of their way to be present for the choir broadcasts or noon organ recitals. Temple Square attracted even more visitors than Yellowstone or other popular national parks in the area.

Exhibits at fairs were another means of sharing the Church's message with the world. An exhibit at the International Hygiene Exposition in 1930 at Dresden, Germany, featured the Mormon health code revealed in the Word of Wisdom. It attracted an average of five thousand visitors per day and resulted in the distribution of over 250,000 pieces of missionary literature. An estimated 2.3 million persons visited the Church's booth at the Chicago Century of Progress Exposition in 1933 and 1934. A changed attitude was reflected as Elder B. H. Roberts, who had been denied the opportunity to speak at Chicago's 1893 Columbian Exposition, was well received as he spoke at the Congress of Religions in conjunction with the 1933 Chicago fair. At the California-Pacific International Exposition held in San Diego during 1935 and 1936, the Church for the first time erected its own exhibit building. The Golden Gate International Exposition was held on Treasure Island in San Francisco Bay in 1939 and 1940. Capital-

Scale model of the Salt Lake Tabernacle on display at Chicago's "Century of Progress" exposition in 1933 helps to tell the Church's story to hundreds of visitors. (Church Archives)

izing on the Tabernacle Choir's popularity, the Church designed its exhibit building in the form of a "miniature Tabernacle" with a fifty-seat auditorium in which missionaries could present illustrated lectures on the history and beliefs of the Church.

Beginning in 1937, the annual Hill Cumorah Pageant became one of the Church's most successful public relations ventures. Featuring a cast composed mostly of missionaries serving in the area, "America's Witness for Christ" was presented on three large stages constructed on the slopes of the hill. It depicted scenes from the Book of Mormon, culminating with the Savior's visit to the ancient inhabitants of America. Just a month before the first pageant was presented, Elder Harold I. Hansen, who had just received his bachelor's degree in drama, entered the Eastern States Mission. He was immediately assigned to help with the final preparations and rehearsals. He believed that his call to that mission at that time resulted from divine guidance. He would continue to be associated with the pageant for the next forty years, most of the time as its director. Over the years, additional stages, lighting, and other technical effects were added. During post-World War II years the annual attendance would regularly top one hundred thousand.

Moves Toward Greater Correlation, 1939-1940

With the stimulation of Church activities during the 1930s came an increased financial burden as well as greater demands on the time and energy of the Saints. To lessen this load, the General Authorities undertook a new study of all Church programs with the goal of correlation and simplification where possible.

In January 1939 the First Presidency affirmed that the real reason for all Church organizations "is to instruct the people in the gospel, to lead them to a testimony of its truthfulness, to care for those in need, to carry on the work entrusted to us by the Lord, to promote culture among the people, and to encourage, foster, and secure among the people the living of righteous lives. . . . The work of the auxiliary organizations and of our educational institutions should be coordinated, unified, and standardized to avoid duplication and overlapping, and to provide the training which is required by the young people." The Presidency therefore appointed a Committee of Correlation and Coordination, headed by three members of the Twelve. The committee's assignment was "to define, to simplify, to intensify, and to correlate the work of each auxiliary and educational group in the Church. . . ."[22]

Following this study, President J. Reuben Clark, Jr., representing the First Presidency, convened a meeting of auxiliary executives on March 29, 1940. He first emphatically declared:

> That the sole ultimate aim and purpose of the Auxiliary organization of the Church is to plant and make grow in every member of the Church a testimony of the Christ and of the Gospel, of the divinity of the mission of Joseph Smith and of the Church, and to bring the people to order their lives in accord-

ance with the laws and principles of the restored Gospel and Priesthood.

That the home is the basis of a righteous life, that no other instrumentality can take its place nor fulfill its essential functions, and that the utmost the Auxiliaries can do is to aid the home in its problems, giving special aid and succor where such is necessary.

President Clark next outlined the specific role each organization was to play in achieving these objectives. He then announced the formation of the Church Union Board of the Auxiliaries to "coordinate, consolidate, eliminate, simplify and adjust the work of the auxiliary organizations" in accordance with the outline he had set forth.[23]

In July 1940 the First Presidency announced that "the auxiliaries had taken the first step in the direction of eliminating duplication and overlapping of classes and meetings by providing for the incorporation into the curriculum of the Sunday School classes the work which had previously been accomplished (since the early 1920s) in the weekly genealogical meetings."[24]

In his presentation to the auxiliaries, President Clark had also proposed the possible merger of existing Church magazines. One action in this direction was discontinuing the *Utah Genealogical and Historical Magazine,* which had been published since 1910, and transferring its material to the *Improvement Era.*

Developments in Administration

During the 1930s the Church continued to grow throughout North America and abroad. This expansion was reflected in two extended trips overseas taken by General Authorities. During a three-month tour, President Heber J. Grant and other Church leaders visited the Saints throughout the missions of Europe. Wherever he went, the president encouraged the Saints to stay where they were and build up the Church there. Large crowds at public meetings and extensive press coverage helped build goodwill for the Mormons in areas where they had generally been unknown or misunderstood. When Presi-

President Heber J. Grant and other Church leaders mark the British Mission's centennial in 1937 at the River Ribble, site of the first baptisms in England. Shown here (front row, from left) are Ruth May Fox, George D. Pyper, J. Reuben Clark, Jr., President Grant, Richard R. Lyman, and Hugh B. Brown. (*Deseret News* photo)

dent J. Reuben Clark, Jr., joined President Grant to commemorate the British Mission's centennial, this marked the first occasion when two members of the First Presidency were in Europe at the same time. Then, in 1938, Elder George Albert Smith of the Council of the Twelve made a six-month visit to the Pacific missions. He was received very warmly by the Saints in the various island missions. A high point was his participation in the Maori Saints' annual "hui tau" conference. As President Grant had done in Europe the year before, Elder Smith not only strengthened Church members in the Pacific, but also developed more favorable attitudes toward the Church through interviews with the press, speaking on the radio, and meeting with governmental officials.

Continued Church growth and a multiplication in the number of stakes and missions around the world placed an ever heavier administrative load on the shoulders of the General Authorities. Consequently, steps needed to be taken to lighten their assignments and to provide more help.

General Authorities and the Auxiliaries

While leading sisters in the Church have served as the presidents of the Relief Society, YWMIA, and Primary, General Authorities served for some years as the superintendents of the Sunday School and YMMIA.

Wilford Woodruff, for example, was serving as superindendent of the YMMIA when he became President of the Church in 1889, and he continued in both capacities. Upon President Woodruff's death in 1898, Lorenzo Snow was sustained in both of these offices. When Joseph F. Smith became President of the Church in 1901, he also became superintendent not only of the YMMIA but also of the Sunday School. Following President Smith's death in 1918, Elder David O. McKay became superintendent of the Sunday School, and Elder George Albert Smith became superintendent of the YMMIA. When Elder McKay was called as Second Counselor in the First Presidency in October, 1934, he was released from the Sunday School superintendency, being succeeded by a non-General Authority. Consistent with this new pattern, the First Presidency decided to release the superintendency of the YMMIA, all three of whom were Apostles. On January 18, 1935, the First Presidency wrote to them:

> For some time past it has been evident that the growth of the Church and the ever-increasing demands upon the time and strength of the General Authorities would make imperative the releasing of members of the First Presidency and of the Council of the Twelve from the direct responsibility of presiding over the general boards of the auxiliary organizations. It has been seventeen years since one of the First Presidency so officiated.
>
> It is now deemed advisable, indeed absolutely necessary, to relieve members of the Twelve of their duties not only as presiding officers, but also as members of the general boards. The duties of the Apostleship, as well as the health of the individuals, demand that this action be taken without further delay.[25]

Beginning in the mid-1930s one or more members of the Twelve were assigned as advisers to each of the auxiliary organizations. This pattern continued until the late 1970s when General Authorities once again were called to form the presidencies of the Sunday School and the Young Men. They were not members of the Twelve, however, but were drawn from the recently expanded ranks of the First Quorum of Seventy.

Assistants to the Twelve

As the number of stakes and missions multiplied, the administrative load carried by the General Authorities increased accordingly. At the close of 1900 there had been forty-three stakes; the one hundredth stake was organized in 1928, and by April 1941 there were 137 of these units. Not only did this mean a greater number of stake conferences to meet, but during the 1930s the Saints had increasingly moved to scattered areas, and stakes had been organized in such distant centers as New York, Washington, Chicago, Seattle, and Honolulu. This was the setting for the decision to create a new group of General Authorities to help shoulder the load. At the April general conference in 1941 the First Presidency announced:

> In the past history of the Church, especially in President Brigham Young's time, it was found necessary for the First Presidency or the Twelve or both to call brethren, frequently designated as counselors, to help carry on their assigned work in the Church.
>
> The rapid growth of the Church in recent times, the constantly pressing necessity for increasing our missions in numbers and efficiency that the Gospel may be brought to all men, the continual multiplying of Church interests and activities calling for more rigid and frequent observation, supervision and direction—all have built up an apostolic service of the greatest magnitude.
>
> The First Presidency and Twelve feel that to meet adequately their great responsibilities and to carry on efficiently this service for the Lord, they should have some help.
>
> Accordingly it has been decided to appoint Assistants to the Twelve, who shall be high priests, who shall be set apart to act under the direction of the Twelve in the performance of such work as the First Presidency and the Twelve may place upon them.
>
> There will be no fixed number of these Assistants. Their number will be increased or otherwise from time to time as the

Assistants to the Twelve were first appointed in 1941. Pictured here are four of the first five men called to this position: (from left) Marion G. Romney, Clifford E. Young, Thomas E. McKay, and Alma Sonne. Not included in this photo is Nicholas G. Smith, who died in 1945. (Church Archives)

necessity of carrying on the Lord's work seems to dictate to be wise.[26]

Initially five men were named Assistants to the Twelve. As the administrative burden continued to increase, their number was enlarged from time to time so that by 1975 two dozen were serving in this office.

Even though the decade of the 1930s is best known in the Church for the formation of the welfare plan, there were many other important strides in refining Church activities. These included improvements in Melchizedek and Aaronic Priesthood programs, efforts to reactivate Church members and to reach out to nonmembers in new ways, and significant moves toward a greater correlation and consolidation of Church activities. These developments have continued to benefit the Saints during succeeding decades.

10 The Latter-day Saints and World War II

Most people hoped that World War I had been the "war to end all wars" and that it had "made the world safe for democracy." After two decades, however, it was obvious that war had not been eradicated from the earth. The world was still recovering from the Great Depression when World War II began in Europe. Under the leadership of Adolf Hitler and the Nazis, Germany sought to expand the "Third Reich" in quest of *Lebensraum,* or room in which to live. During these same years Japan was pushing into China, Southeast Asia, and the Pacific seeking new sources of raw materials and expanded markets for her industries. The United States did not become actively involved in the hostilities until the Japanese attack on the Pearl Harbor naval base in Hawaii on Sunday morning, December 7, 1941. Even as the Great Depression had profoundly affected Latter-day Saint history during the early and middle 1930s, in like manner World War II became the single most important external influence on Church developments during the later 1930s and the 1940s. These tragic circumstances led the Latter-day Saints to ponder their attitudes about war and provided the occasion for the Church to expand its programs for members in military service. The coming of war not only disrupted

Church activities but altered the lives of most Latter-day Saints worldwide.

Ever since the National Socialists or Nazis had gained control in 1933, the Church and its members in Germany had had to walk an increasingly sensitive line. Gestapo agents frequently sat in to observe Church meetings, and most branch and mission leaders were thoroughly interrogated by the police about Mormon doctrines, beliefs, and practices, and were warned not to concern themselves with political matters. Latter-day Saint meetings increasingly had to be canceled during Nazi rallies, and the Church-sponsored Boy Scout program was replaced by the Hitler Youth Movement. Latter-day Saint teachings about Israel were out of harmony with the Nazis' anti-Jewish policies. Copies of Elder James E. Talmage's popular doctrinal work *The Articles of Faith* were therefore confiscated and burned because of frequent references to Israel and Zion. In one town, police ripped out of hymnbooks all pages referring to these topics.

These conditions caused feelings of uneasiness and concern, which led some members to quit coming to Church lest the police cause trouble for them. Among other Saints these worries tended to increase the interest in emigration. Nevertheless, The Church of Jesus Christ of Latter-day Saints was never officially persecuted, nor was it forced to cease functioning, as was the fate of some other small religious groups in Germany. This may have been due at least in part to the Saints' emphasis on the separation of Church and state and on obeying the constituted law of the land.

At least three Nazi policies or programs actually benefited the Church: When Mormon Elders were invited to coach the German basketball teams and to officiate at the 1936 Berlin Olympics, the Church received favorable publicity. When the police banned door-to-door tracting, missionaries were forced to develop a more efficient "friend-to-friend" referral system. The Nazis' emphasis on racial purity stimulated an interest in genealogy. Earlier government officials had often regarded the Mormons as an unpopular sect and so denied them access to vital records; now the Saints were honored as patriotic because of their genealogical research.[1] Nevertheless, the situation for the Church and its missionaries became much more precarious during the later 1930s as Hitler launched his program of expansion.

The Evacuation of Missionaries

As tensions mounted in Europe, the General Authorities became increasingly concerned over the safety of Latter-day Saint missionaries serving there. As early as autumn 1937 Adolf Hitler vowed to expand Germany by annexing Austria and the Sudetenland region of Czechoslovakia, areas both inhabited by large German-speaking populations. In March 1938 Germany carried out the *anschluss* or annexation of Austria. By September of that year Hitler was accusing the Czechs of persecuting the German minority in that country and asserted the right to intervene in their behalf. As troops were massed on both sides of the German-Czech border, war seemed inevitable. On September 14 the First Presidency ordered the evacuation of all missionaries from Germany and Czechoslovakia. At a meeting with Hitler in Munich held September 29 and 30, however, Britain and France capitulated to his annexation of the Sudetenland on the condition that he commit no further aggression. Thus war was averted at least temporarily, and the First Presidency permitted the evacuated missionaries to return to their fields of labor. This brief evacuation had a sobering effect on the missionaries, causing them "to rededicate their efforts with greater fervor than ever to the work of the Lord" and to feel that "Germany was the most wonderful place in the world to work, and that we must not let any time pass without making the most of it."[2]

However, Britain's and France's yielding at Munich to Hitler's demands did not sustain peace for long. By the spring of 1939 Hitler's troops had occupied not only the Sudetenland, but all of Czechoslovakia. Hitler next turned his attention to Poland, demanding greater access through the Polish Corridor to German-populated East Prussia. Echoing his charges against Czechoslovakia a year earlier, Hitler now accused Poland of maltreating its German minority. To strengthen his

European Missions—1938

position, Hitler signed a military pact with Benito Mussolini of Italy, creating the Rome-Berlin Axis.

In the midst of these tensions, Elder Joseph Fielding Smith of the Council of the Twelve received the assignment to tour the missions in Europe and to conduct the annual mission presidents' conference there. Meanwhile, in August 1939 Germany and Russia were concluding a non-aggression treaty and a secret pact to partition Poland, thus clearing the way for a new German offensive. As these tensions mounted in Europe, President J. Reuben Clark's diplomatic background proved to be valuable to the First Presidency. Through his contacts at the State Department, he was able to keep Church leaders apprised of developments in Europe on almost an hour-by-hour basis. Finally, on Thursday, August 24, the First Presidency ordered the evacuation of missionaries from Germany and Czechoslovakia and directed Elder Joseph Fielding Smith, who was still in Europe, to take charge of this operation.

The evacuation of missionaries, particularly from the West German Mission, posed great challenges and provided the setting for what participants in these events regarded as remarkable instances of divine assistance. The First Presidency's telegram arrived Friday morning, August 25. At that time, Elder Smith and Mission President M. Douglas Wood were in Hanover to conduct a conference, but they immediately returned to mission headquarters at Frankfurt. By Friday afternoon they had sent telegrams to all missionaries, directing them to leave at once for Holland. On Saturday morning, however, the Netherlands closed its borders to almost all foreigners, fearing that the influx of thousands of refugees would deplete the already short food supply. At the same time, bulletins broadcast on German radio warned that by Sunday night all railroads would be placed at the disposal of the military, and that no further schedules could be guaranteed for civilian travel.

When the Dutch closed their border a serious crisis resulted that challenged the resourcefulness of Mission President Wood and his missionaries. Knowing that they could take no more than ten marks (about $2.50) out of the country, most

West German missionaries had used their excess funds to purchase cameras or other goods that they could take with them. When they discovered that their rail tickets into Holland could no longer be used, they did not have enough money to buy tickets to Copenhagen, Denmark, the alternate point of evacuation. Several groups of missionaries were therefore stranded at the Netherlands border.

The rescue of these stranded missionaries along the Dutch border was particularly dramatic. In Frankfurt President Wood gave Norman G. Seibold, a missionary and a former football player from Idaho, a very special assignment: "Elder, we have thirty-one missionaries lost somewhere between here and the Dutch border. It will be your mission to find them and see that they get out." The mission president instructed him "to follow his impressions entirely" because there was no way of knowing exactly where the Elders were. After four hours on the crowded train, Elder Seibold arrived at Cologne. "I rode the entire distance from Frankfurt to Cologne standing up," Elder Seibold recalled, "the trains were so crowded. It was almost impossible to get off the train at Cologne because of the crowds."

"Cologne was not his destination," President Wood explained, "but he felt impressed to get off the train there." The huge station was crowded with thousands of people trying to reach their destinations. Elder Seibold continued: "I had no idea where the brethren would be, so I hunted through the station for anyone that looked like a missionary. I jumped up on a baggage cart and whistled 'Do What Is Right,' a favorite mission hymn. I couldn't whistle nor sing, but I did the best I could. We picked up about eight missionaries there."

As he rode along on the train he was impressed to remain on board at some towns, but at others he was impressed to get off and whistle. Elder Seibold continued: "I had the feeling to stop at the station in a small town. . . . I had a premonition to go out of the station into the town, which seemed silly to me at the time. I went inside a restaurant. As surely as someone had taken me by the hand, I was guided there. I found two missionaries who were happy to see me. They had spent their last dime for a soft drink."

Having arrived in Copenhagen by Monday, August 28, President Wood learned that fourteen of his thirty-one missing missionaries had entered Holland safely. That afternoon he received a telegram from the football player stating that the remaining seventeen would arrive in Denmark that evening.[3]

While the West German missionaries were struggling to reach Denmark, quite a different drama was unfolding in Czechoslovakia. On July 10 two Elders had been arrested for exchanging money illegally. The next day two more were also arrested when they happened to come looking for their mission associates at the time the Gestapo were searching the latter's apartment. All four were put in the Gestapo's Pankrac Prison, where political prisoners were held. For the next six weeks Mission President Wallace Toronto worked persistently for the Elders' release. This was not achieved until August 23, the day before the Czech Mission received the First Presidency's directive to evacuate. Most of the missionaries, as well as Sister Toronto and her children, left promptly, but President Toronto remained behind to help the Elders who had been in prison recover their passports and other possessions. As Hitler's armies were massing for their invasion of Poland, all communications with Czechoslovakia were cut off. Sister Toronto recalled: "Naturally I was very upset over the whole thing and expressed my concern and worry to President Joseph Fielding Smith. Seeing that I was very worried and getting more upset by the minute, President Smith came over to me, put his protecting arm around my shoulders and said, 'Sister Toronto, this war will not start until Brother Toronto and his missionaries arrive in this land of Denmark.' "

In Czechoslovakia President Toronto and his missionaries were able to conclude their business by Thursday, August 31. Just before leaving, however, one of the missionaries was rearrested and again thrown into Pankrac Prison. Following quick action by President Toronto and American diplomatic representatives, it was learned that there had been a case of mistaken identity: the missionary had the same name as a man sought by the Germans as a British spy. The Elder was promptly released. At midnight, August 31, the group boarded a special train which had been sent to evacuate the British legation; this was the last train to leave Czechoslovakia. They passed through Berlin early Friday morning, September 1, and that afternoon boarded the last ferry to cross from Germany to Denmark.[4] This was the very day that the Germans commenced their invasion of Poland, the event generally regarded as the beginning of World War II. Thus Elder Joseph Fielding Smith's prophetic promise to Sister Toronto was fulfilled.

In Salt Lake City, the First Presidency continued to monitor the mounting war crisis and soon ordered the evacuation of all missionaries from Europe. Finding passage back to America presented a monumental problem. The Netherlands Mission president was sure that he had divine help in making necessary arrangements: "As I got close to the Holland America Line office I noticed a great crowd of people around the front door. I thought to myself, 'Oh, how am I going to get through that crowd of people.' A voice came to me just as clear as if you and I were talking. It said, 'Telephone.' " President Murdock went directly to a pay phone and called the general manager, with whom he had done business on other occasions. This official told him to come to the back door, where he was admitted.

President Murdock stated, "I need ninety spaces on your first ship going to the United States."

"You don't realize what you are asking," the manager replied. "I'm sorry; our ships are booked up until February." Just then he was called away from the office for a few minutes. While he was gone, the mission president did some urgent praying. When the manager returned, he unexpectedly said: "How did you know we were going to charter a new boat? You can have the first ninety spaces on it." Although President Murdock did not have any money, he was able to book the space simply by signing the name of the Church.[5]

Most missionaries, however, were not fortunate enough to secure passage on passenger liners. Most crossed the Atlantic on cargo ships with makeshift accommodations for two to three hundred passengers each. Typically, the ships' holds were filled with bunks, with only a curtain separating the men's and women's dormitories. President J. Reuben Clark, Jr., regarded the successful evacuation as truly miraculous: "The entire group was evacuated from Europe in three months, at a time when tens of thousands of Americans were besieging the ticket offices of the great steamship companies for passage, and the Elders had no reservations. Every time a group was ready to embark there was available the necessary space, even though efforts to reserve space a few hours before had failed. . . . Truly the blessings of the Lord attended this great enterprise."[6]

In 1940 more areas of the world were drawn into the rapidly expanding war. By June the Low Countries and France had fallen to the Germans, and Britain was preparing to fight for its life. This crisis made the overseas colonies of these countries more vulnerable to attack. In September 1940 Japan signed a ten-year mutual assistance treaty with Germany and Italy and began occupying French Indochina. These developments provided the background for the First Presidency's decision the following month to withdraw all Latter-day Saint missionaries from the South Pacific and South Africa. Unlike the situation in Europe, communications between these areas and Church headquarters in America were not cut off, and mission presidents were permitted to remain in their areas. Missionaries were not evacuated from South America, but after 1941 no new missionaries were sent to that continent, and by 1943 none remained there. Thus, by that time proselyting by regular full-time missionaries was limited to North America and Hawaii, although even in these areas the number of missionaries was drastically reduced as more and more young men were drafted into military service during the war.

The Saints Who Were Left Behind

When the missionaries were withdrawn, local Saints were left on their own, often in isolated circumstances. Many personally witnessed the destruction and death brought by war. Even beyond the actual combat zone, the preoccupation with war was demoralizing and tended to diminish interest in spiritual things. Another problem faced the Saints in the occupied countries: While some felt that the wisest course was to collaborate with the Nazis, others were convinced that their patriotic duty was to resist the German occupation. The Saints had to face these challenges cut off from the General Authorities and mission leaders to whom they had been accustomed to turn for spiritual guidance and strength. Evacuated missionaries were encouraged to write letters of faith and hope to members where they had served, and the mission presidents were given a special assignment to keep in touch through correspondence with the local leaders whom they had left in charge. Unfortunately, however, the war disrupted the mails, and even from neutral Switzerland no letters were received for a period of two years.

Although there were some isolated exceptions, the Saints' faithful adherence to Church doctrines and procedures was actually strengthened during the war. In several areas the contribution of tithes and fast offerings and the attendance at Church meetings increased. In Switzerland local missionaries gave two evenings per week and succeeded in baptizing more converts than the full-time missionaries had done just before the outbreak of the war. Much credit is due the local Saints who assumed responsibilities as the missionaries from America were withdrawn. During prewar years mission presidents had actively prepared the Saints for just such an eventuality. Time and again during his 1937 visit to Europe, President Heber J. Grant urged the Saints to assume their own responsibilities and not to lean so much on the Elders from America. Max Zimmer, who assumed responsibility for the Swiss Mission during the war, is a good example of these capable local leaders. He conducted regular training programs for local priesthood and auxiliary leaders, and distributed current Church periodicals to the Saints.

Of course the greatest suffering was experienced by the Saints in the areas of actual fighting, and local leaders felt they were often inspired as they carried out their responsibilities amid these trying conditions. For example, Hamburg was bombed 104 times during a ten-day period in 1943. During Church meetings it was necessary for a member of each branch presidency to monitor the radio for information about possible air raids. On one Sunday, Branch President Herbert Baarz in Hamburg had not heard anything about a raid, but he felt inspired to close the meeting abruptly and to have the congregation go immediately to the nearest shelter, a ten-minute walk. Branch members had no sooner reached the shelter than bombs hit the area near the meetinghouse.[7]

When regular meeting places were destroyed, the Saints continued to hold religious services in their homes. But in one mission, some 95 percent of the Saints also lost their homes. Local leaders launched a variety of self-help programs to meet this emergency. Mission leaders directed that food, clothing, and household supplies be stockpiled at branch meeting places. The Saints willingly responded, agreeing that all should share alike in whatever was available. "Family after family brought their entire stores . . . and shared them with their brothers and sisters who were destitute." All contributed to a fund with which the Relief Society purchased material to patch or remodel old clothing or to sew new garments. Members in Hamburg also participated in the *loeffelspende* or "spoon contribution," bringing a spoonful of flour or sugar to each Church meeting. Although one spoonful might seem insignificant, when "multiplied by 200 it was sufficient to bake a cake for a young couple for their wedding or to give to a mother who was expecting or nursing a baby."[8]

Impact on North American Saints

While the Saints in North America did not suffer in the way that their counterparts in Europe did, still the war had a substantial impact on Church members and programs. As World War II began, shipyards, aircraft plants, and other defense industries created many new jobs along the West Coast. These economic opportunities lured many Mormons from the Intermountain area to the Pacific Coast. This represented a continuation of the pattern established during the 1920s and accelerated during the depression of the 1930s— that of younger people leaving home in the quest for improved employment opportunities.

This population drain might have been even larger except for two factors: (1) Wartime demands had brought an unaccustomed prosperity even to Intermountain area agriculture. (2)

Establishment of defense industries such as the Geneva steel plant near Provo created new jobs in Utah and surrounding areas. Many who had left the Intermountain area during earlier decades wanted to return and establish their permanent homes in a predominantly Latter-day Saint environment. These improved economic conditions made it possible for them to do so.

These war-stimulated population shifts created several challenges for the Church. Mormon youth were among those seeking employment in defense industry. Near the end of the war, more than half of the priests in the Aaronic Priesthood, most of whom were young men of high school and college age, were living away from home. The General Authorities encouraged local Church leaders to take a special interest in these youth who were deprived of the stabilizing influence of home and family.[9] The coming of new industries to predominantly Mormon areas resulted in a sudden influx of new people into certain communities. While some longtime residents were concerned about the introduction of such a large "outside element," Church leaders encouraged the Saints to fellowship the newcomers and to share the gospel with them where possible. This created a fertile field for the stake missions which had been established just a few years before.

Wartime conditions affected programs sponsored by the Church in still other ways. In January 1942, just a month after the United States entered World War II, the First Presidency announced that all auxiliary institutes and stake leadership meetings were being suspended immediately for the duration of the war. This cutback in leadership instruction came at the very time when Church activities had to reach, more effectively than ever before, the growing numbers of members cut free from the guiding and sustaining influence of home and family. "This action," the Presidency stressed, "places increased responsibility upon the ward and branch auxiliary organizations to see that their work not only does not suffer, but is increased in intensity, improved in quality, and in general made more effective." Auxiliary general boards kept in touch and gave direction by mail, and the home was stressed more as the key to preserving the faith among the youth.[10] The First

Presidency also limited attendance at general conferences to specifically invited priesthood leaders. At the same time, the Tabernacle was closed to the public and the weekly choir broadcasts made without audiences present. Observations of the Relief Society's 1942 centennial had to be postponed and the annual Hill Cumorah Pageant was cancelled for the duration.

Thus, when United States President Franklin D. Roosevelt on April 27, 1942, spoke of the need of wage and price controls, rationing, and increased taxes, Latter-day Saint Church leaders had already taken steps to adapt programs to these conditions.

Elder Harold B. Lee was convinced that the timing of the Church's precautions was the result of revelation. Referring to the January 1942 restrictions on auxiliary meetings and travel, he declared:

> . . . When you remember that all this happened from eight months to nearly a year before the tire and gas rationing took place, you may well understand if you will only take thought that here again was the voice of the Lord to this people, trying to prepare them for the conservation program that within a year was forced upon them. No one at that time could surely foresee that the countries that had been producing certain essential commodities were to be overrun and we thereby be forced into a shortage.

Furthermore, Elder Lee was convinced that Church leaders were inspired when, beginning in 1937, they counseled the Saints to produce and store a year's supply of food. He believed that this helped prepare Church members for rationing and scarcity and anticipated the government's emphasis on "victory gardens."[11]

Church activities were hampered in yet other ways. As building supplies were diverted to military use, construction of meetinghouses and even of the Idaho Falls Temple came to a halt. Perhaps no Church activity felt the impact of war more than did the missionary program. In 1942 the Church agreed not to call young men of draft age on missions. Hence the number of missionaries serving plummeted. While 1,257 new full-time missionaries had been called in 1941, only 261 were called two years later. Before the war, five-sixths of all missionaries were young men holding the offices of elder or seventy; by 1945, most new missionaries were women or high priests. Members living in mission fields again assumed more responsibilities, just as they had done when the number of missionaries dropped during the Great Depression a decade earlier. Throughout North America these Saints accepted calls as local part-time missionaries and assumed greater roles in district or branch organizations.

The Church sponsored special wartime programs and in other ways encouraged its members to patriotically support the war effort. The first Sunday in 1942 was designated as a special day of fasting and prayer. As they had done during World War I, the General Authorities again commended the Saints for their generous contributions to the Red Cross and other charitable funds. Women in the Relief Society put together first aid kits for home use and prepared bandages and other supplies for the Red Cross. During the winter of 1942-43 the Church's twelve- and thirteen-year-old Beehive Girls donated 228,000 hours, collecting scrap metal, fats, and other needed materials, making scrapbooks or baking cookies for soldiers, and tending children for mothers working in defense industries. A special "Honor Bee" award was offered for such service. Then in 1943, Mutual Improvement Association youth in the United States and Canada raised more than three million dollars to purchase fifty-five badly needed rescue boats to save the lives of downed airmen.

The Saints' Attitudes on War

As war engulfed the world, Latter-day Saints again had to examine their feelings relative to the appropriateness of resorting to arms. They were guided by the Book of Mormon's teachings, which denounced offensive wars but condoned fighting "even to the shedding of blood if necessary" in defense of home, country, freedom, or religion (see Alma 43:45-47 and 48:14). During the early years of the Church's history the Saints had been called on to do just that as they were repeatedly driven from their homes by force. Nevertheless, in the midst of these persecutions the Lord called on his people to "renounce war and proclaim peace" (D&C 98:16), and this injunction has continued to shape the Saints' basic feelings about war.

Latter-day Saints in the United States, along with the majority of their fellow citizens, continued to cling to the hope for peace. Speaking in general conference only a month after Hitler's 1939 invasion of Poland, President J. Reuben Clark, Jr., emphatically declared that "nothing is more unrighteous, more unholy, more ungodly than man-declared mass slaughter of his fellow man for an unrighteous cause."[12] "I pray with all the earnestness of my heart," President Heber J. Grant declared the following year, "that our country may not get into war."[13]

In their annual Christmas message issued less than a week after the attack on Pearl Harbor, the First Presidency insisted that only through living the gospel of Jesus Christ would enduring peace come to the world. Echoing the counsel given by President Joseph F. Smith at the outbreak of World War I, the Presidency now exhorted members in the armed forces to keep "cruelty, hate, and murder" out of their hearts even during battle.[14]

The above points were all incorporated in the First Presidency's official statement read at the April 1942 general conference just four months after the attack on Pearl Harbor. This declaration represented the most comprehensive and authoritative review of the Church's attitude on war, and it was widely distributed in pamphlet form. "Hate can have no place in the souls of the righteous," the Presidency declared, emphasizing the Savior's injunction to love one another.

Nevertheless, the Presidency explained that members of the Church were also members of "the body politic," so "must give allegiance to their sovereign," and therefore urged the Saints, "fully to render that loyalty to their country and to free institutions which the loftiest patriotism calls for.

". . . Obedient to these principles," the Presidency continued, "the members of the Church have always felt under obligation to come to the defense of their country when a call to arms was made. . . . In the [First] World War, the Saints of America and of European countries served loyally their respective governments, on both sides of the conflict. Likewise in the present war, righteous men of the Church in both camps have died, some with great heroism, for their own country's sake. . . . The Church has been benefitted by their service and sacrifice.

"Nevertheless, God commanded, 'Thou shalt not kill.' " Addressing this delicate question, the First Presidency explained that if in the course of combat, servicemen "shall take the lives of those who fight against them, that will not make of them murderers, nor subject them to the penalty that God has prescribed for those who kill . . . for it would be a cruel God that would punish His children as moral sinners for acts by them as the innocent instrumentalities of a sovereign whom He had told them to obey and whose will they were powerless to resist.

"This Church is a worldwide Church. Its devoted members are in both camps. . . . On each side they believe they are fighting for home, and country, and freedom. On each side, our brethren pray to the same God, in the same name, for victory." The Presidency conceded "both sides cannot be wholly right; perhaps neither is without wrong."

In conclusion, the First Presidency exhorted: ". . . live clean, keep the commandments of the Lord, pray to Him constantly to preserve you in truth and righteousness, live as you pray, and whatever betides you the Lord will be with you and nothing will happen to you that will not be to the honor and glory of God and to your salvation and exaltation. . . . Then, when the conflict is over and you return to your homes, having lived the righteous life, how great will be your happiness—whether you be of the victors or the vanquished—that you have lived as the Lord commanded."[15]

Latter-Day Saints in Military Service

Heeding the counsel of their Church leaders, Latter-day Saints responded when calls came for military service. By the war's end, the number in military service approached one hundred thousand, or in other words, about one out of every ten Church members.

Even though LDS servicemen's groups were organized

during the Spanish-American War and Elder B. H. Roberts served as a chaplain during World War I, the most complete development of the Church's programs for servicemen came during World War II.

In 1940, over a year before the United States entered the war, the Church appointed Hugh B. Brown, a former stake president (and future General Authority), to serve as servicemen's coordinator. Having attained the rank of major in the Canadian army during World War I, he was able to capitalize on this title in making contact with military authorities. Elder Brown traveled extensively, meeting with LDS servicemen, giving them encouragement, and receiving from them recommendations concerning what the Church could do. His warm personality and deep spirituality made him particularly well suited for this assignment.

A Church Servicemen's Committee was organized in October 1942, with Elder Harold B. Lee, a new member of the Twelve, as chairman. The committee worked with United States military officials to secure the appointments of Latter-day Saint chaplains. Achieving this aim posed a formidable challenge. Army and Navy officials were reluctant to appoint chaplains who did not meet the usual requirements of a professional clergyman. The Army Chief of Chaplains, however, remembered favorably how a local Mormon bishop had cared for the spiritual well-being of the servicemen in his area. Through the committee's efforts military officials gradually approved the appointment of additional LDS chaplains, and by the end of World War II the number peaked at forty.[16]

Certainly forty chaplains were not enough to give religious leadership to the thousands of Latter-day Saints scattered throughout the widely separated theaters of war. As early as the Spanish-American War the Mutual Improvement Association had sponsored servicemen's groups. During the course of World War II this program was revived under the direction of the Servicemen's Committee, and approximately a thousand group leaders served. Once set apart by proper Church authorities, these group leaders could officiate anywhere their services might be needed. Each received a certificate identifying him as "an Elder in the Church" and as "an authorized Group Leader in the Mutual Improvement Association" empowered, with approval of appropriate military officials, "to conduct study classes and other worshipping assemblies. . . ."[17]

The Church sponsored several other measures to benefit members in the service. Servicemen's "homes" were opened in Salt Lake City and California. For servicemen away from home, "budget cards" became "passports" to the social and recreational activities offered by the Church. Members entering military service received pocket-size copies of the Book of Mormon and *Principles of the Gospel.* A miniature version of the *Church Section* carried messages of inspiration, reports of servicemen's activities, and important announcements.

Latter-day Saint servicemen set an outstanding example of faith and devotion. Military officials frequently reported astonishment at the initiative and ability of the Mormon soldiers to conduct their own religious worship without the need for professional clergymen. On Saipan a group of LDS Marines who had no place to meet set to work building their own chapel. German LDS soldiers during the occupation of Norway shared their rations with needy Saints in that land. Similarly, LDS American soldiers helped German Saints to rebuild as the war drew to a close. Always eager to share the gospel, Church members took advantage of opportunities even under wartime conditions. Numerous conversions resulted from Mormon buddies' worthy examples. While in a German prison camp, a Dutch member shared the gospel with a fellow POW who later became the first stake president in their native country. Eldin Ricks, an LDS chaplain, presented a copy of the Book of Mormon to Pope Pius XII at the Vatican.

Elder Ezra Taft Benson lamented the wartime drop in the number of full-time missionaries, but added:

> I cannot help feeling that we are probably doing more total missionary work today than we have ever done in the history of the Church. While our number of full-time missionaries has been reduced, we have, it is estimated, almost one hundred thousand of our young men in the service of their country, hundreds and thousands of whom are doing effective missionary work. . . .
>
> Only this week there came to my office several young men, in the uniform of their country, who were thrilled with the experiences they were having in the mission field, although

in the service of their country. One of them said, "Brother Benson, it is just like being on another mission. Conditions are different, but we have opportunities to preach the gospel, and we are taking advantage of it."[18]

Latter-day Saint servicemen were even responsible for introducing the gospel into new areas of the world. For example, they provided the Church's first contact with the Philippine Islands.[19]

Latter-day Saint servicemen, like many of other faiths, often saw divine protection in the preservation of their lives amid the terrors of combat. For example, Melden J. Smith tells how his life was spared when a copy of the *Improvement Era* in his shirt pocket retarded a machine gun bullet.[20] A widely recounted incident involved two United States marines who were seriously wounded during the invasion of Kwajalein early in 1944. A war correspondent described how the less severely wounded marine, a Latter-day Saint, refused attention until his buddy was helped and then pronounced a blessing on him: "In the name of Jesus Christ and by virtue of the Holy Priesthood which I hold, I command you to remain alive until the necessary help can be obtained to secure the preservation of your life." His life was saved, and his recovery was the "wonder of the medical unit." To testify of the power of the priesthood, President George Albert Smith on several occasions read the United Press account of this story, dateline Honolulu, February 8, 1944.[21]

Of course, the lives of many servicemen were not spared. Why some were saved, even miraculously, and others were not, is difficult or impossible to know. The Servicemen's Committee reported that a total of 5,714 were killed, wounded, or missing in action. Speaking at a 1942 general conference, Elder Harold B. Lee offered one possible justification for the death of faithful Latter-day Saint servicemen: "It is my conviction that the present devastating scourge of war in which hundreds of thousands are being slain, many of whom are no more responsible for the causes of the war than are our own boys, is making necessary an increase of missionary activity in the spirit world and that many of our boys who bear the Holy Priesthood and are worthy to do so will be called to that missionary service after they have departed this life."[22]

The need for military forces continued even after the close of World War II in 1945. The spread of the "Cold War" meant that a large number of Latter-day Saints would always be serving in the armed forces, and the Church would continue its interest in them. Programs developed for servicemen during World War II would continue to play a key role, and they would be supplemented by several important new activities. The Church conducted annual conferences for servicemen beginning in 1953 in Europe and 1967 in Japan. Often attended by more than a thousand, these gatherings would become the largest "retreats" conducted among American military personnel. These conferences featured leadership workshops, recreational activities, and addresses by General Authorities, and were generally climaxed by inspirational testimony meetings. A further boost came with the organization of the first servicemen's stake in 1968; assuming responsibility for a wide range of Church programs contributed substantially to the servicemen's personal spiritual growth. In 1969 the Servicemen's Committee was renamed and its assignment broadened. The Military Relations Committee would be responsible not only for the well-being of men and women while in military service, but also for preparing them beforehand for this experience, and then for reorienting and fellowshipping them following their discharge from the service. The General Authorities announced their commitment to give the growing number of members entering the military service "encouragement and help similar to that given to departing missionaries." To this end, the Church inaugurated in 1970 the practice of conducting orientation seminars for those entering one of the armed services. These sessions reviewed the challenges and opportunities that young men and women would encounter in military service, and provided counsel on how to make the most of this experience.[23] Latter-day Saints who served in the military during these postwar years would also be instrumental in opening doors for the gospel in new parts of the world even as their predecessors had done during World War II.

11 George Albert Smith and Recovery from War

P resident Heber. J. Grant died on May 14, 1945, one week after Germany's surrender in Europe, and just three months before Japan's surrender would bring World War II to its close. His funeral was held in the Salt Lake Tabernacle, which was opened to the public for the first time in over three years, and the building was filled to overflowing. His successor, George Albert Smith, would face the challenging task of leading the Saints during an era when the world needed to overcome hate and to rebuild following the end of the war. President Smith's experience and character suited him well for this task.

George Albert Smith's Earlier Life

The new President was born in Salt Lake City in 1870. When he was almost fourteen years of age, a patriarchal blessing gave him an understanding of the direction his life should take: "And thou shalt become a mighty prophet in the midst of the sons of Zion. And the angels of the Lord shall administer unto you, and the choice blessings of heaven shall rest upon you . . . for thou art destined to become a mighty man before the Lord, for thou shalt become a mighty apostle in the church and kingdom of God upon the earth. . . ."[1]

1870	April 4: Born in Salt Lake City, Utah
1883	Began work in ZCMI's overall factory (age 13)
1891	Special mission in southern Utah for the YMMIA (21)
1892	Married Lucy Emily Woodruff (22)
1892-94	A mission in the southern states (22-24)
1898	Appointed receiver of United States Land Office
1903	Called as a member of the Quorum of the Twelve (33)
1919-21	Presided over European Mission (49-51)
1921-35	Superintendent of Young Men's Mutual Improvement Association
1930	Founded Pioneer Trails Association
1931	Elected a member of the National Executive Board of the Boy Scouts of America (61)
1943	Became President of the Quorum of the Twelve (73)
1945	World War II ended; sustained as President of the Church
1946	Ezra Taft Benson directed reopening work in Europe; Spencer W. Kimball named chairman of Church's Indian Committee
1947	Utah pioneer centennial is celebrated (77)
1951	April 4: Died in Salt Lake City, Utah (81)

On May 25, 1892, he married his childhood sweetheart, Lucy Emily Woodruff, the granddaughter of President Wilford Woodruff. Only a month later, the new husband departed for a two-year mission in the southern states. On at least two occasions he was convinced that his life was spared only through divine intervention—once when a hostile mob fired shots into the house where he was sleeping, and again when he was warned on a dark night to stop just short of the edge of a high precipice.[2] After he had been only a few months in the field, Mission President J. Golden Kimball called Elder Smith to be his secretary. When the president had to be absent for a prolonged period, he placed George Albert Smith in charge of mission affairs.

Nine years later, George Albert Smith's call to the Apostleship came as a complete surprise to him. Because of a particularly busy day at his office, he had not been able to attend general conference. As he came home that afternoon, a woman congratulated him enthusiastically. He was at a loss to know what she was talking about. She told him he had been sustained that afternoon as a new member of the Council of the Twelve Apostles. With characteristic modesty he insisted that she must certainly be mistaken, as he knew nothing at all about it. Becoming flustered, she returned to the Tabernacle to verify what had happened and soon returned to assure him that she had not heard wrong. That evening he confided to his journal: "I was completely dumbfounded and I could hardly believe it possible at this time, although I felt that I might some day succeed my father, as my patriarchal blessing under the hands of Zebedee Coltrin indicated that I might become an apostle. I didn't feel capable or worthy, but if it pleases the Lord I will try to do my full duty. . . ."[3]

Elder Smith became the fourth generation in his family to serve as a General Authority and even in the First Presidency. His great-grandfather, John Smith, the uncle of the Prophet Joseph, served as an assistant counselor to Joseph Smith and as Patriarch to the Church. His grandfather, George A. Smith, after whom the Apostle was named, had been an Apostle and a counselor in the First Presidency to Brigham Young. His father, John Henry Smith, was serving in the Twelve at the time of George Albert's call. These two served together in the Quorum until 1910, when John Henry was called into the First Presidency. This was the only time that a father and a son had served simultaneously in the Council of the Twelve.

Throughout his life George Albert Smith was plagued with illness. A few years after his call to the Apostleship he was convalescing from an especially serious siege when he had a dream in which he saw his grandfather after whom he had been named:

. . . he looked at me very earnestly and said:
"I would like to know what you have done with my name."
Everything I had ever done passed before me as though it were a flying picture on a screen. . . . I smiled and looked at my grandfather and said:
"I have never done anything with your name of which you need be ashamed."
He stepped forward and took me in his arms, and as he did so, I became conscious again of my earthly surroundings. My pillow was as wet as though water had been poured on it—wet with tears of gratitude that I could answer unashamed.[4]

From 1919 to 1921 George Albert Smith presided over the European Mission. In the aftermath of World War I, food was scarce in Europe, and so several countries refused to admit any foreigners. As Elder Smith negotiated with these governments to gain permission for missionaries to enter their borders, he gained experience which would be valuable when he would face similar circumstances following the close of World War II.

Upon his return home, Elder George Albert Smith was called to preside over the Young Men's Mutual Improvement Association. This service continued until 1935, when the First Presidency released all members of the Twelve from auxiliary boards. His interest in the youth was of long standing. At the age of twenty-one he had served four months as a special "MIA missionary" in southwestern Utah, working to stimulate activity among the young men there. From the earliest days of the Boy Scout movement, Elder Smith had been a prime booster. He became an active local Scout council member and was proud to wear his Scouter's uniform. In 1932 he was elected to the national executive committee. Two years later Elder Smith received the Silver Buffalo, the highest award presented by the national Boy Scout organization in recognition of outstanding service. This concern for young people would aid President Smith as he counseled returning servicemen about meeting their challenges following the close of World War II.

George Albert Smith was actively interested in preserving and marking historic sites. In 1930 he founded the Utah

Pioneer Trails and Landmarks Association, and he served as its president until his death. He supervised the erection of more than one hundred substantial markers at historic sites throughout the western United States. Elder Smith linked these activities with his concern for youth. As superintendent of the YMMIA he involved Latter-day Saint young people in numerous projects to suitably mark points of local interest. He saw this as a means to help the youth identify and better appreciate their heritage. Appropriately he would be serving as President of the Church at the time of the pioneer centennial celebration in 1947.

A Christlike love was perhaps the outstanding quality George Albert Smith would bring into his calling as President of the Church. Years earlier Elder Smith had formulated a creed to guide his life:

> I would be a friend to the friendless and find joy in ministering to the needs of the poor. I would visit the sick and afflicted and inspire in them a desire for faith to be healed. I would teach the truth to the understanding and blessing of all mankind. I would seek out the erring one and try to win him back to the righteous and a happy life. I would not seek to force people to live up to my ideals but rather love them into doing the thing that is right. I would live with the masses and help to solve their problems that their earth life may be happy. I would avoid the publicity of high positions and discourage the flattery of thoughtless friends. I would not knowingly wound the feeling of any, not even one who may have wronged me, but would seek to do him good and make him my friend. I would overcome the tendency to selfishness and jealousy and rejoice in the successes of all the children of my Heavenly Father. I would not be an enemy to any living soul. Knowing that the Redeemer of mankind has offered to the world the only plan that will fully develop us and make us really happy here and hereafter I feel it not only a duty but a blessed privilege to disseminate this truth.

After quoting these ideals, Bryant S. Hinckley declared: "You can put this creed in the past tense and it epitomizes his life— this is what he has actually done."[5] Looking back on his life, President Smith affirmed: "I do not have an enemy that I know of, and there is no one in the world that I have any enmity towards. All men and all women are my Father's children, and I have sought during my life to observe the wise direction of the Redeemer of mankind—to love my neighbor as myself. . . ."[6] This capacity to love would prove invaluable to George Albert Smith as he assumed the Presidency of the Church at the very time when the world was turning its attention from war to a quest for a lasting peace. The Council of the Apostles and the Patriarch, meeting in an upper room of the Salt Lake Temple on May 21, 1945, sustained George Albert Smith as the new President of The Church of Jesus Christ of Latter-day Saints.

The Close of World War II

The formal end to World War II came on August 14, 1945, when Japan accepted the Allies' terms for surrender. Even before the war had ended, machinery was set in motion to create a new international organization designed to prevent future conflict. In 1945 at a special conference in San Francisco, the charter for the United Nations was adopted. In contrast to the heated and prolonged debates over the League of Nations following World War I, the United States Senate's approval of participation in the new UN was swift and almost unanimous. The Church did not take an official stand either for or against the new international body. Even though President J. Reuben Clark feared that membership in such a body would compromise the nation's sovereignty, there was none of the active campaigning by prominent Latter-day Saints against the UN that there had been against the League of Nations a quarter century earlier.[7] Nevertheless, Church leaders reminded the Saints that the only hope for enduring peace was the world's acceptance of and adherence to the principles of the gospel of Jesus Christ.

Beginning with the later months of 1945, thousands of Latter-day Saints were discharged from military service. This was the joyous time eagerly anticipated by relatives and sweethearts, and of course by the servicemen themselves, when

"Johnny would come marching home." Nevertheless, the return to civilian life was not free from perils, and the Church took steps to help its members successfully make this transition. The General Authorities encouraged bishops to interview returning servicemen promptly and see that they received callings to Church service. Priesthood quorums sponsored welcome-home parties and assisted with finding employment. The Mutual Improvement Association played a key role in fellowshipping veterans in athletic and social activities.

A high priority for Church leaders following the close of World War II was to reestablish contact with the Saints who had been cut off from any communication for up to six years. Nowhere was this need more pressing than in Europe, where war-caused devastation was so great. Hundreds of Saints were left homeless as cities were destroyed, especially in Germany and Holland. An acute shortage of food compounded the suffering immediately after the war.

Latter-day Saint servicemen in the Allied armies brought the first help to the suffering members.

> . . . I attended Sunday School in the Apeldoorn Branch. With me I brought what food we were able to save from our army rations. After Sunday School we held a "banquet" for the thirty-five members who were present.
>
> "Dear Lord," prayed Brother Dodenbier, "forgive us for holding a feast on thy holy day, but the need is great."
>
> After a song of rejoicing, each person was served one small meat or cheese sandwich, two raisin pancakes, a cup of cocoa. For the children there was the added treat of a small piece of chocolate, the first candy many of them had ever tasted. They were children of the occupation, born during the darkest years of their country's history. The "banquet" was received with an appreciation unknown to us who have never suffered for want of food.
>
> "It has come in answer to our prayers," concluded the branch president.[8]

These contacts often strengthened the faith of the needy Saints as well as of the servicemen providing succor.

Summarizing the impact of Mormon men in the military, Elder Ezra Taft Benson later wrote from Europe: "The willing service and clean, exemplary lives of the LDS servicemen who have been among the peoples of Europe, have left a splendid impression over here."[9]

Hugh B. Brown, president of the British Mission, was the first Church official to visit the European continent following the close of the war. On July 20, 1945, only two months after the formal end of hostilities in Europe, President Brown flew to Paris. There, in the large ballroom of an exclusive hotel, he conducted a meeting which was attended by some 350 servicemen and local Saints. He then continued by train to Switzerland for a hectic series of meetings. At Lausanne, not a member was absent even though the meeting was held during normal working hours. Elder Brown wrote: "The sheer joy of these humble folk at seeing someone from 'Zion' again made me realize how really lonely they had been during the isolation of the war years."[10]

As early as the fall of 1945 the Church was sending relief supplies to Europe. These were addressed to branch presidents or other responsible individuals. The supplies had to be sent through the regular mails, which meant that only small packages were accepted and that the cost was prohibitive. By January 1946 the Church had shipped some thirteen thousand of these packages, besides many more mailed by individuals. In the meantime the Church was seeking means of shipping larger quantities. This would require the special cooperation of government officials. Consequently, President George Albert Smith together with Elders John A. Widtsoe and David O. McKay went to Washington, D.C., where they spent considerable time conferring with ambassadors and other officials of foreign nations. On November 3 President Smith and his party had a twenty-minute interview with United States President Harry S Truman at the White House. President George Albert Smith later reported the following concerning this important occasion:

> When the war was over, I went representing the Church, to see the president of the United States. When I called on him, he received me very graciously—I had met him before—and I said: "I have just come to ascertain from you, Mr. President,

President George Albert Smith confers with U. S. President Harry S. Truman about shipping food and clothing to the suffering peoples of Europe in the wake of World War II. (Church Archives)

what your attitude will be if the Latter-day Saints are prepared to ship food and clothing and bedding to Europe."

He smiled and looked at me, and said: "Well, what do you want to ship it over there for? Their money isn't any good."

I said: "We don't want their money." He looked at me and asked: "You don't mean you are going to give it to them?"

I said: "Of course, we would give it to them. They are our brothers and sisters and are in distress. God has blessed us with a surplus, and we will be glad to send it if we can have the co-operation of the government."

He said: "You are on the right track," and added, "we will be glad to help you in any way we can . . . How long will it take you to get this ready?"

I said: "It is all ready."

The government you remember had been destroying food and refusing to plant grain during the war, so I said to him:

"Mr. President, while the administration at Washington were advising the destroying of food, we were building elevators and filling them with grain, and increasing our flocks and our herds, and now what we need is the cars and the ships in order to send considerable food, clothing, and bedding to the people of Europe who are in distress."

President Truman also gave the Church leaders advice on procedures to follow in arranging for the shipment of the welfare supplies.[11]

Elder Benson's Mission to Europe

On January 14, 1946, the First Presidency announced that Elder Ezra Taft Benson of the Council of the Twelve, who had extensive experience in national agricultural organizations, was called to preside over the European Mission. Elder Benson would reopen the missions in Europe, "attend to the spiritual affairs of the Saints," and "make available food, clothing, and bedding for the members of the Church in these distressed areas."[12]

In Elder Benson's letter of appointment, the First Presidency declared: ". . . your influence [will] be felt for good by all you come in contact with, and . . . you and they [will] be made to feel that there is a power and spirit accompanying you not of man."[13] Events of succeeding months would amply demonstrate the prophetic nature of this promise.

Elder Benson was accompanied by Frederick W. Babbel, who had served in the Swiss-German Mission just before the outbreak of World War II. They left Salt Lake City on January 29, 1946, and arrived in England on February 4. From the beginning of their mission they frequently referred to a scriptural promise which they regarded as being fulfilled in their behalf: "And they shall go forth and none shall stay them, for I the Lord have commanded them" (D&C 1:5). Elder Benson recalled:

> Barriers have melted away. Problems that seemed impossible to solve have been solved, and the work in large measure has been accomplished through the blessings of the Lord.

I remember well our first inquiry as to the time we could set sail, either by plane or boat. We were told it would take three months, that all bookings were filled for that period. Yet within twenty-one days from the time our appointment was announced, we landed at Hurn Airport sixty miles south of London. And in spite of a most acute housing shortage in London, two days thereafter suitable headquarters had been established; how, I do not know, except through the blessings of the Almighty; and had we been free to select a spot for our headquarters, as it developed later, we could not have done better for our purpose.[14]

Elder Ezra Taft Benson became the first strictly civilian American authorized to travel throughout all four occupied zones of Germany. Furthermore, his travels were often characterized by an "amazing series of events" enabling him to meet his demanding schedule. He and his associates accepted these circumstances as manifestations of divine intervention. Typical were his experiences as he traveled with Chaplain Howard S. Badger from Paris to the Hague. He reported that railway officials in Paris advised him that there would be a day's delay because Holland must be entered through the eastern border rather than via a more direct route. Elder Benson continued:

> We were almost resigned to taking the service they recommended. It was then that I noticed a train on one of the tracks preparing to leave. "Where is that train headed?" I asked the stationmaster. "Antwerp, Belgium," he answered. I told him we would take that train and he assured me that we would lose an extra day because all connections between Antwerp and Holland had been cut off as a result of the war.
>
> But I felt impressed to board that train in spite of his protestations.
>
> When we arrived at Antwerp, the stationmaster was very upset and advised us that we would have to back-track somewhat and lose an extra day. Again I saw another train getting ready to leave and inquired where it was going. We were advised that this was a local shuttle-service which stopped at the Dutch border where the large bridge across the Maas river still lay in ruins. I felt impressed that we should board that train in spite of the stationmaster's protests.

When we reached the Maas river, we all had to pile out. As we stood picking up our luggage, we noticed an American army truck approaching us. Brother Badger flagged it down and, upon learning that there was a pontoon bridge nearby, he persuaded them to take us into Holland. When we arrived at the first little village on the Dutch side, we were pleasantly surprised to find this local shuttle-service waiting to take us into The Hague.[15]

One of Elder Benson's early visits was to Karlsruhe, a key German city on the Rhine River. Upon inquiring where the Latter-day Saints might be meeting, the group was directed to an area of almost totally demolished buildings. Elder Babbel wrote:

Parking our car near massive heaps of twisted steel and concrete, we climbed over several large piles of rubble and threaded our way between the naked blasted walls in the general direction which had been pointed out to us. As we viewed the desolation on all sides of us, our task seemed hopeless. Then we heard the distant strains of "Come, Come Ye Saints" being sung in German. We were overjoyed. No strains of music were ever more welcome!

We hurried in the direction of the sound of the singing and arrived at a badly scarred building which still had several usable rooms. In one of the rooms we found 260 joyous saints still in conference, although it was already long past their dismissal time. . . .

With tears of gratitude streaming down our cheeks, we went as quickly as possible to the improvised stand. Never have I seen President Benson so deeply and visibly moved as on that occasion.[16]

Elder Benson later described his feelings during the meeting:

I well remember our first meeting at Karlsruhe. . . . The Saints had been in session for some two hours waiting for us, hoping that we would come because the word had reached them that we might be there for the conference. And then for the first time in my life I saw almost an entire audience in tears as we walked up onto the platform, and they realized that at last, after six or seven long years, representatives from Zion, as they put it, had finally come back to them. Then as the meeting closed, prolonged at their request, they insisted we go to the door and shake hands with each one of them as he left the bombed-out building. And we noted that many of them, after they had passed through the line went back and came through the second and third time, so happy were they to grasp our hands. As I looked into their upturned faces, pale, thin, many of these Saints dressed in rags, some of them barefooted, I could see the light of faith in their eyes as they bore testimony to the divinity of this great latter-day work, and expressed their gratitude for the blessings of the Lord. That is what a testimony does.[17]

Elder Benson felt a sense of urgency in visiting the scattered Saints in what had been East Prussia but was now Polish territory. Repeated visits to the Polish embassy in London, however, failed to secure the needed visas to Warsaw. Elder Babbel reported the latest of these failures to Elder Benson:

> I sensed deeply with him that we were faced with a seemingly insurmountable problem. After moments of soul-searching reflection, during which neither one of us broke the silence, he said quietly but firmly, "Let me pray about it."
>
> Some two or three hours after President Benson had retired to his room to pray, he stood in my doorway and said with a smile on his face, "Pack your bags. We are leaving for Poland in the morning!"
>
> At first I could scarcely believe my eyes. He stood there enveloped in a beautiful glow of radiant light. His countenance shone as I imagine the Prophet Joseph's countenance shone when he was filled with the Spirit of the Lord.

Flying to Berlin, Elder Benson there obtained the necessary clearances for his party to go to Poland, even though he had been told definitely that the Polish Military Mission in Berlin had no authority to provide it.

Upon arriving in Poland, Elder Benson's party drove to a small town where a German branch of the Church had been located.

> Not a sign of life was upon the streets as we entered the little village of Zelbak. . . . Proceeding to the further end of the village we spied the branch chapel—the only Church-owned chapel in all of what was formerly Germany—and upon alighting from our vehicle we asked the only woman in sight if this

was the Mormon chapel and where we might find the branch president.

We had spotted the woman hiding behind a large tree. Her expression was one of fear as we stopped, but upon learning who we were she greeted us with tears of gratitude and joy. . . .

Within minutes the cry went from house to house, "The brethren are here! The brethren are here!" Soon we found ourselves surrounded by about fifty of the happiest people we had ever seen.

Having seen our strange jeep approaching with what they feared to be Russian or Polish soldiers, they had abandoned the street as if by magic. Likewise, when they learned of our true identity and mission, the village became alive with joyous women and children—women and children, because only two of our former twenty-nine priesthood holders remained.

That morning in fast and testimony meeting over one hundred saints had assembled together to bear their testimonies and to petition Almighty God in song, in fasting and prayer, to be merciful to them and let the leaders again come to visit them. Our sudden and unheralded arrival, after almost complete isolation from Church and mission headquarters since early 1943, was the long-awaited answer, so wonderful they could scarcely believe their good fortune.[18]

Elder Benson found the European Saints eager to move forward again in promoting the Lord's work. Nevertheless, substantial problems had to be overcome before Church programs could be reimplemented. Many branches could not be fully organized because so many of their priesthood leaders had been lost during the war. Furthermore, as meetinghouses and homes had been destroyed, the Saints lost not only material possessions but items of spiritual importance as well. In some branches, for example, not even copies of the scriptures remained. Nevertheless, "the faith of the Saints is stronger than ever before," Elder Benson reported. "Everywhere in war-torn Europe, the faithful members of the Church, bereft of earthly possessions, face the future with courage undaunted. This is in great contrast to the melancholy, suicides, and discouragement all around them."[19]

One of Elder Benson's most important assignments was to see that the critical temporal needs of the Saints in Europe were met. Supplying the desperately needed food and clothing posed a substantial challenge to the Church's decade-old welfare program. Its prompt and efficient response, however, provided the occasion for extensive favorable comment. Elder Benson discovered that the needs were great, particularly in the war-affected areas.

An exception was Denmark, where the people appeared to have plenty to eat. The Danish Saints regarded this to be the fulfillment of Elder Joseph Fielding Smith's prophetic promise made at the outbreak of the war—that because Denmark had opened its doors to the missionaries being evacuated from Germany and Czechoslovakia, her people would not want for food during the war. Germany, on the other hand, had been devastated by the war, so her Saints' needs were acute. The German Saints exhibited courage, faith, and resourcefulness in meeting the emergency. During the closing months of the war, Saints in the East German Mission began gathering clothing, hiding it in safe places and sharing it cooperatively. The mission president compared the German members to the early Latter-day Saints who were driven closer together by the difficulties they suffered.[20]

By March 14, 1946, Elder Benson had made necessary arrangements with government and military authorities in Europe to have the relief supplies sent. To supplement the supplies already in storage, the Church launched drives for used clothing and other goods. President George Albert Smith took the lead in demonstrating his love and concern for the suffering Saints in Europe. He donated at least two suits fresh from the cleaners and several shirts still in their wrappings from the laundry. During a visit to Welfare Square to inspect the results of these clothing drives, he took off his own topcoat and laid it on one of the piles of clothing being prepared for shipment to Europe. Despite the protestations of his associates, the weather being quite cool, he insisted on returning to the office without his coat.[21]

Elder Benson reported that military and other officials were amazed at the dispatch with which the shipments arrived from the Church in America. European Church leaders wept for joy and gratitude when they visited the storehouses where

Elder Ezra Taft Benson (right) and Brother Max Zimmer inspect Church welfare supplies sent to Europe by the Saints in America. (*Improvement Era* photo)

the welfare goods had been received. Elder Benson wrote: "I wish you could have seen the clothes as they had them neatly arranged on the floors and in cabinets at the mission home and witnessed the expressions of gratitude, both facial and by word of mouth, from the mission presidency and other Saints."[22] Many wept openly as they examined clothing or ran their fingers through sacks of grain.

In addition to supervising the distribution of these welfare supplies, Elder Benson was also instrumental in extending regular missionary work to Finland. Prior to World War II there had been only infrequent contacts by missionaries from the Swedish Mission with the few scattered Swedish-speaking Saints living in Finland. In 1946, however, Elder Benson directed that regular proselyting be inaugurated in Finland, and then, on July 15, on a beautiful hill near Larsmo, he dedicated and blessed Finland that it might be receptive to the gospel. The following day, a surprising 245 persons attended a meeting in Helsinki and manifested a genuine interest in the Latter-day Saints' message.[23] A separate Finnish Mission would be organized the following year.

Elder Benson returned home in December 1946, having traveled more than sixty thousand miles during his ten-month assignment in Europe. Some ninety-two carloads of welfare supplies, about two thousand tons, had been received and largely distributed. By this time, newly called presidents were directing the work in the missions of Europe. American missionaries "were busily engaged in teaching the restored gospel in all of the pre-war missions of Europe; and where military restrictions did not yet permit their entry, local missionaries had been called to serve full-time and were doing a commendable work."[24]

By the spring of 1947 Church leaders had not yet been able to find a Finnish-speaking member with sufficient experience to serve as president of the new Finland Mission. On a trip to the East, Elder Benson (now back in the United States) got off his train in Chicago to make a special purchase. Even though he had been assured he would have plenty of time, the train left without him. He immediately telephoned the president of the Chicago Stake to have someone pick him up and drive him to the airport. He was picked up by Henry A. Matis, the stake clerk. Matis expressed a particular interest in Finland. Elder Benson learned that Matis had been born of Finnish parents and could speak the language with some fluency. The Apostle had found the man for whom he had been seeking, and Elder Matis was soon called as the first president of the Finnish Mission.[25]

Foundations for Growth in Other Areas

Reopening missionary work in the Pacific did not involve as much effort as in Europe. Although missionaries had been withdrawn, except from Hawaii, mission presidents had been able to remain at their posts. Furthermore, areas served by these missions were never in actual combat zones (except Pearl

Boyd K. Packer, serving in the U. S. Air Force, participates in first Japanese baptisms following the close of World War II. (Photo courtesy of Elder Boyd K. Packer)

Harbor). Following the end of hostilities, therefore, missionaries were again assigned there, without the complications that had been experienced in Europe.

A different situation existed in Japan. The Latter-day Saint mission there had been closed in 1924, long before the outbreak of World War II. By 1945 only about fifty members remained in the Land of the Rising Sun. Latter-day Saint servicemen among the American occupation forces made an important contribution to the future of the Church in Japan. Many were anxious to bless the Japanese people with the spirit and message of the gospel. When three Mormon soldiers were offered a cup of tea in a curio shop in the village of Narumi, they declined and took the opportunity to explain the Church's teachings concerning the sanctity of the body. This led to further gospel conversations, and on July 7, 1946, the shop's proprietor, Tatsui Sato, and his family became the first postwar converts baptized in Japan. The young serviceman who baptized Mrs. Sato was Boyd K. Packer, a future member of the Council of the Twelve.[26] Other convert baptisms fol-

Elder Matthew Cowley, president of the Pacific Mission during the postwar years, had a special love for the Polynesian peoples. He is shown here with local residents.

lowed, and thus foundations were laid for the eventual reopening of the Japanese Mission.

The appointment of Elder Matthew Cowley to be president of the Pacific Mission was announced by the First Presidency on December 7, 1946, just five years after the attack at Pearl Harbor. Elder Cowley had presided for eight years over the New Zealand Mission, including the period of World War II. He had been called to the Council of the Twelve almost immediately following his release from his mission assignment. He would fulfill a function to the missions of the Pacific similar to Elder Benson's in Europe. During the next three years he would travel widely and have many remarkable experiences in the Pacific. On one occasion, for example, he blessed fifty people. On another day he gave blessings to seventy-six, many getting in line as early as 5:00 A.M. "This seemed the usual thing," Elder Cowley noted in his journal. "And they are made well, such is their faith. I know that when I lay my hand upon their heads that they are made whole," he testified. "It is not my faith. I just have faith in their faith."[27] Elder Cowley's deep faith in the gospel of Jesus Christ, his great love for the peoples of the Pacific, and his enthusiastic leadership helped provide the impetus for postwar Church growth throughout the area.

In 1947 the First Presidency called Elder Edward L. Clissold, who had served in Japan as part of the allied occupation forces, to return and open the mission there. Upon his arrival in Tokyo, he found the climate far more conducive for successful missionary work than in former decades. There was a spiritual void that needed to be filled.

Two of President Clissold's most urgent tasks were to get the Japanese Mission formally registered and to find a suitable mission home. Fortunately his earlier experience with the occupation authorities provided him with key contacts with Japanese government officials and others. Still, several weeks of diligent searching, persistent contacting, and frequent fasting and prayer were required before these objectives could be achieved. Finding a home was not easy, so much housing having been destroyed by the war. Finally a building was found in a good location near many embassies, across the street from a beautiful park, and only five minutes from downtown Tokyo. About a year later, when Elder Matthew Cowley was in Tokyo, he dedicated this home, praying that the Lord's work might progress and that temples might be erected in this land. Thirty years later, this home would be torn down to make way for the Tokyo Temple, the first of these sacred structures in the Orient.

On June 26, 1948, the first five missionaries arrived. All five were former servicemen, come to share the gospel with the nation that so recently had been their enemy. By 1949 there would be 135 Church members in Japan.

The second half of the twentieth century would be a period of unprecedented growth for The Church of Jesus Christ of Latter-day Saints. The reopening of missionary work in Europe and in the Pacific were only two of the important foundations for this growth laid during the years immediately following the close of World War II.

The Church continued to gain strength in many new areas of North America where the Saints had been attracted during the war. This was reflected in the creation of several new stakes along the Pacific Coast. In 1947 the formation of the Florida and South Carolina stakes, the first in the South, evidenced progress in that area.

Some important developments in Latin America anticipated the great growth that would soon occur there. In Mexico, a large group of members, responding to the growing spirit of nationalism in their country, in 1936 had demanded a mission president of their own blood and had become disaffected from the regular Church organization. Arwell L. Pierce, who became president of the Mexican Mission in 1942, devoted his major effort to bringing these people back into full harmony with the Church. He repeatedly demonstrated genuine love for them and a spirit of helpfulness as he held out the goal of eventually having a stake in Mexico under local leadership and urged the Saints to unite in working toward that objective. The climax came at a special mission conference in 1946, attended by George Albert Smith, the first Church President ever to visit Mexico. He radiated his Christlike love as he stressed the need for harmony and unity. Former differences were overcome. The fifteen hundred attending the conference were eager to show their love and respect for the prophet and thronged around him. Though ill, President Smith graciously received their attention, further cementing the spirit of unity which would be vital for future progress.[28] In 1947 a new era of growth in Latin America was evidenced as missionary work was extended from Mexico to Central America and as a new mission was opened in Uruguay.

The Church passed a significant milestone in 1947 as its membership reached the one million mark. President George Albert Smith's administration not only witnessed a growth in numbers and geographical expansion, however, but these postwar years were also a significant period of revitalization and refinement for the Church's varied programs and activities.

12 Postwar Resurgence

The Salt Lake Tabernacle was opened to the public on August 13, 1945, for the first time in nearly four years. Audiences were again able to enjoy the daily organ recitals and attend the weekly choir broadcasts. The first general conference without wartime restrictions on travel and attendance convened that October. These developments typified the ushering in of an era when Church activities revived and expanded, and provided the occasion for reevaluating and refining Church programs. In the midst of these postwar developments, the Latter-day Saints also marked the centennial of the Mormon pioneers' arrival in Utah. Hence President George Albert Smith's administration provided the occasion for reflection on past accomplishments as well as looking forward to and preparing for future opportunities.

Revival and Expansion of Church Programs

Missionary work and the construction of Church buildings were undoubtedly the activities most hampered by wartime restrictions. With the ending of hostilities, however, these and other activities not only revived but also expanded in order to better meet the needs of the Saints.

The rapid influx of missionaries after the war pushed their numbers to the new peak of 2,244 in 1946; by 1950 some 5,156 were serving. As had been the case before the war, most missionaries again were young Elders. The sudden explosion in the number of missionaries led to measures designed to enhance their effectiveness. The development of improved proselyting plans in these postwar years will be considered in a later chapter.

As the pace of missionary work picked up, the administrative load of mission presidents increased. Unlike ward bishops, stake presidents, or most other executives in the Church who enjoyed the assistance of two counselors, mission presidents served alone despite their responsibilities for missionaries and members. Therefore in 1947 the General Authorities directed mission presidents to call counselors from among the missionaries and local Melchizedek Priesthood bearers. Elder Spencer W. Kimball later declared that the decision to appoint counselors was a revelation to the Presidency of the Church.[1]

While mission organization was being strengthened and proselyting missionaries were refining their methods, the Church was also taking advantage of other means to share its message with the world. With the end of wartime gasoline rationing and the consequent upsurge in travel, the importance of Temple Square as a missionary tool revived. In 1948 the number of visitors topped the one-million mark for the first time. In that same year the annual Hill Cumorah Pageant, "America's Witness for Christ," resumed. The Church's first major involvement in motion picture production also came during these postwar years. Several Church leaders had been especially impressed with teaching and training films produced by the Walt Disney Studios as part of the war effort. New Latter-day Saint motion pictures appearing during the later 1940s treated Church historic sites, Temple Square, and the welfare program. Likewise, as television developed during the postwar years, the Church was quick to make use of it. The October 1949 general conference was the first to be telecast.[2] A later chapter will consider in greater detail the importance of these media in sharing the gospel with the world.

The shortage of critical materials had brought the Church building program almost to a complete halt during the war. With the return of peace, Latter-day Saints looked forward to the construction of meetinghouses and other badly needed facilities. As materials became available, the Church embarked on an ambitious chapel-building program. By 1949 some two hundred local meetinghouses had been completed, and the total reached nine hundred only three years later. As early as the mid-1950s, more than half of all Latter-day Saint buildings in use had been constructed since the close of World War II. Expenditures for these building projects accounted for more than half of the appropriations from general Church funds during these years.

The need for new buildings was particularly acute at Brigham Young University as it experienced a sudden expansion of its student body following the close of World War II. BYU's prewar enrollment had stood at just less than 3,000, but as more and more young men responded to calls into military service, the student body shrank to a wartime low of only 1,155 during the 1943-44 school year. As the conflict ended and veterans began pouring back onto the campus, the school's enrollment soared to 5,082 for the 1946-47 year and continued to grow. Over 2,200 veterans enrolled as freshmen during the 1946 fall quarter. Thus almost overnight Brigham Young University was transformed from a dormant wartime campus dominated by coeds into a bustling campus on which men outnumbered women for the first time. To meet the resulting housing shortage, BYU purchased twenty-six barracks-type temporary buildings from the Army to provide accommodations for two hundred married students and three hundred single veterans.

The Church's administration building in Salt Lake City was remodeled during 1948 and 1949. A central light well was filled in to create more office space. As a result, all the General Authorities' offices were under one roof for the first time.

In 1937 President Heber J. Grant had announced plans to build a temple in Idaho, and construction got under way two years later. The work moved forward, and on October 19,

1941, the capstone was laid. From the outside the structure appeared to be completed. But less than two months later, the attack at Pearl Harbor propelled the United States into war, and the temple's completion had to be postponed as strategic building materials suddenly became scarce. Finally by mid-1945 the Idaho Falls Temple was completed and ready for dedication. In his dedicatory prayer President George Albert Smith expressed gratitude for the cessation of war and for the coming of peace. He prayed that the peoples of the world might be inclined to live the gospel of Jesus Christ, thereby making the peace permanent and hastening the time of the Lord's coming.

The General Authorities encouraged and gave greater direction to the Saints' temple and genealogical activity. Elder Joseph Fielding Smith, a member of the Quorum of the Twelve and president of the Genealogical Society, was called in 1945 to become president of the Salt Lake Temple and hence to give general supervision to the work of all the Church's temples.

One of the society's most valuable services was the microfilming of vital records from many countries and making them available to genealogical researchers. This project had commenced during the late 1930s but was interrupted with the coming of World War II. It resumed even before the war ended. In March 1945 the Church began microfilming 365 English parish registers that had been sent to Salt Lake City for this purpose. During 1947 Archibald F. Bennett, Secretary of the Genealogical Society, spent four months in Europe conferring with government and religious officials. He was successful in obtaining permission for the society to microfilm records in England, Scotland, Wales, Denmark, Norway, Sweden, Holland, Germany, Finland, Switzerland, northern Italy, and France. George Fudge, who many years later would become Director of the Genealogical Society, was called to inaugurate the work of microfilming records in England. At first he had only a used camera with no light meter, and he had to work alone. Nevertheless, within three months nearly a quarter of a million pages had been filmed. Only occasionally did the Church representatives encounter anti-Mormon opposition from local churchmen. In the wake of war most archivists

George Fudge, who pioneered microfilming of genealogical records in Britain, later managed the Genealogical Department of the Church. (Utah State Historical Society)

were eager to cooperate with the microfilmers in order to ensure that a copy might be preserved in case the original records were destroyed. Furthermore, the society presented each library or church with a copy of the material microfilmed, allowing the public to have access to this information without having to handle the already fragile originals. By early 1950 twenty-two full-time microfilmers were at work in the United States and several European countries. Prior to the war some 3,340 records had been microfilmed and cataloged. By 1950 this total reached 24,579.[3]

Postwar social trends placed stress on the family and caused Church leaders to give added attention to the home. The close of World War II witnessed a sharp increase in the number of marriages, followed by what demographers have called the postwar baby boom. Hence there were probably more new families and new parents than at any previous time in the Church's history. Unfortunately, however, the rate of divorces in the United States almost doubled from 1940 to 1945. Elder Richard L. Evans considered this highest divorce rate in history as one of the appalling "costs of war" and acknowledged that it was a subject very much on Church leaders' minds.[4] It should be no surprise, therefore, to find that the home and family received considerable attention during these critical postwar years. Under the leadership of the General Authorities, therefore, various Church organizations in 1946 inaugurated programs to strengthen families and specifically to promote a regular "family hour."

The same wartime conditions that undermined family stability also posed significant challenges for the youth. The General Authorities had repeatedly instructed local Church leaders to look out for the welfare of these young people. The Granite Stake in Salt Lake City had developed a method of checking on and encouraging the activity of young women, similar to the Presiding Bishopric's program for young men bearing the Aaronic Priesthood. In 1944 the Twelve recommended that all stakes adopt this girls' program. In order to avoid unwanted duplication of effort, responsibility for the LDS Girls Program was formally assumed by the Young Women's Mutual Improvement Association in 1950. Under the leadership of the Young Men's and Young Women's MIAs, new age-group and activity programs were sponsored for the youth. As a result, active Latter-day Saint young people typically spent many wholesome hours in dramatic, cultural, recreational, social, and athletic activities. Road shows, dance festivals, speech competitions, and Churchwide softball and basketball tournaments attracted widespread attention and praise. Involvement in such activities helped the Church's youth retain their religious faith at a time when others were restless in their search for new values and beliefs.

In the spirit of refining activities in order to more adequately meet the needs of the Saints, the General Authorities made adjustments in the sacrament meeting, the Church's basic weekly worship service. Over the years, the practice had developed of having soft instrumental or even vocal music during the passing of the sacrament. In 1946, however, the First Presidency specified that there should be absolute quiet during this time, that nothing should distract the Saints from reflecting on the atonement of Jesus Christ and on the sacred covenants they had made with him.[5] The Church certainly was not opposed to music as such. To the contrary, during these

After moving into its new facilities, dedicated in 1952, the Primary Children's
Hospital developed into one of America's leading pediatric facilities. (Church
Archives)

postwar years Church leaders encouraged special courses of
instruction for Church musicians. A new edition of the Latter-
day Saint hymnal was prepared. Publication of *Recreational
Songs* and *The Children Sing* in 1949 and 1951, respectively,
represented an important new expansion of Latter-day Saint
music literature.

The Church was also taking steps to enhance the temporal
welfare of its members. For some time the Church had operated a few hospitals in the Intermountain area, and during the
years immediately following World War II it took steps to
strengthen this system. Hospitals in Salt Lake City and Ogden
underwent major renovation and expansion. The Church also
cooperated with rural communities in Utah, Idaho, and
Wyoming to open and operate several small hospitals. Then, in
1949, ground was broken for the new Primary Children's Hospital in Salt Lake City. This $1.25-million facility would pro-
vide badly needed hospital care to children of all religions and
races—free of charge to the families unable to pay.

The Day of the Lamanites

The Latter-day Saints have always had an interest in the American Indians and related groups, whom they identify as descendants of the Book of Mormon Lamanites. The scriptures describe great future blessings for these people (see 2 Nephi 30:3-6 and D&C 49:24), and the Saints have always believed that it was their unique responsibility to help the Lamanites realize this glorious destiny. As a result, the Church since its beginning has sponsored missions and other programs to benefit the Lamanites. The 1940s brought a significant expansion of these activities, and many Church members became more involved than ever before in working with the Lamanites.

Modern missionary work among the North American Indians dates from 1936, when the First Presidency directed the Snowflake Stake in northeastern Arizona to open formal missionary work among these people. Soon other stakes became involved.

Missionary work among the Indians received a significant boost in November 1942. George Jumbo, a Navajo Latter-day Saint, had gone to Salt Lake City for back surgery. Before returning home, his wife Mary expressed the desire to meet President Heber J. Grant. Arrangements were made. "Mary stood before him in her beautiful Navajo costume and eloquently pleaded that missionaries be sent to her people. President Grant, eyes filled with tears, turned to Elder George Albert Smith and said, 'The time has arrived for the preaching of the gospel to the Lamanites of the Southwest,' " and directed the Apostle to give more attention to this matter.[6] Early the following year the Navajo-Zuni Mission was organized. The work soon spread beyond these tribes, reaching Indians throughout the United States and Canada. The second half of the twentieth century would also witness very successful missionary work among other Lamanite groups, particularly in Latin America and Polynesia.

While these Indian missionary programs were moving forward, another group of Lamanites was being blessed in quite a different way. Most Spanish-speaking Saints did not

President George Albert Smith took a personal interest in expanding missionary work among the American Indians and other Lamanites. Here he shows the Book of Mormon to two Navajos, Many Turquoise (left) and Manuelito Begay. (*Improvement Era* photo)

understand the full meaning of the temple ceremonies as presented in English, so in 1945 the temple endowment was presented for the first time in a language other than English. Most of the Saints who attended had had to make a substantial economic sacrifice to travel the long distances to Mesa, Arizona, some even giving up jobs to attend. Nevertheless about two hundred gathered, some coming from as far away as Mexico City. At a special Lamanite conference on Sunday, November 4, 1945, President David O. McKay congratulated those who had gathered. The history-making Spanish-speaking endowment sessions commenced two days later.[7] Those who attended discovered that the Church included more than just the small branch with which most of them worshipped each week. During succeeding years the Lamanite conference and Spanish-speaking temple sessions at Mesa became eagerly anticipated annual events.

President George Albert Smith had over the years manifested a special interest in the Lamanites, and soon after he became President of the Church he called Spencer W. Kimball (who had lived among the American Indians), Matthew Cowley (whose service among the Polynesians is well known), and Antoine R. Ivins (who had been reared in Mexico) to give special attention and leadership to these people. "I do not know when I began to love the children of Lehi," Elder Kimball reflected. "It may have come from my patriarchal blessing which was given to me . . . when I was nine years of age. One line of the blessing reads: 'You will preach the gospel to many people, but more especially to the Lamanites. . . .' And now, forty-two years after the promise, President George Albert Smith called me to this mission, and my blessing was fulfilled." Elder Kimball testified that "a great thrill came to me, such as I have had few times in my life."⁸

While touring the Mexican Mission in 1947, Elder Kimball envisioned a glorious future for the Lamanites, which he related at the Lamanite conference in Mesa during November of that year. Some thirty years later, as President of the Church, he would conduct an area conference at Mexico City. As he addressed the large audience, he again told them of his 1947 vision, which he could see well on its way to fulfillment:

> Maybe the Lord was showing to me what great things this people would accomplish.
>
> I could see you children of Lehi with your herds and flocks on thousands of hills.
>
> In my dream I no longer saw you the servant of other people, but I saw you as the employer, the owner of banks and businesses.
>
> I saw the people of Lehi as engineers and builders building lofty bridges and great edifices. I saw you in great political positions and functioning as administrators of the land. I saw many of you as heads of government and of the counties, states, and cities.
>
> I saw you in legislative positions where as good legislators and good Latter-day Saints you were able to make the best laws for your brothers and sisters.
>
> I saw many of your sons become attorneys. I saw doctors, as well as lawyers, looking after the health of the people. . . .

I saw you as owners of newspapers with great influence in public affairs. I saw great artists among you. Many of you I saw writing books and magazines and articles and having a powerful influence on the thoughts of the people of the country. . . .

I saw the Church growing in rapid strides and I saw wards and stakes organized. I saw stakes by the hundreds: I saw a temple. . . ."9

One of the Lamanites' most critical needs has been for education. The postwar years brought the development of Latter-day Saint schools in Polynesia and later in Latin America. Two programs, which had their beginning during the later 1940s, would be of particular benefit to American Indians.

Golden R. Buchanan was a member of the Sevier Stake presidency in central Utah. During the autumn of 1947 he had occasion to observe the deplorable condition of some migrant Indian agricultural workers in the area. Speaking at a stake conference he admonished the Saints to take better care of their Lamanite brethren. Shortly afterwards a member from a neighboring town came to President Buchanan and told him of a teenage Indian girl named Helen John who did not want to return to the reservation with her family but was determined to remain and go to school. "If you'll let me pitch my tent out back of your house," she pleaded to her Latter-day Saint employers, "I promise I won't be any bother to you. I'll take care of myself, but I would like to live where I can go to school with your girls."

President Buchanan was impressed with the idea. "If a program of this sort were undertaken by the Church," he envisioned, "literally hundreds of Indian children would have the privilege of living in LDS homes where they not only could be taught in school but they could be taught the principles of the gospel." He outlined his ideas in a letter to Elder Spencer W. Kimball. Elder Kimball personally invited the Buchanans to take Helen into their home. Several other Indian youth were placed in other homes in the area. The Saints had to overcome prejudices that stemmed from the era of Indian wars in pioneer times. From these beginnings the program grew and became an official Church-sponsored activity in the 1950s. Eventually as many as five thousand students were placed in Latter-day

Saint homes, especially throughout the western United States and Canada. Many of the Indian students achieved marked success in school and became leaders among their people.[10]

By the 1970s, educational opportunities would improve on the reservations, allowing an increasing number of Indian youth to remain at home while going to school. Still, the placement program would represent the key to success for hundreds of other Indian students.

Another special education program designed particularly for Lamanites was the Indian Seminary. When a military hospital near Brigham City, Utah, was converted in 1949 into the Intermountain Indian School, local Church authorities took steps to provide seminary classes for the new Latter-day Saint Indian youths attending the school. A key role was played by Boyd K. Packer, member of one of the local stake high councils (and future member of the Council of the Twelve), who served as the first teacher. In 1949 the Church bought property adjacent to the school's entrance and later erected a seminary building there. By the mid-1950s the need for similar programs at other government Indian schools had become apparent, and in 1955 Indian Seminaries were officially inaugurated as a distinct program of the Church's educational system. Within a few years more than ten thousand Indian students, from kindergarten through the twelfth grade, were being served. Some Indian Seminary classes met daily as did other seminaries, but most were allowed to provide instruction to the Indian students only once a week.

Brigham Young University would also inaugurate specialized programs for Indian students on campus and also to help train those interested in working with Indians. BYU would also sponsor a special institute to conduct research and service projects on numerous Indian reservations aimed at improving the standard of living.

The Pioneer Centennial

In the midst of this postwar revival of Church activity, the celebration of the pioneer centennial in 1947 focused the Saints' attention on their heritage. President George Albert

Smith, who seventeen years earlier had become president of the Utah Pioneer Trails and Landmarks Association, was now appointed chairman of the committee to plan appropriate observances for the pioneer centennial. Few, if any, Church leaders excelled his zeal in commemorating the achievements of the past. It was fitting, therefore, that he should be serving as President of the Church at the time of the 1947 centennial. At the April 1947 general conference, just about all the speakers paid tribute to the faith and courage of the early pioneers and reflected on the accomplishments during the intervening years. During the spring and summer, dozens of musical performances, art exhibits, sporting events, and dramatic productions marked the occasion. The pageant, "Message of the Ages," which had been so popular during the 1930 centennial, was again staged in the Salt Lake Tabernacle. Some 1,400 persons were involved in the production, and a total of 135,000 persons witnessed the twenty-five performances between May 5 and June 5. A musical production, "Promised Valley," was presented in the University of Utah stadium from July 21 through August 10 with more than 85,000 people attending. Featuring the original music of Crawford Gates, this production depicted the frustrations and dedication of the early pioneers. It was presented throughout the Church by local MIA groups, and in later years became a popular annual attraction in Salt Lake City during the summer tourist season.

A feeling of goodwill accompanied the centennial celebrations. During July the nation's governors held their annual meeting in Salt Lake City. President George Albert Smith hosted the group, and the friendship manifested by these leaders was a far cry from the persecutions of a century earlier. Members of the Sons of Utah Pioneers reenacted the original pioneer trek, following the 1846-47 route from Nauvoo, Illinois, to the Salt Lake Valley. Each of their seventy-two vehicles was outfitted with wagon box, canvas cover, and plywood oxen to give the appearance of a covered wagon. The "trekkers" presented programs and were well received in each of the towns where they stopped along the way.

The centennial celebration climaxed on July 24, exactly one hundred years from the day the first pioneer company had

Automobiles made to look like covered wagons attract attention during the Salt Lake City parade that concluded a reenactment of the pioneer trek, part of Utah's 1947 centennial celebration. (Church Archives)

entered the Salt Lake Valley. A gigantic "Days of '47" parade included numerous floats honoring these early founders. On this day the United States Post Office issued a commemorative stamp in memory of the pioneers. The highlight of the celebration was the unveiling of the sixty-foot-high "This is the Place" monument near the mouth of Emigration Canyon. Fifteen separate sculptures honored the early settlers in the Great Basin. It was located near the spot where Brigham Young had gazed out over the valley, recognized it as the Saints' resting place shown him in vision, and therefore declared, "This is the right place, drive on." The entire monument was dedicated by President George Albert Smith.

Reflecting on the significance of the pioneer centennial, the First Presidency declared: "As that small group of pioneers looked upon what appeared to be a sterile desert, so today the Church faces a world lying in moral lethargy and spiritual decline. A sense of responsibility should be and is in the Church today." The Presidency compared the physical dangers faced by the pioneers with the temptations confronting the Church, particularly the youth, in the twentieth century and charged the Saints to be prepared to meet these challenges as their forbears had been.[11]

The Saints' continuing interest in their heritage was reflected in efforts during and following World War II to acquire additional sites of historic importance. In 1944 the Church began purchasing land at Adam-ondi-Ahman in northern Missouri. Not only was this the site of a small Mormon settlement in the late 1830s, but Latter-day Saints also identified this as the place where Adam met his posterity just before his death, where Book of Mormon Nephites had erected an altar, and where a great priesthood conference will convene just before Christ's second coming.[12] In 1946 and 1949 nearly two hundred acres were purchased at Harmony, Pennsylvania, including the banks of the Susquehannah River where John the Baptist had restored the Aaronic Priesthood in 1829. These purchases were made on behalf of the Church by Wilford C. Wood, who had taken great personal interest in researching, identifying, and acquiring historical sites. President George Albert Smith also took a personal interest in acquiring and suitably marking these sites.

The Saints at Mid-Twentieth Century

The midpoint of the twentieth century was reached as the year 1950 came to its close. Just over three months later, President George Albert Smith would die and a new leader would be sustained. Both of these milestones provided the occasion for the Latter-day Saints to reflect on the Church's status— what had been accomplished, and what still lay ahead.

The first half of the twentieth century had been a period of substantial growth for the Saints, Church membership passing the one-million mark only three years before midcentury. At the general conference held in April 1950, President George Albert Smith shared his feelings about this growth: "The Church has increased more during the past year than in any other year since it was organized. . . . How happy we should be," he continued, "not that we have increased in numbers, but that more of our Father's children . . . have been brought to an understanding of the truth."[13]

Not only had there been an increase in the quantity of Church members, but during the years following the close of World War II there was also an improvement in the quality of the Saints' religious activities. This improvement was reflected in the level of participation in Church meetings. Attendance at sacrament meetings, for example, had only improved from 17 percent to 19 percent between 1920 and 1940, but it reached 24 percent in 1950.[14] The postwar refinement in Church activities and the construction of hundreds of new meetinghouses undoubtedly had a positive impact on this trend.

President George Albert Smith had been afflicted with poor health throughout his life. Following a prolonged illness, he died peacefully on his eighty-first birthday, April 4, 1951. Countless individuals, both small and great, paid tribute to the departed leader. Almost all made specific reference to President Smith's great capacity to love his fellowmen. His second counselor, President David O. McKay, affirmed that George Albert Smith had "lived as nearly as it is humanly possible for a man to live a Christ-like life. He found that the answer to the yearning of the human heart for fulfillment lies in living outside oneself by love."[15] President Smith's emphasis on love had heightened the Saints' spirit of unity. Under his leadership there had been a revival, refinement, and resurgence in Church activity and growth. In these and other ways he had helped lay the foundations for the unprecedented growth during the following decades.

13 David O. McKay and His Administration

David O. McKay holds the distinction of having lived more years than has any other President of the Church. His mortal lifetime extended from the days of Brigham Young to the space age. The gold spike completing the first transcontinental railroad was driven only four years before David O. McKay was born, and yet he lived to see the first men land on the moon. The two decades in which he presided over the Church were an era of unprecedented growth and expansion.

David O. McKay's Earlier Life

David O. McKay was born on September 8, 1873, in Huntsville, a small agricultural community in northern Utah. His father and mother were converts who had immigrated from Scotland and Wales, respectively. The wholesome home environment they created was one of the profound influences in young David's life, and he frequently referred to their worthy example in later sermons.

"My home life from babyhood to the present time has been the greatest factor in giving me moral and spiritual standards and in shaping the course of my life. Sincerity, courtesy,

1873   September 8: Born in Huntsville, Utah
1881-83   Father served mission to Britain (ages 7-9)
1897   Graduated from University of Utah (23)
1897-99   Mission in Scotland (24-26)
1899   Became faculty member at Weber Stake Academy in
          Ogden (26)
1906   Member of Twelve and of General Sunday School
          superintendency (32)
1908   Chairman of General Priesthood Committee
1918-34   General Superintendent of the Sunday School
1919-20   Church Commissioner of Education (46-47)
1920-21   Toured Church missions worldwide (47-48)
1922-24   Presided over European Mission (48-50)
1934   Chosen as Second Counselor in the First Presidency
          (61)
1951   April 9: Sustained President of the Church (77)
1952   Toured missions of Europe (78)
1954   Toured missions in South Africa and Latin America
          (80)
1955   Visited missions in the Pacific; dedicated Swiss
          Temple
1956   Dedicated Los Angeles Temple
1958   Dedicated New Zealand and London Temples and
          Church Colleges of New Zealand and Hawaii;
          organized Auckland Stake
1964   Dedicated Oakland Temple
1967   Regional Representatives first called
1970   January 18: Died in Salt Lake City, Utah (96)

consistency in word and deed exemplified in the lives of my parents and others . . . have proved a safeguard and guidance."[1]

David was only seven years old when his father was called to return as a missionary to Great Britain. The two oldest girls in the family had recently died from serious illnesses, and the mother was now expecting another child. Under these trying circumstances David's father felt that he shouldn't leave his wife, and considered asking for a postponement. "Of course you must accept," David's mother insisted; "you need not worry about me. David O. [who was the eldest son] and I will manage things nicely!"[2] During his father's absence, young David learned how to assume responsibility and how to work. As "man of the house," he rapidly matured beyond his years.

An important event occurred when David O. McKay was not quite fourteen years old. During the summer of 1887, John Smith, the Patriarch to the Church, visited the McKays' rural community in order to give patriarchal blessings to the faithful Saints. As he blessed David, Patriarch Smith clearly anticipated the vast contributions this young man would one day make in the Lord's work:

> Thou art in thy youth and need instruction, therefore I say unto thee, be taught of thy parents the way of life and salvation, that at an early day you may be prepared for a responsible position, for the eye of the Lord is upon thee. . . . The Lord has a work for thee to do, in which thou shalt see much of the world, assist in gathering scattered Israel and also labor in the ministry. It shall be thy lot to sit in council with thy brethren and preside among the people and exhort the Saints to faithfulness.[3]

David's quest for spiritual development began early. He later recalled how as a teenager he prayed fervently for a sure testimony: "I had in mind that there would be some manifestation come, that I should receive some transformation that would leave me without doubt." But, as shall be seen, the desired answer would come only after several more years of seeking.[4]

David O. McKay had a well-rounded college experience. Besides attending to his studies, he played the piano for dances, was left guard on the University of Utah's first football team, courted his sweetheart, and graduated as president and valedictorian of his class.

Upon graduating from the university, David had planned to go to work immediately in order to finance the education of other family members. Shortly before graduating, however, he received a mission call to the British Isles. Even though this represented a financial sacrifice for his family, he accepted the call. After being in Scotland for a short time, he was discouraged and homesick. Then one day in Stirling he noticed an inscription on an unfinished building: "Whate'er thou art, act well thy part." He accepted this message "as if it came from One in whose service we were engaged," and he resolved to act well his part as a Latter-day Saint missionary.[5]

David O. McKay's missionary experience brought great spiritual growth that laid the foundation for his lifetime of service. During a very spiritual conference session in Scotland, an unusual feeling of harmony and faith prevailed. One Elder's declaration that there were angels in the room was confirmed by James L. McMurrin, a counselor in the mission presidency. President McMurrin then prophesied the future of several of the missionaries who were present, including David O. McKay, who later wrote: "His words made an indelible impression upon me: 'Let me say to you, Brother David, Satan hath desired you that he may sift you as wheat, but God is mindful of you.' Then he said: 'If you will keep the faith, you will yet sit in the leading councils of the Church.' I knew that the answer to my boyish prayer had come."[6]

Soon after returning from the mission field, David O. McKay married his college sweetheart, Emma Ray Riggs, their sealing being the first one performed in the Salt Lake Temple in the twentieth century. He accepted a teaching position at the Church's Weber Stake Academy in Ogden. His service as a teacher confirmed his love of reading the scriptures and the works of Shakespeare, Robert Burns, and other literary masters, whom he would quote in sermons throughout his life. At the same time he was called to the Weber Stake Sunday School superintendency with particular responsibility for instruction. Here he introduced features which would "find their way into all the Sunday Schools of the Church and which resulted in revolutionizing the teaching throughout the entire organization." For the first time formal outlines were prepared, stake preparation meetings held, and lesson work unified and made progressive from grade to grade.[7]

In April 1906 David O. McKay was called to the Council of the Twelve, at the age of thirty-two. In October of the same

year he became assistant to the General Sunday School superintendent, who was none other than Church President Joseph
F. Smith. Upon the latter's death in 1918, Elder McKay succeeded him as superintendent, and the following year also
became the Commissioner of Education for Church Schools.
In these capacities he influenced the improvement of teaching
throughout the Church. During these same years he profoundly influenced the development of Church programs in
his capacity as chairman of the General Priesthood Committee
and of several other committees appointed to better correlate
the programs of various Church organizations.

At the end of 1920 Elder McKay was assigned by the First
Presidency to make a worldwide tour in order to assess conditions in the Church's far-flung missions. He spent Christmas
of that year with missionaries in Tokyo, Japan.

On January 9, 1921, Elder McKay and Hugh J. Cannon,
his traveling companion, felt they were guided as they located
a secluded cypress grove within the "Forbidden City" at
Peking, China. There, away from the noisy throngs, Elder
David O. McKay blessed the land and its people, that famine
and superstition might be removed, that the government
might become stable, and that missionaries might come who
can "comprehend the Chinese nature, so that in the souls of
this people an appreciation of the glorious gospel might be
awakened."

In Hawaii Elders McKay and Cannon enjoyed some remarkable spiritual experiences. During a prayer, they were
made aware of the presence and blessing of Joseph F. Smith
and George Q. Cannon (the father of Hugh J. Cannon), who
had introduced the gospel to the Islands seventy years earlier.
On another occasion, Elder McKay was impressed to get off a
lookout ledge just before it crumbled into the crater of Kilauea
Volcano.[8] They visited a small missionary-conducted elementary school in the town of Laie where the Hawaii Temple had
been dedicated about a year and a half earlier. As Elder McKay
witnessed a flag-raising ceremony in which students representing many races participated, he was impressed that Laie would
become an educational as well as spiritual center for the

peoples of the Pacific. His prophetic vision would be fulfilled with the opening of the Church College of Hawaii during the 1950s.

One of the last stops in their three-week visit to the Samoan Mission was at the small mountain town of Sauniatu, which had been colonized by the Latter-day Saints. Elder McKay was the first Apostle these people had ever seen. As the last meeting closed, the Saints formed a line so that they might shake hands with the special visitors. They began singing a beautiful Samoan farewell hymn, but their sobbing soon interrupted their singing as they fondly embraced the visitors. Finally, Elder McKay and his party rode off on horseback, but after going only a short distance were prompted to turn back. As they reached the point where the Saints were still gathered, Elder McKay dismounted, and pronounced a beautiful Apostolic blessing on the Samoan Islands and people. After he had ridden away again, the Saints recorded the words of the prayer, and marked the spot with a pile of stones. A year later they erected a permanent stone monument to commemorate this inspiring moment.[9]

At a meeting in New Zealand, Elder McKay faced an audience "that had assembled with unusual expectations." In other meetings he had spoken through a translator, but on this occasion he longed to speak directly to the people. He informed Brother Stuart Meha, who stood at his side ready to translate, that he would speak without a sentence-by-sentence translation. After Elder McKay had spoken for about forty minutes, Brother Meha gave a synopsis in Maori. Several times, however, he was corrected by his Maori listeners—who did not know English but who had understood Elder McKay's words by the gift of tongues.[10]

In the Holy Land, Elder McKay received instructions by telegram to meet J. Wilford Booth, with whom they were to tour the Armenian Mission. Booth had served a mission among those people, and without his knowledge of the area the tour would be impossible. Elders McKay and Cannon had no idea where to meet Booth, but as they were preparing to leave Jerusalem, Elder McKay felt impressed to travel by train rather than by car. While waiting a few minutes on the railway platform at

Haifa, the Apostle met another traveler, who tapped him on the shoulder and asked, "Isn't this Brother McKay?" This stranger turned out to be Brother Booth. They were astonished to have found one another, and realized that they couldn't have met at a better time. "As we recounted to each other our experiences," Elder McKay reflected, "we had no doubt that our coming together was the result of divine interposition."[11]

Before returning home, Elders McKay and Cannon visited the Church's missions in western Europe. By the time they returned to Utah on Christmas Eve of 1921, they had traveled more than twice the distance around the globe. These experiences gave Elder McKay a worldwide vision of the Church's challenges and opportunities, which would be invaluable to him in later years, especially during the rapid growth which would be part of his Presidency.

Elder McKay's missionary expertise was further enhanced as he presided over the European Mission from 1923 to 1925. Using the motto "Every Member a Missionary," he encouraged the European Saints to share the gospel with their neighbors. This slogan would become a well-known emphasis of President McKay's teachings during the 1960s.

An even more important assignment came to David O. McKay in 1934 when he was called to fill a vacancy in the First Presidency of the Church. During the next seventeen years he would serve as the Second Counselor to Presidents Heber J. Grant and George Albert Smith. He carried the responsibility for missionary work and many other Church programs. He served in the First Presidency during the Great Depression of the 1930s and during World War II and its aftermath in the 1940s. This experience gave him further preparation for the greatest calling of all, which would occupy the last two decades of his life.

President McKay's Teachings

President George Albert Smith died on Wednesday, April 4, 1951, just two days before the scheduled opening of general conference. The Saturday sessions of conference were canceled so President Smith's funeral could be held. The conference had been scheduled to conclude on Sunday, but a special "solemn assembly" session convened on Monday, April 9, at which David O. McKay was sustained as the ninth President of the Church. As he accepted this high and holy office, President McKay sounded a theme which would be central to his teachings:

> No one can preside over this Church without first being in tune with the head of the Church, our Lord and Savior, Jesus Christ. He is our head. This is his Church. Without his divine guidance and constant inspiration, we cannot succeed. With his guidance, with his inspiration, we cannot fail. . . .
>
> I pledge to you that I shall do my best so to live as to merit the companionship of the Holy Spirit, and pray here in your presence that my counselors and I may indeed be "partakers of the divine spirit."[12]

President McKay recommended a similar standard of conduct for everyone: "An upright character is the result only of continued effort and right thinking, the effect of long-cherished associations with Godlike thoughts. He approaches nearest the Christ spirit who makes God the center of his thoughts. . . ." President McKay was convinced that "man's chief concern in life should not be the acquiring of gold, or of fame, or of material possessions. It should not be development of physical powers, nor of intellectual strength, but his aim, the highest in life, should be the development of a Christlike character."[13] He believed that in order to live on this loftier plane, man must overcome the more worldly or carnal aspects of his character. The world and individuals need "to be saved . . . from the dominating influence of animal instincts, of passions, of appetites." Selfishness, he believed, was a major cause of man's ills.[14] "The development of our spiritual nature should concern us most," President McKay insisted. "Spirituality is the highest acquisition of the soul, the divine in man; 'the supreme, crowning gift that makes him king of all created things.' It is the consciousness of victory over self and of com-

munion with the infinite. It is spirituality alone which really
gives one the best in life."[15]

This emphasis on spirituality was underscored by a
special experience Elder McKay had during his 1921 world
tour. Aboard his ship in Apia Harbor, Samoa, he witnessed an
unusually spectacular sunset. As beautiful and glorious as this
was, he realized that it did not stir his emotions nearly as much
as do the worthy lives of loved ones. He wrote:

> I then fell asleep, and beheld in vision something infinitely
> sublime. In the distance I beheld a beautiful white city. Though
> far away, yet I seemed to realize that trees with luscious fruit,
> shrubbery with gorgeously-tinted leaves, and flowers in perfect
> bloom abounded everywhere. The clear sky above seemed to
> reflect these beautiful shades of color. I then saw a great con-
> course of people approaching the city. Each one wore a white
> flowing robe, and a white headdress. Instantly my attention
> seemed centered upon their Leader, and though I could see
> only the profile of his features and his body, I recognized him at
> once as my Savior! The tint and radiance of his countenance
> were glorious to behold! There was a peace about him which
> seemed sublime—it was divine!
>
> The city, I understood, was his. It was the City Eternal;
> and the people following him were to abide there in peace and
> eternal happiness.
>
> But who were they?
>
> As if the Savior read my thoughts, he answered by pointing
> to a semi-circle that then appeared above them, and on which
> were written in gold the words:
>
> "These Are They Who Have Overcome The World—Who
> Have Truly Been Born Again!"[16]

As will be seen hereafter, home and family became a
major emphasis in President David O. McKay's teachings. He
felt that the home was the most important place for Latter-day
Saints to manifest the noble attributes of character which grow
out of increased spirituality. He urged husbands to treat their
wives with loving courtesy and respect, and parents to teach
their children through precept and proper example. The
loving relationship between David O. and Emma Ray Riggs
McKay became for the Saints a model of ideal family life. Presi-

dent McKay's declaration that "no other success can compensate for failure in the home" quickly became one of the Church's most widely quoted mottos during the second half of the twentieth century.

President of a Worldwide Church

President David O. McKay's administration was a period of unprecedented growth. By 1950, after one hundred and twenty years of the Church's existence, the number of members reached approximately 1.1 million. During the next two decades, the period of David O. McKay's Presidency, the number of Latter-day Saints almost tripled, reaching over 2.9 million. Taking into account those who had died during this period, it is probable that as many as two-thirds of all Church members living at the beginning of 1970 had known no other President than David O. McKay. When he had taken office in 1951, there were 184 stakes. The five-hundredth stake was organized on the very day he died in 1970. In 1951 the Oahu Stake in Hawaii was the only one outside of continental North America. President McKay would direct the formation of the first South Pacific, European, and Latin American stakes. His personal background suited him well to give leadership during this era of expansion. His mission to Scotland, his round-the-world tour, his service as president of the European Mission, and his responsibility for missionary work as a counselor in the First Presidency all made him personally aware of the Church's worldwide opportunities and responsibilities. His commitment to gaining a broad understanding of the world around him made it easier for him to relate to the wide spectrum of leaders he contacted in the interest of spreading the gospel.

As President McKay's administration opened, however, certain forces were at work that appeared as though they might actually block Church growth. Within the past year, international tensions had led to the closing of Latter-day Saint missions in the Near East and in Czechoslovakia. The 1949 Communist takeover in China and the 1950 outbreak of the Korean War also led to the temporary closing of the Chinese Mission in

Hong Kong. The impact of the Korean War was not limited to the Far East, however. As the United States assumed a major share in the United Nations peacekeeping force, young men were again being drafted into military service. As had been the case during World War II ten years earlier, the number of elders available for missionary service was cut drastically. In contrast to the 3,015 called by the First Presidency in 1950, only 872 were able to receive mission calls in 1952. To make up for the loss in the number of missionary Elders, the General Authorities called upon the seventies quorums throughout the Church to provide a thousand additional missionaries. This would represent a significant sacrifice, inasmuch as typical seventies were older than the elders and most were married and already established in their careers. Nevertheless, the seventies regarded missionary service as their special responsibility and opportunity, so they responded to the call from their Church leaders. Hence many of the missionaries serving during the early 1950s were young married men who had left their wives, families, and jobs behind. Fortunately, by 1953 a negotiated end to the Korean War was at hand, and the Church was able to resume calling more of its younger single men as missionaries. Despite continuing tensions incident to the "Cold War," conditions during the remainder of President McKay's administration were more favorable for Latter-day Saint growth in most parts of the free world.

David O. McKay became the most widely traveled President in the history of the Church. In 1952 he visited the several missions in Britain and on the European continent. The following year he returned to Europe to dedicate sites for the first "overseas" temples—outside of North America or Hawaii. In 1954 he stopped briefly in London on the first leg of a thirty-seven-thousand-mile tour that took him to South Africa and Latin America. On this trip he became the first General Authority ever to visit South Africa (it being the one area he had not visited during his 1921 tour) and the first President of the Church ever to be in South America. Then, in 1955, he traveled throughout the South Pacific, returning to places where he had enjoyed sacred experiences some thirty-four years ear-

Argentine Saints enthusiastically greet President David O. McKay and his wife on their arrival at the Buenos Aires airport in 1954. President McKay was the first President of the Church to visit South America, as well as other parts of the world. (*Improvement Era* photo)

lier. While on this trip he announced plans to construct a temple in New Zealand, which represented yet a further step in making the blessings of the house of the Lord available to the Saints in various parts of the world. A few months later he was in Europe for the fourth time in four years, this time to dedicate the Swiss Temple. In 1958 he returned to the Pacific to dedicate the New Zealand Temple. While in that country, he also organized the Auckland Stake, the first outside of North America or Hawaii and a further evidence of the Church's international growth. Later that same year he was back in Europe to dedicate the London Temple.

Everywhere President McKay went he was greeted with love and respect. He was the first living prophet most of the scattered Saints had ever seen in person. At airport after airport they welcomed him with tear-filled eyes and choked voices as they sang the familiar strains of "We Thank Thee, O God, for a Prophet."

President McKay often felt the reality of divine blessings and guidance as he traveled. In 1955, for example, his flight was delayed because of warnings that a hurricane was headed toward Fiji, their next stop. By the time they reached the area, however, they were able to land safely. Officials in Fiji were puzzled to see how the hurricane "had suddenly reversed its course" at the very time of President McKay's arrival. The President remarked that truly "something very unusual had happened." Heavy tropical rains continued, delaying the McKays' departure from Fiji. Until he unexpectedly met two Elders on the street, President McKay was not aware that Latter-day Saint missionaries had begun working in the area only three months earlier. He immediately arranged to meet with the small group of Latter-day Saints living in Suva. They met at the home of Brother C. G. Smith, who, all alone, had kept the little flock of Saints together for many years. As Brother Smith welcomed God's prophet to his home and to their meeting "he broke down and wept tears of joy and thanksgiving." The congregation with tears in their eyes sang "We Thank Thee, O God, for a Prophet" with feeling and humility, singing "every word as if it were a prayer." President McKay remarked that "this was a significant meeting." He explained that he was not aware that there were Church members in Suva and that his schedule had called for him to be on his way to Tonga by then. He compared this occasion to the meeting at Philippi where the Apostle Paul and his associates had started the first European branch of the primitive Church. He also reported that he had stopped at Fiji in 1921, "but decided that the time was not ripe for the preaching of the gospel to the people of that country" at that time. He declared that circumstances had now caused them to remain so that they might "commence the building up of the Kingdom of God" in Suva. "Surely," he concluded, "God has had a hand in changing our schedule so that we can be with you members of the Church."[17]

President McKay's travels were a source of inspiration to more than just those scattered Saints he visited. The *Church News* carried day-by-day accounts of his experiences, and they

were followed with great interest. Even those in the strong
central areas of the Church found their faith being strengthened as they read about the feelings of faith and gratitude manifested by their fellow Saints in far-flung countries.

The worldwide Church growth which accelerated so
dramatically during President David O. McKay's administration will be the subject of the next chapter. There were, however, other dimensions to Church progress under his leadership. The process of refining Church programs continued,
leading to "Priesthood Correlation" and a renewed emphasis
on the home during the 1960s. These, too, will be treated in
later chapters. Few, if any, Church programs experienced
more growth or development during President McKay's administration than did the educational system.

Educational Expansion During the McKay Years

By the 1930s the Church's educational program had
assumed the basic pattern that would characterize it during
subsequent decades of the twentieth century. Henceforth
growth, especially following World War II, would be the
major feature of its history. As can be seen from the accompanying figures, enrollment in the Church's various educational programs increased approximately fivefold during the
two decades while David O. McKay presided over the Church.
His backbround and personal commitment to education suited
him well to give leadership during this era of phenomenal
growth. At only twenty years of age he became the principal of
the district school in his hometown of Huntsville. He then
completed a three-year teacher-education course at the University of Utah, thus becoming the first President of the Church to
hold a college degree. As has been seen, he served as a teacher
and then as principal of the Church's Weber Stake Academy
and later became superintendent of the Church's entire educational system. His continuing commitment to education was
demonstrated by developments while he served as President
of the Church.

1950	Building missionaries began erecting schools in the Pacific; early-morning seminaries pioneered in southern California
1953	Ernest L. Wilkinson became administrator of all educational programs
1955	Church College of Hawaii opened
1956	First student stake organized at Brigham Young University
1957	Pacific Board of Education organized
1960	Expansion of Church schools in Mexico began
1966	Home-study seminary pilot program inaugurated
1970	Neal A. Maxwell became Church Commissioner of Education

Few individuals had greater impact on Church education during the McKay years than did Dr. Ernest L. Wilkinson. He was an attorney in Washington, D.C., at the time of his appointment as president of Brigham Young University in 1950. Three years later he was also named administrator of the unified Church system including schools, seminaries, and institutes of religion worldwide.[18] In these capacities he would give a dynamic and powerful direction to the entire Church educational program during the next two decades.

Church Schools in the United States

Brigham Young University was not alone in facing the pressures caused by the surging enrollments following the close of World War II. Ricks College, the Church's two-year school in southeastern Idaho, also was affected by the postwar expansion. In 1948 the Church Board of Education approved Ricks's becoming a four-year school. Not only did this provide additional badly needed educational opportunities, but it also allowed the school to accommodate persons seeking to comply with a 1947 Idaho law requiring four years of college train-

Student Enrollment

Year	Seminaries	Institutes	BYU	Other Church Schools
1900			40	
1910			111	
1920	2,980		438	
1930	27,075	321	1,448	
1940	26,128	3,352	2,715	
1950	28,677	4,309	5,429	
1955	38,285	5,558	9,440	
1960	62,253	10,270	11,555	
1965	103,500	30,052	21,286	12,076
1970	132,053	44,005	25,921	17,459 (1968)
1975	174,010	73,643	25,950	15,695
1980	199,317	124,939	27,772	27,449

ing for a public school's teaching certificate. In 1954, however, the board decided to return Ricks to its junior college status. By that time the postwar pressures had lessened, and Wilkinson and his associates were planning a system consisting of a single university supported by other schools.[19]

"After long and careful consideration," the First Presidency wrote, "we have come to the conclusion that Ricks College will be of more service to the Church and have a greater destiny as an integral and permanent part of the Church School System by being a first-class Junior College than by continuing as a relatively small four-year college."[20] A few years later the Church Board of Education announced plans to move Ricks College from Rexburg to Idaho Falls, a larger community offering more employment opportunities and other resources. The hope was to allow a larger number of students to obtain their education close to home. Following persistent efforts by Rexburg residents, however, the board in 1961 decided to leave the school in Rexburg. In later years it would continue to fill an important place in the Church's educational system.

At the time of Ernest L. Wilkinson's appointment as president of Brigham Young University in 1950, he was assured that the First Presidency wanted BYU to become "the greatest educational institution in the world."[21] For the next two decades Wilkinson labored energetically to see this hope realized. As a well-trained lawyer, he argued persuasively and successfully before the board that Brigham Young University needed to expand significantly in order to more effectively meet the educational needs of the Saints. Under his leadership and with the board's backing, BYU launched an unprecedented building program. Major new academic buildings were constructed; the capacity of on-campus student housing was tripled; and other facilities including a motion picture studio, a student center, and a new stadium were also added. During the years 1951 to 1971 the estimated value of BYU's physical plant, including buildings and equipment, soared from just over six million dollars to well over one hundred million.[22] President Wilkinson took steps to see that academic progress kept pace with physical growth. He actively recruited faculty members with doctor's degrees from the prestigious universities of the land. In 1960 BYU offered its own doctorates for the first time. In that same year it also launched the Honors Program, allowing serious students to enjoy contact in small classes with the university's most outstanding faculty members.

The Church activity of students was also a source of concern. In some wards adjacent to college campuses, students sometimes tended to crowd out local members. At the same time, there were other students who did not affiliate with any Church unit when away from home. As early as 1947 two special branches were formed to meet the needs of married and single students, respectively, at Brigham Young University. At first these units were considered experimental, but they soon demonstrated their success by setting the highest attendance record in the East Provo Stake. As enrollment mushroomed, the first complete student stake in the Church was organized at BYU in 1956. This made a unique and significant contribution to life at BYU and to the students' personal development.

Soon student stakes or wards were organized on many other campuses wherever numbers were sufficient. Typically a faculty member or a person from the community would be the

During postwar decades, Brigham Young University grew to become one of the largest privately owned institutions of higher education in the United States. (Photo courtesy of Mark Philbrick, BYU)

bishop, but students would fill most other positions. Thus they gained experience as quorum or auxiliary leaders, teachers, clerks, and so on. Mature students even had the opportunity to serve as counselors in the bishopric or as members of the stake high council. In contrast to campuses of most major universities, which were almost deserted on Sundays except for the handful attending chapel services, at Brigham Young University and Ricks College the buildings where the students wards met were as crowded on Sunday as during the week. The success of these units at Church schools soon led to the organization of student stakes and wards for the benefit of Latter-day Saints attending other universities or colleges. As President Wilkinson reflected on his two decades of leadership at BYU, he declared that the organization of the student stakes and wards was "the most satisfying accomplishment during the time I have been here."[23]

Part-Time Religious Education

While the foregoing developments were occurring on the campuses of the Church's schools, significant progress was also being made in its programs of part-time religious education. Seminaries and institutes were spreading throughout the United States and around the world to meet the needs of high school and college students.

Adaptations in the seminary program made possible the rapid growth in the number of high school students enrolled. Originally all seminaries were of the "released-time" variety. In predominantly Latter-day Saint communities of Utah and adjoining areas a seminary building was erected near the high school and students were released during the regular school day to take a seminary class as one of their electives. As the Latter-day Saints spread beyond the Intermountain states, they increasingly lived in areas where such an arrangement was not possible. Therefore early-morning and home-study programs developed to meet their needs.

Early-morning seminary classes had been inaugurated in Salt Lake City and Pocatello in 1929; the program in the latter location was discontinued after only one year. As early as 1941

Enrollment in Various Types of Seminaries

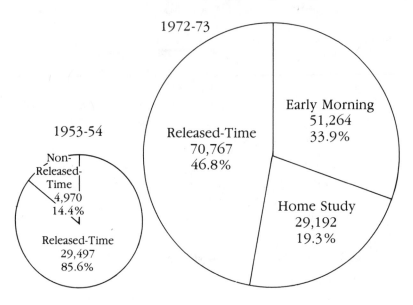

1972-73

1953-54

Released-Time
70,767
46.8%

Early Morning
51,264
33.9%

Home Study
29,192
19.3%

Non-
Released-
Time
4,970
14.4%

Released-Time
29,497
85.6%

Source: Seminaries and Institutes 1972-73 Annual Report
(This does not include the Indian seminary enrollment.)

the institute director in southern California reported that there were five high schools in the Los Angeles area alone having more than one hundred Latter-day Saint students each, and that there were several others approaching that number. However, wartime restrictions precluded any new programs at that time. In 1950 the eleven Los Angeles area stake presidents unanimously urged that early-morning seminaries be started at once.

Formidable obstacles had to be overcome: Most classes would have to serve more than one high school; differences in schedules from one school to another meant that the only possible time for seminary was before school. Classes would have to begin at 7:00 A.M. or even earlier. Almost no chapels were located within walking distance of the high schools, so car pools or other transportation would need to be arranged. In September 1950 six pilot classes were inaugurated; their success led to the addition of seven more classes that same school year. Despite the difficulties of time and distance, the 461 southern California seminary students registered an average attendance of 88 percent that first year. Three years later there were fifty-nine classes achieving an average attendance of 92 percent. This record was a tribute to the devotion of students and their parents who were willing to get up as early as five-thirty in order to attend or help their children attend a religion class before school. During the next quarter century, early-morning classes would make seminary instruction available to Latter-day Saint students in many parts of the world, especially in centers of Church population in the United States and Canada beyond the Intermountain area.[24]

Home-study seminaries were next established where there were not enough students to make a regular daily class possible, where distances were too great to make transportation to and from a seminary class before school feasible, or where there were no Church buildings in which the classes could meet. The first home-study programs were started as pilot projects in the Midwest during the 1966-67 school year. The young people would study their seminary lessons at home during the week and then meet with others in their branch to go over this material with a volunteer teacher as part of their regular meetings on Sunday. Then about once every month or so all the students from a district would gather at a central location under the direction of a full-time seminary coordinator. During the morning they reviewed with him the highlights of their past month's study. In the afternoon the students enjoyed social or recreational activities conducted by MIA leaders, and the local teachers received a preview of the coming month's lessons from the seminary coordinator. These home-study programs have made seminary instruction available to Latter-day Saints no matter where they live throughout the world. A similar home-study institute course for college students was inaugurated in 1972.[25]

Developments Abroad

The worldwide growth of the Church as a whole brought a corresponding expansion in the educational system during the years of President David O. McKay's administration. In the Pacific and in Latin America, two areas of particularly rapid growth, public education was not widely available, so Church leaders were concerned that a substantial portion of the Saints did not have the opportunity for even an elementary education. In these areas, therefore, the Church returned to the practice of nineteenth-century pioneer times—establishing schools to teach the basics of secular education along with religious instruction.

During the early twentieth century several of the Pacific missions had conducted schools, generally small, for the benefit of Latter-day Saint children. An outstanding example was the Maori Agricultural College in New Zealand. Full-time missionaries were called on to act as teachers in these schools. Church growth following the close of World War II heightened the need for these schools to be expanded. During the early 1950s the Church opened the Liahona College in Tonga, the Pesega and Mapusaga high schools in Samoa, the Church College of New Zealand near Hamilton, and several elementary schools in these same countries. Even though two of these schools were called colleges, they included work only to the high school level. As will be seen in a later chapter, buildings for these badly needed schools were constructed through the "building missionary" program that had its beginning at this time in the South Pacific.

The Church College of Hawaii, a four-year institution of higher education at Laie, opened in 1955. The school came to serve about a thousand students, most coming from the Pacific islands. Emphasis was on teacher education, thus making it possible for many Polynesian young people to return to their homelands and become faculty members in the Church schools there. In 1958 President David O. McKay dedicated a complex of fine new buildings on the CCH campus. A thirty-three-foot mosaic on the facade of the administration building depicted the flag-raising ceremony which had prompted Elder McKay to prophesy some thirty-seven years earlier that Laie would one day become the educational center for the Saints in the Pacific. In 1963 the Church opened the Polynesian Cultural Center adjacent to the college campus. It not only helped to preserve and share the unique cultures of several Pacific peoples, but it also became a very popular tourist attraction which created goodwill for the Church and also provided meaningful employment for a large number of CCH Polynesian students. In 1974 the Church College of Hawaii became the Hawaii Campus of Brigham Young University, emphasizing subjects which could be taught more advantageously in the Pacific setting than on BYU's main Provo campus.

At first the Church's schools in the Pacific were operated under the supervision of the respective missions where they were located. By 1957, however, the system had grown to the point that the First Presidency formed a separate Pacific Board of Education to give direction to these schools as a group. Called as chairman of the Board was Wendell B. Mendenhall, who was also head of the Church's building program in the Pacific. Under the Board's leadership, the transition from missionary teachers to a professionally trained faculty accelerated, the process being virtually completed by 1959.[26]

The expansion of the Church's educational program in Latin America also came during these same years. As has been seen, the Juarez Academy in the Mormon colonies of northern Mexico dated from near the turn of the century. Beginning in 1960, however, with the encouragement of President David O. McKay, a system of some forty elementary and secondary schools was established to meet the educational needs of Saints in various parts of Mexico. Over two thousand students, many at the college level, attend the Church's school "Benemerito de las Americas," near Mexico City. Here again, emphasis is on teacher preparation. As in the Pacific, these schools have made a significant contribution to Latter-day Saint activity as a whole, a sizable number of local Church leaders having graduated from them. The Church also operated a few schools in Chile and Peru.

An especially important contribution was made by the Church's literacy program. In some developing areas, people were being called as leaders and teachers who did not know even how to read or write. Under the direction of Brigham Young University, a simple plan was developed to teach these basic skills. In Bolivia, for example, members received fifteen hours of one-to-one instruction teaching them to read Spanish. Having completed this course, an additional four hours of training prepared these people to teach others. In this way hundreds of Latter-day Saints were enabled for the first time to read the scriptures as well as handbooks, lesson manuals, and other Church literature. Not only were many able to obtain better employment, but their self-esteem received a substantial boost. One branch president commented that before he had learned to read, opportunities had been like a closed book for him; now his life was rich and full like an open book.

Guidelines for the Future

With the growth of the Church's schools and other educational programs, it became necessary in 1964 to divide the administrative responsibility. Ernest L. Wilkinson continued as president of Brigham Young University, while Dr. Harvey L. Taylor became "chancellor" of the remainder of the Church educational programs. By June 1970 (just five months after President McKay's death), the General Authorities felt the need to have a more thorough unification of the entire system under one leader. Dr. Neal A. Maxwell, the executive vice president of the University of Utah (and future member of the Council of the Twelve), was appointed commissioner of the Church Educational System.

Commissioner Maxwell and his staff gave thorough consideration to what should be major objectives of the Church's efforts in education. With the approval of the General Authorities, the following report of what had been accomplished under President McKay's leadership, together with guidelines for future developments, was published:

(1) *Literacy and basic education are gospel needs.* Without literacy, individuals are handicapped—spiritually, intellectually, physically, socially, and economically. Education

is often not only the key to the individual member's economic future, but also to his opportunities for self-realization, for full Church service, and for contributing to the world around him —spiritually, politically, culturally, and socially.

In response to special needs there are 75 Church-operated elementary and middle schools and seven secondary schools in Mexico, Chile, Peru, Bolivia, New Zealand, Tonga, Tahiti, Western Samoa, Fiji, and American Samoa. Without such schools, many members in these areas would be almost totally deprived of education. More than 15,200 students are enrolled in these programs.

(2) *Church programs will not duplicate otherwise available opportunities, especially in higher education.* Post-high school education is within reach of a majority of Church members. Of the more than 200,000 members presently enrolled in colleges and universities, only 32,000 of them are in a Church school. However, 50,000 LDS college students on 320 other campuses are enrolled in LDS institutes of religion to receive instruction in religion and enjoy social and cultural opportunities.

The Church has four institutions of higher education. Brigham Young University at Provo, Utah, with 25,000 students; the four-year Church College of Hawaii at Laie, with 1300 students [redesignated BYU Hawaii campus in 1974]; Ricks College (a junior college) at Rexburg, Idaho, with 5100 students; and LDS Business College in Salt Lake City, with 800 students.

(3) *Ultimately, all high school and college-age Latter-day Saints should have access to weekday religious education, in tandem with secular education.* The greatest impact, in terms of numbers of individuals served by Church educational programs, comes from seminary and institute programs, which enroll 190,000 students. Seminary classes (high school level) are held in all 50 United States and 10 other countries. A recent innovation in the seminary system is a home-study program, which today enrolls 10,000 students, and is conducted in the United States, Canada, the British Isles, Germany, Switzerland, Austria, Australia, New Zealand, Guatemala, El Salvador, Brazil, Uruguay, and Argentina.

Commissioner Maxwell anticipated that Church Education in conjunction with priesthood and auxiliary programs could help individual Latter-day Saints to: (1) develop stronger testimonies of the gospel of Jesus Christ, (2) become more effective Church leaders, (3) be more effective parents, (4) give community leadership, (5) develop employment skills and industriousness, and (6) heighten their creative abilities and self-esteem.[27]

Education was only one branch of Church activity that experienced significant development during the administration of President David O. McKay. During an era of unprecedented worldwide growth, missionary work, public relations, temporal resources, correlation of Church organizations, the home and family, and temples, as well as other activities, all took on increasing importance. These will be considered in the following chapters.

14 Growth into a Worldwide Church

The gospel of Jesus Christ is intended to bless all the peoples of the earth. Hence worldwide growth, especially beginning with David O. McKay's administration, was essential to the Church's fulfilling its mission and was also the fulfillment of prophecy. The Old Testament prophet Daniel declared that in the latter days the Lord would set up a kingdom which would fill the earth (read Daniel 2:26-45, esp. verse 44; compare D&C section 65).

One of the clearest and most forceful expositions of the Church's worldwide responsibilities would be set forth in 1974 by President Spencer W. Kimball.

> It seems to me that the Lord chose his words when he said [the gospel must go to] "every nation," "every land," "uttermost bounds of the earth," "every tongue," "every people," "every soul," "all the world," "many lands." Surely there is significance in these words! A universal command! My brethren, I wonder if we are doing all we can. Are we complacent in our approach to teaching all the world? . . .
>
> I believe the Lord can do anything he sets his mind to do. But I can see no good reason why the Lord would open doors that we are not prepared to enter. Why should he break down the Iron Curtain or the Bamboo Curtain or any other curtain if we are still unprepared to enter? I believe we have men who

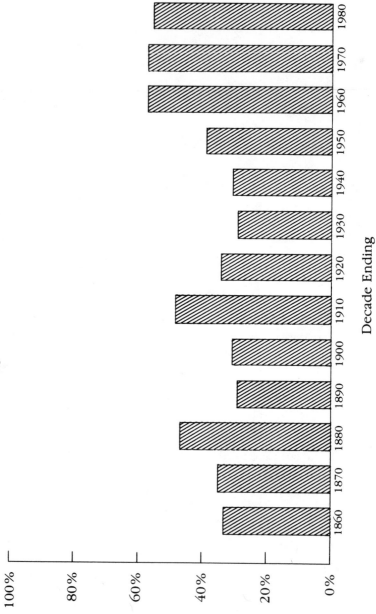

Rate of Growth Per Decade

could help the apostles to open these doors—statesmen, able and trustworthy—but, when we are ready for them.[1]

Following visits to the Far East and Latin America, President Kimball declared that he "seemed to envision a great movement when there would be thousands of local men prepared and anxious and strong to go abroad . . . in great numbers qualifying themselves for missionary service within their own country and then finally in other lands until the army of the Lord's missionaries would cover the earth as the waters cover the mighty deep."

If the Church is to fulfill its mission, it must not only be numerically strong, but its membership must be geographically distributed around the world. The accompanying graphs illustrate the extent to which these requirements are being met. Notice how the Church's rate of growth is increasing; this is in marked contrast to the usual pattern by which the rate of increase drops off as an organization grows larger. Notice also how the Church's members are increasingly widely distributed. This is due to increased missionary success throughout the world and to Church leaders' urging the Saints to remain in their own lands and to build up the kingdom there.

Patterns of Growth

Latter-day Saint growth began in some lands much earlier than in others. By the 1850s missionaries had established lasting footholds in many of the countries of western Europe and in the Pacific. Because large numbers of converts emigrated to America, however, the rate of growth in these areas was not as great as it might otherwise have been. Most Church members were gathering in the Intermountain area of the western United States. The last quarter of the nineteenth century, however, witnessed missions opening or reopening in other parts of North America, in Mexico, and in other parts of the South Pacific.

As has been seen, at about the turn of the century the General Authorities began emphasizing that the need to gather into one place had passed, and that the more important task was to build up the Church in other places around the world.

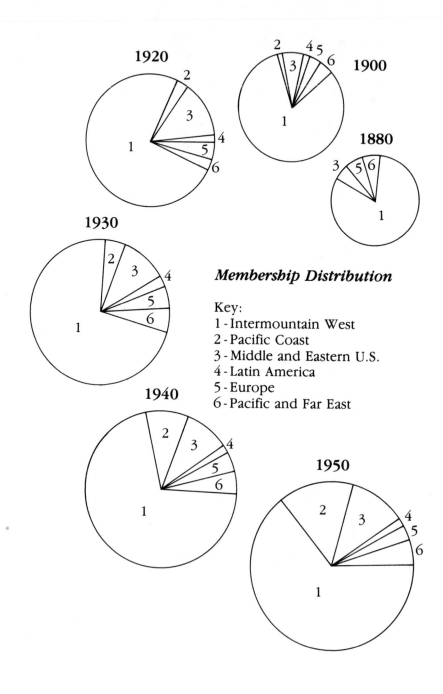

1920

1900

1880

1930

Membership Distribution

Key:
1 - Intermountain West
2 - Pacific Coast
3 - Middle and Eastern U.S.
4 - Latin America
5 - Europe
6 - Pacific and Far East

1940

1950

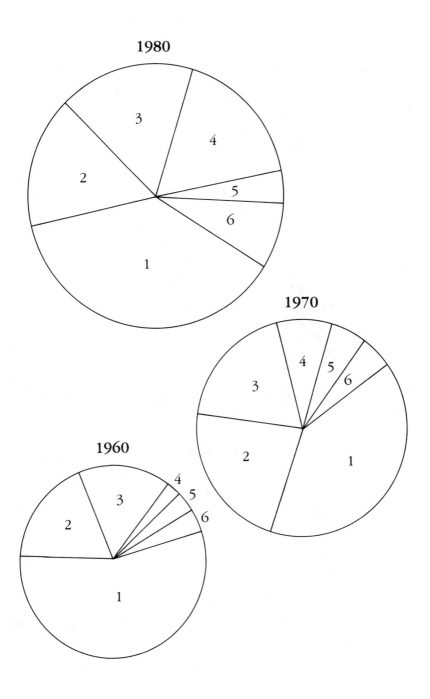

1923	Los Angeles Stake, first outside of Intermountain area
1925	South America dedicated and mission opened
1928	One-hundredth stake organized
1929	Czechoslovak Mission, first in eastern Europe
1934	New York Stake, first in eastern U.S.
1935	Oahu Stake organized in Hawaii
1936	Chicago Stake, first in Midwest
1938	Portland and Seattle stakes, first in Northwest
1947	Florida Stake, first in South; Finland Mission opened; membership passed one million
1953	Houston and Dallas stakes, first in Southwest
1958	Auckland Stake, first outside U.S. and North America
1959	Andes Mission opened in western South America
1960	Manchester Stake, first in Europe
1961	First Latin American stake formed in Mexico City
1962	Korean Mission organized
1966	Sao Paulo Stake, first in South America; Italian Mission opened
1969	Southeast Asia Mission organized
1970	500th stake organized; Tokyo and Johannesburg stakes, first in Asia and Africa respectively; Spain Mission opened
1972	International Mission formed; Jerusalem Branch organized
1975	Indonesia and Utah missions created; ten new stakes formed in Mexico City on a single weekend
1978	Membership passed four million
1979	1000th stake organized at Nauvoo

A new era of growth followed the close of World War I. Many Saints in the Intermountain area began an exodus, particularly to southern California, in quest of improved economic opportunity. Elder David O. McKay's yearlong inspection tour of the Church's far-flung missions in 1921 brought a heightened worldwide vision. A door was opened to the gospel in

South America when German immigrant Saints in Argentina actively shared the gospel with their neighbors. During the 1930s preaching also began among German immigrants in Brazil, but as World War II approached, that government's restrictions on the use of German in public meetings led the missionaries to give more attention to the Portuguese-speaking majority. The interwar years also brought the inauguration of missionary work in Czechoslovakia in eastern Europe.

The impact of World War II on Church growth was both negative and positive. As has been seen, proselyting continued during the war only in North America and Hawaii, and even in these areas the missionary force was reduced to a skeleton crew. The Saints in Europe demonstrated faith and devotion as they withstood the intense suffering brought by the conflict; never before had such a large number of Church members lived within an active war zone. As Latter-day Saints around the world assumed more responsibility for local Church activity, they gained experience that would prove valuable in the years of rapid growth which would follow. The positive role Latter-day Saint servicemen played in carrying the gospel to new areas, particularly to southern Europe and eastern Asia, has been described in an earlier chapter. These areas, together with predominantly Lamanite Central America and western South America, became important new mission fields during the second half of the twentieth century.

Unprecedented growth and expansion characterized the years following the close of World War II. During the 1950s, 1960s, and 1970s the Church's membership increased more than 50 percent each decade, far exceeding the rates of growth during the previous century. This growth was especially strong along the United States' West Coast and in Latin America.

The establishment of new stakes is probably a better measure of true Church progress than is a mere increase in membership. The scriptures have identified "stakes" as sources of strength. The prophet Isaiah, seeing the latter-day glory of Zion, wrote figuratively about her preparation for rejoicing: "Enlarge the place of thy tent, and let them stretch forth the curtains of thine habitations: spare not, lengthen thy cords, and *strengthen thy stakes*" (Isaiah 54:2, italics added; compare D&C 82:14, 115:5-6, and 133:9). In contrast to a mis-

Percentage of Church Members Living in Stakes

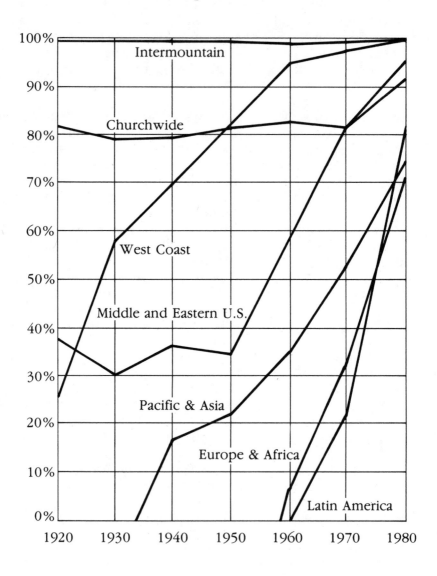

Melchizedek Priesthood Bearers
(as a percentage of total numbers of Church members in the area)

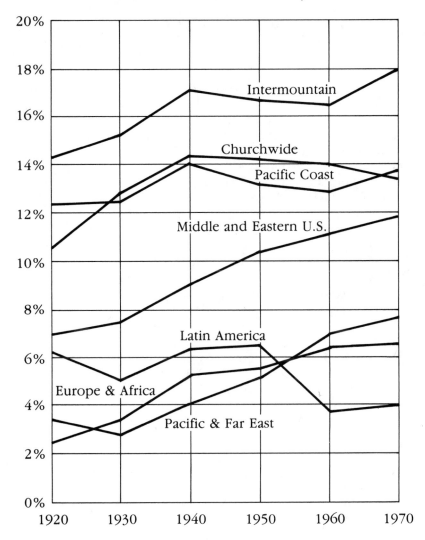

sion district, which generally must *receive* strength and leadership *from* the church, a stake is able to *give* strength and stability *to* the Church, just as stakes support a tent. Church leaders have pointed out that "stakehood" is the ideal for which every mission district is preparing. Stakes cannot be organized until there is not only sufficient membership but also leaders trained and experienced in operating the full programs of the Church. Hence, the formation of new stakes and the consequent increased percentage of Church members living in stakes is a reliable measure of maturity and development in Church activity and spirituality. One of the greatest barriers to this progress is the lack of the Melchizedek Priesthood bearers required to provide the necessary leadership. During the brief period 1958 to 1961, the first South Pacific, European, and Latin American stakes were created. The first stakes in Asia and Africa were organized in 1970. As the thousandth stake was organized in 1979, these units were strengthening the Saints in many parts of the world.

Another evidence of mature growth is the erection of temples. The unprecedented pace of temple construction in the late 1970s and early 1980s (to be described in a later chapter) reflected the increasing spirituality of the Saints around the globe. Yet another evidence of the Church's growing international strength is the appointment of General Authorities from areas outside of Anglo-America. Beginning in 1975 these Church leaders have been called from such diverse areas as the Netherlands, Germany, England, Japan, and Argentina.

Perhaps the greatest benefit of Church growth is seen in the lives of the Saints around the world. Elder Gordon B. Hinckley declared:

> It is my judgment that the work today is on a more stable basis in Europe than it has ever been. We have stakes of Zion. We have strong missions. We have capable local leaders. We have Regional Representatives of the Council of the Twelve from those nations. We have mission presidents coming out of those lands, and missionaries who are working among their own people as well as going to other lands to serve. There is stability in the work in Europe such as I think we have never before had. This is most encouraging.[2]

While the Church was growing rapidly in some parts of the world, formidable barriers still remained in others. The postwar spread of communism closed large sections of the world to the gospel. Furthermore, local laws made other countries inaccessible. Nevertheless, as the final quarter of the twentieth century was dawning, even these obstacles were beginning to be overcome. An ever-increasing number of faithful Latter-day Saints were living in almost every nation of the earth as a result of government, military, or business assignments. In 1972 the new International Mission was organized to meet the special needs of these scattered members. Largely through the efforts of David M. Kennedy, special consultant on diplomatic affairs, the Church during the later 1970s began sending "special representatives" to countries where traditional missionaries would not be allowed. These mature and experienced couples were careful to observe local laws and customs while making friends for the Church and helping to strengthen the few Saints who might be living in the area.

Following the 1978 revelation authorizing priesthood eligibility for all races, missionary work was opened in West Africa. Here hundreds of people had already become interested in the Church primarily through correspondence, and upon the arrival of the missionaries whole congregations were baptized within a few weeks.

Although the Church's growth in recent decades has been phenomenal, still there is ample room and a pressing need for much more expansion. During the 1970s Church membership passed the four million mark, but the estimated world population was about four billion. Hence, only one in a thousand was being blessed by the gospel of Jesus Christ and the program of the restored Church.

The Church in Many Lands

As the Church increasingly became a worldwide movement, it faced ever more diverse circumstances and challenges. Although the gospel provides universal ideals and truths, these must be understood and applied by members who live in quite distinct environments and cultures. Therefore, Church programs must be flexible enough to take into account the unique customs and aspirations of Latter-day Saints in many nations. Saints in different parts of the world face unique challenges. In many parts of Europe prosperity has contributed to religious indifference; although some countries require their citizens to pay taxes to support established state churches, attendance at their Sunday services has slumped to less than 5 percent. High taxes and other economic pressures make having more than one or two children a real sacrifice and require many mothers to be employed outside of the home. Lax moral standards and liberal laws on pornography also threaten to undermine strong families. In European society drinking is an accepted part of life which faithful Latter-day Saints must reject; and because so many diverse languages are spoken by peoples living in relatively close proximity to one another, Church conferences, temple sessions, and other activities must generally be multilingual.

The Polynesians of the South Pacific have been characterized as the sweetest and most lovable people on earth. Their spirituality is evidenced by remarkable healings and inspiring manifestations of the gift of tongues. Traditions describe how their forbears sailed in primitive craft thousands of miles from the Americas to the South Pacific. Latter-day Saints in Polynesia therefore identify themselves with the peoples of the Book of Mormon. Families are important to the Polynesians, as evidenced by elaborate genealogies memorized and recited orally or intricately carved in wood. The Church has flourished among these people. Nowhere outside of Utah is there a higher ratio of Church members to the total population, 13 percent in Samoa and approximately 20 percent in Tonga, compared to only 1 percent in the United States as a whole. In 1974 Samoa became the first country in the world to be completely covered by stakes. Nevertheless, life in this "tropical paradise" is not always easy. In some areas dependence on a single crop often provides only a meager living. In the past, LDS missionaries had to face opposition by governments strongly influenced by Europe-based missionary societies. Transportation is still a practical challenge faced by Church leaders, as they need to visit local units on separate islands.

The Saints in Latin America face yet a different set of challenges. Perhaps nowhere else in the world is another, single religion so pervasively reflected throughout the culture—place names, holidays, and so on. Hence, conversion to the restored gospel represents more of a change to the convert than in areas where religion is not so closely identified with everyday life. Revolutions in Mexico during the mid-nineteenth century brought greater religious freedom, helping to set the stage for the gospel's introduction there. Another series of revolutions in the early twentieth century, however, provided the circumstances leading to the martyrdom of two Latter-day Saints near Mexico City. Such difficulties have generally strengthened the faith and resourcefulness of the Saints. Church members in Latin America, especially in Mexico, Central America, and western South America, regard themselves as being among the descendants of the Nephites and Lamanites described in the Book of Mormon and hence as heirs to the great promises contained in that volume. In no other area was there greater Church growth during the third quarter of the twentieth century: Church membership in Latin America skyrocketed from less than 9,000 in 1950 to over 650,000 just three decades later. In 1950 only .8 percent of all Latter-day Saints lived in Latin America, while by 1980 the figure had reached 16.4 percent. Such rapid growth has posed significant challenges as well as opportunities, notably in providing adequate leadership and buildings.

Missionaries carrying the gospel to the Orient feel they are entering almost a different world. Christianity is not the dominant religion, but rather is only a very small minority. Not even the familiar alphabet is used, so languages seem strange and terrifying. Despite these cultural differences, the gospel has taken root in several of the nations of Asia, and the Church is beginning to experience rapid growth there. Latter-day Saint emphasis on the importance of families has struck a responsive chord in the hearts of many whose families for generations have revered their ancestors.

Challenges Posed by Worldwide Growth

Translation and Distribution of Church Literature

Making the Church's programs accessible to an expanding worldwide membership has created yet another formidable challenge. One of the greatest needs has been to provide Church literature in the native languages of the growing numbers of Saints around the world. During the Church's first century almost all translation was done by the staff in the various overseas mission offices. It was not until 1939 that Eduardo Balderas became the first full-time translator assigned to work at Church headquarters in Salt Lake City. Just after World War II he was joined by a few others who were brought to Salt Lake City from several of the missions of Europe. In more recent years, however, the responsibility for translation has been increasingly transferred to local areas.

In 1963 the distribution of supplies by various Church organizations was consolidated. Then in 1965 the Presiding bishopric was given responsibility for the translation of Church literature, and in the following year these two operations were brought together in one department. "In approaching such an assignment," Presiding Bishop Victor L. Brown observed, "one first begins by developing an organization. This involves people. It is my conviction that the Lord has touched the hearts and the lives of men and women in many lands who have been preparing for such a work, and then he has led us to them." The original charge was to see that Spanish-speaking members receive materials "at the same time they were received by the members of the Church in the center stakes." This assignment was soon expanded to include Portuguese and other languages of Europe. The Polynesian languages of the South Pacific were added at a later date.[3]

Officials estimated that twelve thousand pages of material[4] had to be translated yearly into each language:

Melchizedek Priesthood and home teaching	1000 pages
Aaronic Priesthood youth and adults	1000
Genealogy manuals	150
Relief Society	650
Sunday School	2700

Young Men and Young Women	3100
Primary	1700
Books or other general materials	1800

Bishop Brown explained that translation poses a very demanding challenge and requires extensive preparation:

> There are many words and terms in English that cannot be translated directly into other languages. The translator must have the ability to transfer the author's meaning from one language and culture to another with an absolute minimum of distortion. This is most difficult. It is even difficult sometimes to be sure one understands the author's intent in English.
>
> Take, for instance, the translator who received a Relief Society lesson for translation. In the lesson was a recipe calling for "Chicken of the Sea." Every Relief Society sister knows that "Chicken of the Sea" is a brand of tuna fish—that is, every sister in the United States. The translator checked her encyclopedia and other reference books. She checked the library and university. Finally, in desperation, she translated "Chicken of the Sea" as "hen of the ocean."

The speaker then testified that translators often recognize divine assistance in their exacting task. He spoke of one of them who was assigned to translate some children's hymns.

> Music is most difficult to translate, and *The Children Sing* is no exception. In this case, however, the translator could not write fast enough to keep up with the flow of words as they came to her. There was no doubt in her mind as to the source of her inspiration.[5]

By 1970 a worldwide organization had been developed with publishing plants and distribution centers in Manchester, England; Copenhagen, Denmark (for the Scandinavian languages); Liege, Belgium (for French and Dutch literature); Frankfurt, Germany (for German and Italian); Mexico City (for Spanish); Sao Paulo, Brazil (for Portuguese); Auckland, New Zealand (for the Polynesian area); Tokyo (for Japanese); Seoul (for Korean); and Hong Kong (for Chinese and southeast Asian languages); as well as the center in Salt Lake City. These international facilities enable the Church to avoid the delays and expense of long-distance shipping, as well as eliminating the problems of bringing imported materials through customs.

A high-quality monthly magazine has been another important means of instructing and inspiring Church members throughout the world. Over the years most missions had developed publications of their own. The Church's magazines director explained:

> The idea for a unified magazine for the non-English-speaking peoples of the Church was developed by Elder Howard W. Hunter of the Council of the Twelve in 1966 when he was supervising the European Mission.
>
> As he traveled from one mission to another and observed the workings of the mission staffs, Elder Hunter noted the great amount of time that was being spent by mission presidents and missionaries in producing mission magazines. Also, he was concerned because the magazines varied so much in quality and in content. He then set about to unify and correlate the efforts going into the publications with the goal in mind of saving precious missionary hours, cutting expenses, and at the same time upgrading the quality of the publications.[6]

Material for this "unified magazine" is selected from the *Ensign,* the *New Era,* and the *Friend.* The English manuscript, together with necessary graphics, is sent from Church headquarters to the areas concerned for translation and publication. Space is provided in the magazine for news or other features of local interest. The magazine first appeared in nine European languages in 1967. It is now issued in a total of seventeen languages, including the English edition for American Indians. The unified magazine retains such traditional names as *La Liahona* (Spanish), *Der Stern* (German), and *L'Etoile* (French).

Chinese	*Shengtao che sheng*	The Voice of the Saints
Danish	*Den danske Stjerne*	The Danish Star
Dutch	*Der Ster*	The Star
English (for American Indians)	*The Liahona*	The Liahona

Finnish	*Valkeus*	The Light
French	*L'Etoile*	The Star
German	*Der Stern*	The Star
Italian	*La Stella*	The Star
Japanese	*Seito No Michi*	The Way of the Saints
Korean	*Songdo Wi Bot*	The Friend of the Saints
Norwegian	*Lys over Norge*	Light over Norway
Portuguese	*A Liahona*	The Liahona
Samoan	*O Le Liahona*	The Liahona
Spanish	*La Liahona*	The Liahona
Swedish	*Nordstjarnan*	North Star
Tahitian	*Te Tiarama*	The Star
Tongan	*Ko E Tuhulu*	The Torch

Providing the full range of Church curriculum materials has placed members speaking various languages on more of an equal footing than ever before. Members in Europe were pleased to point out that they were actually the first to commence new courses of study each year—being ahead of the Saints in Salt Lake City because of the difference in time. One mission president had stated that members in his area were ready to be organized into a stake but were only waiting for necessary handbooks and other materials to be translated. The great expansion of non-English stakes has come since the Church enlarged its translation program. Because the Lord indicated that "every man shall hear the fulness of the gospel in his own tongue, and in his own language" (D&C 90:11), those involved in Church translation feel that their service is a "literal fulfillment of prophecy."[7]

Other Challenges

Growth into a worldwide Church has posed yet other challenges. Chapels must be provided for wards and branches throughout the earth. During the later twentieth century the number of these local congregations was increasing by several hundred each year. Even if an average of two congregations shared each meetinghouse, about one new building needed to be completed every day just to keep up with the new units being created. The Church's rapid growth came at a time when construction costs were escalating. This compounded the financial burden placed on the Church and its members.

The growing number of Saints in distant lands needed access to temples to obtain the eternal blessings available only in these holy places. Yet an increasing share of these Saints lived hundreds or even thousands of miles from the nearest temple, so going to the house of the Lord often wiped out their life's savings.

Worldwide growth has also affected the planning of Church programs. Members living in diverse circumstances have a variety of social, intellectual, physical, and spiritual needs. No longer can activities be planned for a single and rather homogeneous group in western America. Church writers have had to keep an international audience in mind. More flexibility has had to be built into manuals and hand-books. This in turn has placed added responsibility on local leaders who had to suit the implementation of Church pro-grams to meet local needs.

The sheer growth in the number of stakes and missions places an increasingly heavy administrative load on the Church's leadership. More conferences need to be conducted. More local leaders need to be called and trained.

Thus, it is apparent that the Church's organization and programs have had to be flexible enough to respond to the varied challenges of international growth. Just as revelation through living prophets led the Saints in meeting the chal-lenges of the past, so also is divine guidance evidenced in meeting present-day opportunities, needs, and responsibilities of growth and expansion worldwide. Later chapters will con-sider how these challenges are being met.

15 Sharing the Gospel

From the beginning, Latter-day Saints have been a missionary-minded people, eager to share the message of the restored gospel. They have been seriously mindful of the Savior's injunction to his ancient Apostles, "Go ye into all the world and preach the gospel to every creature" (Mark 16:15). Their own commitment to missionary work has been authorized and strengthened by latter-day exhortations and promises: "Now behold, a marvelous work is about to come forth among the children of men. . . . For behold the field is white already to harvest; and lo, he that thrusteth in his sickle with his might, the same layeth up in store that he perisheth not, but bringeth salvation to his soul." (D&C 4:1-4.) ". . . the thing which will be of the most worth unto you will be to declare repentance unto this people . . ." (D&C 15:6). "And if it so be that you should labor all your days in crying repentance unto this people, and bring, save it be one soul unto me, how great shall be your joy with him in the kingdom of my Father! And now, if your joy will be great with one soul that you have brought unto me into the kingdom of my Father, how great will be your joy if you should bring many souls unto me!" (D&C 18:15-16.)

Each year thousands of Church members volunteer for missionary service. Approximately three-fourths of them are

young men about nineteen years of age. Most of the remaining
missionaries are either young women or older couples who
have reached retirement age. Although this service is a broadening experience, missionaries are willing to give approximately two years of their lives and to pay their own expenses primarily because of their faith that they represent the true
Church of Jesus Christ restored by divine authority in these
latter days. They are also motivated by the conviction that they
are preaching his gospel and that its teachings actually have the
power to change the lives of men and women for the better.
These Latter-day Saint missionaries have largely been responsible for the Church's worldwide growth as described in the
preceding chapter.

Proselyting Methods

"The harvest truly is plenteous," the Savior exclaimed to
his disciples, "but the laborers are few" (Matthew 9:37). The
same can be said of the present dispensation as well. Consequently, Church leaders have always urged the Saints to be
well prepared and to give their best efforts in the Lord's service. During the Church's first century, door-to-door "tracting" had been the missionaries' primary method of contacting
people. The object was to leave a religious tract at every home,
hoping for a possible discussion later if individuals had any
questions from their reading. Often weeks would go by without any apparent results from the missionaries' efforts.

Several twentieth-century mission presidents compiled
materials to help missionaries be more effective in their work.
Two early examples were 1924 suggestions on contacting
people at the door in "On Tracting," by President B. H.
Roberts of the Eastern States Mission, a member of the First
Council of the Seventy, and further instructions by Elder John
A. Widtsoe of the Council of the Twelve, president of the
European Mission, in "The Successful Missionary." The con-
tent of all these publications was incorporated into *The Mis-
sionary's Handbook,* which appeared in 1937.

Another publication in that same year was destined to
have a long-lasting impact on Latter-day Saint missionary

Level of Missionary Service

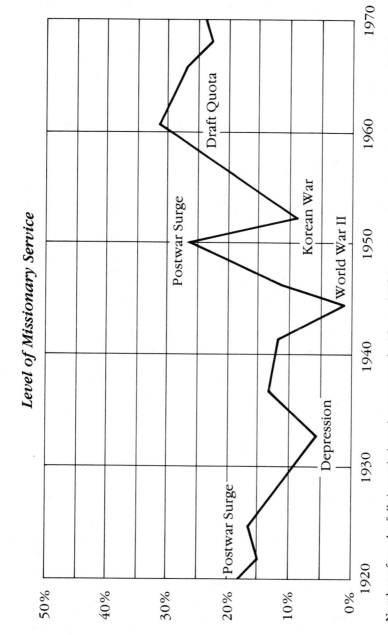

Number of regular full-time missionaries compared with one-half the estimated number of male members 20-24 years of age (approximately the number of young men and women available for missionary service).

1925	Missionary home in Salt Lake City began providing instruction
1929	Tabernacle Choir inaugurated weekly network broadcasts
1933	LDS booth at Chicago's Century of Progress exhibition
1935	Church had its own building at California-Pacific Exposition in San Diego; Radio, Publicity and Mission Literature Committee formed
1936	Shortwave radio beamed First Presidency's message to Europe
1937	Missionary Handbook and LeGrand Richards's proselyting outline published
1939	Church exhibit at Golden Gate International Exposition in San Francisco
1947	Richard L. Anderson developed improved proselyting methods in Northwestern States Mission
1952	First official proselyting outline published by the Church
1957	Church Information Service established
1961	Worldwide mission presidents seminar; missionary language training inaugurated at BYU
1964	Church pavilion opened at New York World's Fair
1972	Public Communications Department organized
1973	*Uniform System for Teaching Families* adopted
1978	All missionaries began receiving instruction at Missionary Training Center near BYU

work. As LeGrand Richards, a future Presiding Bishop and member of the Council of the Twelve, concluded his presidency of the Southern States Mission, he left with each missionary a copy of *The Message of Mormonism*. This outline was prepared to assist the missionaries in their study and presentations of the gospel in a systematic and logical manner. In twenty-four weekly topics the missionary could cover the

Elder Richard L. Anderson pioneers improved proselyting methods while serving as a missionary in the Northwestern States Mission during the later 1940s. (Photo courtesy of Richard L. Anderson)

Restoration and basic doctrines of the gospel. Under each topic President Richards outlined key scriptures, listed tracts or other available reading matter, and suggested questions which should be answered in the discussion. During the next several years many other missions adopted this plan. Repeated requests for copies eventually led Elder Richards to enlarge his material and to publish it in book form, under the title *A Marvelous Work and a Wonder.* This has become one of the most popular Latter-day Saint doctrinal works of the twentieth century, selling more copies than any other Church book except the Book of Mormon.[1]

Following the close of World War II the Church's full-time missionary force soared from an average of 477 in 1945 to 2,244 a year later. This meant that there were many new missionaries in the field who lacked experience and who could profit from some help and direction. To help meet this need, Roy W. Doxey, president of the Eastern States Mission, authored his "Missionary Guide." Without question the most widely circulated postwar proselyting outline was that pre-

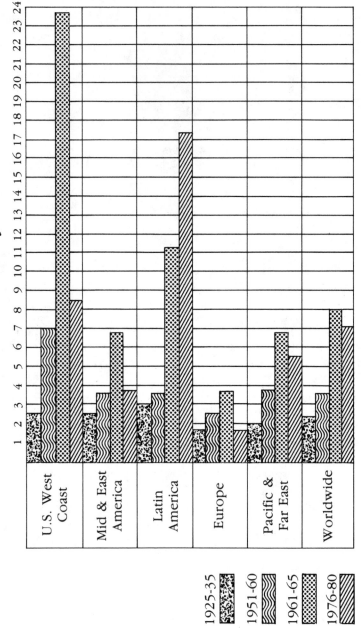

Converts Per Missionary

1 2 3 4 5 6 7 8 9 10 11 12 13 14 15 16 17 18 19 20 21 22 23 24

U.S. West Coast

Mid & East America

Latin America

Europe

Pacific & Far East

Worldwide

1925-35

1951-60

1961-65

1976-80

Data compiled by Richard O. Cowan from annual mission reports pared by Richard L. Anderson, a young Elder who arrived in the Northwestern States Mission in the fall of 1946.

Elder Anderson built on a teaching program he had worked out as a stake missionary while in the military service. Under this program, rather than merely handing out tracts at the door, the missionaries' objective was to get inside the homes in order to present their message. Placing copies of the Book of Mormon was another important goal. Fifteen doctrinal discussions were arranged in a logical sequence to bring conversion. These discussions stressed a careful study of the scriptures and the bearing of testimony. Elder Anderson gained some key ideas from earlier successful missionaries. As these improved methods were adopted throughout the mission, the results were apparent. The number of converts per missionary climbed from 1.87 in 1946 to 5.72 in 1949. In this latter year the Northwestern States Mission baptized 1,001 converts, thus becoming the first mission in the Church to exceed one thousand baptisms during a single year.

The first proselyting plan published officially by the Church for use in all missions worldwide appeared in 1952. *A Systematic Program for Teaching the Gospel* condensed the missionaries' presentation into only six discussions. The plan's preface explained: "Experience has shown that it is not always necessary to take people through an extended series of lessons before they become converted to the Church. Agreement may be gained on . . . fundamental doctrines in a relatively short time through a logical presentation of gospel principles, fortified by scripture, together with reading, convincing testimony, and sincere prayer."[2]

In 1961 Church leaders convened the first worldwide seminar for mission presidents. Under the leadership of the General Authorities the mission presidents pooled their experience in refining proselyting methods. The result was a new missionary plan, *A Uniform System for Teaching Investigators.* Using President David O. McKay's slogan of "Every Member a Missionary," stress was placed on the Saints' role in finding and fellowshipping potential converts. Church members were admonished to lead exemplary lives that would win the respect of others and open the way for gospel discussions. For some time the referral system, in which the Saints gave names of interested friends to the missionaries, had proved successful. Now the Saints were encouraged to invite nonmembers into their homes for "group meetings" to hear the missionaries' message. This method proved even more successful and had at least two important advantages: (1) Missionaries could use their time much more efficiently. One mission president reported that in contrast to tracting, in which missionaries had spent 90 percent of their time looking for contacts and only 10 percent teaching, the cooperation of Church members enabled the missionaries to spend 90 percent of their time actually teaching the gospel and only 10 percent hunting. (2) The same families who first introduced nonmembers to the missionaries could also fellowship these friends as they became converted to the gospel and help them make the transition from one way of life to another and often from one circle of friends to another.[3]

A new missionary outline which appeared in 1973 reflected the growing emphasis on the family. *The Uniform System for Teaching Families* suggested that missionaries might introduce the gospel by working with nonmember parents in presenting family home evenings. Seven proselyting discussions then taught the following gospel principles:

1. *The Restoration.* The Lord has shown his love and concern for all his children in our time by appearing to a prophet, revealing the Book of Mormon, and restoring his church with his authority and power. One can discover the truth of these things by reading and pondering the teachings in the Book of Mormon and praying sincerely.

2. *Eternal progression.* As we are obedient to the commandments of the Lord, we earn the right to live with him forever in the celestial kingdom.

3. *Continuing revelation and individual responsibility.* God spoke to many prophets in ancient times and he speaks to prophets today. We will be blessed as we follow the counsels of the living prophet and other priesthood leaders.

4. *Truth versus error.* Knowledge of truth helps us to become free. Our Heavenly Father wants each of his chil-

dren to learn and live the truth. He has given us several ways to discern truth from error. As we apply the first four principles and ordinances of the gospel, we will begin our preparation to enter the kingdom of God.

5. *Obedience to the Lord's commandments brings his blessings.* Commandments are guidelines to happy living, given because of God's love for us. By obeying them, we can have peace in this life and eternal life with our families; we can become like God.

6. *Our relationship to Christ.* Jesus Christ is our Creator, Savior, and Redeemer—the Light and Life of the world. By him we shall be judged. His atoning sacrifice assures each of us a resurrection from death and opens the way to redemption from sin. (In 1982 this discussion would be moved to the first position in order to give more prominence to the Latter-day Saints' faith in the Savior.)

7. *Membership in the kingdom.* After baptism, which is the gate to the straight and narrow path leading to eternal life, we must press forward with determination to serve the Lord and obey his commandments.

The missionary was encouraged to seek guidance from the Lord's Spirit to know the best order in which to present these discussions to each individual family. A set of visual aids was also provided to enhance the effectiveness of these lessons.[4]

Missionary Preparation

Following World War I, as new missionaries came to Salt Lake City to be endowed and set apart, President Heber J. Grant and his counselors recognized the need to provide a suitable place for them to stay, where the environment would be conducive to reading the scriptures and other appropriate learning activities. In 1924 the First Presidency approved a "Church Missionary Home and Preparatory Training School." Homes on State Street just north of the Beehive House were purchased, and the first group of missionaries entered March 4, 1925.

Before leaving for their respective fields, the missionaries spent a week at the home receiving instructions on Church

Beginning in 1925, the Salt Lake Missionary Home provided orientation for outgoing missionaries. Junius F. Wells is shown here addressing a group of missionaries outside the home in June 1925. (Church Archives)

programs and points of doctrine, being trained in etiquette and other practical skills, and hearing messages of inspiration from the General Authorities.[5] Over the years other facilities have been provided, and the instructional program has been refined to provide the best possible orientation for outgoing missionaries.

A further step in missionary preparation was taken in 1961. Elders were experiencing lengthy delays in obtaining visas to enter Argentina and Mexico. A special language training program was set up for them at BYU to take advantage of this waiting period.

The aim was "to place a missionary in the field ready to speak the language," explained Ernest J. Wilkins, the program's first director. The daily schedule was full of intensive instruction emphasizing conversation. The "Live Your Language" program encouraged the missionaries to speak only in the tongue they were learning.

In addition to language instruction, there was opportunity to practice the missionary discussions with native speakers

Architect's rendering of the new complex in Provo, Utah, designed for the training of missionaries. (Photo courtesy of BYU Physical Plant Dept.)

posing as contacts. Furthermore, the Elders and Sisters adhered to standards of missionary dress and conduct, so were able to develop proper habits and attitudes even before reaching the field.

Because of its success, the program was organized as a formal mission in 1963, and all going to Spanish- or Portuguese-speaking countries were sent first to BYU for training. In 1964 German was added to the program, and more than a dozen other languages have followed since.

The Language Training Mission was expanded in 1969 to include instruction in Dutch and the Scandinavian languages at Ricks College, and training in the languages of the Pacific and Orient at the Church College of Hawaii. Four years later, however, Church leaders announced that all of these activities were to be consolidated at BYU and ground was broken for a $15-million complex near the Provo campus.

Beginning in 1976 all missionaries called to non-English missions reported directly to the LTM rather than first receiving training at the Missionary Home in Salt Lake City. Then in 1978 all full-time missionaries began to receive their complete orientation at the Provo facility rather than in Salt Lake City. Those going to English missions received four weeks of training (later reduced to two) in missionary discussions and procedures. Those assigned to non-English missions continued to receive eight weeks of instruction in their language as well as in missionary matters. The name Language Training Mission was changed to Missionary Training Center to reflect its broadened function.[6]

Meanwhile, missionary orientation centers were established at scattered locations around the world. They served missionaries called from lands far removed from the United States. The first of these opened in São Paulo, Brazil, in 1977. It was designed to provide training for missionaries called from South America to serve in Brazil or Portugal; with the opening of the São Paulo Temple missionaries were able to receive the blessing and instructions of the endowment, and their orientation period was extended from three days to one week.

Public Relations

To supplement the personal contacts by proselyting missionaries, the Church has employed a variety of other methods, including the mass media, to present its message to the world. Visitors' centers and broadcasting have played an especially important part in improving the public's understanding of the Church and its people during the twentieth century.

Bureaus of Information or Visitors' Centers

The Church's system of visitors' centers had its beginning at the dawning of the twentieth century with the 1902 "Bureau of Information" on Temple Square in Salt Lake City. As the volume of travel increased during the years following World War II, the annual number of visitors to Temple Square soared past the million mark. Only Yellowstone National Park attracted more visitors in the Intermountain West. During the 1960s and 1970s the Church built two new commodious structures on Temple Square, each equipped to effectively teach various facets of the gospel message and program.

In the light of this success, the Church continued its program of opening visitors' centers at other historic sites. Likewise, because of the positive response to the Hill Cumorah Pageant, additional pageants at other locations have become means of sharing the gospel with the public.

The restoration of the old Mormon city of Nauvoo began during the 1960s. This ambitious project was patterned after the very successful restoration of the colonial city of Williamsburg in Virginia. The objective was to depict interesting facets of Nauvoo life in the 1840s when this was the largest city in the state of Illinois, but more important, to communicate the faith of the Saints who sacrificed to build the city and then to leave it in the face of religious persecution.

The Church has also found opportunities to share the gospel message with the public at fairs and expositions. As has been seen, the Church sponsored exhibits at several major fairs during the 1930s. More than three million people visited the Mormon pavilion at the New York World's Fair during 1964 and 1965. For this exhibit the BYU Motion Picture Studio produced a new film, entitled "Man's Search for Happiness," depicting the Latter-day Saint concept of life before and following mortality. Experience gained at the New York fair enabled the Church to transform its bureaus of information, renamed "visitors' centers," into more effective tools for teaching the gospel. At Joseph Smith's birthplace in Vermont, for example, guides had formerly stressed the exact location of the family home relative to a nearby township boundary line. Now they emphasized Joseph Smith's prophetic calling in restoring the gospel of Jesus Christ.

Radio and Television

As radio broadcasting began to develop in the 1920s, the Church was quick to use this new medium as an aid in declaring its message to the world. As early as 1922 President Heber J. Grant delivered a message by radio, and two years later sessions of general conference were broadcast. The weekly nationwide broadcasts of the Salt Lake Tabernacle Choir, which were to become the oldest continuous network programs in the history of radio, began in 1929. Richard L. Evans (not yet a General Authority) joined the program the following year; for over four decades his well-known "sermonettes" made many friends for the Church.[7] In addition to these activities in Salt Lake City, members and missionaries around the world prepared special programs for presentation on local stations.

As television was perfected during the years immediately following World War II, the Church did not delay in making use of this new means of communication. General conference sessions were carried from the Tabernacle by closed-circuit TV to other buildings on Temple Square as early as April 1948, and in October of the following year the conference was broadcast by television for the first time. Television coverage of conference was extended to California by the late 1950s, and in 1962 sessions were carried from coast to coast for the first time. The Church paid the cost of getting the conference broadcast to the local stations, many of which in turn donated air time as part of their public service activity. In recent decades, therefore, speakers at general conference have been conscious that they were not only addressing the congregation of a few thousand in the Tabernacle, but rather a potential audience of many millions.

Yet another medium of communication has carried conference proceedings. Since 1952 the general priesthood session has been transmitted by closed-circuit direct-wire to an increasing number of selected stake centers and other Church buildings. Thus well over a thousand separate groups of priesthood bearers throughout the United States and Canada as well as in Australia, New Zealand, and several other countries can have the privilege of simultaneously participating in this conference session.

Church leaders early became interested in international broadcasting. At the April 1936 general conference, the three members of the First Presidency beamed a message to Europe via shortwave radio. In 1962 conference broadcasts were inaugurated, in English to Europe and Africa and in Spanish to Latin America. In more recent years, however, emphasis has shifted to providing general conference and other Church programs for broadcast on standard local radio stations around the world. The perfection of communications satellites during the 1970s has made it possible to relay radio or television programs to distant points on the earth for broadcast locally. By 1980 the Church was equipping selected stake centers with their own satellite-receiving antennas, making it possible for the Saints gathered there to see as well as hear conference proceedings as well as other broadcasts directly from Church headquarters.

Over the years the Church has developed materials to be used by the media. For example, the Radio, Publicity, and Mission Literature Committee distributed radio programs, film strips, and literature needed both in and out of the Church. As demands increased, a division of labor was effected in 1957 and the Church Information Service came into being to handle nonmember contacts. Its primary objective was to promote missionary work by projecting an accurate image of the principles and activities of the Church.

To accomplish this goal, CIS maintained a photo library, coordinated publicity for special events such as conferences or temple dedications, prepared feature articles on phases of Church activity in which the public was most interested—welfare plan, family home evening, youth activities, and so forth —and provided posters, displays, and other help for local open houses or other public relations.

A hosting service was also created to entertain important visitors to Church headquarters, including government or business officials, heads of other churches, artists, or entertainers. These groups were taken to such points of interest as Temple Square and Welfare Square. These visitors often appreciated being entertained in individual Latter-day Saint homes as well as attending Church services in local wards.[8]

In 1972 these and related activities were consolidated under the Department of Public Communications. Important assignments included producing radio and television programs, maintaining good press relations, directing the work of

LDS visitors' centers, and coordinating pageants. This department also was to promote the work of local public relations
representatives appointed in each stake and mission.[9]

The Public Communications Department has sought new
ways of using the mass media to create a climate in which the
public would want to learn more about the Church. In 1976
television stations across the nation carried an hour-long
professionally produced program featuring wholesome family
life. Viewers were invited to write or telephone for a free
brochure (a condensed version of the family home evening
manual) that could help them improve relationships within
their own families. Then, beginning in 1978, the Church sponsored special inserts in the *Reader's Digest* which explained
Latter-day Saint views on the family and other gospel topics.[10]
In addition, Bonneville International, the Church's broadcasting arm, produced a series of half-minute television and radio
announcements urging better communications and more love
in the family. These "Homefront" messages were identified as
coming from "The Church of Jesus Christ of Latter-day Saints,
the Mormons." They were carried on stations throughout the
United States and abroad as a public service, and have earned
several broadcasting awards for their excellence. Response to
these efforts has been quite favorable, thus helping to create a
better understanding, and a more positive image of the Church
—a climate in which missionary work can enjoy greater success.

The Church's Popular Image

The public's attitude about the Church, its programs, and
its members, have exerted a powerful influence on the course
of Latter-day Saint history. Popular misunderstanding during
the Church's early decades led to intense persecution and
suffering. During the last half of the nineteenth century, the
relative isolation of the Latter-day Saints in the Rocky Mountains made misunderstanding and misrepresentation more
likely. Articles published in nationally circulated periodicals
reflected the predominantly negative image during this period.
Joseph Smith was portrayed as an ignorant farm boy, and the

Shifts in Popular Attitude

(shading represents periods when more than usual attention was given Mormonism)

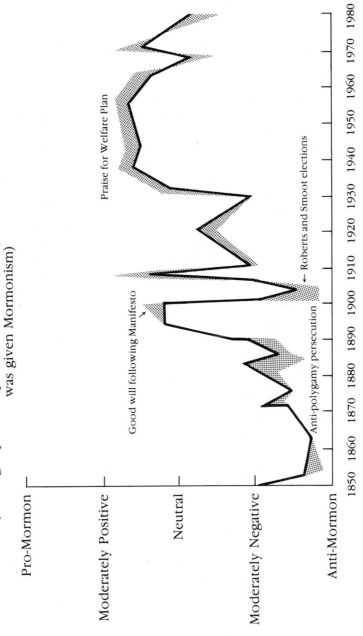

religion he founded was branded an "impostor." Plural marriage was the practice most widely condemned in the press. Furthermore, nationalistic writers regarded Mormon convert immigrants as "ignorant foreigners," and described the ecclesiastical "hierarchy" as a "menace" to the rest of the country.

Following President Wilford Woodruff's 1890 Manifesto officially announcing the suspension of plural marriage, Mormonism cooled as a controversial issue. The periodical press began to recognize in the Mormon people some of the virtues then being advocated by the American populist movement—industry, thrift, temperance, self-reliance, and so forth. In 1893 the Tabernacle Choir drew goodwill and favorable publicity during its concert tour to Chicago's Columbian Exposition. It was also during this decade that Utah finally became a state.

As has been seen, during the Progressive Era the election of two General Authorities, B. H. Roberts and Reed Smoot, to the United States House and Senate respectively, sparked a revival of earlier agitation against the Latter-day Saints. As a result of these attacks, the national magazines portrayed a less positive image of the Mormons.

After Reed Smoot was finally given his Senate seat in 1907, however, Mormonism again declined as a controversial issue. With the coming of World War I, the American public tended to forget old charges. The Mormon Church and people amply demonstrated their loyalty during the war crisis. In the following decade Latter-day Saints began moving away from the traditional centers of Mormon population, seeking greater economic opportunities. As the Saints thus became more integrated with American national life, the nation began to exhibit a more sympathetic understanding of the Saints.

During the decade beginning in 1930, the Church's centennial year, two new features were seen in the popular image which have characterized it ever since. Although the long-range trend had been toward a more favorable image, it was not until these years that it crossed the line from a predominantly negative to a more positive character. The second new feature was a strong interest in the programs of the Church rather than in its theology. This change reflected a general shift seen in twentieth-century American religion—interest in the "social gospel" and its program for social salvation rather than in traditional emphasis on personal salvation through the atonement of Jesus Christ.

In 1936 the Mormon Church Welfare Program attracted widespread admiration. During the next two years the titles of four-fifths of all magazine articles treating Mormonism made specific reference to the new Church security program. Observers praised the Church for taking positive steps to satisfy the temporal as well as the spiritual needs of its members. This praise was especially pronounced when Mormon welfare assistance was the most prompt and effective relief at the time of several major disasters. Admiration for the welfare program helped to confirm the new positive image of the Latter-day Saints. Magazine articles have also reflected an interest in other Church programs, especially its cultural and recreational activities and its excellent program for the youth.

During the second half of the twentieth century more and more Latter-day Saints were achieving prominence in government service, in professional circles, and in a variety of other fields. These individuals have had a very positive influence on the public's attitude. While praising them for their achievements, the press almost always explicitly identifies them as Mormons. The virtues of their religion are often described as contributing to their personal success. For example, articles about golfer Johnny Miller or the Osmond family often discuss the Mormon health code in the Word of Wisdom as well as the gospel's emphasis on family solidarity.

Even though there have been a few negative themes in recent years, such as misunderstandings about the Church's position on blacks and on women's rights, the popular attitude has continued to be largely positive. The importance of this fact is seen in the large number of converts who first became interested in the restored gospel because of favorable publicity about the Tabernacle Choir, prominent Latter-day Saints, or Church programs. Along with the key roles being played by the Church public relations organization and proselyting missionaries, the wholesome examples set by individual Latter-day Saints everywhere must be acknowledged as one of the most important factors in bringing others to a faith in the gospel of Jesus Christ.

16 Temporal Affairs

Even though the ultimate goals of the Church are spiritual, there are many temporal concerns involved in making its religious programs available. These include providing the essential financial support and also dealing with legal, business, and other matters generally regarded as temporal. Modern tools, such as the computer, have facilitated this aspect of the Church's administration.

The Church's worldwide growth, especially during the years following World War II, required that increasing attention be given to these matters. For example, the postwar expansion of stakes and wards in North America, as well as rapid growth in the mission field, created an unprecedented need for buildings. As such demands on the Church's financial resources mounted, the General Authorities were blessed with divine guidance as they made decisions concerning the expenditure of these sacred funds.

Church Economics

A Book of Mormon prophet spoke of the appropriate role of worldly wealth in doing good (see Jacob 2:17-19), and in the

The Lord's Law of Revenue

Percentage of tithing and other
general Church funds spent
for various purposes,
based on 1925–55
statistics

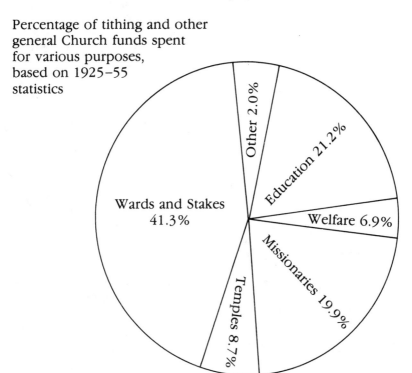

present dispensation the bishop was directed to establish a
storehouse where material means might be accumulated for
the benefit of the poor (see D&C 42:30-36).

Tithing may be described as "the Lord's law of revenue"
(see D&C 119:1-4). Concerning the importance of these funds,
President Henry D. Moyle of the First Presidency declared:

> . . . Truly we are in the day and age when we can and we
> are and we will preach the gospel to every nation, kindred,
> tongue, and people. And that is what the Lord has indicated he
> would permit us to do, through our own diligence in these
> latter days. And that is just the beginning. As I see the tremen-
> dous growth and development of the church in all of its rami-

fications . . . I say to myself, "We are just beginning to scratch the surface." But we cannot get below the surface, and we cannot even scratch the surface (and by that I mean take the benefit of all of the opportunities that present themselves to us day by day to preach this gospel and to save souls), without the payment of the tithes of the Latter-day Saints.

We are grateful. The increase in the tithes in the last 15 years has been tremendous, but I say to you my brethren . . . that the day has come . . . to double the tithes of the church. We're not going to leave the President of the Church in the position where he has to say "no" to any opportunity the Lord presents us, to continue to establish His Church and kingdom here upon this earth. He will hold us as his leaders (holding the keys of Presidency) responsible. And what was done in the days of President Snow can be accomplished today. So far as I am concerned it is just as urgent for us to meet this problem. While we have no immediate financial difficulties, we do have so many means by which we can present our message to the world that we need more and more funds with which to do it. . . .

And I tell you my brethren that the plans that are being forecast for the future are nothing short of phenomenal, and I know with all my heart and soul just as sure as I know the gospel is true that the Lord will not be pleased if we do not make these funds available. . . .[1]

Section 120 in the Doctrine and Covenants provided for a "committee on the disposition of tithes" to oversee the expenditure of these sacred funds. President J. Reuben Clark, Jr., explained how this and related bodies operate:

> . . . Tithing is now administered in the following way:
> Under the direction of the First Presidency a budget is drawn up, as nearly as may be at the first of the year, which includes all of the proposed expenditures of the tithing. This budget is the result of the careful consideration of the departments which are responsible for the expenditure of the funds.
> This budget is then taken before the Council on the Disposition of the Tithes, composed, as the revelation provides, of the First Presidency, the Council of the Twelve, and the Presiding Bishopric. This council considers and discusses the budget so submitted, approving or disapproving, as the case may be, individual items, but finally passing the budget.

> The approved budget as it comes from that meeting is then turned over to the Budget and Appropriations Committee, composed of the First Presidency, three members of the Council of the Twelve, representing that council, and the Presiding Bishopric. This committee then passes upon and authorizes the expenditures of tithing. So that there is a complete check upon all of the tithing which is paid into the Church. None of it is expended except upon the approval and authorization of this committee.[2]

Concerning this later committee, Presiding Bishop Joseph L. Wirthlin testified:

> This committee meets once a week. . . . And over the fifteen years that I have had the privilege of being a member of this committee, I have been inspired and thrilled by the careful appropriating of Church funds. Civil government could well afford to follow the example of the expenditure committee of the priesthood government of the Lord Jesus Christ.[3]

To provide continuity and more effective economic administration, and to lessen the load carried by the First Presidency, the Church established several corporation entities: (1) The Corporation of the President of the Church was to hold tax-free properties mostly at Church headquarters. (2) The Corporation of the Presiding Bishopric was to hold ecclesiastical properties mostly away from headquarters. (3) In 1922 President Heber J. Grant organized Zions Securities Corporation to manage revenue-producing properties; on these strictly investment properties, the Church voluntarily pays taxes although it could generally claim a nonprofit exemption. (4) Cooperative Securities Corporation was set up during the Great Depression to coordinate the management of welfare program properties.[4]

The Building Program

A substantial portion of the Church's expenditures has been for buildings. Providing adequate facilities so that members living in the growing number of stakes, wards, and branches could participate in the full Church program has

posed a major challenge. In addition, more specialized buildings for educational, welfare, genealogical, and administrative
activities have been required. The need for additional buildings was particularly acute during the era of rapid Church
growth following World War II. In 1965, for example, there
were 2,219 Church buildings in existence; of these, 2,034 were
chapels in the stakes and missions. At the same time, 556 new
chapels, or more than 27 percent of those then in existence,
were under construction. In 1964 more than 60 percent of all
Church buildings then in service had been constructed during
the previous decade.[5]

A unique program resulted when the Church encountered a labor shortage when attempting to erect school buildings in the South Pacific just after World War II. Beginning in
1950, the Church resolved the problem by calling young men
as "building missionaries" to donate their labor for two years.
They learned necessary skills as they worked under the direction of experienced builders, most of whom had been called
on special missions from the United States or Canada. Not only
were the needed buildings completed, but the young men
gained self-confidence as they learned a valuable trade.[6]
During the early 1960s this program spread to other parts of
the world, especially to Europe and Latin America. As economic conditions changed, however, the need for this type of
service declined, and by the 1970s most Church buildings
were being constructed by regularly contracted workmen.

To coordinate the Church's widespread building program, a General Building Committee was called in 1955. New
chapels and their sites, normally recommended by local
Church leaders, were evaluated by the Committee's real estate
division, which considered each site's size and location before
giving approval. The number of members and projected
growth were weighed in determining chapel size and type.
Following approval, funds for each project were appropriated
by the Committee on Expenditures. Over the years, in addition
to their tithing the Saints contributed a substantial share of the
money needed for erecting their chapels. As well as making
large cash contributions to the building fund, ward or branch
members donated many hours of service in a wide variety of

fund-raising projects. The exact ratio of local to general Church funds depended on the size, activity, and economic strength of the congregation. In 1982, however, the General Authorities announced that thereafter the local share would not exceed 4 percent of the total cost, and that local units must demonstrate faithfulness in tithe paying in order to have a building project approved.[7] This decision placed emphasis on tithing as the primary source of funding for Church buildings. Rather than asking already faithful tithe payers to contribute additional building funds, more people were encouraged to share in the blessings and opportunities of paying tithing. Members of the Building Committee also worked with local architects in finalizing plans and in supervising and inspecting construction. In 1972 the Building Committee and the Real Estate and Maintenance departments were merged to form the new Physical Facilities Department under the supervision of the Presiding Bishopric.

The architecture of Latter-day Saint buildings has been influenced by a variety of factors both inside and outside the Church. General architectural trends as well as individual architects have left their mark. Because many early Church members came from the northeastern United States, Mormon architecture for over a century reflected the style of the New England Colonial meetinghouse.

Probably the most important influence on chapel design has been the expansion of Church programs. In pioneer times Mormon chapels were simple meeting halls that accommodated a variety of community activities. By the turn of the century, they typically included a chapel or assembly room, a few smaller rooms for instructional or other purposes, and perhaps an "amusement hall" in the basement. The development in the Church's cultural and recreational programs called for a larger "cultural hall" to accommodate dances as well as basketball games; a well-equipped stage was needed for dramatic presentations. The multiplication of priesthood and auxiliary organization age groupings necessitated a larger number of classrooms. Over the years specialized rooms have been provided for children's worship, seminary, the Boy Scouts, and Relief Society.

The need for economy has been another concern. During the Great Depression of the 1930s, Church leaders repeatedly counseled against unnecessary extravagance. The increasing popularity of the "contemporary" building style in recent years is due in part to its comparatively low cost of construction. Experience in designing and erecting hundreds of chapels enabled the building committee to develop a series of standardized plans which incorporated the most desirable features and were engineered to minimize construction costs. "Generally a simple, pleasant design is incorporated into our meeting-houses," Elder John H. Vandenberg, managing director of physical facilities, explained. "We build our buildings to be of a type that can easily be maintained and take the wear-and-tear of normal use."[8] Cost has also been saved by designing almost all post-World War II meetinghouses to serve two or more congregations. Finally, "expandable chapels" were designed to be built one phase at a time, thus reducing the initial cost and more fairly distributing the total expense among all members of a growing congregation.

Explosive Church growth in the later twentieth century as well as a sudden rise in petroleum prices and an energy crisis brought even a greater need for economy. This was one of the reasons for consolidating the schedule of Church meetings in 1980. This simplification of activities, in turn, paved the way for more compact chapel designs. The "new generation of meetinghouses" was announced in 1981. The use of movable partitions brought greater flexibility in meeting the needs for classrooms of varying sizes. Having a portable rather than a fixed stage not only saved room but also facilitated special musical and theater-in-the-round productions. Such innovations reduced the size of a typical ward meetinghouse from 19,000 to 14,000 square feet. Church officials estimated that these new buildings would cost from 20 percent to 30 percent less to construct, and the greater use of insulation plus other improvements in design would make them 15 percent to 20 percent more energy efficient.[9]

Although the vast majority of the Church's building projects have been local chapels, a few larger structures have also been erected. These include temples, the twenty-six-story office building in Salt Lake City, a combined chapel and office building in Manhattan, the Missionary Training Center complex, and various major buildings on the Brigham Young University campus.

Varied Departments Behind the Scenes

As the Church's multimillion membership has expanded worldwide, many administrative needs have developed. These needs have been met by several behind-the-scenes agencies which make a vital contribution to the success of better-known Church activities.

The first commandment given to the Church in 1830 was to keep a history (see D&C 21:1). Early Church historians kept their records in their own homes until space was provided for the Church historian's office in the new administration building in 1917. This office's functions were enlarged with the organization of the Historical Department in 1972. Over the years, hundreds of thousands of record books had been submitted by ward, stake, and mission clerks. Arranging, preserving, and making these and other records available became the responsibility of the Library-Archives Division. Acquiring other key historical documents and maintaining a general reference library have been valuable services. The History Division (later known as the Joseph Fielding Smith Church History Institute at BYU) was charged with researching and writing Church history; in addition to work done by its own staff, this division encouraged research by scholars throughout the world.[10]

The Legal Department's team of attorneys, at Church headquarters as well as abroad, has handled a variety of problems for many Church departments, each lawyer specializing in a different area. Taxation, for example, became increasingly important as laws narrowed available exemptions. As the Church acquired property worldwide, lawyers verified titles and determined zoning regulations. Obtaining formal governmental recognition was particularly critical; without this status, the Church cannot own property or even conduct religious services in many countries. Wilford W. Kirton, the Church's chief attorney, testified that the Lord has helped to open doors. For example:

> Until recently, only the Catholic Church was recognized in Spain. Others had no legal status, were not allowed to hold public worship services and were forbidden to make any proselyting attempts.
>
> During the 1960s, however, the Spanish government relaxed its laws and enacted what is termed a "religious freedom law," permitting those faiths which had been in existence in the country prior to the passing of the law the right to operate publicly.
>
> On the basis of this, the Church contacted government officials in Spain with a request for legal recognition. The answer came in the form of a refusal on the grounds that the Church was not existent in Spain prior to the passing of the new law.
>
> However, the decision was reversed when it was discovered that U.S. servicemen stationed at NATO bases in Spain had been conducting Church meetings on the bases for many years. In the process, they had converted sufficient Spanish people working at the bases to constitute a legal "presence" for the Church.
>
> The Spanish Mission was quickly organized and represents a rapidly growing area of the Church today.[11]

The Central Purchasing Department handled all Church buying, saving money through bulk purchasing and by eliminating unnecessary paper work. Branch offices have been established in such distant countries as England, Mexico, and New Zealand.[12]

Seeing that information is prepared and delivered on time is the business of the Printing and Mailing Department. The Church-operated Deseret News Press had become the Intermountain West's largest publisher of books, magazines, forms, and related materials. In 1980 it phased out all commercial work and became known as the Printing Services Division of the Materials Management Department, thereafter devoting its full capacity to Church printing needs.[13]

The Personnel Department was charged with seeing that positions are filled and also with upgrading the quality of Church employees. In 1968 there were eighteen hundred full-time and five hundred hourly employees in the Genealogical Society, the Presiding Bishopric's office, distribution centers, and dozens of other Church organizations or departments.[14]

The Financial and Statistical Reports Department receives thousands of reports every month. Statistical summaries and averages are prepared for general Church organizations as well as for regional or stake conference use.

Membership records have helped Church leaders be aware of those for whom they are responsible. Before 1907, when a person moved from one location to another, he was given his membership record to deliver in person to his new bishop or branch president. In that year, however, the practice began of sending the records to Church headquarters for forwarding to the new wards or branches when members moved. A further development in 1941 established a duplicate master file in the Membership Department; whenever a member moved, his record in this file was compared with the record received from his former ward or branch and the master copy was updated. This enabled general Church leaders to find within a few moments the latest available information on any member. This operation required a large staff of dedicated workers noted for their initiative and attention to details.

In 1968 ward clerks began "auditing" records of Church members to verify accuracy and completeness. This information was then entered into the computer, which could automatically update records as new ordinances were performed, and print ward lists of members, special lists by age groups, and so forth. Thus Church leaders could have immediate access to more current and complete information about the members for whom they were responsible.[15]

Beginning in 1970 Church financial records also were computerized. Preparing receipts on special typewriters enabled an "optical scanner" to record the information directly into the computer without the need for posting entries by hand. The computer could then keep a record of contributions in the various currencies of the world and periodically print lists of contributors and amounts for the use of general and local Church officials.[16]

The Church's extensive use of electronic computers dates back to the early 1960s when a computer center was first established at Church headquarters. A few years later this operation was organized as an independent business, and in 1980 it became the Data Processing Division. It is used by Genealogy, Finance, Building Operation and Maintenance, Real Estate, Distribution, Materials Management, Member and Statistical Records, Purchasing, Translation, Auditing, Historical, Public Communications, Personnel, Welfare, and Missionary departments, as well as by the Church Educational System. The Historical Department has used the computer to prepare indexes of periodicals and registers of manuscript materials. The Church magazines and the *Church News* keep track of subscriptions by means of the computer. Through the computer, the Quorum of the Twelve's scheduling officer has arranged visits by General Authorities to well over a thousand stake and other local conferences every year.[17]

Modern tools such as the computer and these varied behind-the-scenes departments at headquarters have enabled the Church to keep up with its phenomenal growth and to more effectively fulfill its worldwide mission.

17 The Unfolding of Priesthood Correlation

As Church programs expanded during the twentieth century, the General Authorities have felt keenly the responsibility to be certain that all Church programs were effectively pursuing the objective of perfecting the Saints. This concern became particularly acute during the decades of rapid international expansion of Church membership following the end of World War II. Because each organization planned its own program and was anxious to do all possible to bless those it served, some unnecessary duplication had inevitably resulted. At the same time, other key areas may not have been receiving enough emphasis. As has been seen, Church leaders during the twentieth century repeatedly gave attention to these concerns and made adjustments in Church activities and programs as needed.

The most thorough correlation effort began in 1960 when the First Presidency directed the Priesthood Committee of the Twelve under Elder Harold B. Lee to conduct "an exhaustive prayerful study" of all programs in the light of the Church's ultimate objectives, "so that the Church might reap the maximum harvest from the devotion of the faith, intelligence, skill, and knowledge of our various auxiliary organizations and priesthood committees."[1]

1906	President Joseph F. Smith looked forward to time when the priesthood would more fully assume its role in the Church
1907	Committee on Adjustments recommended consolidating programs and magazines and stressed the importance of the home
1908	General Priesthood Committee appointed: introduced weekly ward priesthood meetings and specific ages for ordination to offices in the priesthood
1912	Correlation Committee appointed to reduce duplication among the auxiliaries
1920	Correlation-Social Advisory Committee coordinated priesthood and auxiliaries; stressed that auxiliaries were to be helps to the priesthood, and that all programs must meet the needs of Church members
1928	"Priesthood-Auxiliary Movement" sought to simplify Church activities by uniting priesthood and auxiliary meetings
1929	Primary and Religion Classes consolidated; MIA magazines merged
1938	Committee of the Twelve to study Church programs
1940	First Presidency clarified role of each organization and stressed that "the home is the basis of the righteous life"; genealogy class amalgamated into the Sunday School; separate genealogical magazine discontinued
1948	Correlation of Church activities again studied

Correlation at the Churchwide Level

Elder Lee and his committee recognized that more was needed than simply ensuring that all gospel topics were being treated adequately in the Church's curriculum. They realized that an organization was needed at the all-Church level to bring about the desired correlation of its varied programs and activities. Elder Lee announced the results of the study at the fall general conference in 1961 and stressed basic principles that would guide priesthood correlation. He quoted Paul's comparison of the Church to a perfectly functioning body (see 1 Corinthians 12:14-28). He then explained that a similar passage in latter-day scripture had served as the text for his committee's work:

> Therefore, let every man stand in his own office, and labor in his own calling; and let not the head say unto the feet it hath no need of the feet; for without the feet how shall the body be able to stand?
>
> Also the body hath need of every member, that all may be edified together, that the system may be kept perfect. (D&C 84:109-110.)

Elder Lee concluded that this meant:

> ... first, that each organization was to have its specific function, and it was not to usurp the field of the other, which would be like the eye saying to the hand, "I have no need of thee." Second, that each sub-division is of equal importance in the work of salvation, just as each part of the physical body is essential to a complete human being. Third, that all may be edified or educated together; and fourth, that the system may be kept perfect, or in other words, that within the framework of the Lord's plan of organization for the salvation of his children, the Church will perform as a perfectly organized human body, with every member functioning as it was intended.

Elder Lee cited another fundamental principle which had been given in a communication from the First Presidency: "The home was the basis of a righteous life and . . . no other instrumentality can take its place nor fulfill its essential functions and . . . the utmost the auxiliaries can do is aid the home in its problems, giving special aid and succor where such is necessary. . . ."[2]

Thus, as Elder Lee later defined it: "Correlation means merely to place the priesthood of God where the Lord said it was to be—as the center and core of the Church and kingdom

of God—and to see that the Latter-day Saint homes also have their place in the divine plan of saving souls."[3]
    Elder Lee announced:

> . . . It is the feeling now of the First Presidency and the Council of the Twelve, . . . that there should be presently more coordination and correlation between the activities and programs of the various priesthood quorums and auxiliary organizations and the educational system of the Church. . . . In the adoption of such a program, we may possibly and hopefully look forward to the consolidation and simplification of church curricula, church publications, church buildings, church meetings, and many other important aspects of the Lord's work.[4]

The realization of these hopes would be achieved step by step over the following two decades.
    As he made his announcement, Elder Lee explained that an all-Church coordinating council would "formulate policy which would govern the planning, the writing, co-ordination, and implementation of the entire Church curriculum." This group included the executives of the auxiliaries and other Church organizations.
    Three age-group committees, representing children, youth, and adults, were to "plan, write, provide, and coordinate curricula and activities" for their respective age groups.[5]
    If the Church is to be compared to a perfectly functioning human body, suggested Elder Gordon B. Hinckley, these correlation committees "might be likened to the nervous system whose responsibility is to keep the various aspects of the great teaching program of the Church operating harmoniously together."[6]
    Elder Lee explained that the auxiliary organizations would continue to implement the programs developed by the correlation committees, thus unnecessary duplication would be avoided, and the Gospel could be taught more effectively to all the members of the Church.[7]
    In April 1963 four committees were added to this organization with the mission of giving leadership to the following key priesthood programs: home teaching and home evening, genealogy, missionary, and welfare.
    Specific aspects of this organizational structure have been changed from time to time. During the early 1970s the re-

All-Church Correlation Organization—1963

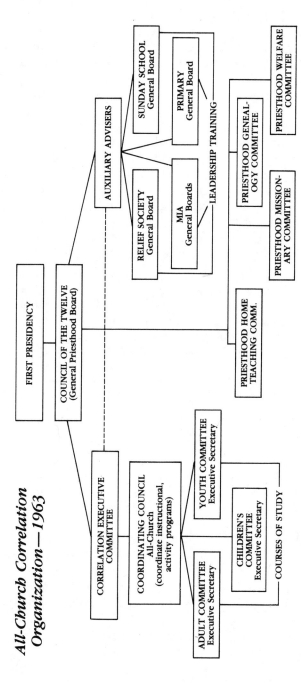

The original chairmen of these Correlation committees were:

- Correlation Executive Committee and All-Church Coordinating Council — Harold B. Lee
- Children's Committee — Gordon B. Hinckley
- Youth Committee — Richard L. Evans
- Adult Committee — Marion G. Romney (later succeeded by Thomas S. Monson)

- Priesthood Home Teaching Committee — Marion G. Romney
- Priesthood Genealogy Committee — Nathan Eldon Tanner (later succeeded by Howard W. Hunter)
- Priesthood Missionary Committee — Joseph Fielding Smith (later succeeded by Spencer W. Kimball)
- Priesthood Welfare Committee — Bishop John H. Vandenberg

(Source: Conference Report, April 1963, p. 12)

sponsibility for developing instructional materials for all age groups was assigned to a single department. In 1975 Correlation became a distinct department with major responsibilities for reviewing all written materials and for evaluating the effectiveness of Church programs and activities. Despite these changes, however, basic principles remained the same: Under central priesthood direction, curricula and activities for all Church members are planned, prepared, reviewed, and evaluated. The Correlation Department thus exercised a judicial type of function, seeing that the policies and programs approved by the First Presidency and the Twelve were being carried out as intended for the maximum benefit to the Saints.

In 1962 Elder Richard L. Evans, a member of the Twelve working with the correlation effort, described major features of the program which would be carried out Churchwide:

> . . . The Gospel [will] be taught as completely as possible at least three times during these three age levels of life: children, youth, and adults. Within these major groupings there will be many minor groupings, taking into account school associations, social interests, priesthood ages, missions, marriage, and other factors. . . . The basic program of the various age groups will be made flexible enough to meet the varying needs and circumstances of individuals and of wards and stakes and branches and missions of different sizes and circumstances.[8]

Correlation at the Local Level

Although significant strides had been taken in coordinating the planning of programs at the all-Church level, more still needed to be done at the ward and stake levels in implementing these activities. Teachers in one organization did not often have the occasion to coordinate lessons and activities with those teaching the same age group in other organizations. In fact, the age grouping often varied from one organization to another.

To implement the desired correlation, a priesthood executive committee and a ward correlation council were established at the ward level in 1964. The priesthood executive committee consisted of the bishopric and priesthood quorum leaders; this weekly meeting enabled the bishop and key priesthood leaders to give correlated direction to all ward activities. The monthly ward council meeting included the above leaders plus auxiliary and other organization leaders; here they could correlate schedules and activities and, most important of all, discuss how the ward's programs could best meet the specific needs of individual members or families. Similar organizations were implemented at the stake level three years later.

A key step in implementing priesthood correlation at the local level was the inauguration of home teaching in 1964. Prior to this time, several Church organizations were involved in contacting families in their homes. Under the direct supervision of the bishopric, "ward teachers" had been assigned to visit several families, each month presenting a message published for use throughout the Church. Melchizedek Priesthood quorums were also responsible for making regular contacts with their members. A given family might also receive visits from auxiliary teachers interested in enlisting family members in their respective activities. All these contacts were now consolidated or coordinated through the home teachers. President David O. McKay explained: "Through the priesthood quorums, and under the bishop's direction, Home Teaching takes the message of the gospel, the message of life and salvation and brotherly love, into the home, wherein lies the first and foremost opportunity for teaching in the Church."

Home teaching included regular visits to all Church members, contacting quorum members, fellowshipping and encouraging new members and the inactive, helping parents to improve gospel instruction in the home, and correlating all enlistment activities; it also provided a channel for two-way communication between the home and the priesthood and ward leaders.[9]

Elder Harold B. Lee appraised the true position of home teaching in this way: "Home teaching isn't just one of the programs. . . . Home teaching is the instrument by which we see to it, through the priesthood, that every program in the Church is made available to parents and their children."[10] Or, as one of the manuals described home teaching: "This program emphasizes that every family head is responsible for the spiritual welfare of his family and that it is the responsibility of the priesthood, through the Home Teachers, to make available all of the resources of the Church to every Church member and to help each member in achieving his spiritual goals."[11] To provide further help to the heads of families, the Church in 1965 began publishing yearly family home evening manuals. This program will be the subject of the following chapter.

A 1964 handbook explained a fundamental channel of communication which guided implementation of the organization at the local level:

> . . . Priesthood correlation involves the carrying out of priesthood or church activities by individual members of families, presided over by the parents, who are presided over by priesthood leaders, who in turn are presided over by bishops. The bishops are presided over by stake presidents, who are presided over by the General Authorities of the Church. These . . . constitute what we might call the pipeline of priesthood correlation. All priesthood activities should properly recognize and be funneled through this line of authority as it is revealed from our Father in Heaven. This line of authority should govern and correlate in such a way that the resources of the Church may be brought through this power to serve the individual members of the Church. Thus, we might become one as we have been advised. . . .
>
> Auxiliary officers and other members of the Church in the various areas of life activity who are not officially in this line of authority should, when called upon by the priesthood officers, sustain priesthood and Church activity."[12]

Some Further Accomplishments

Since the 1960s the General Authorities have continued the process of refining, correlating, and even consolidating Church activities. These later developments have built on the foundations of "priesthood correlation" laid during that decade.

Seventies were given the major responsibility for missionary work in the stakes, and the formerly separate stake missions came to be much more closely identified with the

Priesthood
Line of Authority—1967

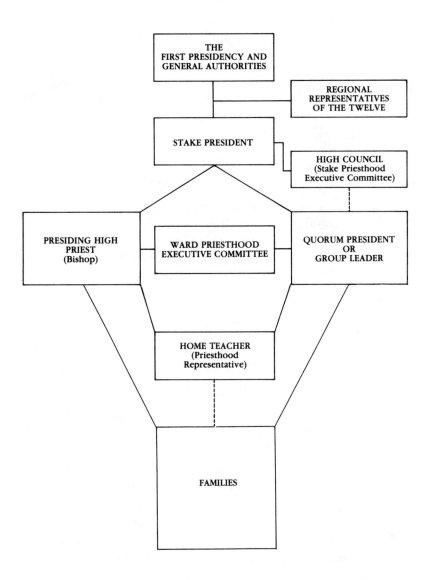

1960	First Presidency directed Priesthood Committee to make exhaustive study of all Church courses and activities
1961	Announcement of organization to plan and prepare programs for children, youth, and adults under direction of the priesthood
1962	Curriculum for children, youths, and adults outlined
1963	Priesthood Committees established to give direction to home teaching, missionary, genealogical, and welfare activities
1964	Above four functions placed under local priesthood quorum leaders; home teaching implemented; ward priesthood executive committees and correlation councils formed
1965	Family home evening manuals published; priesthood and auxiliary lessons specifically designed to strengthen parents
1967	Unified dates established for starting Church programs and age groupings standardized
1970	Aaronic Priesthood and YMMIA leadership consolidated
1971	All magazines for adults, youth, and children, respectively, merged under the priesthood; responsibility for producing all instructional materials consolidated into single department
1974	Seventies quorums' and stake missions' leadership combined
1975	Separate Correlation Department responsible for reviewing and evaluating curriculum and activities
1980	Ward meetings consolidated

seventies quorums. "Perhaps the door has opened as widely as it has ever been for the work of the seventies," Elder Harold B. Lee remarked, "and we thank the Lord for the work of our leaders in the seventies quorums."[13] By 1974 the stake mission presidency and the seventies quorum presidency had become one and the same.[14]

An important improvement came in 1967 with the adoption of a uniform Church year. Previously, some organizations had commenced their lesson work at the beginning of the local school year, while others operated on a calendar year basis. Now all Church organizations, both priesthood and auxiliary, would begin and finish their courses of instruction at the same time. Furthermore, the age groupings were standardized from one organization to another. All this facilitated a greater coordination of curriculum materials and of the Church's programs in general.

Other refinements brought together similar activities formerly conducted by separate organizations. In many wards, for example, each auxiliary had maintained its own collection of teaching aids. Beginning in 1967 a single "meetinghouse library" was established to serve all the organizations meeting in a given Church building. Over the years several of the auxiliaries had developed teacher-training programs to enhance this most vital aspect of their work. Beginning in 1970, a teacher development director was called to coordinate these efforts in each ward. He was responsible for teaching a basic course in instructional methodology as often as necessary to meet the needs of new and existing teachers in all Church organizations. Each organization then presented follow-up "in-service" instruction tailored to its specific programs and needs as part of its regular ward and stake leadership or preparation meetings. As already noted, the various auxiliary organizations published their own magazines throughout most of the twentieth century. Beginning in 1971, however, three new magazines— the *Friend* for children, the *New Era* for youth, and the *Ensign* for adults—were published directly under the supervision of the General Authorities. Material in these magazines supported all Church programs serving their particular age group. At the ward level, this eliminated the need for several separate persons to represent the different Church publications; a single magazine director now was called to promote the regular use of all three Church magazines.

The Church's program for the youth underwent both expansion and restructuring. As part of the increased emphasis on missionary work during the early 1960s, "youth missionary committees" had been created in many parts of the Church.

These committees brought young people together to motivate and coordinate their efforts in sharing the gospel with their peers. Many ward bishops recognized in these gatherings a golden opportunity to enlist the youth themselves in planning and promoting the Church's youth programs. General Church leaders also recognized the value of involving the youth, and by 1967 were directing that these "bishop's youth councils" meet monthly in each ward.[15] A major reorganization came when the formerly separate Aaronic Priesthood and the Young Men's Mutual Improvement Association programs were merged in 1970. Rather than have one group of leaders teach the boys during priesthood meetings and another group conduct week-night activities for them, the quorum advisers became the ward Young Men's presidency, responsible for both instruction and activity. The number of women required to staff the Young Women's program was similarly reduced. From their beginnings in the nineteenth century, the Young Men's and Young Women's Mutual Improvement associations had conducted educational, cultural, social, and recreational programs for all Church members twelve years of age and above. A major redefinition came in 1974 when Church leaders transferred responsibility for adult programs to Melchizedek Priesthood quorums and the Relief Society. This left Young Men and Young Women leaders free to concentrate on the unique needs of the youth.[16]

Perhaps the most thorough restructuring of all would come in 1980 when not only leadership assignments but actual meetings and activities would be consolidated. For decades priesthood meeting and Sunday School had met during the morning on Sundays, and sacrament meetings had been held during the afternoon or evening. Relief Society meetings for women, Primary activities for children, and MIA instruction and activities for youth had taken place during the week. The Junior Sunday School was amalgamated into the Primary Association as part of the 1980 consolidations. All basic ward meetings—priesthood, Relief Society, Young Women, Primary, Sunday School, and sacrament meeting—were streamlined to fit into a single three-hour block on Sunday morning or afternoon. Such long-standing traditions as the Sunday

School's half-hour opening exercises were discontinued. Only a youth activity night, monthly Relief Society homemaking meetings, and occasional activities for children would continue during the week. Although this new plan had obvious energy-saving advantages, the First Presidency explained that a more basic consideration was to give families more time for scripture study and other activities in the home.[17] With this move, the Church again demonstrated its commitment to strengthening families, which had been one of the prime objectives of priesthood correlation during the 1960s.

18 Strengthening the Family

Emphasis on the home and family was a major feature in the teachings and leadership of President David O. McKay. As the priesthood correlation program unfolded, Church leaders focused on the home as the most effective place for teaching and applying gospel principles. Strong homes, they believed, would provide the surest defense against the temptations of modern life, which at the same time were undermining the institution of the home and family. In the face of increasing challenges to the home, the General Authorities took steps to strengthen the family in its vital role in today's world.

Teaching the Gospel in the Home

The scriptures in all ages have affirmed that parents have the primary responsibility to teach their children. An Old Testament proverb admonished: "Train up a child in the way he should go: and when he is old, he will not depart from it" (Proverbs 22:6). In his great concluding discourse, the Nephites' King Benjamin counseled his people that those who were truly converted would not permit their children to "transgress the laws of God, and fight and quarrel one with another, and serve the devil," but rather they would "teach them to walk in the ways of truth and soberness [and] to love one another, and to serve one another" (Mosiah 4:14-15). Latter-day revelations have commanded parents to bring up their children "in light and truth," and to teach them "to pray, and to walk uprightly before the Lord," warning that if they fail to do so, "the sin [will] be on the heads of the parents" (see D&C 68:25-28; 93:40). Twentieth-century prophets have echoed this same message. For example, President Heber J. Grant cautioned:

> I have heard men and women say that they were going to let their sons and daughters grow to maturity before they sought to teach them the principles of the gospel, that they were not going to cram the gospel down them in their childhood, before they were able to comprehend it. When I hear men and women say this, I think they are lacking faith in the principles of the gospel and do not comprehend it as they should. The Lord has said it is our duty to teach our children in their youth, and I prefer to take His word for it rather than the words of those who are not obeying His commandments. . . . I may know that the gospel is true, and so may my wife; but I want to tell you that your children will not know that the gospel is true, unless they study it and gain a testimony for themselves. Parents are deceiving themselves in imagining that their children will be born with a knowledge of the gospel.[1]

President David O. McKay further explained that "the character of the child is formed largely during the first twelve years of his life when he spends sixteen times as many waking hours in the home as in school, and more than a hundred times as many hours in the home as in the Church." He concluded, "Every child is, to a great degree, what he is because of the ever constant influence of home environment and the careful or neglectful training of parents. . . ."[2]

President McKay therefore testified:

> When one puts business or pleasure above his home, he that moment starts on the downgrade to soul-weakness. When the club becomes more attractive to any man than his home, it is time for him to confess in bitter shame that he has failed to measure up to the supreme opportunity of his life and flunked

in the final test of true manhood. No other success can compensate for failure in the home. The poorest shack in which love prevails over a united family is of greater value to God and future humanity than any other riches. In such a home God can work miracles and will work miracles.[3]

President Joseph Fielding Smith taught that "the primary function of a Latter-day Saint home is to insure that every member of the family works to create the climate and conditions in which all can grow toward perfection." This requires a substantial commitment of time and energy on the part of parents. "Do you spend as much time making your family and home successful as you do in pursuing social and professional success? Are you devoting your best creative energy to the most important unit in society—the family?" President Smith insisted that "parent and child must be willing to put family responsibilities first in order to achieve family exaltation."[4]

President Harold B. Lee warned: "Keep your home ties strong. . . . The greatest of the Lord's work you brethren will ever do as fathers will be within the walls of your own home."[5]

President Spencer W. Kimball reflected the teachings of these earlier prophets: "The Church's long-standing concern for children and its massive commitment in time and energy and resources to improve their lot are well documented. We are constantly seeking ways to strengthen families and bless children. . . ." President Kimball believes that "the greatest blessing we can give our own children" comes through "the simple processes of training them in the way of the Lord. Home life, proper teaching in the home, parental guidance and leadership," he said, "are the panacea for the ailments of the world and its children. They are the cures for spiritual and emotional diseases and the remedy for its problems." He echoed earlier cautions against parents leaving the training of their children to others. As important as the school, the Church, and other agencies may be, "they never can adequately take the place of the influence of the mother and the father. Constant training, constant vigilance, companionship, and being watchmen of our own children are necessary in order to keep our homes intact and to bless our children in the Lord's own way." "All should work together," President Kimball concluded, "to make home a place where we love to be, a place of listening and learning, a place where each member can find mutual love, support, appreciation, and encouragement."[6]

Latter-day prophets have not only stressed the urgent responsibility to teach children in the home, but they have also promised divine assistance to parents who faithfully discharge this sacred obligation.

President Wilford Woodruff declared:

> Our children should not be neglected; they should receive a proper education in both spiritual and temporal things. That is the best legacy any parents can leave to their children. We should teach them to pray, and instill into their minds while young every correct principle. Ninety-nine out of every hundred children who are taught by their parents the principles of honesty and integrity, truth and virtue, will observe them through life.[7]

President Joseph F. Smith likewise counseled:

> Do not let your children out to specialists in these things, but teach them by your own precept and example, by your own fireside. Be a specialist yourself in the truth. Let your meetings, schools, and organizations, instead of being our only or leading teachers, be supplements to our teaching and training in the home. Not one child in a hundred would go astray, if the home environment, example and training, were in harmony with the truth in the gospel of Christ, as revealed and taught to the Latter-day Saints.[8]

Family Home Evening

Although the Church's family home evening program flowered during the 1960s, its seeds were established much earlier. As early as the days of Brigham Young, the First Presidency had instructed parents to gather their families together "if not every day, at least as often as they can" in order to "interrogate them respecting their associations, their words, and actions," and to teach them the gospel.[9]

In 1909 Granite Stake in Salt Lake City inaugurated a weekly home evening. Two thousand attended the special meeting where the plan was announced. Church President Joseph F. Smith addressed the group and declared that the "inspiration" of the stake presidency in "setting apart at least one evening in a week for the especial use and benefit of the families of the Saints, is of the greatest importance. . . ."[10] The success of this activity undoubtedly contributed to the First Presidency's recommending a similar program Churchwide six years later.

President Joseph F. Smith anticipated priesthood correlation's emphasis on the home. In 1915 he and his counselors issued instructions which became the frequently quoted charter for the Church's subsequent emphasis on the family:

> We advise and urge the inauguration of a "Home Evening" throughout the Church, at which time fathers and mothers may gather their boys and girls about them in the home and teach them the word of the Lord. They may thus learn more fully the needs and requirements of their families. . . . This "Home Evening" should be devoted to prayer, singing hymns, songs, instrumental music, scripture-reading, family topics and specific instruction on the principles of the gospel, and on the ethical problems of life, as well as the duties and obligations of children to parents, the home, the Church, society and the nation. For the smaller children appropriate recitations, songs, stories and games may be introduced. Light refreshments of such a nature as may be largely prepared in the home might be served.
>
> Formality and stiffness should be studiously avoided, and all of the family should participate in the exercises.
>
> These gatherings will furnish opportunities for mutual confidence between parents and children, between brothers and sisters, as well as give opportunity for words of warning, counsel and advice by parents to their boys and girls. They will provide opportunity for the boys and girls to honor father and mother, and to show their appreciation of the blessings of home so that the promise of the Lord to them may be literally fulfilled and their lives be prolonged and made happy. . . .
>
> If the Saints obey this counsel, we promise that great blessings will result. Love at home and obedience to parents will increase. Faith will be developed in the hearts of the youth of

Israel, and they will gain power to combat the evil influence and temptations which beset them.[11]

For the next fifty years home evenings were promoted primarily by local Church leaders and to some extent by the auxiliaries. From time to time the General Authorities reminded the Saints of their responsibility and blessing in conducting these family gatherings. In 1936 the First Presidency commended these local activities: "In this day when socials, parties, dinners, business interests, etc., all tend to lead away from home association," the Presidency declared, "the adoption of a home evening is highly advisable."[12] Then, in the midst of the strains on family life which accompanied the close of World War II, Church leaders launched an especially important effort to again revive the family home evening. In a 1946 circular letter, the Quorum of the Twelve reviewed previous home evening programs beginning with the First Presidency's 1915 instructions and then announced the appointment of a special committee composed of General Authorities and auxiliary representatives to plan home-centered activities. Ward teachers taught families the importance of regular gatherings. The Sunday School demonstrated how this could be done. Through the *Children's Friend* the Primary offered suggestions every month. The Relief Society published a pamphlet entitled "The Family Hour," which was distributed by the society's visiting teachers. It was not until 1965, however, that the Church launched an ongoing promotion of family home evening, including the publication of lesson manuals distributed to every family each year.

Elder Harold B. Lee announced this new emphasis at the general conference in October 1964. He first reviewed what had been done the previous fifty years. Elder Lee quoted from the First Presidency's 1940 statement that indicated the direction the Church's program should go: "The home is the basis of the righteous life, and no other instrumentality can take its place nor fulfill its essential functions; the utmost the auxiliaries can do is to aid the home in its problems, giving special aid and succor where such is necessary." He cited the examples of the Sunday School, whose program of "gospel living

in the home" featured a series of articles in the *Instructor*
magazine. Similarly the "Primary Home Partnership" sought to
carry into the home the lessons taught to the children by that
auxiliary.

Elder Lee then announced that 1965 would bring "some
definite steps taken to strengthen the hands of the parents in
carrying out these great God-given admonitions in placing
stress upon the teaching of the gospel in the home." The first
step was to provide a manual containing weekly lessons to be
taught in the home. Throughout the year the various Church
organizations published suggestions for home activities. The
Relief Society provided specific help for mothers, and the
priesthood quorums provided training for fathers. All was correlated into a single effort entitled "Teaching and Living the
Gospel in the Home." Elder Harold B. Lee testified that this
new program had come as a result of inspiration given through
President David O. McKay: "My mind has been filled with the
realization that in 1964 and the year just preceding, we have
been receiving as pertinent and important divine direction as
has ever been given to the Church in any similar period in its
history through the prophet and leader who now presides as
the President of this Church."

Elder Lee concluded: "I say to you Latter-day Saint
mothers and fathers, if you will rise to the responsibilities of
teaching your children in the home, . . . the day will soon be
dawning when the whole world will come to our doors and
will say, 'Show us your way that we may walk in your path' "
(see Micah 4:1-2).[13]

Elder Alvin R. Dyer later bore his testimony that "truly the
righteous, well-ordered home, if the leaders of nations could
accept it, is the panacea for their most serious problems. Here
is God, if we all will but accept it, communicating with his
children and pointing the way."[14]

In the preface to the first family home evening manual,
President David O. McKay declared that "the problems of
these difficult times cannot better be solved in any other place,
by any other agency, by any other means, than by love and
righteousness, and precept and example, and devotion to duty
in the home."[15]

The renewed emphasis on family home evenings beginning in 1965 has brought blessings to Latter-day Saints around the world. (Church Visual Resources Library)

A later manual contained this promise: "Families who prayerfully prepare and constantly hold their weekly Home Evenings, and who work together during the week to apply the lessons in their lives, will be blessed. There will be better feelings between husband and wife, between parents and children, and among children. In such homes the Spirit of the Lord will be made manifest."[16]

Encouraged by such promises, Latter-day Saint parents around the world took steps to teach their children. Whether the family home evenings were taking place in a New York City apartment, a Navajo hogan, or in a Polynesian thatched house, certain common elements were usually present: Family members took turns in conducting the program, offering prayers, leading the singing, or even presenting the lesson. Families often combined these elements of their home evenings with special recreational activities, and almost always with refreshments. In 1971 Church leaders announced that

Monday evenings were being designated as the time for these family gatherings, and that no other Church activities were to be scheduled on that night.[17]

Family-Related Current Issues

The second half of the twentieth century witnessed a general disintegration of many traditional social institutions and values, and a growing disregard for moral standards. These trends were in marked contrast to the Latter-day Saints' continuing emphasis on the sanctity of the home and of family relationships. The resulting conflict between the world's and gospel standards prompted the General Authorities to declare official positions on several contemporary issues affecting the family.

Pornography

In 1966 the First Presidency lamented the growing flood of pornography:

> The circulation of pornographic pictures, books, magazines, and films in nearly every community has now reached an alarming stage. Its detrimental effect upon standards of morality is becoming so serious that all thoughtful people must unite to combat it.
>
> Financially interested persons, claiming "the right to sell whatever the public will buy," merchandise their questionable wares with no regard for the consequences.
>
> We are unalterably opposed to sexual immorality and to all manner of obscenity. We proclaim in the strongest terms possible against the evil and wicked designs of men who would betray virtuous manhood and womanhood, enticing them to thoughts and actions leading to vice, the lowering of standards of clean living, and the breaking up of the home.

The First Presidency therefore called on government officials "to do all in their power to curb this pernicious evil" and called on the Latter-day Saints and others "to join in a concerted movement to fight pornography wherever it may be found, whether in books and magazines, on the screen or in materials sent through the post office."[18]

In many areas local groups of Church members responded by mounting campaigns to protest indecency or other forms of pornography in their communities. Some picketed theaters which were showing pornographic motion pictures, while others gathered signatures on petitions requiring higher moral standards for material shown on cable television.

Birth Control

By the 1960s a variety of contraceptive devices and especially the birth control pill were gaining in popularity. These were used by both unmarried and married couples to avoid unwanted pregnancies. Thus the use of contraceptive devices not only encouraged sexual immorality but also threatened one of the basic functions of the family. During the two decades between 1955 and 1975, the annual number of births per thousand in the United States dropped from twenty-five to only fifteen. In 1969 the First Presidency wrote:

> We seriously regret that there should exist a sentiment or feeling among any members of the Church to curtail the birth of their children. We have been commanded to multiply and replenish the earth that we may have joy and rejoicing in our posterity. . . .
>
> However, we feel that men must be considerate of their wives who bear the greater responsibility not only of bearing children, but of caring for them through childhood. To this end the mother's health and strength should be conserved and the husband's consideration for his wife is his first duty, and self-control a dominant factor in all their relationships.
>
> It is our further feeling that married couples should seek inspiration and wisdom from the Lord that they may exercise discretion in solving their marital problems, and that they may be permitted to rear their children in accordance with the teachings of the gospel.[19]

Abortion

Like the spreading popularity of contraceptive devices, the growing number of abortions contributed to the declining birthrate and was also undoubtedly linked to the growing tide of immorality. When various groups challenged local laws restricting the availability of contraceptives and of legalized abortions, the highest court in the land ruled in 1972 that no legal barriers may be placed in the way of performing abortions during the first three months of pregnancy.

"In view of a recent decision of the United States Supreme Court," the First Presidency wrote, "we feel it necessary to restate the position of the Church on abortion in order that there be no misunderstanding of our attitude." The Presidency then declared:

> The Church opposes abortion and counsels its members not to submit to, be a party to, or perform an abortion except in the rare cases where, in the opinion of competent medical counsel, the life or health of the woman is seriously endangered or where the pregnancy was caused by forcible rape or incest and produces serious emotional trauma in the victim.
>
> Even then it should be done only after counseling with the presiding priesthood authority and after receiving divine confirmation through prayer.
>
> Abortion must be considered one of the most revolting and sinful practices in this day, when we are witnessing the frightening evidence of permissiveness leading to sexual immorality.
>
> Members of the Church guilty of being parties to the sin of abortion must be subjected to the disciplinary action of the councils of the Church as circumstances warrant. In dealing with this serious matter, it would be well to keep in mind the word of the Lord stated in the 59th section of the Doctrine & Covenants, verse 6, "Thou shalt not steal; neither commit adultery, nor kill, nor anything like unto it."[20]

During the 1970s the rate of abortions continued to soar. The United States government noted that by 1977, there were 568 abortions performed for every 1,000 live births.[21] In the face of such developments, the First Presidency in 1976 reaffirmed their foregoing counsel in a follow-up statement.[22]

Other Threats to the Family

While pornography, birth control, and abortions could be linked to the decline in moral standards, two other problems—divorce and homosexuality—threatened the very existence of the family itself. In the United States during 1925, there were 1.5 divorces per thousand people. By 1965 the divorce rate had risen to 2.5; during the next decade it almost doubled, rising to 4.9 in 1975, and it has continued to climb. The growing number of divorces was even a source of concern in predominantly Latter-day Saint areas. In Salt Lake County, for example, half as many divorces as marriages were being recorded. It was in this setting that President David O. McKay spoke out against this family-destroying trend. In the April 1969 general conference he declared:

> In the light of scripture, ancient and modern, we are justified in concluding that Christ's ideal pertaining to marriage is the unbroken home, and conditions that cause divorce are violations of his divine teachings. Except in cases of infidelity or other extreme conditions, the Church frowns upon divorce. . . .
> A man who has entered into sacred covenants in the house of the Lord to remain true to the marriage vow is a traitor to that covenant if he separates himself from his wife and family just because he has permitted himself to become infatuated with a pretty face and comely form of some young girl who flattered him with a smile.[23]

President Spencer W. Kimball would later voice similar concerns. He noted that in the mid-1970s, 24 percent of the Saints were marrying out of the Church, and that on the average only one in seven of these nonmember spouses was ever baptized. Although 46 percent of Saints married in the temple, one in ten of even these marriages ended in divorce. "Every divorce is the result of selfishness on the part of one or the other or both parties to a marriage contract," President Kimball asserted. He was appalled at the number of children who had to grow up without the essential benefit of having both parents in the home. He acknowledged that the record among the Saints was better than that of the population as a whole, but was "chagrined that there should be any divorce following a temple marriage. . . . The divorce itself does not constitute the entire evil," he continued, "but the very acceptance of divorce as a cure is also a serious sin of this generation."[24]

Another threat to the traditional family came with the increased prominence of homosexuality, especially during the

1970s. While in earlier years this practice had been prohibited by civil laws as well as by the scriptures, it came increasingly to be described simply as an "alternate life-style" which should be and was legalized in many localities. As early as 1973, Church leaders branded homosexuality "as sin in the same degree as adultery and fornication." Seven years later, in a "Special Message to All Latter-day Saints," President Spencer W. Kimball denounced the various forms of immorality then so widely prevalent. Concerning homosexuality he warned:

> The unholy transgression of homosexuality is either rapidly growing or tolerance is giving it wider publicity. If one has such desires and tendencies, he overcomes them the same as if he had the urge toward petting or fornication or adultery. The Lord condemns and forbids this practice with a vigor equal to his condemnation of adultery and other such sex acts. And the Church will excommunicate as readily any unrepentant addict.
>
> Again, contrary to the belief and statement of many people, this sin, like fornication, is overcomable and forgivable, but again, only upon a deep and abiding repentance, which means total abandonment and complete transformation of thought and act.[25]

The Equal Rights Amendment

Few family-related issues have generated more discussions both in and out of the Church than did the proposed "Equal Rights Amendment" to the United States Constitution. Proposed by Congress in 1972, the amendment would provide that "equality of rights under the law shall not be denied or abridged by the United States or by any State on account of sex." On the surface this provision appeared commendable, and at first attracted widespread support. A more careful analysis, however, raised several concerns. Individual Church officers began voicing these concerns, but at the same time other groups of members organized to promote the "ERA." In 1976 the First Presidency issued an official statement opposing passage of the proposed amendment. The Presidency's statement first took pains to point out the Church's basic interest in women's opportunities and rights:

From its beginnings, The Church of Jesus Christ of Latter-day Saints has affirmed the exalted role of woman in our society. In 1842, when women's organizations were little known, the Prophet Joseph Smith established the women's organization of the Church, the Relief Society, as a companion body of the Priesthood. The Relief Society continues to function today as a vibrant, worldwide organization aimed at strengthening motherhood and broadening women's learning and involvement in religious, compassionate, cultural, educational, and community pursuits. In Utah, where our Church is headquartered, women received the right to vote in 1870, fifty years before the Nineteenth Amendment to the Constitution granted the right nationally.

The Presidency deplored the fact that there had been "injustices to women before the law and in society," but firmly insisted that the proposed Equal Rights Amendment was not the answer.

While the motives of its supporters may be praiseworthy, ERA as a blanket attempt to help women could indeed bring them far more restraints and repressions. We fear it will even stifle many God-given feminine instincts. It would strike at the family, humankind's basic institution. ERA would bring ambiguity and possibly invite extensive litigation. Passage of ERA, some legal authorities contend, could nullify many accumulated benefits to women in present statutes.

We recognize men and women as equally important before the Lord, but with differences biologically, emotionally, and in other ways. ERA, we believe, does not recognize these differences. There are better means for giving women, and men, the rights they deserve.[26]

In 1980 the Church circulated with its magazines a special pamphlet detailing reasons for opposing the amendment. There was concern that passage of the ERA would undermine the husband's traditional responsibilities to support his wife and family, that women might be required to serve in combat on an equal basis with men, and that too much responsibility for interpreting details of the law was being shifted away from local officials to federal judges. The pamphlet pointed out that having an honest difference of opinion with Church authorities on such an issue did not constitute apostasy, but warned that trying to impose one's views on others, publicly criticizing the Church's leaders and policies and seeking to create division could lead to a person becoming "imbued with the spirit of apostasy" and being found "fighting against God and the authority which He had placed here to govern His Church."[27]

Although the Equal Rights Amendment was not ratified by the 1982 deadline, Church leaders anticipated that threats to the family would not cease. They therefore continued to encourage the Saints to strengthen family relationships as a protection against the challenges that lay ahead.

19 Joseph Fielding Smith and Harold B. Lee

The brief administrations of Joseph Fielding Smith and Harold B. Lee as Presidents of the Church during the early 1970s represented in each case the capstone of long and significant service to the Church. Each set a record for presiding for a shorter period than any of his predecessors—Joseph Fielding Smith serving as President of the Church for two and a half years, and Harold B. Lee occupying the position for only a year and a half. They are considered together in this chapter, not just because their administrations were so brief, but because most of the significant developments of this period cannot be confined to the leadership of either of these men alone. These years saw not only continued key developments of earlier decades, but also witnessed the defining of policies and new patterns of activity that would become increasingly important in later years.

Two Latter-day Prophets

Joseph Fielding Smith

Joseph Fielding Smith was born in Salt Lake City in 1876, just one year before the death of President Brigham Young. While other boys occupied their time with hunting, fishing, or

1876	July 19: Born in Salt Lake City
1899	Mission to England (age 22)
1901	Became clerk in Church historian's office; called as assistant Church historian five years later
1910	Sustained as member of the Quorum of the Twelve (33); began editing genealogical magazine
1915-35	Counselor to Salt Lake Temple president
1921-70	Served as Church historian
1922	*Essentials in Church History* published
1934-63	President of the Genealogical Society
1939	Directed withdrawal of missionaries from Europe (63)
1945-49	Presided over Salt Lake Temple
1951	Became president of the Council of the Twelve
1965	Became counselor to David O. McKay in the First Presidency (89)
1970	Sustained President of the Church (93)
1972	July 2: Died in Salt Lake City (nearly 96)

playing ball, young Joseph Fielding was more interested in reading. He had read the Book of Mormon twice before he reached ten years of age. He often carried a pocket edition of the New Testament which he could read in every available spare minute, and he began early to commit favorite scriptural passages to memory. Many years later he concluded that he had "received more pleasure and greater satisfaction out of the study of the scriptures, and reading of the Lord Jesus Christ, and of the Prophet Joseph Smith, and the work that has been accomplished for the salvation of men, than from anything else in all the world."[1] Joseph Fielding Smith inherited these interests from his father, after whom he was named. (To avoid confusion, the father is generally known as Joseph F. Smith and the son as Joseph Fielding Smith.) Only four years after Joseph Fielding was born, his father was called as a counselor to President John Taylor. Joseph F. Smith had personally experienced the exodus from Nauvoo following his own father's martyrdom and had participated in the colonization of the Great Basin; he passed on to his son a keen interest in the history of the Church. Joseph F. Smith was also a clear and powerful expounder of gospel doctrines, a quality for which his son would also be known. Young Joseph Fielding Smith found in his father's library many of the volumes from which he learned so much.

When Joseph Fielding Smith was twenty years of age, he received a patriarchal blessing from his uncle, John Smith, the Patriarch to the Church and the half-brother of his father. This blessing foreshadowed key activities and qualities of Joseph Fielding Smith's later life:

> It is thy privilege to live to a good old age and the will of the Lord that you should become a mighty man in Israel. . . . It shall be thy duty to sit in counsel with thy brethren and to preside among the people. It shall be thy duty also to travel much at home and abroad by land and water, laboring in the ministry, and I say unto thee, hold up thy head, lift up thy voice without fear or favor as the Spirit of the Lord shall direct, and the blessing of the Lord shall rest upon thee. His spirit shall direct thy mind and give thee word and sentiment that thou shall confound the wisdom of the wicked and set at nought the counsels of the unjust.[2]

In 1899 Joseph Fielding Smith commenced a two-year mission to England. Upon his return he served as a home missionary, as a member of his stake high council, and as a member of the Young Men's Mutual Improvement Association general board. He accepted employment as a clerk in the Church historian's office, where he would make a substantial contribution during succeeding decades.

In 1910 Elder Joseph Fielding Smith was sustained as a member of the Council of the Twelve, and was ordained an Apostle by his father, President Joseph F. Smith. In that same year he became secretary of the Genealogical Society of Utah, serving in various administrative capacities and eventually as president of that organization until 1963. He launched the *Utah Genealogical and Historical Magazine,* helped direct the formation of the Temple Records Index Bureau and the creation of the family group sheets used so widely throughout the

President Joseph Fielding Smith's doctrinal and historical writings constitute a
significant part of his legacy to the Church. (Church Visual Resources Library)

Church, and directed the inauguration of the society's widespread microfilming program. During much of this time he also
served in the presidency of the Salt Lake Temple. These experiences brought him into personal contact with the Church's
important genealogical and temple activity, a theme which
became prominent in his teachings and writings.

Elder Smith was sustained as Church historian and
recorder in 1921, a position in which he would serve until
being sustained as President of the Church a half century later.
Under his direction, report forms were standardized, countless
ward and stake histories were collected and cataloged, and
other significant steps were taken to preserve the history of the
Church. Soon after becoming Church historian, he published
Essentials in Church History, which would be the most widely
read single-volume LDS history for many years to come. This

work reflected his philosophy that history should record virtuous events and at the same time help us profit from the mistakes of the past. Nevertheless, he believed history must be accurate.[3]

Despite his many pressing ecclesiastical duties, Elder Joseph Fielding Smith was a prolific author. In *The Way to Perfection,* published in 1931, he placed human history in the context of scriptural doctrines, emphasizing developments in early dispensations as well as prophesied latter-day events. An especially significant and widely cited volume was *Teachings of the Prophet Joseph Smith.* First published in 1938, it contained chronologically arranged extracts from doctrinal sermons and writings of the Church's founder. Elder Smith's own teachings were compiled and published in the three-volume set, *Doctrines of Salvation,* 1954-1956. In all, Joseph Fielding Smith's writings filled twenty-five volumes.

Elder Smith's writings and sermons often cast him in the role as a defender of the faith against false notions, a role foreseen in his patriarchal blessing. To him, a proper understanding of the scriptures was essential. As he forcefully expounded revealed gospel truths, he gained the popular reputation of being stern and unyielding. Those who were close to him, especially his family, saw quite a different side of his personality. After twenty-four years of marriage, his wife Ethel wrote:

> I have often thought when he is gone people will say, "He is a very good man, sincere, orthodox, etc." They will speak of him as the public knows him; but the man they have in mind is very different from the man I know. The man I know is a kind, loving husband and father whose greatest ambition in life is to make his family happy, entirely forgetful of self in his efforts to do this. He is the man that lulls to sleep the fretful child, who tells bedtime stories to the little ones, who is never too tired or too busy to sit up late at night or to get up early in the morning to help the older children solve perplexing school problems. When illness comes the man I know watches tenderly over the afflicted one and waits upon him. It is their father for whom they cry, feeling his presence a panacea for all ills. It is his hands that bind up the wounds, his arms that give courage to the sufferer, his voice that remonstrates with them gently when

they err, until it becomes their happiness to do the thing that will make him happy.

The man I know is most gentle, and if he feels that he has been unjust to anyone the distance is never too far for him to go and, with loving words or kind deeds, erase the hurt. He welcomes gladly the young people to his home and is never happier than when discussing with them topics of the day—sports or whatever interests them most. He enjoys a good story and is quick to see the humor of a situation, to laugh and to be laughed at, always willing to join in any wholesome activity.[4]

As he assumed the leadership of the Church in 1970, President Joseph Fielding Smith affirmed that the Latter-day Saints "join with men of good will in all churches in expressing love and concern for the temporal and spiritual well-being of all our Father's children," trusting that God would "bless all the officers and teachers and members of our Father's church so they may serve him in righteousness, faithfully, and effectively; and bless the world and all men everywhere that they may turn to Him in righteousness and find peace, happiness, and purpose in life."[5] These thoughts reflected the spirit of Joseph Fielding Smith's Presidency. President Smith assumed the reigns of leadership at the age of ninety-three, the greatest age at which any Church President had entered that office. Many Church members expected this to be a period of waiting, until a younger man might again provide dynamic leadership. These expectations proved to be wrong. With the help of his two able counselors, Harold B. Lee and N. Eldon Tanner, President Smith directed the implementation of a variety of improvements in Church activities and programs. He traveled widely, conducting conferences, dedicating buildings, and in other ways strengthening the Church and its members. One reason why he was able to follow such a demanding schedule was that he enjoyed his work. On one sunny afternoon his sister found him busy in his office. She chided him for working too hard, citing the examples of several former Church leaders who had always taken naps in the afternoon. "Yes," responded President Smith, "but look where they are now."[6] After serving for two and one-half years, President Joseph Fielding Smith died peacefully just two weeks short of his ninety-sixth birthday.

Harold B. Lee

Following President Smith's death, Harold B. Lee was sustained as the eleventh President of the Church. Like his predecessor, President Lee had already made significant contributions that had a far-reaching impact on the Church and its programs.

Growing up on a farm in southeastern Idaho taught Harold B. Lee many valuable character traits and provided experience from which he could draw in his later life. "We began to do chores shortly after daybreak so we could start with the day's work by sunup. When the day's work was finished we had yet to do our evening chores, usually by the aid of a lantern."[7] While gaining an appreciation for hard work, he learned an even more important lesson as a boy. One day he had the urge to explore an old broken-down shed, but he heard a voice warning: "Harold, don't go over there." Elder Lee later recalled: "I looked about to see who was speaking my name. My father was way up at the other end of the field. He could not see what I was doing. There was no speaker in sight. Then I realized that someone that I could not see was warning me not to go over there. What was over there, I shall never know, but I learned early that there are those beyond our sight that could talk to us."[8]

After attending the Church-operated Oneida Stake Academy, he qualified as a teacher at the Albion State Normal School. He began his teaching career at age seventeen in the small, rural one-room Silver Star School. A year later he became principal of the district school, some of whose students were older than he was. Harold's interests were varied. While in school he had played basketball and participated in debates. He also played the trombone and piano in dance bands in and around his community.

After serving in the Western States Mission, Harold B. Lee moved to Salt Lake City, where he completed his college education by attending summer sessions at the University of Utah and through taking extension and correspondence courses. He became successively principal of two schools and then district manager of a library supplies company. In 1932 he was

1899	March 28: Born in Clifton, Idaho
1916	Began teaching school (age 17); became principal the following year
1920	Called to Western States Mission
1923-28	School principal in Salt Lake City
1930	Became president of Pioneer Stake (31)
1932	Appointed as member of Salt Lake City Commission
1935	Called to direct Churchwide implementation of the welfare plan (36)
1941	Became member of the Quorum of the Twelve (42)
1962	Directed development of the priesthood correlation program
1970	Set apart as First Counselor in the First Presidency (70)
1972	Became President of the Church (73)
1973	December 26: Died in Salt Lake City (74)

appointed a member of the Salt Lake City Commission with responsibility for streets and public properties.

The activities and contributions for which Harold B. Lee is remembered, however, lay in a different area. In 1930 he became president of the Pioneer Stake at the age of thirty-one. He presided during the Great Depression, and the members of his stake, located on the west side of Salt Lake City, were particularly hard hit. Under Harold B. Lee's leadership, the stake developed a series of innovative projects to produce and preserve needed food and other supplies for the destitute. President Lee was also concerned about the social and recreational needs of his stake members. The stake constructed a gymnasium, using materials from a demolished business building, and then set up a stakewide budget plan to provide wholesome Church-sponsored activities for all, regardless of their financial status. It was because of this background that the First Presidency in 1935 appointed Harold B. Lee to develop the Churchwide welfare plan announced the following year. During the next several years he traveled widely, counseling with local leaders concerning the implementation of the welfare program. Thus he was already widely known and respected when he received his next significant calling.

On April 6, 1941, Harold B. Lee was sustained as a member of the Council of the Twelve Apostles. He later related a sacred experience he had during the week immediately following his call:

> It was on the day or so following conference that President Stephen L Richards, who was then chairman of the Church radio and publicity committee, approached me and said, "Brother Lee, next Sunday is Easter, and we have decided to ask you to give the Sunday night radio talk, the Easter talk, on the resurrection of the Lord." And then he added, "You understand now, of course, that as a member of the Council of the Twelve, you are to be one of the special witnesses of the life and mission of the Savior and of that great event." The most overwhelming of all the things that have happened to me was to begin to realize what a call into the Council of the Twelve meant.
>
> During the days which followed, I locked myself in one of the rooms over in the Church Office building, and there I read the story of the life of the Savior. As I read the events of his life, and particularly the events leading up to and of the crucifixion, and then of the resurrection, I discovered that something was happening to me. I was not just reading a story; it seemed actually as though I was living the events; and I was reading them with a reality the like of which I had never before experienced. And when, on the Sunday night following, after I had delivered my brief talk and then declared, simply, "As one of the humblest among you, I, too, know that these things are true, that Jesus died and was resurrected for the sins of the world," I was speaking from a full heart, because I had come to know that week, with a certainty which I never before had known.[9]

Visits to stake conferences, tours of missions, and assignments to advise auxiliary organizations all broadened Elder Lee's experience. As World War II broke out, he was called as the first chairman of the Church's Servicemen's Committee. Elder Lee was particularly responsive to the challenges and needs of the younger members of the Church. In 1945 he gave a series of radio addresses which were subsequently published as a book, *Youth and the Church*. A revised version of this volume, *Decisions for Successful Living*, appeared in 1973. By 1960 Elder Harold B. Lee had become chairman of the General Priesthood Committee of the Twelve. It was in that year that the First Presidency directed him and his committee to conduct an exhaustive review of the Church's programs and curriculum. The result of this study was the Priesthood Correlation effort of the 1960s. In the priesthood session of several successive general conferences Elder Lee introduced and explained such significant developments as ward correlation councils and priesthood executive committees, home teaching, and family home evenings.

There was another dimension to Elder Lee's preparation. During the Great Depression he had learned empathy as he shared the suffering of those over whom he presided. Then, during the 1960s, he personally experienced deep sorrow as he lost his wife and then one of his two daughters through death. Reflecting on these tragic experiences and on the words of the Prophet Joseph Smith, Harold B. Lee concluded:

> These thoughts now running through my mind begin to give greater meaning to some of the experiences in my life, things that have happened which have been difficult for me to understand. At times it seemed as though I too was like a rough stone rolling down from a high mountainside, being buffeted and polished, I suppose, by experiences, that I too might overcome and become a polished shaft in the quiver of the Almighty.[10]

That for which Elder Lee was being prepared became obvious when President Joseph Fielding Smith passed away on July 2, 1972, and Elder Lee succeeded to the leadership of the Church. At a press conference, he declared that the Church's greatest challenge was to keep up with the worldwide growth in its membership. President Lee declared on this occasion that his most important message to the Saints was that they should keep the commandments of God. "The safety of the church lies in the members keeping the commandments. There is

The First Presidency from 1970 to 1972: (from left) Harold B. Lee, Joseph Fielding Smith, and N. Eldon Tanner. (Church Archives)

nothing more important that I could say. As they keep the commandments, blessings will come."[11] President Harold B. Lee would lead the Church for only a year and a half before his unexpected death on December 26, 1973. Though brief, his administration continued the important trends that had been inaugurated by his predecessors.

The Early 1970s: An Era of Consolidation

The four years during which Joseph Fielding Smith and Harold B. Lee presided saw the Church continue its worldwide growth. During this period membership climbed from 2.8 to 3.3 million. Early in 1970, on the very day when President David O. McKay died, the five-hundredth stake was organized. During that same year sixty-four of these units were formed (the previous record was twenty-nine). These included stakes in Tokyo, the first in Asia; Johannesburg, the first in Africa; and Lima, the first on the west coast of South America. Efforts to sustain this growth through sharing the gospel also continued. Over six million people visited the Church's pavilion at "Expo '70" in Osaka, Japan. This made the Church's programs and teachings more widely known than ever before in Japan and other countries of eastern Asia. In 1972 the Church opened a visitors' center in San Diego at the terminus of the Mormon Battalion's epic march, and also opened a special public relations office in New York City. The following year a complex of restored buildings was dedicated in Nauvoo, and Japanese-language tours were inaugurated at the Hawaii Temple visitors' center.

Yet the early 1970s was not merely an era of growth and expansion. These years also witnessed a consolidation of administrative responsibilities at Church headquarters, a continuing effort to improve the Church's varied programs, and an intensified desire to help each individual member cope with the mounting challenges of the modern world.

Consolidating Church Administration

The rapid growth of the Church around the world during the 1950s and 1960s placed mounting responsibilities on the General Authorities. There were more stake conferences to attend, and more local leaders to call, train, and supervise. (How this challenge was met will be the subject of a later chapter.) One step taken during the early 1970s was to increase the number of the Assistants to the Twelve; this group of General Authorities grew from eleven to eighteen in 1974. Church leaders also adopted the policy of delegating whatever responsibilities they could. In 1970, for example, Neal A. Maxwell was appointed commissioner of the Church's educational system. Not yet a General Authority, he was serving as executive vice president of the University of Utah. He assumed responsibility for all the facets of the Church's education programs and thus helped to lighten the load carried by the General Authorities.

As the Church's administrative structure expanded to meet these growing needs, the First Presidency carefully considered the best way to organize it. They employed two nationally known business consulting firms to make in-depth studies, the findings of which became the basis for some important reorganizations at Church headquarters. The reports pointed out that the General Authorities, particularly the Twelve, were carrying extensive responsibility for dozens of Church agencies or programs. They recommended that these activities be grouped into several large departments, and that responsibility for day-to-day operations be delegated to full-time executive directors. In 1972, therefore, the new Internal Communications Department brought together the preparation, publication, and distribution of magazines, lesson manuals, and instructional materials intended for use within the Church. (Many of these responsibilities were later transferred to the Presiding Bishopric's office.) During that same year, the External Communications Department (later renamed Public Communications) coordinated the Church's visitors' centers, broadcasting, and other public relations activities. Similarly, in 1973 the Church's Welfare, Social Services, and Health programs became part of the new Welfare Services Department.

The International Mission was another example of consolidation of responsibilities. Beginning in 1972, this unit met the needs of the hundreds of Latter-day Saints living in parts of the world where there were no organized stakes or missions. At about this same time, Lee S. Bickmore, an active Church member who was chairman of the board and chief executive officer of Nabisco, was named special consultant to the First Presidency for business operations, finances, building, communications, and other related activities.[12]

A tangible consolidation of Church administration came with the construction of the Church's $31-million twenty-eight-story office building in Salt Lake City. When this facility was occupied in 1972, departments that had been located in rented space in a dozen buildings in downtown Salt Lake City were housed under a single roof for the first time. This not only made for efficiency of operation but also enhanced a feeling of unity—each agency seeing itself as more clearly an integral part of the total Church program.

Completed in 1972, the 28-story Church Office Building provides much-needed facilities at the headquarters of a growing worldwide Church. (*Deseret News* photo)

Refining and Consolidating Church Activities

The principles of priesthood correlation, enunciated so clearly during the 1960s, continued to guide the development of Church activities during the following decade. In several instances, formerly separate programs were consolidated into a single organization. As noted in an earlier chapter, an outstanding example during the early 1970s was the uniting of the Aaronic Priesthood and the Young Men's Mutual Improvement Association programs and a similar streamlining of the Young

Women's organization. Another consolidation affected the important task of training teachers. A single teacher development program under the direction of the bishop served all Church organizations. Beginning in 1971 the Church published only three magazines—one each for children, youth, and adults. This consolidated production and circulation of these magazines was now handled by a single staff under the direction of the General Authorities. As has been seen, a corresponding reduction in personnel was also accomplished at the local level.

Other changes during this period involved abandoning long-standing names of Church programs. After ninety-nine years, the title "Deseret Sunday School Union" was replaced by the more current designation "Sunday School of The Church of Jesus Christ of Latter-day Saints." The former title was descriptive of how the Churchwide organization had been formed through the uniting of separate local Sunday Schools in pioneer times, but this meaning became less significant during an era of worldwide growth.[13] Other traditional names discontinued during these years included "Trail Builders" (nine- to eleven-year-old boys in Primary), "M-Men" and "Gleaners" (young single adults), and even the name "Mutual Improvement Association" itself. The newer names were generally simpler, more descriptive, and less provincial than their predecessors. However, the shift from "Senior Aaronic" to "Prospective Elder" represented a basic restructuring of this program. The former title seemed to reflect a man's past failure to advance beyond the lesser priesthood, while the new name reflected the hope for future progress. Giving the elders quorum responsibility for reactivating these men placed them in the mainstream of priesthood activity and associations. Recently returned missionaries, usually found in the elders quorums, could employ the same skills in working with their inactive brethren as they had used in teaching nonmembers.[14]

President Joseph Fielding Smith's interest in gospel scholarship was reflected in another refinement of Church activity. Within a few weeks of his death the adult Gospel Doctrine class in Sunday School began a systematic study of the standard works. Theretofore a variety of manuals had been prepared for this class, but beginning in 1972 the scriptures themselves became the sole text. The Old Testament, the New Testament, the Book of Mormon, and the Doctrine and Covenants were studied in rotation, two years (and later only one year) being spent on each. The Pearl of Great Price was studied in conjunction with relevant sections of the other works. Latter-day Saints took scripture study seriously more than ever before. Not only did they read the week's assignment for the Gospel Doctrine class, but the scriptures were cited more frequently in sermons and other instructions, and an increasing number of Saints could be seen with their copies of the standard works open during meetings. Church leaders anticipated a spiritual resurgence as a result of the Saints' added contact with the word of God.

Under the leadership of Presidents Smith and Lee, the momentum in temple activity continued to build. In 1972 the Provo and Ogden temples were dedicated. These immediately became the most productive temples in terms of the number of ordinances performed. Construction of the Washington Temple, largest ever built by the Church, was commenced. The thorough remodeling of five existing temples was also announced. As will be seen in the following chapter, the level of ordinances performed soared to new heights, and a new system of submitting names promoted a resurgence in genealogical activity.

Responding to New Needs

The postwar decades had witnessed a general disintegration of institutions and traditions that in earlier years had brought stability and security. Crime rates increased. Growing numbers of divorces were breaking up families. A larger proportion of the population was living in an urban rather than a rural environment. Large cities typically were impersonal and were characterized by a hectic life-style which placed added emotional strain on the individual. In contrast to farming communities where the family was central to economic survival, the cities presented an extensive array of attractions pulling individuals in a variety of directions away from the family. Even though the gospel offered a defense against these social problems, the Latter-day Saints were not totally immune.

President Harold B. Lee was concerned about these problems, so he stressed the need of blessing each member with the program of the Church. Paraphrasing a passage from latter-day revelation (D&C 84:109-110), he declared: "The Church indeed, hath need of every member that all may be edified so that the system may be made perfect, and every member has a deep need to participate fully in the Church. . . ." He stressed that the Church and its programs were designed to strengthen and bless the members, that they were means to this end rather than being the end in themselves. Paraphrasing Mark 2:27, President Lee asserted that "man was not made for the Church: but the Church was made for man." "We need appropriate involvement for every individual," President Lee counseled, "because there is little individual progress without participation, for it is participation by everyone which permits us to apply the principles of the Gospel."15 This concern for meeting the needs of each member was reflected in the Church's efforts to help the Saints cope with the new challenges they were facing.

The Doctrine and Covenants instructed the Saints to "remember in all things" the "sick and afflicted" as well as the "poor and the needy" (see D&C 52:40). It can be seen that some of the twentieth century's greatest challenges lie in the areas of physical health and emotional well-being. To meet these challenges the Church established its health and social services programs.

Health Services

The importance of physical and emotional health is affirmed by the scriptures. Healing is one of the gifts of the Spirit, and many of the Lord's miracles were of this nature. The Apostle Paul taught that we are the "temple of God" and that this temple must be kept holy (see 1 Corinthians 3:16, 17). In our own day the Lord has revealed the Word of Wisdom, which is concerned with the "temporal salvation of all saints in

the last days" (see D&C 89:2). Church programs as well as
teachings have focused on the physical well-being of Latter-
day Saints.

Health needs were critical as the Mormon pioneers con-
quered the desert wilderness. Later, with the help of a dollar-a-
month contribution by Relief Society and MIA members, the
Deseret Hospital provided the first nurses' training and mater-
nity care in the Intermountain area. In 1890, after only eight
years of operation, this badly needed institution was forced to
close because of financial problems. In 1905 the new LDS Hospital opened in Salt Lake City. Fifty thousand dollars of the
$180,000 construction cost had come from the estate of Wil-
liam H. Groves, a wealthy dentist who had left this amount for
the establishment of a Mormon hospital. Over the years the
hospital's facilities and equipment were enlarged and modern-
ized, and its staff became noted in such areas as heart surgery.[16]

Other hospitals were added in Utah, southeast Idaho, and
southwest Wyoming, bringing the total in the Church system
to fifteen. An administrator was appointed in 1962 to provide
central coordination for the system; in 1970, under the direction of President Joseph Fielding Smith, a health services commissioner was named to head a legally distinct corporation
under the leadership of the Presiding Bishopric.

The early 1970s, however, witnessed a new emphasis in
the Church's health program. In 1971 a new *Health Services
Handbook* outlined the fundamental objectives and the basic
procedures for this expanding program.

> Health services for worthy members in need have primar-
> ily been provided in the United States. There are, however,
> challenges facing the entire Church today that relate to the
> health of a worldwide membership. The purpose of priesthood
> correlation of health services is to assist priesthood leaders and,
> through them, Church members to meet these challenges suc-
> cessfully. . . .[17]

In accordance with these concerns, the Church in 1971
called its first "health missionaries." These missionaries performed traditional proselyting duties along with providing
special medical instruction. Their first task was to identify the

Health Services missionaries bless Guatemalan Saints and friends through principles of nutrition, sanitation, and first aid. (*Ensign* photo)

greatest medical needs of both Church members and nonmembers in an area. They then developed programs to be implemented through existing Church organizations to meet these needs.

Most programs sponsored by government agencies or other religious groups have featured clinics for the curing of illness; doctors worked long hours "doing much for a few but nothing for many." In contrast to this pattern, LDS health missionaries emphasized prevention of illness. By enlisting Church members to help in teaching basic health principles and sanitation, the missionaries were able to reach thousands. The Church has sent its health missionaries into parts of the world where the need is greatest. By the end of the program's second year, 200 health missionaries were serving, but many more were needed.[18]

In later years they received a wider variety of assignments and were called welfare services missionaries or missionaries with special assignments.

This new direction in the Church's health activities was reflected in yet another far-reaching change announced by the First Presidency in 1974:

> . . . After a thorough study and consideration, the Council of the First Presidency and Quorum of the Twelve has decided to divert the full efforts of the Health Services of the church to the health needs of the worldwide church membership.
>
> As a result of that decision, and because the operation of hospitals is not central to the mission of the church, the church has also decided to divest itself of its extensive hospital holdings, including the 15 hospitals that have been operated in Utah, Idaho, and Wyoming by the Health Services Corporation.
>
> The growing worldwide responsibility of the church makes it difficult to justify provision of curative services in a single, affluent, geographical locality.
>
> In past years, the church responded to the appeal of communities to save an existing facility or to build a hospital because their health needs seemingly could not be met in any other way.
>
> Today, however, there are other ways that these needs can be met. It is no longer necessary for the church to be involved in hospital ownership or management.
>
> The First Presidency also affirmed that the decision "in no way signifies loss of interest or concern on the part of the church for the sick and afflicted."
>
> "To the contrary," they said, "it provides greater flexibility as the church assists members and others everywhere with their temporal needs. . . ."

An independent and self-perpetuating corporation, Intermountain Health Care, was established to own and operate these hospitals.[19]

Social Services

Over the years the Church had established three special programs to meet specific twentieth-century social challenges: (1) The Relief Society Social Welfare Department, established in 1919, served as an adoption agency and provided foster homes for disadvantaged children. (2) The Indian student placement program under the chairmanship of Elder Spencer W. Kimball had extended the advantages of attending good schools and living in a wholesome LDS family environment to thousands of Lamanite youth since the mid-1950s. (3) Under Elder Thomas S. Monson's direction, the "youth guidance" program worked to prevent problems and to make foster care or day camps available to youth in need. All three of these programs were required by law to employ licensed professional social workers. In 1969 they were unified to form the new Social Services Department.[20]

From this beginning, the program expanded to provide a wide variety of services: Young people with severe social or emotional problems received, together with their parents, short-term professional counseling. Foster care was provided in extreme cases to youth when their home situation was such that a wholesome family relationship was not possible. The goal was to have them return home as soon as the problem was resolved. Summer day camps provided helpful experiences in coping with social situations for disturbed children between the ages of eight and fourteen. Indian student placement also continued to be provided through the Social Services Department. Special foster homes aided unwed parents in the process of repentance, encouraging them to marry where appropriate. The Church's adoption agency helped create families for barren couples and found Latter-day Saint homes for children. Services to Church members in prison and their families included counseling and rehabilitation; special home evenings were arranged for the inmates. In working with members having drugs or alcohol problems, Church social services coordinated with public agencies and also provided instruction for local Church leaders.[21]

Concerning the efficacy of this help, President Harold B. Lee testified:

> Our social services program has already been a great blessing to our Church members. This program seeks to respond to many problems that beset our members in an affluent society and it will no doubt increase in its importance, because so many of the problems which this cluster of agencies deals with are

symptomatic of our time. Members may need counseling more than clothing, and members who, through bishops, are referred to any agency in our social services program should feel no more hesitancy in asking for help of this kind than we should in requesting help through the priesthood welfare program.[22]

In areas where Church membership is more concentrated, particularly in the western United States and Canada, the Church established social service agencies. These employed professionally trained and licensed personnel, and operated in accordance with government regulations.[23]

The social services handbook distinguished the roles of professional counselors and that of the regular ecclesiastical structure of the Church. Priesthood officers typically dealt with the kind of social or emotional problems that could be remedied by the demonstration of warmth, firmness, and love. On the other hand, state and local laws usually required that professionally trained social workers conduct such licensed services as adoptions, foster care arrangements, and counseling with severe types of social-emotional disturbance. To carry on these licensed services and to meet legal requirements, the Church in 1973 organized a legally separate Social Services Corporation.[24]

Also in 1973 the general Church welfare program, health services, and social services were brought together to form the new Welfare Services Department under the supervision of the Presiding Bishopric. This was intended to "unify activities in meeting the total needs of the whole man."[25]

At the ward level, welfare services committees were organized to coordinate the work of the bishopric, the Relief Society, and the priesthood quorums in meeting the needs of Church members.

Basic lines of priesthood communication were followed in relation to the social and health programs.

> Any member of the Church experiencing conflicts in his personal life should first seek assistance and support from his family. As additional help is required, he may, with the assistance of his home teacher and quorum leader, consult with his bishop. The bishop endeavors to aid the member on a ward level through utilizing the ward family or other special re-

sources he feels appropriate. If additional help is needed, the bishop counsels with his stake president, who aids through the use of stake or other resources he may select. If additional help is needed beyond this level, the stake president authorizes contact with the Social Services Department, which is able to provide the full range of social services.[26]

In areas where members are too scattered for LDS social services agencies to be organized, Church leaders were instructed to identify local professional counselors who could provide help consistent with gospel standards.

Meeting Other Needs

Over the years the Church had published literature in braille or in recorded form for blind Latter-day Saints. A concern for the unique needs of the handicapped continued and even expanded. Bishops received instructions on how to involve handicapped members more fully in Church activities. Sighted companions were invited to help blind teachers prepare their lessons. Home teachers assisted members confined to wheelchairs to get to church. Young people learned sign language in order to interpret services for deaf friends. The number of special branches for the deaf expanded throughout the United States. A special conference in 1972 considered how better to meet the needs of deaf Latter-day Saints. A film was produced to teach how priesthood ordinances can be performed without the use of speech. A new dictionary was compiled in order to standardize signs used to interpret unique gospel or Church-related terms to the deaf.[27]

The early 1970s was an era of growing minority consciousness. Ethnic groups became increasingly proud of their unique heritages. The Church took steps to meet the special needs of these groups. In 1970 the name of the Indian Committee was changed to "Committee for Lamanites and Other Cultures" to reflect a broader scope. This committee did not administer programs of its own, but rather coordinated efforts of existing Church organizations in behalf of various minority groups. The committee considered how gospel principles could be taught more effectively in terms of the understanding of the various cultural groups. It also sought to identify and help preserve contributions from each culture which might benefit Church members as a whole.[28]

In 1972 President Harold B. Lee and his counselors instructed local priesthood leaders to assume the responsibility for adequately meeting the needs of minority groups residing within their boundaries. Special attention was given to those not speaking the language of the majority. As a result, translation facilities, special classes taught in the minority language, or even separate branches or wards were provided as needed. Although special needs were to be met, the basic goal was to involve minority members as fully as possible in the mainstream of Church activity.

Another group with special needs was the growing number of single adults. While in 1900 only 1 percent of Church members over twenty-five years of age were divorced, this proportion increased more than fivefold by 1975. Traditional couple-oriented activities did not adequately meet the needs of single, widowed, or divorced members.

President Harold B. Lee expressed a special concern for these people:

> We have found that we have been neglecting some of our adult members—those over eighteen who have not yet found their companions, or who are perhaps widowed or divorced. They have been saying to us, "But you have no program for us." Instead of our saying, "Sorry, we can't do anything for you except through our existing MIA or Relief Society programs," we have said to them, "We want to find out what you need." It is still the same gospel, but we are endeavoring to reach those for whom we have had no adequate programs.[29]

An outgrowth of this concern was the creation of the new Young Special Interest program for singles twenty-six through forty years of age, and the revitalization of Special Interest activities for older single Latter-day Saints.

The aging constitute yet another group that can best be helped through the regular Church organization at the local level. During the twentieth century the proportion of the United States population over sixty-five has increased from 4 percent to more than 10 percent. The challenges faced by these senior citizens are complicated by the fact that 17 percent of the men and 51 percent of the women over sixty-five are alone, most being widows and widowers. Because these experienced older Saints have much to contribute and want to feel needed, bishops were encouraged to see that they are involved in Church activity. Local Church leaders have developed a variety of ways to use home teachers and others to creatively meet the needs of their older members.

The formation of social, health, and related programs in the twentieth century illustrates how, under inspired direction, the Church is able to respond to new needs as they may arise.

20 Temples and Temple Work

Temple building and temple activity have been important and unique characteristics of the Latter-day Saints' religion since the beginning. This was likewise true of the Lord's people in earlier dispensations. Nevertheless, the later twentieth century has witnessed remarkable developments in this sacred service, an unprecedented number of temples having been constructed around the world. At the same time, new methods have enhanced the presentation of the sacred ordinances for which temples are built. Furthermore, modern inventions have significantly expedited the demanding genealogical research required to identify persons for whom temple ordinances are to be performed. Despite these exciting developments, however, the basic nature and purpose of temples have remained the same.

What Is a Temple?

Latter-day Saints regard their temples as quite different from ordinary chapels or other houses of worship. The scriptures, both ancient and modern, describe temples as unique places of revelation and communion between God and man.

In his inspired dedicatory prayer of the Kirtland Temple, Joseph Smith referred to the Saints' having sacrificed and endured "great tribulation" to build that edifice "that the Son of Man might have a place to manifest himself to his people" (D&C 109:5). For a similar purpose the Lord later directed the Saints in Nauvoo to "build a house to my name, for the Most High to dwell therein. For there is not a place found on earth that he may come to and restore again that which was lost unto you, or which he hath taken away, even the fulness of the priesthood." (D&C 124:27-28.)

This function of temples suggests the importance of personal worthiness as a requirement for those who enter. The Lord promised:

> And inasmuch as my people build a house unto me in the name of the Lord, and do not suffer any unclean thing to come into it, that it be not defiled, my glory shall rest upon it;
>
> Yea, and my presence shall be there, for I will come into it, and all the pure in heart that shall come into it shall see God.
>
> But if it be defiled I will not come into it, and my glory shall not be there; for I will not come into unholy temples. (D&C 97:15-17.)

Elder James E. Talmage of the Council of the Twelve accepted this general definition of temples as places of contact between our Heavenly Father and his children; but he also pointed out: "A temple, however, is characterized not alone as the place where God reveals Himself to man, but also as the House wherein prescribed ordinances of the Priesthood are solemnized."[1]

Elder John A. Widtsoe described the temple as a "place of instruction" and explained that "if we enter the temple in the right spirit and are attentive, we go out enriched in gospel knowledge and wisdom." It is a place of peace because we may leave the "turbulent world" outside and concentrate on "things of the spirit." Temple covenants contribute to a "high resolve to lead lives worthy of the gifts of the gospel." Temple blessings are eternal in scope and conditioned only on the participant's faithfulness. In the temple "every person may receive revelation to assist him in life."[2]

Elder Boyd K. Packer declared that "temples are the very center of the spiritual strength of the Church." This strength is not only available to the Church as a whole, Elder Packer explained, but also to individual Latter-day Saints: "When members of the Church are troubled or when crucial decisions weigh heavily upon their minds, it is a common thing for them to go to the temple. It is a good place to take our cares. In the temple we can receive spiritual perspective. There, during the time of the temple service, we are "out of the world."[3]

The endowment is at the heart of temple worship. "The instruction given in the endowment," Elder Packer explained, "provides a firm perspective, a point of reference by which a person may gauge all his learning and wisdom, both spiritual and temporal; by which he may gather things together, determine their true meaning and significance, and fit them into their proper places."[4] Elder James E. Talmage pointed out that it comprises a course of instruction which reviews important phases of the history of mankind, including the creation of the world, the fall of Adam and Eve, and conditions we face in the present world. It teaches the plan of salvation, Elder Talmage explained, including "the absolute and indispensable condition of personal purity and devotion to the right in the present life and a strict compliance with gospel requirements."[5] When the Prophet Joseph Smith gave the first endowment in this dispensation in 1842, he recorded that he had spent the day with the brethren instructing them in "all those plans and principles by which any one is enabled to secure the fullness of those blessings which have been prepared for the Church of the Firstborn, and come up and abide in the presence of the Eloheim in the eternal worlds."[6]

Latter-day Temples
Revealed Development in Temple Design

An important precedent was set when the Lord directed that the first temple of this dispensation be built "not after the manner of the world," but according to a pattern which he

1836	Kirtland Temple dedicated; sealing keys restored
1840	Baptisms for the dead inaugurated
1841	Sealing of living couples first performed
1842	Endowment for the living given in Joseph Smith's private office
1846	Nauvoo Temple dedicated; sealing of living children to parents commenced
1855	Endowment House dedicated in Salt Lake City; first sealings of deceased couples
1877	St. George Temple dedicated; endowments for the dead and sealing of deceased children to parents inaugurated
1884	Logan Temple dedicated
1888	Manti Temple dedicated
1893	Salt Lake Temple dedicated
1894	Genealogical Society organized

would reveal (see D&C 95:13-14). As Elder James E. Talmage reflected on the design of temples, both ancient and modern, he concluded: ". . . direct revelation of temple plans is required for each distinctive period of the Priesthood's administration, that is to say for every dispensation of Divine authority. While the general purpose of temples is the same in all times, the special suitability of these edifices is determined by the needs of the dispensation to which they severally belong. There is a definite sequence of development in the dealings of God with man throughout the centuries."[7] Therefore the temple buildings themselves constitute a tangible record of God's progressive revelations concerning the scope of temple work. Understanding how temple design developed during the nineteenth century can provide the background for what has happened in this century.

The Kirtland Temple, for example, was built before temple ordinances as we have them today had been restored. In fact, Elijah restored the sealing keys, so important in temple work, only one week following the dedication of this temple.

Thus the Lord directed that the Kirtland Temple be designed for general worship and educational purposes (see D&C 95:15-17). Elder Orson Pratt later testified that the Lord had "revealed the pattern according to which that house should be built, pointing out the various courts and apartments, telling the size of the house, the order of the pulpits, and in fact everything pertaining to it was clearly pointed out by revelation. God gave a vision of these things, not only to Joseph, but to several others, and they were strictly commanded to build according to the pattern revealed from the heavens."[8]

The Prophet Joseph Smith first taught the doctrine of baptism for the dead in 1840.[9] Thus, when the Nauvoo Temple was built, it not only followed the pattern of the Kirtland Temple—two large rooms plus smaller rooms in the attic— but it also added a baptismal font in the basement.[10] The endowment was first given by Joseph Smith in his office in 1842. Following the Prophet's martyrdom, when the Nauvoo Temple was sufficiently completed, these endowments were given in the large room on the attic level.

Within a few days of the pioneers' arrival in the Salt Lake Valley, Brigham Young designated the site where the temple would stand, and the city was laid out from that point. During the forty years the Salt Lake Temple was under construction, three other Utah temples were erected and dedicated. The earliest of these, in St. George (dedicated in 1877), followed the Nauvoo pattern. As interest in temple work increased, however, expanded facilities specifically designed for giving the endowment instructions were needed.

". . . The Lord is not confined to an exact pattern in relation to these Temples," Elder Orson Pratt explained, ". . . but He will construct His Temples in a great variety of ways, and by and by, when the more perfect order shall exist we shall construct them, through the aid of revelation, in accordance with the Temples that exist in yonder heaven."[11] As early as 1855, the Endowment House, a temporary adobe structure erected on Temple Square in Salt Lake City, had set a new pattern, providing separate lecture rooms where different phases of man's eternal life might be taught as part of the endowment presentation. The lower portion of the Logan,

The Los Angeles Temple, shown here nearing completion, was dedicated in 1956. (Photo courtesy of Paul L. Garns)

Manti, and Salt Lake temples (all completed during the last two decades of the nineteenth century) followed a similar plan and also included the traditional large priesthood assembly room on their upper floor.

The next four temples—Hawaii, Alberta, Arizona, and Idaho Falls, all built during the first half of the twentieth century—represented Church expansion in the Intermountain West and also in the Pacific. These temples were smaller, included lecture rooms specifically designed for presenting the endowment, but did not have the large assembly rooms.

The Los Angeles Temple, dedicated in 1956, was the largest such structure the Church had built to that date. It represented extensive Latter-day Saint progress in southern California, and included not only the individual endowment rooms, but also a large priesthood assembly room on the upper floor.

The Swiss Temple, dedicated in 1955, inaugurated a new concept in temple building. President David O. McKay announced that this would be "but the first of several such temples" for the benefit of the far-flung membership of the Church, and that by building smaller temples it would be possible to build more of them.[12] The construction of this first "overseas" temple marked a major turning point in Church history. Previously the European Saints had felt they needed to "gather" to America, where they could receive their temple blessings. Now they realized that they could heed the General Authorities' counsel to stay where they were, build up the Church in their own lands, and enjoy all the benefits of the gospel program, including temple blessings, in Europe. Furthermore, beginning in the Swiss Temple the use of motion pictures made it possible to present the endowment as effectively in one room as in the series of four separate rooms required in earlier temples. The use of films also made it easier to present the endowment in the several languages spoken by the patrons of this temple.

The New Zealand and London temples (1958) were very similar to the Swiss Temple in design. The Oakland Temple (dedicated in 1964) employed the same principle but provided two lecture rooms where separate groups could receive the endowment simultaneously. The Provo, Ogden, and Washington, D.C., temples were designed to provide six such lecture rooms, where six separate groups could receive the endowment instructions at once.

Divine Guidance in Locating Temples

By means of revelation the Lord has participated in the process of selecting the sites on which these temples were to be built. Concerning the Nauvoo Temple, an 1841 revelation declared: "I will show unto my servant Joseph all things pertaining to this house . . . and the place whereon it shall be built. And ye shall build it on the place where you have contemplated building it, for that is the spot which I have chosen for you to build it." (D&C 124:42-43.) Similarly, President Brigham Young declared that he had seen in vision not only the

1910	*Utah Genealogical and Historical Magazine* inaugurated
1911	One-millionth endowment for the dead performed
1919	Hawaii Temple dedicated
1923	Alberta Temple dedicated at Cardston
1924	Temple Index Bureau organized to avoid duplication of ordinances
1927	Arizona Temple dedicated at Mesa
1938	St. George Temple reopened after yearlong remodeling; Genealogical Society began using microfilms
1941	Ten-millionth endowment for the dead performed
1945	Idaho Falls Temple dedicated
1955	Swiss Temple dedicated, first "overseas" temple and first to use films
1956	Los Angeles Temple dedicated
1958	New Zealand and London temples dedicated; first branch genealogical library opened
1961	Records Tabulation, using computer, provided names to temples
1964	Oakland Temple dedicated
1965	Three-generation assignment given to Church members
1969	Individual entry system for submitting names for temple work inaugurated
1972	Ogden and Provo temples dedicated in Utah
1974	Washington Temple dedicated
1975	Arizona and St. George temples rededicated following thorough reconstruction
1978	Sao Paulo Temple dedicated; name-extraction program introduced Churchwide
1979	New four-generation assignment given to LDS families
1980	Seven new temples announced; Tokyo and Seattle temples dedicated

design but also the building site for the Salt Lake Temple; he also declared that the Manti Temple site had been selected and dedicated by the ancient prophet Moroni.[13]

Latter-day Saints can also point to evidence of similar divine help in selecting and obtaining temple sites during the twentieth century. The Saints in northern California, for example, often spoke of what they regarded as a prophetic statement concerning a temple in their area. During the summer of 1924 Elder George Albert Smith was in San Francisco attending regional Boy Scout meetings. On that occasion he met with W. Aird MacDonald, who was president of the Church's small branch across the bay in Oakland. They met at the Fairmont Hotel high atop San Francisco's Nob Hill. MacDonald later recalled:

> From the Fairmont terrace we had a wonderful panorama of the great San Francisco Bay, nestling at our feet. The setting sun seemed to set the whole eastern shore afire, until the Oakland hills were ablaze with golden light. As we admired the beauty and majesty of the scene, President Smith suddenly grew silent, ceased talking, and for several minutes gazed intently toward the East Bay hills.
> "Brother MacDonald, I can almost see in vision a white temple of the Lord high upon those hills," he exclaimed rapturously, "an ensign to all the world travelers as they sail through the Golden Gate into this wonderful harbor." Then he studied the vista for a few moments as if to make sure of the scene before him. "Yes, sir, a great white temple of the Lord," he confided with calm assurance, "will grace those hills, a glorious ensign to the nations, to welcome our Father's children as they visit this great city."[14]

In 1934 the Church's second stake in the San Francisco Bay area was organized in Oakland, the San Francisco Stake having been formed seven years earlier. At about this time a committee, headed by Eugene Hilton, was formed to locate a site in the area envisioned by Elder Smith. Hilton later recalled that the Chamber of Commerce and city officials eagerly cooperated. As the relative merits of several sites were weighed, "one particular spot always seemed to impress us as 'the one.' " Even though this site was definitely not for sale, two other sites offered free of charge were turned down. Just after World War II had started, however, the owners of the choice site found that their plans for developing it were blocked because necessary building materials were now restricted. They therefore offered the land to the Church. Hilton, who by this time had become stake president, regarded this as an answer to prayer.[15]

The erection of both California temples would not come until the period of international growth in Church membership and accelerated temple building during the 1950s and 1960s under the leadership of President David O. McKay.

At the dedication of the Swiss Temple in 1955, President David O. McKay specifically acknowledged gratitude to the Lord for answering prayers for guidance in selecting the site for that temple and for "overruling matters that brought about the consummation of this beautiful temple."[16]

In 1952 the First Presidency and the Twelve had decided that a temple should be erected in Europe, and the presidents of the missions there agreed that the temple should be located in or near Bern, the capital of Switzerland. President McKay approved a site, but despite several months of negotiations with the owners no definite agreement could be reached. "Finally, during a sleepless night in October" the Swiss Mission president, Samuel E. Bringhurst, recalled, "the thought occurred that perhaps there was a reason for the delay, and that we should pray for a decision, and leave the matter with the Lord." He therefore asked all the missionaries to fast, "that we might receive a decision concerning the proposed temple site." The following day he was notified that the property was no longer for sale. "This answer so quickly, while a little disappointing, was a wonderful testimony to all of us."[17] The mission president reported these developments to President McKay, who replied:

> As I read your letter stating that all effort had failed and a negative decision had been rendered, I was not surprised, but at first disappointed; however, strangely enough, my disappointment soon disappeared and was replaced by an assurance that the Lord will overrule all transactions for the best good of his Church, not only in Switzerland but throughout Europe.[18]

Meanwhile, President Bringhurst and his real estate agent found another property site in the Bern area. "As we walked over it," President Bringhurst testified, "all doubt seemed to leave and we felt certain we were on the site the Lord wished for the first European temple. . . . At this time we learned why the Lord did not allow us to purchase the first site." The construction of a new highway preempted the key section of the original site. The new property included twice the area and was purchased for half the cost.

At about this same time, steps were being taken to obtain a temple site in the South Pacific. In 1954 President McKay appointed Wendell B. Mendenhall, who was then directing the Church's Pacific building program, to a special confidential mission to investigate possible temple sites. Elder Mendenhall looked over various properties in New Zealand, but did not feel satisfied that he had seen the temple site yet. He related:

> Then one day I felt I should go to Hamilton to visit the college. While in the car on the way, the whole thing came to me in an instant: The temple should be there by the college. The Church facilities for construction were already there, and that was the center of the population of the mission. Then, in my mind, I could see the area even before I arrived, and I could envision the hill where the temple should stand. As soon as I arrived at the college and drove over the top of the hill, my whole vision was confirmed. In my heart I felt that the Lord had especially made this hill for his temple, everything about it was so majestic and beautiful.

About ten days later President McKay arrived in Hamilton. Elder Mendenhall first met him in the presence of others, so nothing could be said about the question of a temple site. Elder Mendenhall described their first visit to the hill:

> As we drove up the road, there was that noble hill. We directed our travel around the back of it to the farm lands. After we stepped from the car and were looking around, President McKay called me to one side. By the way he was looking at the hill, I could tell immediately what was on his mind. I had not said a word to him. He asked, "What do you think? I knew what his question implied, and I simply asked in return, "What do you think, President McKay?" And then in an almost

prophetic tone he pronounced, "This is the place to build the temple."

The owners of this choice hill had previously indicated that they did not wish to sell their property. One morning, following President McKay's departure from New Zealand, Elder Mendenhall again met with them. They still were not willing to sell. By afternoon, however, Elder Mendenhall had convinced them to change their minds. His account continues:

> Elder [George] Biesinger [supervisor of Church construction in New Zealand] and I had gone over the property very thoroughly and had put a valuation on it by breaking it down into various lots and acres. We met with the attorney and he overpriced the property considerably. After discussing the matter for about an hour, he said, "Would you be willing to consider this purchase if I break this property down my way and arrive at its valuation?" And we hazarded the chance and said, "Yes."
>
> He figured the property his way, not knowing what was in our hearts or that we had our own valuation on paper in our pockets. He passed his paper to us. We looked at it. It was exactly the same figure, right to the penny, we had figured that morning before going to his office. At five-thirty that evening we had the signed papers.[19]

Worldwide Expansion in Temple Building

The 1970s was a decade unprecedented in terms of the amount of temple construction. The Washington Temple, the largest erected in the present dispensation, was dedicated in 1974. Not only did it include six lecture rooms for presenting the endowment, but it was the second twentieth-century temple to have the large priesthood assembly room on an upper floor. A year earlier, the Arizona and St. George temples closed for renovation. They were redesigned to present the endowment by means of motion pictures. So complete was the rebuilding that in 1975 the Arizona and then the St. George temples were reopened for public open houses and then rededicated, the first time this had ever been done. The Hawaii and Logan temples were similarly remodeled and rededicated later in the decade.

The Washington D. C. Temple, completed in 1974, is the largest temple built by the Church in this dispensation. (Church Visual Resources Library)

The year 1975 also brought the announcement of three new temples—São Paulo, Brazil, the first in South America; Tokyo, the first in Asia; and Seattle, the first in the Pacific Northwest. Latter-day Saints in these and other scattered areas around the world had eagerly looked forward to a time when they might have a temple and temple blessings closer at hand. ("I have an important announcement," President Spencer W. Kimball began at the 1975 Brazil area conference, even before the opening hymn or prayer. The Saints gave him their full attention. "A temple will be built in Brazil," he announced, as a painting of the future temple was unveiled. A gasp could be heard throughout the hall. "It will be built [here] in São Paulo." By then tears filled the eyes of many as they wept for joy.)[20] In

1977 temple plans were also announced for Mexico City and American Samoa, and in 1978 for the Jordan River Temple in the southern part of the Salt Lake Valley. This temple-building decade climaxed with the 1980 announcement of seven new temples. They were to be built in Atlanta (first in the southeastern United States), Argentina, Chile, Australia, Tonga, Tahiti, and Western Samoa (the site having been shifted from American Samoa when the decision was made to erect several temples in the South Pacific instead of only one). President Spencer W. Kimball declared: "There now begins the most intense period of temple building in the history of the Church. We look to the day when the sacred ordinances of the Church, performed in the temples, will be available to all members of the Church in convenient locations around the globe."[21]

Consistent with this expectation, Church leaders in the early 1980s would announce plans to construct yet more temples, even including one behind the Iron Curtain in East Germany. An unprecedented number of temples (six) would be dedicated during 1983. By mid-1984 there would still be twenty-one more temples either being planned or under construction. Prior to President Kimball's administration, the record had been three temples being built at once—when the Salt Lake, Logan, and Manti temples were under construction during the 1880s. Completion of these new temples would bring the total to forty-seven—compared to only fifteen in service when President Kimball began his administration. Furthermore, for the first time in the Church's history, temples would be located on every continent.

This increase in the number of temples was made possible by building much smaller structures, as President David O. McKay had anticipated over a quarter-century earlier. The largest of these new temples would be only the size of a typical stake center.[22]

Prior to this time, many families in widely scattered parts of the world had sacrificed most of their material possessions in order to make the once-in-a-lifetime trip to their nearest, yet distant, temple: Almost a full year's wages were required to take a Tahitian family to the New Zealand Temple. A shoemaker in Costa Rica had to sell his automobile and his full stock of shoes in order to take his wife and seven children to the Mesa Temple so that their family might be sealed for eternity; during the eight-thousand-mile round trip their group had to sleep in chapel cultural halls each night and change buses every time they crossed into a new country. These and other Saints in similar circumstances were willing to make such sacrifices because of their burning desire to receive the sacred blessings available only in temples. In some countries, such as Korea, governmental restriction on travel actually prevented couples from leaving the country at the same time, making it impossible for them to be sealed. In other cases, parents with limited funds had to make the painful decision of which of their children they would be able to take with them to the temple.[23] As the new temples began to dot the earth, such sacrifices became increasingly unnecessary. Derek Metcalfe, director of temples, anticipated that a new kind of sacrifice would now be required. "As more temples are built worldwide, the sacrifice will be one of time as members attend local temples with far greater frequency."[24]

The Genealogical Society and Its Programs

As early as 1842 Joseph Smith had warned that "the earth will be smitten with a curse unless there is a welding link of some kind or other between the fathers and the children. . . . For we without them cannot be made perfect; neither can they without us be made perfect." (D&C 128:18.) The Prophet also taught that "the greatest responsibility in this world that God has laid upon us is to seek after our dead," and that "those Saints who neglect it" do so "at the peril of their own salvation."[25] The Latter-day Saints consequently went to work seeking genealogical records of their forbears. In 1888 the *Deseret News* created the "Latter-day Saints' Genealogical Bureau" to promote the cooperative sharing of information. Many of the Saints came to feel that they should be "adopted" or sealed to prominent Church leaders as a means of assuring eventual exaltation. In 1894, however, President Wilford Woodruff in general conference made the following statement:

> When I went before the Lord to know who I should be adopted to (we were then being adopted to prophets and apostles), the Spirit of God said to me, "Have you not a father, who begot you?" "Yes, I have." "Then why not honor him? Why not be adopted to him?"

President Woodruff then instructed:

> We want the Latter-day Saints from this time to trace their genealogies as far as they can, and to be sealed to their fathers and mothers. Have children sealed to their parents, and run this chain through as far as you can get it. This is the will of the Lord to his people.[26]

In November of that same year a group of top Church leaders met and organized the Genealogical Society of Utah (renamed Genealogical Society of the Church in 1944 and more recently known as the Genealogical Department) with the purpose of establishing and maintaining a genealogical library for the use of Church members and others, and of disseminating information on genealogical matters.[27]

Growth of the Society

From this early beginning, the Church's Genealogical Society has grown in stature and holdings to become recognized internationally as one of the major genealogical organizations of the world.

In 1911, Nephi Anderson, an early leader in the Church's genealogical activities, prophesied remarkable future growth:

> I see the records of the dead and their histories gathered from every nation under heaven to one great central library in Zion—the largest and best equipped for its particular work in the world. Branch libraries may be established in the nations, but in Zion will be the records of last resort and final authority. Trained genealogists will find constant work in all nations having unpublished records, searching among the archives for families and family connections. Then, as temples multiply, and the work enlarges to its ultimate proportions, this Society, or some organization growing out of this Society, will have in its care some elaborate, but perfect system of exact registration and checking, so that the work in the temples may be con-

ducted without confusion or duplication. And so throughout the years, reaching into the Millennium of peace, this work of salvation will go on, until every worthy soul that can be found from earthly records will have been searched out and officiated for; and then the unseen world will come to our aid, the broken links will be joined, the tangled threads will be placed in order, and the purposes of God in placing salvation within the reach of all will have been consummated.[28]

Use of the microfilm made the fulfillment of Anderson's prophecy possible. Genealogical Society cameras have filmed vital records all over the world, making available information which otherwise would likely have remained inaccessible. This project began in the eastern United States just before the outbreak of World War II. Expansion overseas had to wait until the years immediately following the close of the conflict. Microfilming has been carried on in Europe, Latin America, the South Pacific, the Far East, and even behind the Iron Curtain. By the end of 1980, the Society's library included 1,024,000 hundred-foot rolls of microfilm, equivalent to 4,927,000 volumes of three hundred pages each. At that time it was acquiring records from thirty-six countries.[29] The advent of the microfilm also made the establishment of branch libraries practical. Beginning in 1964, the number of these branches has grown to well over two hundred. Microfilm copies of materials in the main library can be circulated inexpensively as needed.[30] In 1968 some 140,000 patrons used the facilities of the main library in Salt Lake City, while 212,000 utilized the branches.

One of the Genealogical Department's major tasks is to procure and organize the records that identify persons for whom ordinances are performed in the temples. Earlier, as more temple work was performed, the duplication of these ordinances had increased. To solve this problem, data was copied by hand from temple records onto index cards. This tremendous task began in 1922. This project led to the creation of the Temple Records Index Bureau in 1924. Beginning three years later, it checked all records for accuracy and duplication before clearing names for temple ordinance work.

The computer has become an indispensable tool in genealogical research. When in 1961 more names were needed for the temples, Genealogical Society employees extracted vital information from selected parish and civil records. These names were then automatically alphabetized and printed by the computer. This "records tabulation" program generated hundreds of thousands of additional names for temple work.

In 1969 the "name tabulation" program enabled Church members to submit names of individual ancestors for computer processing. Heretofore only names grouped into families had been accepted for temple work. This greater freedom allowed the Saints to accelerate their genealogical activity, so many more names were added to the Church's growing computerized International Genealogical Index.

Encouraging the Saints' Genealogical Activity

Over the years the Genealogical Society sponsored classes, published instructions, and in other ways sought to stimulate Church members' involvement in genealogical activity. In 1965, Church leaders challenged individuals to fill out family group forms for the seven families in the first three generations of their pedigrees. Church officials hoped that this practical experience with actual genealogical forms might spark an interest in further family research and would also generate additional names for temple work, resulting in an extensive file of genealogical information to aid future researchers.[31] During the following year, those who had completed this assignment were challenged to complete the eight family group forms corresponding to the fourth generation of their pedigrees.

In 1974, Church leaders stressed two other basic responsibilities. Latter-day Saints were to keep a personal or family "book of remembrance," which should be a sacred history of spiritual, ecclesiastical, or other significant experiences. The Saints were also to see that temple blessings were made available to all members of their immediate as well as direct-line ancestral families. A record of completed ordinances was to be included in the book of remembrance.[32]

By the mid-1970s, more than three million endowments for the dead were being performed annually, but less than one million names were being supplied by the Latter-day Saints' own genealogical research. The difference was being made up through the records tabulation program by staff members of the Genealogical Department at Church headquarters. The General Authorities felt the need to increase the amount of temple work, but even more to expand the Saints' role in providing names for temple ordinances. In 1978 President Spencer W. Kimball declared:

> I feel the same sense of urgency about temple work for the dead as I do about the missionary work for the living, since they are basically one and the same. I have told my brethren of the General Authorities that this work for the dead is constantly on my mind.
>
> The First Presidency and the Council of the Twelve recently gave careful consideration as to how we can lengthen our stride in this tremendously important responsibility. We announce a twofold emphasis.
>
> First, all members should write a personal history and participate in a family organization. Also, we want to emphasize again and place squarely upon the shoulders of these individuals and their families the obligation to complete the four-generation program. Families may extend their pedigree beyond the four generations if desired.
>
> Secondly, we are introducing a Church-wide program of extracting names from genealogical records. Church members may now render second-mile service through participating in this regard in extracting these names in this program supervised by the priesthood leaders at the local level.[33]

Church leaders subsequently explained that the four-generation assignment should be completed by families rather than by individuals. Adult brothers and sisters and their parents would verify the accuracy and completeness of the family group forms, and then submit them with their pedigree charts for at least four generations. This information was to become the basis of a new "ancestral file" compiled by the Genealogical Department.[34]

Because duplication of ancestral lines compounds, and because genealogical records are much more difficult to locate beyond the fourth generation, research beyond this point can best be done by the whole Church working together rather than by individual families. Rather than several individual members searching endless hours for the same records, volunteers would extract all names from the original record. These names, Elder J. Thomas Fyans explained, would then be alphabetized by the computer in "telephone book" fashion for easy reference.[35] The Saints' involvement in this "extraction" program would help achieve the goal of each temple district supplying its own names for temple ordinance work. Furthermore, "temple service centers" were established in conjunction with the São Paulo, Tokyo, and Mexico City temples to expedite the local processing of these names for temple work.[36] Elder Boyd K. Packer looked forward to the time when the computer would make clearing names for temple ordinances as easy as making an airplane reservation over the phone.[37] Thus, such modern tools as the microfilm and the computer have made almost limitless what can be accomplished in uniting families and providing for them the ordinances of exaltation.

21 Spencer W. Kimball and His Administration

Because of Elder Spencer W. Kimball's former battles with health problems, some Latter-day Saints conjectured that his administration would be even shorter than the previous two, and that it would bring little in the way of new developments or progress. Those who entertained such ideas were in for a great surprise. Few periods in Church history have witnessed more significant developments than has the administration of President Spencer W. Kimball.

Earlier Life

Although he was born in Salt Lake City, Spencer W. Kimball spent his formative years in the Gila Valley of southeastern Arizona. His life was not easy, but it was full of character-building experiences. Elder Boyd K. Packer wrote:

> The Lord . . . was not just preparing a businessman, nor a civic leader, nor a speaker, nor a poet, nor a musician, nor a teacher—though he would be all of these. He was preparing a father, a patriarch for his family, an apostle and prophet, and a president for His church. There were testings along the way—examinations in courage and patience, that few would have passed.[1]

1895	March 28: Born in Salt Lake City, Utah
1898	May: The Kimball family moved to Thatcher, Arizona (age 3)
1906	Patriarchal blessing promised him a great work among the Lamanites; October 18: His mother died (11)
1914	June 6: Ordained a priest by his father, Andrew Kimball; September 15: Ordained an elder; October 16: Ordained a seventy by his uncle, President J. Golden Kimball of the First Council of the Seventy; October 16: Called to the Swiss-Austrian Mission, but due to World War I was sent to the Central States Mission (19)
1918	January 1: Named stake clerk of the St. Joseph Stake; entered banking business (22)
1924	Called as second counselor in the stake presidency (29)
1934	Released as counselor and sustained again as clerk of the St. Joseph Stake (39)
1938	Called as president of the Mount Graham Stake (42)
1943	Sustained as a member of the Quorum of the Twelve (48)
1946	Appointed as chairman of the Church Indian Committee (51)
1957	One and one-half vocal cords removed due to throat cancer (62)
1969	*The Miracle of Forgiveness* published (74)
1972	Underwent open heart surgery (77)

These trials included suffering a facial paralysis for several months as a boy, and losing his mother when he was only eleven years old.

Following his return from the Central States Mission, Spencer married Camilla Eyring, who was teaching school in the area. He soon became a community leader as he entered banking, real estate, and related enterprises. Church responsibilities also came to him early. These he accepted willingly, and through them he enriched the lives of many. When he was only twenty-three years of age, his father, Andrew Kimball, who was president of the St. Joseph Stake, called Spencer to be the stake clerk. At that time, this position was very demanding, because stake clerks were required to handle many financial and reporting matters later taken over by the Presiding Bishopric. A few years later Andrew Kimball died, and the new stake president called Spencer to be one of his counselors. Spencer later recalled:

> Some of my relatives came to President Grant, unknown to me, after I had been chosen, and said, "President Grant, it's a mistake to call a young man like that to a position of responsibility and make an old man of him and tie him down." Finally, after some discussion, President Grant said very calmly, but firmly, "Well, Spencer has been called to this work, and he can do as he pleases about it," and, of course, when the call came, I accepted it gladly, and I have received great blessings therefrom.[2]

For over ten years, Spencer served both as a counselor in the stake presidency and as stake clerk because no qualified replacement could be found for him as clerk. Finally, the stake president decided to release Spencer as a counselor and retain him as stake clerk. Although he would lose some of the responsibility and honor to which he had become accustomed as a member of the stake presidency, Spencer felt good about the change, as it didn't matter to him where he served. "I'd like to serve wherever I am called."[3] When the stake was divided just a few years later, Spencer became president of the new Mount Graham Stake. He was serving in this capacity when his call to the Apostleship came in 1943. Despite his excellent preparation, Spencer W. Kimball humbly felt unprepared for this high call. In his first general conference address, Elder Kimball described the period of soul searching through which he had just passed:

> As I came home at noon, my boy was answering the telephone and he said, "Daddy, Salt Lake City is calling."
> I had had many calls from Salt Lake City. They hadn't ever worried me like this one. I knew that I had no unfinished busi-

Elders Spencer W. Kimball (left) and Ezra Taft Benson are called to the Quorum of the Twelve Apostles in October 1943. (*Church News* photo)

ness in Salt Lake City, and the thought came over me quickly, "You're going to be called to an important position." Then I hurriedly swept it from my mind, because it seemed so unworthy and so presumptuous, and I had convinced myself that such a thing was impossible by the time that I heard President Clark's voice a thousand miles away saying: "Spencer, this is Brother Clark speaking. The brethren have just called you to fill one of the vacancies in the Quorum of the Twelve Apostles."

Like a bolt of lightning it came. I did a great deal of thinking in the brief moments that I was on the wire. There were quite a number of things said about disposing of my business, moving to headquarters, and other things to be expected of me. I couldn't repeat them all, my mind seemed to be traveling many paths all at once—I was dazed, almost numb with the shock; a picture of my life spread out before me. . . .

I sensed immediately my inability and limitations and I cried back, "Not me, Brother Clark! You can't mean that!" I was virtually speechless. My heart pounded fiercely.[4]

During the next several weeks Spencer went to all those with whom he had had business dealings, wanting to be sure before he embarked on his new calling that everything was right between him and them. This was also a period of spiritual preparation.

I remember reading that Jacob wrestled all night, "until the breaking of the day," for a blessing; and I want to tell you that for eighty-five nights I have gone through that experience, wrestling for a blessing. Eighty-five times, the breaking of the day has found me on my knees praying to the Lord to help me and strengthen me and make me equal to this great responsibility that has come to me.[5]

On one occasion during this period, Elder Kimball went fasting to the top of a high mountain in order to be alone.

Hot tears came flooding down my cheeks as I made no effort to mop them up. I was accusing myself, and condemning myself and upbraiding myself. I was praying aloud for special blessings from the Lord. I was telling Him that I had not asked for this position, that I was incapable of doing the work, that I was imperfect and weak and human, that I was unworthy of so noble a calling, though I had tried hard and my heart had been right. . . .

. . . There was one great desire, to get a testimony of my calling, to know that it was not human and inspired by ulterior motives, kindly as they might be. How I prayed! How I suffered! How I wept! How I struggled!

After several hours of pleading, the desired answer came.

My tears were dry, my soul was at peace. A calm feeling of assurance came over me, doubt and questionings subdued. It was as though a great burden had been lifted. . . . I felt nearer my Lord than ever at any time in my life.[6]

With his background in banking, Elder Kimball became an important member of the committees that prayerfully considered how the sacred tithing funds of the Church should be spent. Perhaps the assignment that was closest to his heart, however, was his appointment as chairman of the Church's Indian Committee. As has been seen, Elder Kimball regarded this calling as a fulfillment of his patriarchal blessing.

Elder Kimball's masterful discourses had a particularly powerful impact. Using vivid imagery, he effectively taught the Saints their responsibilities. In his near-poetic expressions he usually stressed one of two themes—the importance of personal purity, and the Saints' opportunity and obligation to work with the Lamanites. In one sermon, he described how a small parasitic plant had killed a large, beautiful tree. "How like the mistletoe is immorality. The killer plant starts with a sticky sweet berry. Once rooted, it sticks and grows—a leaf, a branch, a plant. It never starts mature and full grown. It is always transplanted in infancy." In the same talk he cautioned that sin does not seem repulsive at first:

> Who ever said that sin was not fun? Who ever claimed that Lucifer was not handsome, persuasive, easy, friendly? Who ever said that sin was unattractive, undesirable, or nauseating in its acceptance? Transgression wears elegant gowns and sparkling apparel. It is highly perfumed, has attractive features, a soft voice.[7]

On another occasion he counseled:

> Sinful habits may be compared to a river which flows slowly and placidly at first, then gains speed as it nears the falls over the precipice. . . . In the stream of sin, it is relatively easy to repent at first, but as the sin becomes more and more entrenched the overcoming becomes increasingly difficult.
>
> If one ignores the roar of the falls below, he is doomed; if he will not listen to the warnings given him, he is sucked into the swift current to destruction.[8]

Elder Kimball likewise used a graphic comparison to teach Church members their responsibility to assist the Lamanites:

> A sail plane furnishes thrills and exhilarating experience to pilots in the great empty sky. . . .
> But there is one thing the glider lacks. It has no engine; it cannot lift itself into the sky. An airplane tows it aloft some two

or three thousand feet and the tow line is cut loose and the glider is then free to soar and to bank and to rise and to descend.

The sail plane is like the Lamanite; the tow plane, like the gospel and the Church; the tow line, like the programs of the Church. . . .

The Lamanite must have initial help—a power beyond himself. The Church and its people can give this lift. The organizations of the Church and its individuals can tow them aloft. We shall not need to worry much about them after they are soaring in the clouds and have the feel of accomplishment and security.[9]

Serious health problems plagued Elder Kimball during his adult years. Following his call to the Twelve, he suffered a series of heart attacks, and the doctors ordered him to have more rest. He chose to spend several weeks with some of his Indian friends at their camp among the pines in the northern Arizona mountains.

One morning he was missing from camp. When he did not return for breakfast, Brother Polacca and other Indian friends began to search. They found him several miles from camp, sitting beneath a large pine tree with his Bible open to the last chapter of the Gospel of John. In answer to their worried looks, he said, "Six years ago today I was called to be an Apostle of the Lord Jesus Christ. And I just wanted to spend the day with Him whose witness I am."[10]

In 1951 his voice was remarkably restored through a blessing by three General Authority colleagues. Six years later, however, throat cancer was diagnosed, and the doctors recommended that Elder Kimball's vocal cords be removed in order to save his life. He feared that the operation might rob him of his voice altogether, that never again could he bear his testimony as a special witness for Jesus Christ. "Shall I ever speak at another temple dedication?" he agonized. "Shall I ever preach again?" He wondered what he could do after the operation. "Shall I ever fit into the program again, the great work to which I was called by the Lord through President Heber J. Grant back in 1943?" Following much prayer and fasting, Elder Kimball underwent the operation, which proved to be less radical than had originally been thought necessary. Nevertheless, Elder Kimball continued to worry: "Will I ever return to [full] activity with the loss of my vocal cord and my weak, poor voice? Will the Brethren give me service? Will my gruff fringe voice be an affront to the people?"[11]

A long period of recuperation and readjustment followed. Elder Boyd K. Packer, a colleague in the Quorum of the Twelve, later recalled: "The [old] voice was all but gone, but a new one took its place. A quiet, persuasive, mellow voice, an acquired voice, an appealing voice, a voice that is loved by the Latter-day Saints."[12]

In 1972, when earlier heart ailments flared up again, Elder Kimball underwent a particularly complicated open-heart operation. With the faith of many and through the outstanding skill of a devoted Latter-day Saint surgeon, Dr. Russell M. Nelson (a future member of the Twelve), Elder Kimball's life was again spared.

These difficulties did not stop Spencer W. Kimball from setting an example of devoting long hours of hard work to his calling. "Prominently displayed on President Kimball's desk," observed Elder Robert L. Simpson, "is a slogan which reads simply, 'DO IT.' With this inspired leader, personal convenience comes second. Everything is done to meet the Lord's convenience."[13] His example for work has become legend and established an example for us all to follow. For instance, sixteen- to eighteen-hour days were not uncommon. Many times while traveling to conferences, he would have his portable typewriter in his lap, papers spread out on the seat beside him, so he could take advantage of every minute to answer the many letters he had received.

His personal character and all these experiences helped to prepare Spencer W. Kimball to meet the challenge of giving leadership to the whole Church worldwide.

President Kimball's Dynamic Administration

Following the unexpected death of President Harold B. Lee on December 26, 1973, Spencer W. Kimball became the twelfth President of the Church. "We will, in large measure,"

The First Presidency and the President of the Quorum of the Twelve speak to the press about their hopes for the future as they assume Church leadership in December 1973. Pictured are (from left) N. Eldon Tanner, Spencer W. Kimball, Marion G. Romney, and Ezra Taft Benson.

he humbly announced, "carry forward the same program, which we have helped in a small way to make. . . ." President Kimball continued: "I anticipate no major changes in the immediate future, but do hope to give increased emphasis to some of the programs already established."[14] Despite this modest declaration, President Kimball's administration would be noted for numerous and significant innovations.

"Lengthen Our Stride"

Rapid Church growth continued. As President Kimball's administration began, Church membership exceeded 3.3 million, having doubled in the last fourteen years. In his first Presidential address to the Regional Representatives, he challenged the Church to "lengthen our stride" in carrying the gospel to *all* the earth. As was seen in chapter 14, President Kimball outlined how this could be done. Elder W. Grant Bangerter recalled that many who came to the Regional Representatives seminar recalled the powerful leadership of President Harold

1973	December 30: Ordained and set apart as the President of the Church (age 78)
1974	April 4: Gave a major address to Regional Representatives of the Twelve on expanding missionary work (79)
1975	Announced plans for temple construction in Brazil, Japan, Mexico, and Washington State; rededicated the renovated Arizona and St. George temples (80)
1976	Two visions added to standard works of the Church; Assistants to the Twelve became members of the First Quorum of the Seventy
1977	February-March: Conducted area conferences in Mexico, Guatemala, Costa Rica, Peru, Chile, Bolivia, and Colombia (81); August 24: Dedicated the land of Poland (82)
1978	Announced revelation extending priesthood blessings to all worthy male members (83); BYU performing group tours Soviet Union for first time; emeritus status given to designated General Authorities
1979	Thousandth stake organized at Nauvoo; new edition of Bible published with LDS study aids
1980	Sesquicentennial commemorated; ward meetings consolidated; construction of seven new temples announced

B. Lee, and were lamenting that "things would not be the same." These apprehensions, however, were soon dispelled.

As he [President Kimball] proceeded with his address, however, he had not spoken very long when a new awareness seemed suddenly to fall on the congregation. We became alert to an astonishing spiritual presence, and we realized that we were listening to something unusual, powerful, different from any of our previous meetings. It was as if, spiritually speaking, our hair began to stand on end. Our minds were suddenly vibrant and marveling at the transcendent message that was coming to our ears. With a new perceptiveness we realized that

President Kimball was opening spiritual windows and beckoning to us to come and gaze with him on the plans of eternity. It was as if he were drawing back the curtains which covered the purpose of the Almighty and inviting us to view with him the destiny of the gospel and the vision of its ministry.

When President Kimball concluded his address, having spoken for over forty-five minutes, President Ezra Taft Benson echoed the feelings of all present as he declared with a voice filled with emotion: "Truly there is a prophet in Israel."[15]

In order to promote this worldwide expansion of the gospel, President Kimball called David M. Kennedy to be a special consultant on diplomatic affairs. Kennedy, who had served in a stake presidency in Chicago, had ample background for his significant new assignment. He had been chairman of the board and chief executive officer of one of the United States banks most heavily engaged in international business. He had also served as Secretary of the Treasury and as ambassador at large for the United States. In succeeding years he played a key role working with governments of many nations in order to resolve problems which had hindered the Church's activities there.[16] He was instrumental in arranging for mature couples to serve as "special representatives" of the Church in countries where traditional missionary work was not yet possible. An outstanding achievement in 1977 was the granting of legal status and the official recognition of the Church in Poland. This came as the result of efforts by local Latter-day Saints and through several visits by David M. Kennedy to Polish government officials. This, in turn, opened the way for a visit by President Kimball to Warsaw where he "dedicated the land of Poland and blessed its people that the work of the Lord might go forth."[17]

Similar negotiations with the government of Israel led to the Church's developing the five-acre Orson Hyde Memorial Garden on the western slope of the Mount of Olives, overlooking the old city of Jerusalem.[18] President Kimball had expressed the feeling that the time had come for the Jewish people to receive the gospel. Consequently a special series of discussions were developed for the use of missionaries. Emphasizing a spiritual rather than intellectual approach, they taught that Joseph Smith's experience was consistent with that of the Old

President Spencer W. Kimball (center), his wife, and their traveling companions are accompanied by Minister Kazimierz Kakol (next to President Kimball) and other Polish officials during an August 1977 visit to dedicate the land of Poland for the preaching of the gospel. (Photo from the personal journal of President Spencer W. Kimball)

Testament prophets, that the Book of Mormon is a second record of God's dealings with the house of Israel, and that Jesus Christ is the prophesied Messiah. These were not designed primarily for use in the country of Israel, where proselyting is restricted, but rather with the large Jewish populations in major United States cities and elsewhere around the world.[19]

President Kimball gave emphasis to the importance of every young man being worthy and prepared to serve a mission. In 1976, the Language Training Mission moved into a beautiful new multibuilding complex near Brigham Young University campus. Two years later, all missionaries, including those who did not need to learn a foreign language, began receiving their instruction at this facility, which was renamed the Missionary Training Center. At this same time, new missionary orientation centers were established at such locations as in

Brazil, Chile, Mexico, New Zealand, and Japan in order to enhance the preparation of local young men and women called to serve in those areas.

Student performing groups from Brigham Young University became another effective means of building good will for the Church. In 1978 the Young Ambassadors presented their music and dance variety shows in Poland and the Soviet Union. Before their tour, the performers spent several weeks studying the cultures and languages of the peoples they would visit. They learned enough to announce their numbers in the local language and to greet members of the audience individually following the performances. They were eager to communicate the spirit of the gospel by setting a good example and by radiating a feeling of heartfelt love. In both countries the performers were well received and were permitted to tape an extended program for later release on nationwide television. In the following year, another group of Young Ambassadors made similar preparation for a tour of mainland China. Here again their performances were highly appreciated, whether by the working people at impromptu performances in factories, or by those able to attend presentations in the most prestigious concert halls of the country.[20]

Perhaps nothing has had a greater impact on the worldwide spread of the Church than did the 1978 revelation received through President Kimball extending the priesthood to worthy males of all races. Over a period of several months the General Authorities had discussed this topic at length in their regular temple meetings. In addition, President Kimball frequently went to the temple, especially on Saturdays and Sundays when he could be there alone to plead for guidance. "I wanted to be sure," he reflected later.

Then, on June 1, 1978, nearly all the General Authorities gathered, fasting, for their regular monthly meeting in the temple. After this three-hour meeting, which was filled with spiritual uplift and enlightenment, President Kimball invited his counselors and the Twelve to remain while the other General Authorities were excused. When the First Presidency and the Twelve were alone, he again brought up the possibility of conferring the priesthood on worthy brethren of all races. He expressed the hope that there might be a clear answer received one way or the other. "At this point," Elder Bruce R. McConkie recalled, "President Kimball asked the brethren if any of them desired to express their feelings and views as to the matter in hand. We all did so, freely and fluently and at considerable length, each person stating his views and manifesting the feelings of his heart. There was a marvelous outpouring of unity, oneness, and agreement in the council."[21] After a two-hour discussion, President Kimball asked the group to unite in formal prayer and modestly suggested that he act as voice. He recalled:

> . . . I told the Lord if it wasn't right, if He didn't want this change to come in the Church that I would be true to it all the rest of my life, and I'd fight the world . . . if that's what He wanted. . . . I had a great deal to fight, myself largely, because I had grown up with this thought that Negroes should not have the priesthood and I was prepared to go all the rest of my life till my death and fight for it and defend it as it was. But this revelation and assurance came to me so clearly that there was no question about it.[22]

Elder McConkie described what happened:

> It was during this prayer that the revelation came. The Spirit of the Lord rested mightily upon us all; we felt something akin to what happened on the day of Pentecost and at the dedication of the Kirtland Temple. From the midst of eternity, the voice of God, conveyed by the power of the Spirit, spoke to his prophet. . . . And we all heard the same voice, received the same message, and became personal witnesses that the word received was the mind and will and voice of the Lord.[23]

Reflecting on this experience, President Spencer W. Kimball and President Ezra Taft Benson and others of the Twelve concurred that none of them "had ever experienced anything of such spiritual magnitude and power as was poured out upon the Presidency and the Twelve that day in the upper room in the house of the Lord."[24]

The impact of this revelation was far-reaching. Faithful black Latter-day Saints rejoiced as they received long-hoped-for ordination to the priesthood, mission calls, calls to serve in bishoprics or stake presidencies, and, of course, the eternal blessings of the temple. In November 1978, just five months

Joseph Freeman, Jr., the first black to receive the priesthood following President Kimball's 1978 revelation, prizes with his family the blessings of the temple. (Photo by Eldon K. Linschoten)

after the revelation came, the First Presidency called two experienced couples to open missionary work in the black nations of Nigeria and Ghana.

The Church's rate of growth accelerated under the leadership of President Kimball. By the early 1980s over a quarter of a million new members were being added every year. In 1982 Church membership passed the five-million mark. This expansion resulted in several key administrative changes. The number of General Authorities continued to be expanded, and in 1976 the First Quorum of the Seventy was organized and took its place with the First Presidency and the Quorum of the Twelve in the revealed administrative structure of the Church. Members of this quorum became administrators of geographical areas, a new level of units introduced into the ecclesiastical chain of command. Then, in 1978, several members of this quorum were designated Emeritus General Authorities, and their workload reduced substantially. Changes were also made in the pattern of conferences conducted by the General Authorities: General conferences were shortened from three days to two, auxiliary conferences at Church headquarters were eliminated, area conferences became more numerous for a time, and the number of stake conferences was cut in halves —reduced from four to two a year. These changes, which eased the load carried by the General Authorities, will be considered in depth in later chapters.

Developments in modern technology also had a profound impact on Church administration. For years the availability of jet aircraft had enabled the General Authorities to travel to distant parts of the world within a matter of hours. The perfection of satellite communication provided a new medium by which Church members could receive counsel from the General Authorities.

Activity Patterns Reshaped

President Kimball's administration also witnessed a significant reshaping of Latter-day Saint activity patterns. As has been seen, regular weekly meetings of local congregations were consolidated in 1980 into a single three-hour block on Sundays. This step was taken at a time when a worldwide energy shortage had caused travel and heating costs to soar. This change, however, was not just an economizing measure. The consolidation enabled families to spend more time together and permitted the Saints to reach out through greater participation in community affairs.

The worldwide expansion in temple building, discussed in the previous chapter, accelerated dramatically under President Kimball's leadership. Previous to his Presidency, no more than three temples had been under construction at any one time. Announcements of new temples by President Kimball, however, pushed the total of temples being planned or under construction to twenty-two in 1982.

As has been seen, this increase in temple building was accompanied by a new direction in the Saints' genealogical responsibility. Here, again, modern technology had its impact. Using computers, the name extraction program, introduced in 1978, made the gathering of names much more efficient. As noted in the previous chapter, President Kimball declared that he felt "the same sense of urgency about temple work for the dead" as he did about "missionary work for the living."[25]

The standard works of the Church underwent significant development in at least two ways under President Kimball's leadership. First, three new items were added to the scriptural canon—the first additions to the standard works in nearly three-quarters of a century. Two of these additions, which became sections 137 and 138 of the Doctrine and Covenants, shed light on the subject of life after death. Concerning their importance, Elder Bruce R. McConkie declared: "Their contents have been known; their provisions have been in force; their principles have been widely taught. But now, at this hour, with their addition to the formal scriptures of the saints, they become a new commandment—they become a new divine pronouncement both to say and to do all that is required in the soul-expanding doctrine of salvation for the dead."[26] The third new item to be added was the official announcement of President Kimball's 1978 revelation on priesthood. Reflecting on these additions to the scriptures, Elder McConkie said: "Nothing is better known or more greatly appreciated than the fact that the canon of scripture is not now and never will be full. God speaks and his people hear. His words and his works are without end; they never close."[27]

The issuing of new editions constituted the second major scripture-related development of President Kimball's administration. In 1979, a new edition of the King James Bible appeared. Although the biblical text itself was not changed, this new edition featured an improved footnote system, references to related passages in the other standard works, more meaningful chapter headings, a 598-page Topical Guide and concordance, and a 194-page dictionary section that reflects unique understandings available through latter-day revelation. Two years later a new edition of the Book of Mormon, the Doctrine and Covenants, and the Pearl of Great Price "triple combination" became a companion to the new edition of the Bible. It contained many of the same improvements. Elder Boyd K. Packer regarded these improvements as extremely important:

> These references from the four volumes of scripture constitute the most comprehensive compilation of scriptural information on the mission and teachings of the Lord Jesus Christ that has ever been assembled in the history of the world. . . .
>
> With the passing of years, these scriptures will produce successive generations of faithful Christians who know the Lord Jesus Christ and are disposed to obey His will. . . .
>
> . . . They will develop a gospel scholarship beyond that which their forebears could achieve. . . .
>
> As the generations roll on, this will be regarded, in the perspective of history, as the crowning achievement in the administration of President Spencer W. Kimball.[28]

A Warning Voice

When the mantle of the Church's presidency fell upon Spencer W. Kimball, his speaking style shifted noticeably. Whereas previously he would devote an entire talk to developing a single theme, as prophet he felt the responsibility to raise a warning voice on a variety of concerns. He declared that a major problem facing the Church was worldliness, "the pattern of life to which too many of our people gear their lives. . . . The encroachment of the world into our lives is threatening! How hard it seems for many of us to live in the world and yet not of the world. . . . You have come here [to conference] seeking guidance. It is the purpose of your leaders to give that direction. As the brethren speak, you will feel the inspiration of our Lord. The gospel gives purpose in our lives. It is the way to happiness."[29]

President Kimball sounded a clear trumpet call, giving the Saints the guidance and direction they so badly needed in the face of worldly pressures. His keynote addresses at the first two general conferences after he became President of the Church each raised the warning voice on a wide range of topics. For example, he reaffirmed the Saints' political responsibilities to elect wise leaders and to obey constitutional law, and cautioned the Saints against allowing political differences to sow the seeds of disunity. He challenged the Saints to clean up and repair their homes and farms. He urged them to plant gardens, store food, and avoid waste. He also reminded them of the virtues of work, industry, and thrift. At the same time he urged the Saints to keep the Sabbath holy, refraining from shopping on that day. He decried the growing incidence of taking the name of the Lord in vain. "Profanity is the effort of a feeble brain to express itself forcibly." He counseled against the use of playing cards. He reminded the Saints of their long-standing belief in the Word of Wisdom, and declared that "the Church has consistently opposed the improper and harmful use of drugs or similar substances under circumstances which would result in addiction, physical or mental impairment or in lowering moral standards." He also warned the Saints to have nothing to do with apostate polygamy cults.

Many of President Kimball's teachings were centered in the family. "All normal people should marry," he declared. "(There could be a few exceptions.) All normal married couples should become parents." "We call upon all people to accept normal marriage as a basis for true happiness." President Kimball counseled that owning one's own home and avoiding debt brings stability to the family. He was concerned about other forces that tended to break families apart. "Most divorces are unwarranted and come of weakness and selfishness and often result in great unhappiness for the divorced persons and also almost irreparable damage and frustration to the unfavored children, who are torn and disturbed." He saw selfishness as a prime cause of family breakups. The Lord planned "for a father and a mother to rear their children. Certainly any who deprive their children of a parent will have some very stiff questions to answer." President Kimball saw immoral or improper use of the body as a major threat to family happiness: "The human body is the sacred home of the spirit child of God, and unwarranted tampering with or defilement of this sacred tabernacle can bring only remorse and regret. We urge: stay clean, uncontaminated, undefiled." Abortion was a related evil. "Certainly the terrible sin of premeditated abortion would be hard to justify. . . . We place it high on the list of sins against which we strongly warn the people."

The President also spoke out against the sin of homosexuality, the "unisex" attempts to blur the distinction between masculine and feminine, the practice of couples living together without marriage, and the performing of vasectomies as a means to limit the birth of children.

President Kimball gave special emphasis to the responsibility of parents to teach the gospel of Jesus Christ to their children, including such virtues as honor, integrity, and honesty. "The home is the teaching situation. Every father should talk to his son, every mother to her daughter. Then it would leave them totally without excuse should they ignore the counsel they have received." President Kimball particularly stressed the importance of the mother's role: "Motherhood is near to Divinity. It is the highest, holiest service to be assumed by mankind. It places her who honors its holy calling and service next to the angels."[30] Many of President Kimball's warnings ran diametrically counter to the prevalent norms of the world.

Under President Kimball's leadership, the Church responded to issues raised by the women's movement, which gained prominence during the 1970s. The Church's stand on the proposed Equal Rights Amendment has been considered in an earlier chapter. Although this stand was approved by the vast majority of Latter-day Saints, a small but vocal minority could not accept it.[31]

On the positive side, Church leaders were aware of the pressures facing Latter-day Saint women as more and more attention was focused on the role of women generally. Articles in national magazines increasingly extolled women who found fulfillment in business or professional careers, and saw traditional roles in the home as demeaning drudgery.

In 1978, the Church inaugurated annual meetings for women, preceding the fall general conferences. Like the priesthood sessions for men, these special sessions originated in the Salt Lake Tabernacle and were carried by closed circuit to hundreds of meetinghouses throughout the United States and in other countries. Speaking at the first of these sessions, President Spencer W. Kimball observed: "Much is said about the drudgery and confinement of the woman's role. This is not so. There is divinity in each new life, challenge in raising each child. Marriage is a partnership." He challenged the women to be full and contributing partners with their husbands in marriage. He urged women to have programs of self-improvement, to reach for new levels of achievement and self-fulfillment. "Let there be no question in your mind about your value as an individual. . . . We want our sisters to be scholars of the scriptures as well as our men."[32] Because many women would face the challenge of earning a living for themselves or for their families, Church leaders encouraged them to qualify themselves for this role through education, without losing sight of their primary role as mothers in the home.

Thus President Spencer W. Kimball came to be respected as a powerful leader who provided specific and timely counsel on the major questions and challenges facing the Saints. This leadership together with the far-reaching innovations during his administration made this an especially exciting and significant period of progress for the Church in the twentieth century.

22 The General Authorities

No study of the Church's progress in the modern era would be complete without a consideration of the General Authorities. The "Brethren" play a special role in directing Latter-day Saint affairs. Not only do they possess the usual qualifications of organizational executives, but all are accepted as inspired leaders and some are specifically sustained as "prophets, seers, and revelators." Although the basic structure of the Church's hierarchy was defined by revelations through the Prophet Joseph Smith during the early 1830s, there have been significant developments in later years, including the twentieth century.

Presiding Councils

At the time of the Church's sesquicentennial in 1980, four specific groups were sustained as General Authorities: the First Presidency, the Quorum of the Twelve, the First Quorum of the Seventy, and the Presiding Bishopric. During earlier years two other positions—Patriarch to the Church and Assistants to the Twelve—had also been included. Each of these offices had its specific responsibilities and functions in Church government.

The First Presidency

President Joseph Fielding Smith explained that the First Presidency constitutes the "supreme governing power of the Church," presiding over all other councils and quorums. He testified that members of the Presidency are the "living oracles of God" authorized to proclaim and interpret the doctrines and laws of the Church. "No part of the work of the Church is beyond their authority," he declared.[1] The pattern of a presidency at the head of the Church was seen in the New Testament. Three of the Twelve—Peter, James, and John—received special keys of authority on the Mount of Transfiguration (Matthew 17:1-3; see also D&C 7:7).

Latter-day revelations shed further light on the calling and authority of the mortal head of the Church. He actually holds two offices at once: President of the Church, and President of the High Priesthood or Presiding High Priest. He is to "preside over the whole church" and to be recognized as a "seer, a revelator, a translator, and a prophet, having all the gifts of God which he bestows upon the head of the Church." (See D&C 107:9, 65-66, and 91-92.) The First Presidency came into being in this dispensation in 1832 when Joseph Smith called two counselors to assist him in presiding over the Church.

The principles governing the selection of a new President of the Church were clarified just before the turn of the century. These were considered in chapter 1. Although the established pattern of succession is regarded as inspired, the Twelve still seek confirming inspiration each time they approach the selection of a new President. For example, Elder Bruce R. McConkie described the temple meeting following President Harold B. Lee's unexpected death in 1973:

> Each member of the Council in turn, specifically and pointedly, expressed himself to the effect that now was the time to reorganize the First Presidency of the Church, that there should not be further delay, that the effective and proper operation of this great organization that we have from the Lord needed this administrative arrangement. Each one in turn expressed himself that President Spencer W. Kimball [the senior Apostle and President of the Twelve] was the man whom the Lord wanted to

preside over the Church; there was no question whatever about that. There was total and complete unity and harmony. The prayer that was in the heart of every person present was "Lord, show unto thy servants whom thou hast chosen to be President of the Church." We did not want to do anything other than what the Lord wanted done.

President Young is quoted as having said, following the death of the Prophet, "I don't care who presides in the Church. All I want to know is what the Lord thinks about it." The Lord made manifest his will in that day, and that's all we wanted to know for our day. And when we met for this most recent reorganization, the Lord made manifest his will to us. It was as though the voice of God had said to each one of us individually and to all of us collectively: "Let my servant Spencer step forth and receive the full power of the presiding priesthood in my Church and kingdom."

And so after there had been full expression and consideration, Elder Ezra Taft Benson, the next one in seniority to President Kimball, made the formal motion that the First Presidency of the Church be reorganized; that President Spencer W. Kimball be sustained, ordained, and set apart as the President of the Church; as the prophet, seer, and revelator to the Church; and as the Trustee-in-Trust. This motion was adopted unanimously.

At this point President Kimball made a speech of acceptance—a very sweet, humble, appropriate expression. President Kimball was willing to accept the will of the Lord and the mantle of leadership that had fallen upon him.

At this point, he chose his first counselor, President N. Eldon Tanner, who responded appropriately and sweetly; he then chose President Marion G. Romney to be the second, who similarly responded. Following these appointments, Brother Benson was sustained as the President of the Council of the Twelve. And then all those present placed their hands upon the head of President Kimball, and he was ordained and set apart, with President Benson being mouth, to serve as President of the Church and as the prophet, seer, and revelator for this time and season.[2]

A new President may or may not select the same counselors as his predecessor. Presidents John Taylor and Joseph F. Smith selected new counselors; Joseph Fielding Smith retained only one of the former counselors; while Heber J. Grant,

George Albert Smith, and Spencer W. Kimball kept both. In one case the former First Counselor was called to be the new Second Counselor. If the senior Apostle has been called as First or Second Counselor in the First Presidency, he has still been sustained as President of the Twelve, and the next member of the Quorum in seniority has been sustained as Acting President of the Twelve.

Revelations in the Doctrine and Covenants specify that the basic structure of the First Presidency consists of the President and two counselors (see D&C 107:22, 124:25-26). As special circumstances have dictated, however, this group has been enlarged. On December 5, 1834, for example, Joseph Smith ordained Oliver Cowdery as "Assistant President."[3] At the time of the Church's organization in 1830, Oliver had been sustained as "second elder," next in authority to Joseph. He was now called not only to assist the Prophet in Church administration but also to stand as a second witness. Oliver Cowdery had been present with Joseph Smith when the priesthoods and keys had been restored. Then in 1841, following Cowdery's apostasy, the Prophet's brother Hyrum was called to occupy this position. The Lord promised to show Hyrum by revelation the things of which he was to bear record (see D&C 124:94-96). Thus the two brothers who were martyred at Carthage in 1844 were the two Presidents and also the two witnesses who sealed their testimonies with their blood. The special need for an Assistant President was thus fulfilled, and this office has not been continued.[4]

The First Presidency has also been expanded through the President's calling additional counselors. Joseph Smith called a total of six between 1837 and 1843, and in 1866 and 1873 Brigham Young also called six "assistant counselors." This pattern was not repeated for almost a century. In 1961 President David O. McKay called Elder Hugh B. Brown as an additional counselor; and when President J. Reuben Clark died a few months later, Elder Brown filled the vacancy as a regular counselor in the First Presidency. Then in 1965 President McKay called Elders Joseph Fielding Smith and Thorpe B. Isaacson, and in 1968 Elder Alvin R. Dyer, as additional counselors. They were released from this calling upon President McKay's death in 1970. No other additional counselors were appointed until 1981, when President Spencer W. Kimball named Elder Gordon B. Hinckley to this position.

The Quorum of the Twelve Apostles

The title of Apostle comes from the Greek word *apostolos,* a person sent forth. Jesus sent his original Twelve out to preach (see Matthew 10:5-42), and latter-day revelation identifies the Apostles as "special witnesses of the name of Christ in all the world" (D&C 107:23). Hence the Twelve have played a key role in the Church's worldwide missionary effort. The Twelve or "traveling presiding high council," were also to constitute an administrative body next in authority to the First Presidency and were responsible to "build up the church and regulate all the affairs of the same in all nations." (D&C 107:24 and 33.) "It is their right to know the truth and to have an abiding witness," President Joseph Fielding Smith affirmed. He explained that being "special witnesses" is "an exacting duty upon them, to know that Jesus Christ is in very deed the Only Begotten Son of God, the Redeemer of the world, and the Savior of all those who will confess their sins, repent, and keep his commandments."[5]

The Quorum of the Twelve together with the First Presidency constitute the administrative body that gives direction to the Church's activities worldwide. The group normally meets in the Salt Lake Temple each Thursday. President Spencer W. Kimball described the spirit and business of these meetings:

> When in a Thursday temple meeting, after prayer and fasting, important decisions are made, new missions and new stakes are created, new patterns and policies initiated, the news is taken for granted and possibly thought of as mere human calculations. But to those who sit in the intimate circles and hear the prayers of the prophet and the testimony of the man of God; to those who see the astuteness of his deliberations and the sagacity of his decisions and pronouncements, to them he is verily a prophet. To hear him conclude important new devel-

opments with such solemn expressions as "the Lord is pleased;" "that move is right;" "our Heavenly Father has spoken," is to know positively.[6]

President Harold B. Lee explained that once a month this meeting is expanded to include all of the General Authorities.

> . . . On the first Thursday of every month a very important meeting is held in an upper room of the temple where all the General Authorities come fasting. The first part of the meeting is a business meeting, at which time all proposals for new ideas or new methods or new undertakings are brought forward, after having been processed through the month preceding, for the perusal and consideration of all the General Authorities of the Church. At that meeting, then, action is taken, and by that action it then becomes the official action of the General Authorities of the Church—which must be considered to be the constitution of the Church and kingdom of God upon the earth.[7]

As has been the case with the First Presidency, the Quorum of the Twelve has been supplemented from time to time. Following Brigham Young's death in 1877, the two brethren who had served as his counselors in the First Presidency were sustained as counselors to the Twelve during the interval prior to the formation of a new First Presidency. Then in 1938 when Presiding Bishop Sylvester Q. Cannon was released, he was sustained as an "associate" to the Twelve; when a member of the Twelve passed away the following year, Elder Cannon filled the vacancy in the Quorum. In 1967 President David O. McKay called Elder Alvin R. Dyer to be an Apostle, although there was no vacancy in the Quorum of the Twelve. The following year Elder Dyer became one of the additional members of the First Presidency.

The First Quorum of the Seventy

The revelation in Doctrine and Covenants section 107 assigned the Seventy a key role in assisting the Twelve to build up and regulate the Church worldwide. (Read verse 26 and also note the almost identical language in verses 33 and 34 describing the roles of the Twelve and Seventy, respectively.)

The original quorum of the seventy was created in 1835. Only its seven presidents, which came to be known as the

"First Council of the Seventy," were recognized as General Authorities. By the mid-1840s there were nine quorums of seventy, each having seven presidents. These sixty-three presidents, as well as being members of their own quorums, became members of the first quorum and were in turn presided over by the First Council. As the number of quorums rose over the years, there was no attempt to identify specific individuals as members of the first quorum, but rather the First Council was recognized as presiding generally over all seventies throughout the Church.

As the number of stakes and missions expanded during the 1930s, some Church leaders mentioned the possibility of adding General Authorities to the First Quorum of the Seventy in order to assume part of the growing administrative load. Nevertheless, as President Spencer W. Kimball later explained: "In 1941 five high priests were called to assist the Twelve Apostles in their heavy work and to fill a role similar to that envisioned by the revelations for the First Quorum of Seventy. The scope and demands of the work at that time did not justify the reconstitution of the First Quorum of Seventy."[8] Consequently, as has been seen, in 1941 five high priests were called to serve as "Assistants to the Twelve."[9] Over the years as the Church continued to grow, the number of these was enlarged as need dictated.

Responsibilities of the First Council of the Seventy were also increased. In 1961 President David O. McKay announced that members of the First Council of the Seventy were being ordained high priests and explained:

> Under the direction of the Twelve Apostles, the First Council of Seventy go to all parts of the world to set in order the affairs of the Church. That means ordaining high priests, setting apart presidents of stakes, high councilmen, setting apart presidents of high priests quorums, etc., and doing other things necessary for the advancement of the work. The First Presidency and Twelve recently agreed that the First Seven Presidents of Seventy under appointment by the Twelve, should have power to set in order all things pertaining to their assignment; and this is an official announcement that they are so authorized.[10]

For the time being, the practice continued of calling into the First Council only those who were currently seventies.

In 1975 President Spencer W. Kimball announced that the time had come to begin organizing the First Quorum of the Seventy and that three new General Authorities were being called to this body "to assist in the carrying forth of the work of the Lord, especially in the missionary area."[11] All three were seventies at the time of their call. In April 1976 four more were added, three being high priests and one an elder at the time; they were to have the same authority as Assistants to the Twelve.

At the October Conference in 1976, President Kimball explained:

> Commencing a year ago, brethren other than the First Council of Seventy were called into the First Quorum of Seventy. Since the functions and responsibilities of the Assistants to the Twelve and the Seventy are similar, and since the accelerated worldwide growth of the Church required a consolidation of its administrative functions at the general level, the First Presidency and the Quorum of the Twelve, with concurrence from the Assistants and the First Quorum of Seventy, have felt inspired to call all of the Assistants to the Twelve into the First Quorum of Seventy . . . and to restructure the First Council of Seventy. A total of thirty-nine members constitute 'a quorum to do business.' With this move the three governing quorums of the Church defined by the revelations, The First Presidency, the Quorum of the Twelve, and the First Quorum of Seventy, have been set in their places as revealed by the Lord. This will make it possible to handle efficiently the heavy work load and to prepare for the increasing expansion and acceleration of the work anticipating the day when the Lord will return to take direct charge of his Church and Kingdom.[12]

At the next several general conferences a few more members were added to the First Quorum of Seventy. These brethren assumed an important role in Church administration during the later 1970s.

The Presiding Bishopric

Although the Church's first bishop was called as early as 1831, the full concept of a Presiding Bishopric giving direction to other bishops was not fully implemented for over two decades.[13] Former Presiding Bishop Joseph L. Wirthlin explained the essential responsibility assigned to this group of General Authorities:

> From the installation of the first Presiding Bishop until the present time, those who have been called to the Presiding Bishopric have been concerned with the material interests of the Church and its members. They have administered the law of consecration; received, distributed, and accounted for the contributions and tithes of the people; looked after the poor; comforted the weary; admonished and exhorted to good works those who faltered; provided and maintained adequate places of worship; and accounted for the records of membership, activity, and advancement of all members of the Church.[14]

Although during the Church's first century and a half most General Authority callings have been lifetime appointments, this was not always the case with the Presiding Bishopric. Of the first sixteen brethren leaving the Bishopric during the twentieth century, three died in office, eight were called to other General Authority assignments, and five were released.

Patriarch to the Church

On December 18, 1833, the Prophet Joseph Smith gave the first patriarchal blessings in this dispensation. On that occasion he also ordained his father to the patriarchal priesthood "to hold the keys of blessing on the heads of all the members of the Church, the Lord revealing that it was his right to hold this authority." The Prophet later explained that "an Evangelist is a Patriarch, even the oldest man of the blood of Joseph or of the seed of Abraham," and that wherever the Church is established, patriarchs should be ordained to bless the posterity of the Saints.[15]

The office first held by Joseph Smith, Sr., came to be known as the Patriarch to the Church. In accordance with revealed instructions, other patriarchs have been ordained as stakes have been established around the world (see D&C 107:39). Each of these was assigned to give blessings to those living within his particular stake, while the Patriarch to the Church had worldwide jurisdiction. His specific role was to give blessings to Church members residing in missions or in other areas where no stake patriarchs were available. The Patriarch to the Church did not have any presiding authority over the local patriarchs.[16]

In 1979 the First Presidency announced that "because of the large increase in the number of stake patriarchs and the availability of patriarchal service throughout the world, we now designate Elder Eldred G. Smith as a Patriarch Emeritus, which means that he is honorably relieved of all duties and responsibilities pertaining to the office of Patriarch to the Church."[17] Since that time, several experienced brethren, some having the capability of speaking foreign languages, have been called on a short-term basis to give patriarchal blessings in specified sections of the world where stake patriarchs are not available.

Emeritus General Authorities

The first designation of "Emeritus General Authorities" had come a year earlier, in 1978. The First Presidency explained:

> The very rapid growth of the Church across the world, with the attendant increase in travel and responsibility, has made it necessary to consider a change in the status of some of the Brethren of the General Authorities. Some of our associates have served for many years with complete and unselfish dedication, and they deserve every honor and recognition for such devoted service. It is felt advisable at this time to reduce somewhat the load of responsibility that they carry. . . . It is out of consideration for the personal well-being of the individuals, and with deep appreciation for their devoted service, that this designation will be given from time to time to designated members of the General Authorities.[18]

At the time of the 1978 announcement, seven members of the First Quorum of the Seventy became Emeritus General Authorities, and others were given this status in subsequent years. A further step would be taken in 1984, when the Church put into effect the practice of calling men to serve in the First Quorum of the Seventy for from three to five years, after which they would be honorably released. During the tenure of

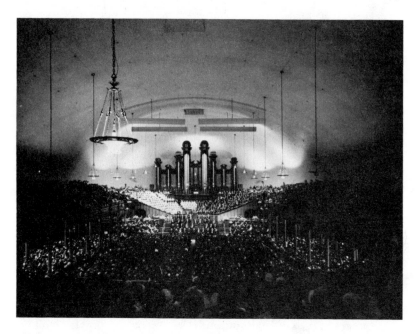

Latter-day Saints from around the world throng the Salt Lake Tabernacle during general conference to receive counsel and direction from their inspired leaders. (Church Archives)

their service they would be General Authorities in every sense, "with every right, power, and authority to function." President Gordon B. Hinckley explained that this new procedure would "provide a constant infusion of new talent and a much widened opportunity for men of ability and faith to serve in these offices."[19]

Follow the Brethren

The Latter-day Saints' respect for their Church leaders is heightened by revealed instructions. At the organization of the Church, the Lord instructed the Saints to accept the Prophet's words "as if from mine own mouth" (D&C 21:4-5; see also 1:38). A later revelation declared that whatever those in authority speak "when moved upon by the Holy Ghost shall be scripture" (D&C 68:2-4). Reflecting on this latter passage, President J. Reuben Clark concluded: "We can tell when the speakers are 'moved upon by the Holy Ghost,' only when we, ourselves, are 'moved upon by the Holy Ghost.' In a way, this completely shifts the responsibility from them to us to determine when they so speak."[20]

Not all groups of General Authorities possess the same authority. Members of the First Presidency and the Quorum of the Twelve are specifically sustained as "prophets, seers, and revelators." Concerning the importance of this, President Clark explained:

> In considering the problem involved here, it should be in mind that some of the General Authorities have had assigned to them a special calling; they possess a special gift; they are sustained as prophets, seers, and revelators, which gives them a special spiritual endowment in connection with their teaching of the people. They have the right, the power, and authority to declare the mind and will of God to his people, subject to the over-all power and authority of the President of the Church. Others of the General Authorities are not given this special spiritual endowment and authority covering their teaching; they have a resulting limitation, and the resulting limitation upon their power and authority in teaching applies to every other officer and member of the Church, for none of them is spiritually endowed as a prophet, seer, and revelator. Furthermore, as just indicated, the President of the Church has a further and special spiritual endowment in this respect, for he is the Prophet, Seer, and Revelator for the whole Church.
>
> Here we must have in mind—must know—that only the President of the Church, the Presiding High Priest, is sustained as Prophet, Seer, and Revelator for the Church, and he alone has the right to receive revelations for the Church, either new or amendatory, or to give authoritative interpretations of scriptures that shall be binding on the Church, or change in any way the existing doctrines of the Church. He is God's sole mouthpiece on earth for the Church of Jesus Christ of Latter-day Saints, the only true Church. He alone may declare the mind and will of God to his people. No officer of any other Church in the world has this high right and lofty prerogative.
>
> So when any other person, irrespective of who he is, undertakes to do any of these things, you may know he is not

'moved upon by the Holy Ghost,' in so speaking, unless he has special authorization from the President of the Church.[21]

Elder Marion G. Romney testified:

Today the Lord is revealing his will to all the inhabitants of the earth, and to the members of the Church in particular, on the issues of this our day through the living prophets, with the First Presidency at the head . . . what the Presidency say as a Presidency is what the Lord would say if he were here, and it is scripture. It should be studied, understood, and followed, even as the revelations in the Doctrine and Covenants and other scriptures.[22]

The Church's regular general conferences are important occasions when this inspired counsel may be received. As early as 1946, Elder Harold B. Lee counseled: "As the Latter-day Saints go home from this conference, it would be well if they consider seriously the importance of taking with them the report of this conference. Let it be the guide to their walk and talk during the next six months. These are the important matters the Lord sees fit to reveal to this people in this day. . . ."[23] Elder Spencer W. Kimball similarly urged the Saints to get the printed report of the most recent conference (such as is published in the *Ensign* magazine) and "underline the pertinent thoughts and keep it with you for continual reference. No text or volume outside of the standard works of the Church," he declared, "should have a more prominent place on your personal library shelves."[24]

23 Administering the Worldwide Church

The Church's accelerated expansion worldwide has presented challenges as well as opportunities. The mushrooming number of stakes and missions around the globe has placed an increasingly heavy administrative load on the General Authorities. The Church has, however, taken significant steps to meet this administrative challenge, especially under the leadership of President Spencer W. Kimball.

As early as 1967 Elder Harold B. Lee spoke of the challenges arising from the Church's rate of growth, and the need to prepare for the prophesied "hastening of the Lord's work." He pointed out that the Church required its first seventy years to reach a quarter of a million members, but that during the 1960s a like number was added every two or three years. (By the early 1980s, nearly a quarter of a million new members— children blessed and converts baptized—were being added every year.) Just as important as the growth in total numbers was the increasingly pronounced regional distribution of Church membership. Elder Lee cited examples of rapid increases in various sections of the world and concluded that "we have no choice but to think regionally." He referred to research by Dr. Howard Nielsen of Brigham Young University indicating that by the year 2000 the Church should have in ex-

1961	Number of mission areas expanded
1964	Welfare regions assumed added priesthood functions
1965	*Priesthood Bulletin* inaugurated; two levels of General Authorities supervised areas
1967	Regional Representatives called
1970	Bishops' training course provided
1971	Church's first area conference held in England
1975	Regions placed under areas; auxiliary general conferences discontinued
1976	Regional Representatives given "limited line authority"
1977	Delineation between temporal and ecclesiastical responsibilities at Church headquarters; general conferences shortened to two days
1979	Frequency of stake conferences reduced; area and regional councils formed

cess of ten million members. "By 1985," Elder Lee continued, "depending on our effectiveness and external events, we should have 1,000 stakes and nearly 10,000 wards." (The thousandth stake was actually organized six years ahead of that projection.) The General Authorities would need to appoint some two hundred new stake presidents each year, conduct five stake reorganizations each weekend, and clear fifty to sixty names for the office of bishop each week. He also pointed out that by 1985 there could be nearly two hundred missions and some thirty thousand full-time missionaries serving.[1] The fact that these milestones were actually reached sooner than had been predicted serves to underscore the challenges this growth has brought.

Strengthening Local Leaders

As the Church has grown worldwide, the General Authorities have delegated more responsibility to local leaders. Stake presidents, for example, were given the authority to set apart full-time missionaries, to ordain seventies and to select and set apart seventies quorum presidencies, and to dedicate chapels. With these added duties has come the need to provide more training. Elder Dean L. Larsen, chairman of the Church's curriculum committee, observed in 1974:

> Perhaps the greatest single challenge is to establish and maintain a system of Church government that is universal. It must be administered by local Church leaders who are called to serve without material compensation, and who come from an almost infinite variety of circumstances. Many are virtually without experience in administrative affairs. Most outside the stakes close to Church headquarters have only a limited tenure of experience in Church membership and service. Every level of education is represented among these local leaders, yet they are expected to learn and to administer a code of inspired principles, procedures, and policies that are determined by the General Authorities of the Church. . . .
>
> It is virtually impossible for those at Church headquarters who draft handbooks of policies and procedures to make provisions for every possible contingency that may arise in localized situations, where customs and personal relationships are so varied. When correct principles are understood by local leaders, however, it is often possible for them to resolve their problems in a way uniquely suited to their special needs without violating the spirit of unity and common purpose that prevails throughout the Church.[2]

As Elder Larsen pointed out, the rapid growth of the Church has necessitated more and more delegation of responsibility to local leaders. This same worldwide growth, however, meant that those called to preside in the districts and branches as well as in the stakes and wards had increasingly little background in Church administration and activity. In Mexico City, for example, stake presidents during the early 1970s were comparatively young men in their thirties who had been members of the Church for only about ten years on the average; about half had not served on missions. (This was in marked contrast to the typical stake president serving in the predominantly Latter-day Saint Intermountain West, who was in his fifties or sixties, had been a member of the Church all his life, and who usually had previously served as a bishop and a member of the stake high council.) Therefore, the General

Authorities gave special attention to the need for training these local leaders to assume their ever more important responsibilities.

Bishops have assumed an increasingly important role as the shepherds of their flocks as well as administrators of ward activities. In the early 1970s approximately 32 percent of Church members resided in missions or in stakes within missions. Many bishops were, therefore, called with comparatively little training in Church leadership. In 1970 the General Authorities developed a new program to help further qualify the thousands of bishops in the Church for their vital work.

The *General Handbook of Instructions* listed fifty-eight distinct duties for bishops; in addition, they had to learn how to utilize effectively such new programs as social services or military relations. One purpose of the training course was to help bishops use their limited time more efficiently. The average bishop spent twenty-six hours per week in Church service, including twelve hours in meetings or attending other activities, and eight hours in personal visits or interviews.[3]

Printed bulletins have also provided channels of communication and instruction from the General Authorities to local Church leaders. Beginning in 1965 the bimonthly *Priesthood Bulletin* carried information about all Church programs, including those sponsored by the Presiding Bishopric and the auxiliaries. In later years a more frequent bulletin consolidated the kind of current instructions formerly sent out in separate mailings by the Church's varied organizations and departments.

As effective as these channels of printed communication might be, personal contact was still most important. Over the years, contacts between the General Authorities and local Church leaders have come through two means: (1) supervisory assignments over missions and stakes, and (2) visits to stake and other conferences.

Worldwide Supervision of Missions and Stakes

During the twentieth century two new levels of administration have developed—"areas" for missions, and "regions" for stakes. In the 1960s they assumed an increasingly impor-

tant role, and during the 1970s they became a regular part of
the Church's administrative line of authority.

Mission Areas

In 1837 the Church's first overseas mission was opened in
Great Britain. Missionary work commenced in France in 1849
and in Scandinavia the following year. Within a few years the
work has spread to all the major countries of Europe. All these
missions were, from the beginning, under the jurisdiction of
the British Mission president. Thus Elder Franklin D. Richards,
who presided in Britain at the midpoint of the nineteenth
century, bore the title "President of the British Isles and
Adjacent Countries." Subsequently, British Mission presidents,
most of whom were General Authorities, were designated as
presidents of the "European Mission." This arrangement continued until 1929, when a separate president was called to preside over the British Mission; like the presidents of the missions
on the continent, he would serve under the direction of the
European Mission president.[4]

World War II interrupted the work in Europe; but early in
1946, just after the end of the war, Elder Ezra Taft Benson was
sent to Europe to supervise the reopening of the mission there.
Later the same year Matthew Cowley was named president of
the Pacific Mission. Elder Cowley was to continue residing in
Salt Lake City and would supervise the missions in the Pacific
area by means of correspondence and periodic visits.

As conditions stabilized after a few years, these two supervisory or administrative missions were discontinued—the
Pacific Mission in 1949 and the European Mission in 1950.

During the 1950s, however, the Church entered an era of
unprecedented growth worldwide. These conditions made it
desirable to reopen the European Mission in 1960. As the work
continued to grow, this mission was divided to form the West
European Mission in April 1961.

On the occasion of the first worldwide mission presidents' seminar in June of that year, the South American Mission, the third of these area administrative units, was formed,
with headquarters in Montevideo, Uruguay. In addition, six
other General Authorities, who were to remain in Salt Lake

City, received assignments to administer mission areas. Of these nine administrators, three were members of the Twelve, five were Assistants to the Twelve, and one was a member of the First Council of the Seventy. Four of their administrative areas were within the United States and Canada, while the other five were abroad.[5]

The number of mission areas was further expanded in 1965, and distinct administrative assignments were given to two levels of General Authorities. The world was divided into twelve large areas, five in the United States and Canada and seven abroad. An assistant to the Twelve or a member of the First Council of the Seventy served as a supervisor for each area under the direction of a member of the Twelve. All lived in Salt Lake City.[6] By 1971 the number of these area supervisors had grown to nineteen.

Meanwhile, the number of stakes had continued to multiply. The total had passed two hundred in 1952, and by the end of 1966 there were 425 stakes. The increased number of these units posed another administrative challenge, which was solved through the development of "regions."

Regions and Regional Representatives

Regions as Church administrative units had come into being in 1936 to coordinate the functioning of the welfare program. By the early 1960s, more than fifty such regions had been organized. The *Church News* announced that these welfare regions were being realigned to serve expanded purpose, with a number of new regions added for a total of seventy. Beginning in 1964 these "priesthood regions" correlated the implementation of home teaching, missionary, genealogical, and welfare activities.[7]

The First Presidency announced a further development on the regional level in 1967:

> As many of you will remember, in 1941, it became necessary for the First Presidency and the Twelve to provide for additional brethren or help with the work of overseeing and setting in order an evergrowing, world-wide Church. Thus in the General Conference of April 1941, Assistants to the Twelve were named and sustained, "to be increased or otherwise from

time to time as the necessity of carrying on the Lord's work seems to dictate.''

Since then the world-wide demands of the Church have increased in ever greater degree and it is felt by the First Presidency and the Twelve that a further provision for guidance and direction is now needed.

What, therefore, is now proposed is the calling of as many brethren as may be necessary, to be known as Regional Representatives of the Twelve, each, as assigned, to be responsible in some aspects of the work to carry counsel to and to conduct instructional meetings in groups of stakes or regions as may be designated from time to time.

These Regional Representatives of the Twelve will not be General Authorities, as such, but will serve somewhat as do stake presidents, giving full Church service time for greater or lesser periods of service as circumstances may suggest.

Fuller details will be in evidence as this plan proceeds under the guidance of the First Presidency and the Twelve.[8]

Initially sixty-nine men were called as Regional Representatives. (By the mid-1970s the number had doubled.) Most had served as members of stake presidencies, and many had also been mission presidents or members of one of the general priesthood committees. Most were assigned to regions near their homes, although a few had to travel long distances because of the need for special language ability.

Regional Representatives received instruction concerning priesthood and auxiliary programs at special seminars conducted in connection with the Church's general conferences in Salt Lake City. They then provided training in these programs to stake and ward leaders at regional meetings.

In 1972, twenty-nine experienced brethren were called as "Mission Representatives" to give special attention to proselyting. By 1974 this assignment was amalgamated with that of the Regional Representatives.[9]

Areas and Regions Integrated

In 1975 regions and stakes were placed under the direction of area supervisors for the first time. Several of the Assistants to the Twelve were assigned to move overseas and to personally direct the missions and regions in their assigned areas.[10] By the following year there were eleven of these brethren living abroad and serving as resident General Authority Area Supervisors. As these new units were stabilized, most of these area directors were able to return to Church headquarters.

In 1976 stakes in the United States and Canada were also placed under the jurisdiction of General Authority Area Supervisors, and the number of areas in these two countries was increased to nineteen.[11]

In 1977 the Twelve delegated to the First Quorum of the Seventy the immediate responsibility for the supervision of specific geographical areas. All area leaders were members of this quorum. At about this same time, the Seventies also received responsibility for directing the various ecclesiastical programs and departments at Church headquarters. This left the Twelve free to give broad attention to the Church's spiritual affairs worldwide.

An important step in 1979 was the organization of councils to determine policy and give direction at various levels of Church organization. "With the increased growth and internationalization of the Church and the great responsibility to promote the ecclesiastical and temporal work throughout the world in a more unified fashion," President N. Eldon Tanner announced, councils were being organized at the area and region levels as well as at the all-Church, stake, and ward levels.[12]

During the later 1970s the responsibilities of the Regional Representatives continued to increase. At first, their assignment had been to serve strictly in a "staff" or advisory capacity. In 1976, however, they were given "limited line authority," which meant that in addition to conducting the annual regional instructional meetings the Regional Representatives would also be accountable for Church progress within their regions and would conduct regular priesthood interviews with stake presidents.[13] Then in 1979, for the first time, seven men were called to serve full time as Regional Representatives and to live within their assigned areas in Latin America or western Europe.[14] In this way they could provide badly needed training and support for local leaders in newly organized stakes.

Responsibility for Church Programs

The General Authorities have been responsible not only for giving direction to Church units worldwide, but also for administering the numerous and varied departments and committees at Church headquarters. In 1977 the First Presidency announced a delineation between responsibility for ecclesiastical and temporal matters, respectively: "The Lord has made it clear that the Council of the Twelve, under direction of the First Presidency, has special responsibility for administering the ecclesiastical affairs of the Church, including responsibility to direct the functioning of the newly organized First Quorum of the Seventy, the third governing quorum of the Church. Under the direction of the First Presidency, the Presiding Bishopric has been given responsibility for administering the temporal affairs of the Church." Areas to be administered by the Twelve included priesthood and auxiliary programs, as well as the missionary, temple and genealogy, and leadership-training activities. Departments under the Presiding Bishopric's jurisdiction included translation and distribution, physical facilities, data processing, financial, purchasing, membership records, and reporting. The mission of these "temporal" departments is to serve and support the ecclesiastical programs of the Church.[15]

Developments in Conference Patterns

Conferences held throughout the stakes have been one of the most important means of strengthening local leaders (see D&C 20:61-62). As the number of stakes multiplied, the General Authorities were able to attend these conferences less frequently. Beginning in 1964, members of the four priesthood committees as well as members of auxiliary general boards were appointed to visit half of the stake conferences each year. Then, in 1968, General Authorities were assigned to attend only two conferences in each stake during the year, the other two being under the direction of the stake president. By 1975, Regional Representatives were given authority to conduct one conference in each stake annually.[16]

Beginning in the 1970s, area conferences such as this one in Montevideo, Uruguay, provided spiritual strength to Church members around the world. (Church Visual Resources Library)

At the same time, bringing the leaders of these widespread units to the general conferences held at Church headquarters became an ever greater economic burden. In addition, it became more difficult to find seats in the Salt Lake Tabernacle for the throngs who traveled long distances to hear the messages of Church leaders. The Church, therefore, inaugurated area conferences in 1971, sending a group of General Authorities to meet the Saints in a given part of the world. At first, only one of these conferences was held each year: 1971, Manchester, England; 1972, Mexico City, Mexico; 1973, Munich, Germany; 1974, Stockholm, Sweden. Four area conferences met in 1975: Sao Paulo, Brazil; Buenos Aires, Argentina; Tokyo, Japan; and Seoul, Korea. These area conferences became an increasingly important link between the General Authorities and the growing Church membership worldwide.

Since the beginning of the twentieth century, Church auxiliaries had conducted annual conferences in Salt Lake City, at which they presented the coming year's programs and provided training and inspiration for local officers and teachers. However, at the MIA conference in 1975, President Spencer W. Kimball pointed out that only a very small proportion of local auxiliary leaders could afford to attend the annual conferences at Church headquarters, and that existing facilities were inadequate to house all who should attend. Therefore, these auxiliary conferences were being discontinued. Leadership training was to be provided instead in the regional meetings conducted by the Regional Representatives of the Twelve beginning in June 1976.

Similarly, beginning in 1977 general conferences were shortened from three to two days. General sessions would be scheduled for the first weekend of April and October, respectively. This meant that the spring conferences would not necessarily include April 6, the anniversary of the Church's organization and a traditional general conference date. Limiting the general sessions to the weekends facilitated attendance for stake presidents and others who often could not leave employment responsibilities during weekdays. The General Authorities regularly conducted the seminars for Regional Representatives on the Friday immediately preceding the general conference weekend.[17]

At the other end of the spectrum, beginning in 1979 the number of conferences held annually in each stake was reduced from four to two. This was done "to ease burdens of time, travel, and money upon members of the Church." One of the conferences each year was to be conducted by a General Authority, and the other by the stake's Regional Representative.

While conferences at the general and stake levels were being reduced, more emphasis was placed on area conferences. President Kimball announced that beginning in 1979 these conferences would be conducted in the United States and Canada for the first time.[18] These changes lessened the time Church leaders were required to spend holding conferences, but at the same time provided expanded contacts between Church members and the General Authorities. The perfection of satellites and other communications media in the future will provide a new source of immediate contact between General Authorities and the far-flung membership of the Church, and may therefore reduce the need for Church leaders to travel so widely.

24 The Destiny of the Church

A t the Church's sesquicentennial conference in 1980, Elder Bruce R. McConkie
spoke of the Church's progress to date and of its future destiny. Using symbolic terms, he likened the Church's present
achievements to standing on a majestic and glorious mountain
peak: "From where we stand, on the peak of 150 years of
progress, the view is glorious indeed." The stone foreseen by
the prophet Daniel is rolling forward towards its destiny of filling the whole earth. (See Daniel 2:34-35.) Prophet after
prophet labors to prepare the faithful for the Savior's second
coming. "Our joy and rejoicing is not in what lies below,"
Elder McConkie continued, "not in our past—great and glorious as that is—but in our present and in our future." Our sor-
rows and sufferings are not all behind us, he cautioned. "We
shall yet be tempted with more severe trials . . . than we have
ever known before. . . ."

"From the top of the peak . . . we can look forward, crest
upon crest, to the Zion of God which one day will be ours if
we walk in the course charted by those who have gone
before." Unfortunately, not all will attain this goal. "We weep
for those in the true Church who are weak and wayward and
worldly and who fall by the wayside as the caravan of the kingdom rolls forward."

Elder McConkie anticipated the time when the gospel would be preached with success in all nations. "We see the Lord break down the barriers so that the world of Islam and the world of communism can hear the message of the Restoration." He looked forward to stakes being organized throughout the earth. In temples, which will dot the earth, "those of every nation and kindred and tongue and people can receive the fullness of the ordinances of the house of the Lord and can qualify to live and reign as kings and priests on earth a thousand years." There will be a rich outpouring of the Holy Spirit, together with revelations, gifts, and miracles. Because of this, Elder McConkie emphasized, faithful souls are "born again, . . . sanctified by the power of the Spirit, and they prepare themselves to dwell with God and Christ and holy beings in the eternal kingdom.

"Truly the world is and will be in commotion," Elder McConkie concluded, "but the Zion of God will be unmoved. The wicked and ungodly shall be swept from the Church, and the little stone will continue to grow until it fills the whole earth."[1]

Prophecies in the Doctrine and Covenants and other scriptures similarly speak of these future conditions through which the Church must pass before the glorious second coming of Christ. The consistent message is a "voice of warning" to the Saints to prepare for that which is to come. Church organizations and programs are intended to aid in this preparation.

In 1823, Moroni declared "that the time was at hand for the Gospel in all its fullness to be preached in power, unto all nations that a people might be prepared for the Millennial reign."[2] During the 1960s a member of one of the priesthood correlation committees recalled:

> I sat in a meeting at 47 East South Temple and heard President N. Eldon Tanner say, "Brethren, we are sending you out to the conferences of this Church. We send you forth to teach, and not to be taught." Then he said, "You go out and prepare the people for the second coming of Jesus Christ." We sat there with those chills just going up and down our spines when we heard a prophet say this.[3]

But before these glorious events occur, prophecy indicates, the world must pass through a period of tribulations. The programs of the Church are designed to fortify the Saints for these difficulties. Elder Harold B. Lee explained:

> Almost imperceptibly we see the hand of the Lord moving to do things, and this I construe to be a consolidation of the forces of the Lord under the direction of the prophet, just as in an army, in order to meet a superior force of the enemy in numbers, the forces of our opposition to the forces of evil must be consolidated in order to give them the most effective possible defense.
>
> We are in a program of defense. The Church of Jesus Christ was set upon this earth in this day ". . . for a defense, and for a refuge from the storm, and from wrath when it should be poured out without mixture upon the whole earth." (D&C 115:6.) [Therefore we are instructed] "to move forward," that we consolidate to make more efficient and more effective the work of the priesthood, the auxiliaries, and the other units in order that we may conserve our time, our energy, and our efforts toward the prime purpose for which the Church itself has been organized.[4]

Elder Thomas S. Monson regarded priesthood correlation, emphasized beginning in the 1960s, as the inspired means by which those objectives can be achieved:

> Though our objectives may at times appear unattainable, though the resources of that evil one loom overpowering, and though discouragement threatens, and weaknesses handicap, yet that blessing brought by correlation—even united effort—will bring us the victory we so much seek.
>
> We can take strength from the example of Gideon. You will remember how Gideon and his army faced the overwhelming strength of forces vastly superior in equipment and in number. . . . The outcome of that mighty battle is recorded in one short sentence: "And they stood every man in his place. . . ." (Judges 7:21), and the victory was won.
>
> Today, we are encamped against the greatest array of sin, vice, and evil ever assembled before our eyes. Such formidable enemies may cause lesser hearts to shrink or shun the fight. But the battle plan whereby we fight to save the souls of men is not our own. It was provided to our leader, even President David

O. McKay, by the inspiration and revelation of the Lord. Yes, I speak of that plan which will bring us victory, even the Correlation Program of the Church. And as we do battle against him who would thwart the purposes of God and degrade and destroy mankind, I pray that each of us will stand in his or her appointed place, that the battle for the souls of men will indeed be won. . . . [5]

President Hugh B. Brown expressed his appreciation for the priesthood correlation program and then added this prophetic declaration:

It seems to me that of all the signs of the times (and they are ominous and on every side) this is one of the significant signs of the times—that the Church of Jesus Christ, the kingdom of God, is massing its forces, getting ready for that which is to follow. . . .

I want to say to you, brethren, that in the midst of all the troubles, the uncertainties, the tumult and the chaos through which the world is passing, almost unnoticed by the majority of the people of the world, there has been set up a kingdom, a kingdom over which God the Father presides, and Jesus the Christ is the King. That kingdom is rolling forward, as I say, partly unnoticed, but it is rolling forward with a power and a force that will stop the enemy in its tracks while some of you live.

Do you want to be among those on the side of Christ and his apostles? . . .

Now is the time to make a resolution to that effect and to prepare to put yourselves in a position where you can do the will of God, keep control of yourselves, and control your passions and your appetites and those other things that lead downward into forbidden paths. [6]

If we are to meet President Brown's challenge, Zion must be established on earth before Christ comes. In 1834, the Lord outlined what is required for us to be prepared to fulfill this goal:

. . . it is expedient in me that mine elders should wait for a little season for the redemption of Zion—

That they themselves may be prepared, and that my people may be taught more perfectly, and have experience, and know more perfectly concerning their duty, and the things which I require at their hands.

And this cannot be brought to pass until mine elders are endowed with power from on high.

In summary the Lord then declared: "But first let my army become very great, and let it be sanctified before me...." (D&C 105:9-11, 31). How are we doing?

We have seen that there has been tremendous growth during the twentieth century, that the Lord's "army" truly is becoming "very great." Yet, has it filled the earth? In 1978 Church membership passed the four million mark, but there were approximately four billion people living on the earth at the time. This meant that there was only about one Latter-day Saint for every thousand of the earth's inhabitants. Obviously there is room and need for further growth.

Is the Lord's "army" or Church sufficiently sanctified? President Wilford Woodruff declared:

> The parable of the ten virgins is intended to represent the second coming of the Son of Man, the coming of the Bridegroom to meet the bride, the Church . . . and I expect that the Savior was about right when he said, in reference to the members of the Church, that five of them were wise and five were foolish; . . . if he finds one-half of those professing to be members of his Church prepared for salvation, it will be as many as can be expected, judging by the course that many are pursuing.[7]

Available statistics do not measure worthiness or sanctification directly. Nevertheless, faith and devotion are reflected in the levels of Church activity. Information presented in this volume indicates that there has been substantial progress during the twentieth century in such matters as attendance at meetings, missionary service, or temple ordinances performed. Yet here again there is ample room for further improvement.

Latter-day Saints in the twentieth century should find the Church's progress thrilling. Truly the kingdom is rolling forth. Yet much more remains to be accomplished. Each Church member has the opportunity and responsibility to contribute to the kingdom's forward momentum. Elder Harold B. Lee once challenged: "If we can get the priesthood now to come alive and to put into gear the full strength of the priesthood, we shall see some of the most wonderful developments and some of the greatest things happen to the forces which the Lord can set in motion that we have ever known in this dispensation."[8]

The challenge to all Latter-day Saints, then, is to catch the vision of the Church's mission and destiny, that they may help to realize the fulfillment of the Prophet's inspired petition (D&C 65:6) in which he prayed, "May the kingdom of God go forth, that the kingdom of heaven may come, that thou, O God, mayest be glorified in heaven so on earth."

Notes

Chapter 1. The Turn of the Century: Lorenzo Snow

1. *Deseret Evening News,* January 1, 1901, p. 5.

2. Eliza R. Snow, *Biography and Family Record of Lorenzo Snow* (Salt Lake City: Deseret News Co., 1884), pp. 7-9.

3. Ibid., p. 46; Orson F. Whitney, "Lives of Our Leaders—Lorenzo Snow," *Juvenile Instructor* 35 (January 1900): 4.

4. Lorenzo Snow's journal as quoted in Preston Nibley, *Presidents of the Church* (Salt Lake City: Deseret Book Co., 1959), p. 195; LeRoi C. Snow's statement quoted in Deta Peterson Neeley, *A Child's Story of the Prophet Lorenzo Snow* (Salt Lake City: Deseret Book Co., 1968), p. 90.

5. Quoted in Reed E. Durham and Steven H. Heath, *Succession in the Church* (Salt Lake City: Bookcraft, 1970), pp. 103-4.

6. LeRoi C. Snow, "An Experience of My Father's," *Improvement Era* 36 (September 1933): 677, 679.

7. Ibid.

8. Ibid.

9. Journal History of the Church, September 13, 1898, p. 2; see also *Improvement Era* 36 (September 1933): 677.

10. Quoted in *Conference Report,* April 1970, p. 124.

11. John A. Widtsoe, *Evidences and Reconciliations* (Salt Lake City: Bookcraft, 1960), p. 264.

12. *Conference Report,* April 1970, pp. 118-19.

13. Ibid., pp. 122-24.

14. Joseph Fielding Smith, *The Life of Joseph F. Smith* (Salt Lake City: Deseret News Press, 1938), pp. 310-11.

15. Leonard J. Arrington, *Great Basin Kingdom* (Cambridge, Mass: Harvard University Press, 1954), pp. 400-401.

16. LeRoi C. Snow, "The Lord's Way Out of Bondage," *Improvement Era* 41 (July 1938): 401, 439-41.

17. B. H. Roberts, *A Comprehensive History of The Church of Jesus Christ of Latter-day Saints: Century I,* 6 vols. (Salt Lake City: The Church of Jesus Christ of Latter-day Saints, 1930), 6:359-60.

18. *Conference Report,* October 1903, p. 7.

19. Roberts, *Comprehensive History,* 6:377.

20. Ibid., p. 379.

21. See, for example, Journal History of the Church, January 19, 1899, pp. 2-5; Frederick Jackson Turner, *The Frontier in American History* (New York: Holt and Co., 1920).

22. "First Presidency to Netherlands Mission," December 14, 1907, in James R. Clark, comp., *Messages of the First Presidency*, 6 vols. (Salt Lake City: Bookcraft, 1965-75), 4:165.

23. *Millennial Star*, September 15, 1921, p. 585.

24. *Report of Mexico City Area Conference*, 1972, p. 45.

Chapter 2. The Church in the Progressive Era

1. B. H. Roberts, *A Comprehensive History of the Church*, 6 vols. (Salt Lake City: The Church of Jesus Christ of Latter-day Saints, 1930), 6:334.

2. Ibid., pp. 134-37.

3. Russell R. Rich, *Ensign to the Nations* (Provo, Utah: Brigham Young University Publications, 1972), pp. 472-73.

4. Francis T. Plimpton at Amherst College, quoted in *Reader's Digest*, June 1958, p. 142.

5. James R. Clark, comp., *Messages of the First Presidency*, 6 vols. (Salt Lake City: Bookcraft, 1965-75), 4:84-85.

6. Quoted in Joseph Fielding Smith, *Life of Joseph F. Smith* (Salt Lake City: Deseret News Press, 1938), pp. 378-80.

7. Roberts, *Comprehensive History*, 6:407-8.

8. Alfred Henry Lewis, "The Viper on the Hearth," *Cosmopolitan*, March 1911, pp. 439-50.

9. *Conference Report*, October 1907, pp. 5-6.

10. George F. Richards, "Why Are Mormon Missionaries Expelled from Germany," *Improvement Era* 13 (September 1910): 1004; as cited in Gilbert Scharffs, *Mormonism in Germany* (Salt Lake City: Deseret Book Co., 1970), p. 70.

11. James B. Allen and Glen M. Leonard, *The Story of the Latter-day Saints* (Salt Lake City: Deseret Book Co., 1976), pp. 473-74.

12. Roberts, *Comprehensive History*, 6:435-41.

13. Roberts, *Comprehensive History*, 1:v, vi, x.

14. "Mr. Roosevelt to the Mormons," *Collier's*, April 15, 1911, p. 28; reprinted in *Improvement Era* 14 (June 1911): 715-18.

15. Roberts, *Comprehensive History*, 6:477-78.

Chapter 3. Joseph F. Smith: An Era of Transition

1. Quoted in Preston Nibley, *Presidents of the Church* (Salt Lake City: Deseret Book Co., 1959), pp. 232-33.

2. Joseph Fielding Smith, *Life of Joseph F. Smith* (Salt Lake City: Deseret News Press, 1938), pp. 160-63.

3. Ibid., pp. 170, 173.

4. Ibid., pp. 288-91.

5. *Conference Report,* April 1907, pp. 5-6.

6. B. H. Roberts, *A Comprehensive History of the Church,* 6 vols. (Salt Lake City: The Church of Jesus Christ of Latter-day Saints, 1930), 6:426-30.

7. Smith, *Life,* pp. 425-27; *Conference Report,* October 1911, pp. 129-30.

8. Smith, *Life,* pp. 427-28.

9. Ibid., p. 397.

10. Rey L. Pratt, "History of the Mexican Mission," *Improvement Era* 15 (April 1912): 493, 498.

11. *Der Stern,* August 1, 1906, p. 332; see also Serge F. Ballif, *Conference Report,* October 1920, p. 90.

12. *Conference Report,* October 1915, p. 8.

13. N. B. Lundwall, *Temples of the Most High* (Salt Lake City: Bookcraft, 1947), p. 173.

14. *Conference Report,* October 1920, pp. 136-37.

15. James R. Clark, comp., *Messages of the First Presidency,* 6 vols. (Salt Lake City: Bookcraft, 1965-75), 4:199-206.

16. "The Father and the Son: A Doctrinal Exposition by the First Presidency and the Twelve," June 30, 1916; Clark, *Messages,* 5:26-34.

17. Joseph F. Smith, *Gospel Doctrine* (Salt Lake City: Deseret Book Co., 1966), pp. 67-68.

18. Quoted in *Improvement Era* 19 (February 1916): 369.

19. *Conference Report,* April 1917, p. 3.

Chapter 4. Priesthood and Auxiliary Expansion

1. *Deseret News Weekly,* April 17, 1852, p. 2.

2. *Deseret Evening News,* April 9, 1894.

3. James R. Clark, comp., *Messages of the First Presidency,* 6 vols. (Salt Lake City: Bookcraft, 1965-75), 3:282.

4. *Conference Report,* April 1906, p. 3.

5. Ibid., p. 19.

6. *Conference Report,* April 1907, p. 5; B. H. Roberts, "Seventies Council Table," *Improvement Era* 11 (November 1907): 63, 65.

7. Clark, *Messages,* 4:195.

8. "The Publications of the Church," an address given to seminary and institute teachers at BYU, July 8, 1958, p. 1.

9. Society for the Aid of the Sightless, Minutes, pp. 1-2, Church Archives, Historical Department, The Church of Jesus Christ of Latter-day Saints, Salt Lake City, Utah.

10. Carol Anne Schuster, "LDS Church Services to the Blind Through the Society for the Aid of the Sightless: The Talmage Era" (master's thesis, Brigham Young University, 1972), pp. 21-50.

Chapter 5. Heber J. Grant Begins His Administration

1. Francis M. Gibbons, *Heber J. Grant: Man of Steel, Prophet of God* (Salt Lake City: Deseret Book Co., 1979), p. 13.

2. Heber J. Grant, *Gospel Standards,* comp. G. Homer Durham (Salt Lake City: Improvement Era, 1941), pp. 11-12.

3. Ibid., pp. 342-43.

4. Bryant S. Hinckley, *Heber J. Grant: Highlights in the Life of a Great Leader* (Salt Lake City: Deseret Book Co., 1951), pp. 40-42; Heber J. Grant, "Work, and Keep Your Promises," *Improvement Era* 3 (January 1900): 196-97; "Learning to Sing," *Improvement Era* 3 (October 1900): 886-90.

5. Heber J. Grant, Diary, Dec. 20, 1931, MS, Church Archives, Historical Department, The Church of Jesus Christ of Latter-day Saints, Salt Lake City, Utah; hereafter cited as Church Archives.

6. Heber J. Grant in *Conference Report,* October 1922, pp. 2-3; Ronald W. Walker, "Young Heber J. Grant and His Call to the Apostleship," *Brigham Young University Studies* 18 (Fall 1977): 121-26.

7. James R. Clark, comp., *Messages of the First Presidency,* 6 vols. (Salt Lake City: Bookcraft, 1965-75), 2:348.

8. Heber J. Grant to Mrs. Parley Fenn, Feb. 13, 1931, MS, Church Archives.

9. Preston Nibley, *The Presidents of the Church* (Salt Lake City: Deseret Book Co., 1959), p. 305.

10. Joseph Anderson, *Prophets I Have Known* (Salt Lake City: Deseret Book Co., 1973), p. 25.

11. Ibid., pp. 20, 30.

12. Heber J. Grant, "Settlement," *Improvement Era* 44 (January 1941): 9, 56.

13. Quoted in Emerson R. West, *Profiles of the Presidents* (Salt Lake City: Deseret Book Co., 1974), p. 232.

14. Clark, *Messages,* 5:291.

15. *Conference Report,* June 1, 1919, p. 4.

16. Grant, Diary, May 19, 1931, Dec. 31, 1935, MS, Church Archives.

17. Anderson, *Prophets,* p. 20.

18. Gibbons, *Heber J. Grant,* pp. 174-75.

19. Grant, *Gospel Standards,* p. 196.

20. California Mission Manuscript History, October 29, 1921, Church Archives.

21. Joseph Smith, Jr., *Teachings of the Prophet Joseph Smith,* sel. Joseph Fielding Smith (Salt Lake City: Deseret Book Co., 1938), p. 363.

22. A. Theodore Tuttle, "South America: Land of Prophecy and Promise," *Improvement Era* 66 (May 1963): 352-60.

23. First Presidency statement in *Conference Report,* April 1930, pp. 3-13.

24. B. H. Roberts, *A Comprehensive History of the Church,* 6 vols. (Salt Lake City: The Church of Jesus Christ of Latter-day Saints, 1930), 6:537.

Chapter 6. Charting the Course in Education

1. *Conference Report,* October 1915, p. 4.

2. Board of Education minutes, March 15, 1920, MS, Church Archives.

3. Board of Education minutes, February 3, 1926; *Conference Report,* April 1926, p. 4.

4. Board of Education minutes, February 3 and March 18, 1926.

5. Jerry C. Roundy, *Ricks College: A Struggle for Survival* (Rexburg, Idaho: Ricks College Press, 1976), pp. 113-51.

6. Joseph F. Merrill, "Brigham Young University, Past, Present and Future," *Deseret News,* December 20, 1930, Section 2, p. 3.

7. *Enrollment Resume 1963-64* (Provo, Utah: Brigham Young University, 1965), p. 2.

8. I. L. Williamson, "On the Existing Relationship Between Religious Seminaries and Public High Schools in the State of Utah," report to the Utah State Board of Education, January 8, 1930; Journal History of the Church,

May 3, 1930, p. 4, and September 24, 1931, p. 3, MS, Church Archives; Board of Education minutes, November 4, 1931.

9. J. Wylie Sessions, interview with author, July 29, 1965.

10. G. Homer Durham, "University Religious Training and the LDS Deseret Clubs, *Weekday Religious Education* 1 (March 1937): 1-2.

11. Ernest L. Wilkinson and W. Cleon Skousen, *Brigham Young University: A School of Destiny* (Provo, Utah: Brigham Young University Press, 1976), pp. 196-209.

12. James R. Clark, comp., *Messages of the First Presidency*, 6 vols. (Salt Lake City: Bookcraft, 1965-75), 4:205; see the discussion in chapter 3 herein.

13. Wilkinson and Skousen, *Brigham Young University*, pp. 211-12.

14. Joseph F. Smith, editorial, *Juvenile Instructor* 46 (April 1911): 209.

15. Ernest L. Wilkinson, ed., *Brigham Young University: The First One Hundred Years*, 4 vols. (Provo, Utah: Brigham Young University Press, 1975), 2:262-69.

16. Quoted in Clark, *Messages*, 6:47-58; *Improvement Era* 41 (September 1938): 520.

17. Wilkinson, *Brigham Young University*, 2:360.

18. *Souvenir of the Dedication of the Joseph Smith Building, Brigham Young University Quarterly* 28 (November 1, 1941): 1; Proceedings of the Dedicatory Service in Founders' Day Report, October 16, 1941, MS, BYU Archives.

19. *Utah Economic and Business Review*, December 1974, p. 58, citing 1940 U.S. Government census data.

20. E. L. Thorndike, "The Origin of Superior Men," *Scientific Monthly* 56 (May 1943): 424-33; "Utah as Birthplace of Scientists," *Improvement Era* 43 (October 1940): 606.

Chapter 7. Temporal Concerns and Current Issues

1. Joseph F. Smith, *Gospel Doctrine* (Salt Lake City: Deseret Book Co., 1966), p. 209.

2. Thomas G. Alexander, "Between Revivalism and the Social Gospel: The Latter-day Saint Social Advisory Committee, 1916-1922," *Brigham Young University Studies* 23 (Winter 1983): 19-39.

3. First Presidency circular letter, January 27, 1969.

4. First Presidency circular letter, July 1, 1979.

5. *Conference Report,* October 1951, pp. 114-15.

6. *Conference Report,* October 1919, p. 17.

7. James B. Allen, "Personal Faith and Public Policy: Some Timely Observations on the League of Nations Controversy in Utah," *Brigham Young University Studies* 14 (Autumn 1973): 77-98.

8. *Church News,* March 17, 1979, pp. 7, 13.

9. In James R. Clark, comp., *Messages of the First Presidency,* 6 vols. (Salt Lake City: Bookcraft, 1965-75), 5:244-45.

10. Ibid., p. 250.

11. Ibid., p. 260.

12. First Presidency statement, June 28, 1959, in *Church News,* July 11, 1959, p. 3.

13. Heber J. Grant to W. B. Wardle, May 8, 1931, First Presidency Letterbooks, Church Archives.

14. *Conference Report,* October 1908, p. 8.

15. Heber J. Grant to the President of the Association Against the Prohibition Amendment, May 31, 1930, First Presidency Letterbooks, Church Archives.

16. Kirk H. Porter and Donald Bruce Johnson, *National Party Platforms, 1840-1964* (Urbana: University of Illinois Press, 1966), pp. 332, 348-49.

17. Clark, *Messages,* 5:309-10.

18. *Conference Report,* October 1933, p. 6.

19. Ibid., October 1935, p. 30.

20. Heber J. Grant to Leo J. Muir, September 22, 1941, Muir Papers, Brigham Young University Library.

21. *Conference Report,* April 1942, p. 11.

22. Ibid., October 1943, p. 47.

23. *Deseret News,* May 11, 1968, p. 1.

24. Thomas G. Alexander, "The Economic Consequences of the War: Utah and the Great Depression of the Early 1920s," in *A Dependent Commonwealth: Utah's Economy from Statehood to the Great Depression,* ed. Dean May (Provo, Utah: Brigham Young University Press, 1974), pp. 57-89.

25. *Conference Report,* April 1928, pp. 3-4, and April 1934, pp. 4-5.

26. Ibid., October 1933, p. 65.

27. Ibid., p. 5; see also Presiding Bishop Sylvester Q. Cannon's comments, pp. 33-35.

28. Ibid., October 1934, p. 6.

29. Ibid., April 1935, p. 93.

30. David O. McKay to Congressman Ralph R. Harding, June 15, 1961, in *Church News,* November 10, 1962, p. 3.

31. Clark, *Messages,* 6:18.

32. Heber J. Grant to J. Harold Long, August 23, 1934, First Presidency Letterbooks, Church Archives; *Conference Report,* October 1919, pp. 13-14.

33. First Presidency statement, *Deseret News,* November 29, 1941; compare *Deseret News,* June 25, 1963; see also David O. McKay, "On Unionism," *Improvement Era* 40 (August 1937): 496.

Chapter 8. The Welfare Plan

1. *Conference Report,* October 1930, p. 103.

2. James R. Clark, comp., *Messages of the First Presidency,* 6 vols. (Salt Lake City: Bookcraft, 1965-75), 5:331-34; for a discussion of President Clark's role in formulating the Welfare Plan, see D. Michael Quinn, *J. Reuben Clark: The Church Years* (Provo, Utah: Brigham Young University Press, 1983), pp. 251-78.

3. *Conference Report,* April 1941, p. 121; October 1972, p. 124; *Church News,* August 26, 1961, p. 8.

4. *Deseret News Church Section,* April 25, 1936, p. 1; in Clark, *Messages,* 6:10-13.

5. *Conference Report,* October 1936, pp. 3-4.

6. Ibid., p. 103.

7. Ibid., April 1937, p. 26.

8. J. Reuben Clark, Jr., *Church Welfare Plan,* a discussion before the Citizens' Conference on Government Management at Estes Park, Colorado, June 20, 1939 (Salt Lake City: General Church Welfare Committee, n.d.), pp. 11-21.

9. J. Reuben Clark's statement, November 1933, recounted by John A. Widtsoe in an interview with Lauritz G. Petersen, December 1, 1940, written summary in Church Archives.

10. William E. Berrett, "Teaching by the Spirit" and "Revelation," addresses at BYU, June 27, 1966, and June 27, 1956.

11. *Conference Report,* April 1943, p. 126.

12. Ibid., April 1941, p. 121.

13. Ibid., October 1942, p. 57.

Chapter 9. New Strides in Church Activity 1928-1941

1. *Improvement Era* 31 (January 1929): 257.

2. *Conference Report,* April 1906, p. 3.

3. *Improvement Era* 31 (June 1928): 744-45, 794.

4. Council of the Twelve circular letter, November 11, 1927, in *Juvenile Instructor* 61 (November 1927): 620-21.

5. *Juvenile Instructor* 62 (November and December 1928): 620-26, 681; 63 (June 1928): 299-309; *Improvement Era* 31 (June 1928): 792-94.

6. Council of the Twelve circular letter, March 12, 1928, in *Improvement Era* 31 (April 1928): 516-19.

7. First Presidency circular letter, May 29, 1929, in James R. Clark, comp., *Messages of the First Presidency,* 6 vols. (Salt Lake City: Bookcraft, 1965-75), 5:267-68.

8. *In the Realm of Quorum Activity,* Second Series, 1931, p. 3.

9. *A Guide for Quorums of the Melchizedek Priesthood,* 1928, p. 4.

10. Minutes of the Aaronic Priesthood Convention held April 4, 1931, p. 3., MS, Church Archives.

11. Ibid.

12. Ibid., pp. 4, 9-10.

13. General Priesthood Committee minutes, December 12, 1911, p. 265.

14. *Improvement Era* 28 (May 1926): 687.

15. *Instructor's Manual and Lesson Outline for Adult Aaronic Priesthood Classes,* 1936, pp. 7-8; *Deseret News Church Section,* June 6, 1936, p. 4; *Improvement Era* 36 (November 1933): 812.

16. *Church News,* September 18, 1982, p. 10.

17. *Deseret News,* April 6, 1931, p. 1; report by president of the French Mission, Mission Annual Reports 1933, p. 240, MS, Church Archives.

18. Heber J. Grant to Leah Widtsoe, October 13, 1933, First Presidency Letterbook, MS, Church Archives.

19. Letter from J. Golden Kimball to the Seventies, January 31, 1934, MS, Church Archives.

20. Letter of Rudger Clawson, President of the Council of the Twelve, to stake presidents, April 24, 1936, MS, Church Archives.

21. *Deseret News Church Section,* March 4, 1939; July 17, 1937.

22. First Presidency to Elders Joseph Fielding Smith, Stephen L Richards, and Albert E. Bowen, January, 1939, MS, Church Archives.

23. J. Reuben Clark, Jr., "Memorandum of Suggestions," MS, Church Archives.

24. Board minutes of the Genealogical Society of Utah, 5:159, MS, Church Archives; see also *Improvement Era* 43 (August 1940): 480.

25. First Presidency letter, January 18, 1935, in *Improvement Era* 38 (March 1935): 134.

26. *Conference Report,* April 1941, pp. 94-95.

Chapter 10. The Latter-day Saints and World War II

1. Gilbert Scharffs, *Mormonism in Germany* (Salt Lake City: Deseret Book Co., 1970), pp. 80-81; Joseph M. Dixon, "Mormons in the Third Reich: 1933-1945," *Dialogue: A Journal of Mormon Thought* 7 (Spring 1972): 71-85; see also reports by presidents of the German missions in Mission Annual Reports, 1933-1939, MS, Church Archives.

2. Reports by President Alfred C. Rees of the East German Mission and M. Douglas Wood of the West German Mission, Mission Annual Reports, 1938, pp. 256 and 736, MS, Church Archives.

3. M. Douglas Wood, interview with author, February 3, 1978; M. Douglas Wood in *Conference Report,* April 1940, pp. 79-81; David F. Boone, "The Worldwide Evacuation of Latter-day Saint Missionaries at the Beginning of World War II" (master's thesis, Brigham Young University, 1981), pp. 35-43.

4. Martha Toronto Anderson, *A Cherry Tree Behind the Iron Curtain* (Salt Lake City: Martha Toronto Anderson, 1977), pp. 31-32; Czechoslovak Mission Manuscript History, June-December 1939, Church Archives.

5. Franklin J. Murdock Oral History, interviews by Gordon Irving, 1973, typescript pp. 54-55, Oral History Program, Church Archives.

6. *Conference Report,* April 1940, p. 20.

7. Scharffs, *Germany,* pp. 104-5.

8. Frederick W. Babbel, *On Wings of Faith* (Salt Lake City: Bookcraft, 1972), pp. 110-11; Scharffs, *Germany,* p. 111.

9. Lee A. Palmer to the Presiding Bishopric, September 21, 1944, LeGrand Richards papers, Church Archives.

10. First Presidency circular letter, January 17, 1942, in *Improvement Era* 45 (February 1942): 74.

11. *Conference Report,* April 1943, pp. 127-28.

12. *Conference Report,* October 1939, pp. 11, 13; see also D. Michael

Quinn, *J. Reuben Clark: The Church Years* (Provo, Utah: Brigham Young University Press, 1983), pp. 201-3.

13. James R. Clark, comp., *Messages of the First Presidency,* 6 vols. (Salt Lake City: Bookcraft, 1965-75), 6:96.

14. Ibid., pp. 140-41.

15. *Conference Report,* April 1942, pp. 90-96.

16. Joseph F. Boone, "The Roles of The Church of Jesus Christ of Latter-day Saints in Relation to the United States Military, 1900-1975" (Ph.D. diss., Brigham Young University, 1975), pp. 548-52; see also Richard Maher, *For God and Country: Memorable Stories from the Lives of Mormon Chaplains* (Bountiful, Utah: Horizon Publishers, 1976).

17. Ibid., pp. 698-99.

18. *Conference Report,* April 1945, pp. 108-9.

19. Lowell Eliason Call, "LDS Servicemen in the Philippine Islands" (master's thesis, Brigham Young University, 1955).

20. Melden J. Smith, "An Escape From Death," *Improvement Era* 49 (September 1946): 568, 580.

21. Roy W. Doxey, *Prophecies and Prophetic Promises from the Doctrine and Covenants* (Salt Lake City: Deseret Book Co., 1970), pp. 97-98.

22. *Conference Report,* October 1942, p. 73.

23. *Church News,* February 8, 1969, p. 3; June 10, 1972, pp. 3, 13.

Chapter 11. George Albert Smith and Recovery from War

1. Quoted in Glen R. Stubbs, "A Biography of George Albert Smith, 1870-1951" (Ph.D. diss., Brigham Young University, 1974), p. 29.

2. Ibid., pp. 55-57.

3. Quoted in Stubbs, "George Albert Smith," p. 83.

4. George Albert Smith, "Your Good Name," *Improvement Era* 50 (March 1947): 139.

5. Bryant S. Hinckley, "Superintendent George Albert Smith," *Improvement Era* 35 (March 1932): 295.

6. George Albert Smith, "After Eighty Years," *Improvement Era* 53 (April 1950): 263.

7. J. Reuben Clark, Jr., "Our Dwindling Sovereignty," address at the

University of Utah, February 13, 1952, in *Stand Fast by Our Constitution* (Salt Lake City: Deseret Book Co., 1962), p. 118. See also James B. Allen, "J. Reuben Clark, Jr., on American Sovereignty and International Organizations," *Brigham Young University Studies* 13 (Spring 1973): 117-42; Stanley A. Taylor, "J. Reuben Clark, Jr., and the United Nations," ibid., pp. 185-95.

8. Frank B. Jex, "As I Saw the Church in Holland," *Improvement Era* 49 (June 1946): 400.

9. *Church News,* March 23, 1946, p. 6.

10. *Church News,* August 25, 1945, pp. 8, 12.

11. George Albert Smith in *Conference Report,* October 1947, pp. 5-6; see also *Church News,* November 10, 1945, p. 1, and November 17, 1945, p. 1.

12. *Improvement Era* 49 (February 1946): 67; *Church News,* January 19, 1946, p. 1.

13. Quoted by Frederick W. Babbel, *On Wings of Faith* (Salt Lake City: Bookcraft, 1972), p. 46.

14. Ezra Taft Benson in *Conference Report,* April 1947, p. 153.

15. Babbel, *On Wings of Faith,* pp. 7-8.

16. Ibid., p. 36.

17. Ezra Taft Benson in *Conference Report,* April 1947, pp. 153-54.

18. Babbel, *On Wings of Faith,* pp. 131-34, 148-49.

19. Report by Ezra Taft Benson in *Conference Report,* April 1947, pp. 152-57; see also Babbel, *On Wings of Faith,* pp. 25-26.

20. Report by Richard Ranglack, *Church News,* November 24, 1945, pp. 5, 9.

21. Joseph Anderson, *Prophets I Have Known* (Salt Lake City: Deseret Book Co., 1973), p. 103.

22. Special report to the First Presidency, October 22, 1946, in European Mission Manuscript History, p. 70, Church Archives.

23. Babbel, *On Wings of Faith,* pp. 126-38.

24. Ibid., p. 168.

25. Ibid., pp. 129-30.

26. Harrison T. Price, "A Cup of Tea," *Improvement Era* 65 (March 1962): 161 ff.; see also Spencer J. Palmer, *The Church Encounters Asia* (Salt Lake City: Deseret Book Co., 1970), pp. 65-69; Boyd K. Packer in *Conference Report,* April 1975, p. 155.

27. Henry A. Smith, *Matthew Cowley: Man of Faith* (Salt Lake City: Bookcraft, 1954), p. 160.

28. *Church News,* June 1, 1946, p. 1; June 15, 1946, pp. 2-3.

Chapter 12. Postwar Resurgence

1. *Church News,* April 12, 1947, p. 1; statement by Spencer W. Kimball quoted in James R. Clark, comp., *Messages of the First Presidency,* 6 vols. (Salt Lake City: Bookcraft, 1965-75), 6:256-58.

2. Melvin K. Johnson, "A History of the Temple Square Mission of the Church of Jesus Christ of Latter-day Saints to 1970" (master's thesis, Brigham Young University, 1971), pp. 50-51; David K. Jacobs, "The History of Motion Pictures Produced by The Church of Jesus Christ of Latter-day Saints" (master's thesis, Brigham Young University, 1967), pp. 69-99; *Church News,* October 5, 1949, pp. 1, 12-13.

3. *Church News,* March 3, 1945, p. 5; January 26, 1946, p. 1; and October 25, 1947, p. 1; George H. Fudge Oral History, pp. 1-3, Oral History Program, Church Archives; *Improvement Era* 53 (April 1950): 273.

4. *Conference Report,* April 1948, p. 166.

5. *Church News,* May 11, 1946, p. 1.

6. Ralph W. and Emma B. Evans, "The Navajo-Zuni Mission," MS, Church Indian Committee files, p. 3.

7. *Church News,* November 10, 1945, p. 1.

8. *Conference Report,* April 1947, pp. 144-45.

9. *Church News,* February 19, 1977, p. 3; compare December 20, 1947, p. 9.

10. Golden R. Buchanan Oral History, interviews by William G. Hartley, 1974, Church Archives, pp. 3-12.

11. First Presidency Centennial message, *Improvement Era* 50 (July 1947): 422-23.

12. See Alvin R. Dyer, *The Refiner's Fire* (Salt Lake City: Deseret Book Co., 1960), pp. 111-30.

13. *Conference Report,* April 1950, pp. 5-6.

14. *Church News,* March 14, 1981, pp. 7-10; see chart in chapter 4 herein.

15. *Church News,* April 11, 1951, p. 10.

Chapter 13. David O. McKay and His Administration

1. Quoted in *My Kingdom Shall Roll Forth* (Salt Lake City: The Church of Jesus Christ of Latter-day Saints, 1979), p. 110.

2. Llewelyn R. McKay, *Home Memories of President David O. McKay* (Salt Lake City: Deseret Book Co., 1956), pp. 5-6.

3. Quoted in Preston Nibley, *The Presidents of the Church* (Salt Lake City: Deseret Book Co., 1959), p. 389.

4. David O. McKay, "Personal Testimony," *Improvement Era* 65 (September 1962): 628-29.

5. Clare Middlemiss, comp., *Cherished Experiences from the Writings of David O. McKay* (Salt Lake City: Deseret Book Co., 1967), p. 174.

6. McKay, "Personal Testimony," p. 629.

7. Bryant S. Hinckley, "David O. McKay," *Improvement Era* 35 (May 1932): 389 ff.

8. Middlemiss, *Cherished Experiences,* pp. 50-56.

9. Ibid., pp. 63-65.

10. Ibid., pp. 73-74.

11. Ibid., pp. 79-83.

12. *Conference Report,* April 1951, p. 113.

13. Ibid., October 1953, p. 10; Jeanette McKay Morrell, *Highlights in the Life of President David O. McKay* (Salt Lake City: Deseret Book Co., 1966), p. 240.

14. David O. McKay, "The World Needs to Be Saved from Dominating Animal Instincts," *Instructor* 97 (June 1962): 181-82.

15. *Conference Report,* October 1936, p. 103.

16. Middlemiss, *Cherished Experiences,* pp. 108-9.

17. *Church News,* January 22, 1955, p. 2; January 29, 1955, p. 2.

18. Ibid., July 11, 1953, p. 2.

19. Jerry C. Roundy, *Ricks College: A Struggle for Survival* (Rexburg, Idaho: Ricks College Press, 1976), pp. 168-72, 178-79.

20. Open letter of the First Presidency to the administration, faculty, students and friends of Ricks College, April 7, 1955, quoted in ibid., p. 184.

21. Ernest L. Wilkinson and W. Cleon Skousen, *Brigham Young University: A School of Destiny* (Provo, Utah: Brigham Young University Press, 1976), p. 433.

22. Ibid., p. 592.

23. Ernest L. Wilkinson, remarks at BYU devotional assembly, March 9, 1971, p. 7.

24. William E. Berrett, "A General History of Week-day Religious Education: The Seminaries and Institutes of Religion," MS, Church Educational System Archives.

25. *Church News,* December 1, 1973, p. 12.

26. Leon R. Hartshorn, "Mormon Education During the Bold Years" (Ph.D. diss., Stanford University, 1965), pp. 185-88.

27. "Report for 1971 from the Commissioner of Education of The Church of Jesus Christ of Latter-day Saints."

Chapter 14. Growth into a Worldwide Church

1. Spencer W. Kimball, "When the World Will Be Converted," *Ensign* 14 (October 1974): 3ff.

2. Gordon B. Hinckley, "Here We Build Our Zion," *Ensign* 13 (August 1973): 6.

3. Victor L. Brown in *Conference Report,* April 1967, pp. 35-37.

4. *Church News,* October 6, 1965, p. 11.

5. Victor L. Brown in *Conference Report,* April 1967, pp. 35-36.

6. Doyle L. Green, "The Church Sends Its Messages to the World Through the Unified Magazine," *Improvement Era* 72 (August 1969): 4-7.

7. Victor L. Brown in *Conference Report,* April 1967, pp. 35, 37.

Chapter 15. Sharing the Gospel

1. *Church News,* May 27, 1978, p. 5.

2. *A Systematic Program for Teaching the Gospel,* 1952, p. 6.

3. *Church News,* June 3, 1961, p. 7.

4. *Ensign* 3 (September 1973): 90-91.

5. Journal History, January 17, 1925, p. 2; February 3, 1925, p. 3; September 9, 1926, p. 3; LeRoi Snow, "The Missionary Home," *Improvement Era* 31 (May 1928): 552-54.

6. *Church News,* February 15, 1969, pp. 8-10; December 15, 1973, p. 3; January 3, 1976, p. 3; September 9, 1978, p. 10.

7. See Gordon B. Hinckley, "Twenty-five Years of Radio Ministry," *Church News,* April 26, 1947, pp. 4-5.

8. *Church News,* July 14, 1973, p. 5.

9. Ibid., July 8, 1972, p. 15; February 17, 1973, p. 3; February 24, 1973, p. 4.

10. Ibid., November 27, 1976, p. 3; February 25, 1978, p. 3.

Chapter 16. Temporal Affairs

1. Henry D. Moyle, address to special bishops' session of general conference, April 5, 1963.

2. *Conference Report,* October 1943, p. 12 (current committee titles inserted); compare *Conference Report,* April 1982, p. 22.

3. Ibid., April 1953, p. 99.

4. John A. Widtsoe, *Priesthood and Church Government* (Salt Lake City: Deseret Book Co., 1938), pp. 256-57; Harold B. Lee, address at welfare conference session, October 3, 1970, pp. 1-2.

5. Summary of Projects as of April 3, 1956, Building Committee Papers, Historical Department Archives; Harold W. Burton, Supervising Church Architect, interview with author, January 28, 1964.

6. David W. Cummings, *Mighty Missionary of the Pacific: The Building Program of the Church* (Salt Lake City: Bookcraft, 1961).

7. *Church News,* April 3, 1982, p. 3.

8. Ibid., August 12, 1972, p. 4; *Conference Report,* April 1972, p. 10.

9. "New Generation of Meetinghouses," *Ensign* 11 (November 1981): 108-10.

10. *Church News,* February 5, 1966, p. 10; January 15, 1972, p. 3; March 18, 1972, p. 3; Guide to the Historical Department, pp. 2-3.

11. *Church News,* January 9, 1971, pp. 4, 7.

12. Ibid., April 17, 1971, p. 3.

13. Ibid., January 2, 1971, p. 9; May 3, 1980, p. 14.

14. Ibid., March 2, 1968, p. 7.

15. Ibid., May 30, 1964, p. 9; November 2, 1968, pp. 8-9, 12.

16. Ibid., December 13, 1969, p. 3.

17. Ibid., June 2, 1979, pp. 8-9, 14.

Chapter 17. The Unfolding of Priesthood Correlation

1. Quoted in *Conference Report,* April 1963, pp. 82-83.

2. Ibid., September 1961, pp. 77-79.

3. *Priesthood Genealogical Research Seminar* (Provo, Utah: Brigham Young University, 1968), p. 55.

4. *Conference Report,* September 1961, p. 79.

5. Ibid., September 1961, pp. 79-81.

6. Ibid., October 1962, p. 72.

7. Ibid., September 1961, p. 80.

8. Ibid., October 1962, pp. 74-76.

9. *Home Teaching Handbook,* 1963, preface and pp. A1-2.

10. Ibid., 1967, p. 1.

11. *Initial Training for Priesthood Home Teachers,* 1963, p. 1.

12. *Suggested Outlines for Stake Priesthood Leadership Meeting,* 1964, p. 9.

13. *Conference Report,* September 1967, p. 101.

14. *Church News,* October 19, 1974, p. 10.

15. Ibid., December 31, 1966, pp. 8-9; May 3, 1969, p. 4.

16. Ibid., June 23, 1973, p. 3; June 30, 1973, p. 6.

17. Ibid., February 2, 1980, p. 3.

Chapter 18. Strengthening the Family

1. Heber J. Grant, *Gospel Standards,* comp. G. Homer Durham (Salt Lake City: Improvement Era, 1941), p. 155.

2. Quoted in *Conference Report,* October 1962, p. 78.

3. Ibid., April 1964, p. 5.

4. *Ensign* 1(January 1971): 1.

5. *Conference Report,* April 1973, p. 130.

6. Ibid., April 1979, pp. 4-5, 115.

7. Wilford Woodruff, *Discourses of Wilford Woodruff,* comp. G. Homer Durham (Salt Lake City: Bookcraft, 1946), pp. 267-68.

8. Joseph F. Smith, *Gospel Doctrine* (Salt Lake City: Deseret Book Co., 1956), p. 302.

9. James R. Clark, comp., *Messages of the First Presidency,* 6 vols. (Salt Lake City: Bookcraft, 1965-75), 2:288.

10. Granite Stake Presidency, *Home Evening Bulletin,* January 1927, p. 43.

11. Clark, *Messages,* 4:338-39.

12. Quoted in *Conference Report,* October 1947, p. 26.

13. Ibid., October 1964, pp. 80-87, 137.

14. Ibid., October 1965, p. 19.

15. *Family Home Evening Manual,* 1965, p. iii.

16. Ibid., 1967, pp. iii-iv.

17. *Church News,* October 10, 1970, p. 3.

18. Ibid., February 26, 1966, p. 3.

19. First Presidency circular letter, April 14, 1969, quoted in *My Kingdom Shall Roll Forth* (Salt Lake City: The Church of Jesus Christ of Latter-day Saints, 1979), p. 114.

20. *Church News,* January 27, 1973, p. 7.

21. U.S. Government, Department of Health Education and Welfare, Public Health Service, Center for Disease Control, "Abortion Surveillance, 1977," p. 33.

22. See, for example, *Church News,* June 5, 1976, p. 3.

23. *Conference Report,* April 1969, p. 8.

24. Spencer W. Kimball, *Marriage and Divorce* (Salt Lake City: Deseret Book Co., 1976), p. 9.

25. *Priesthood Bulletin,* February 1973, pp. 2-3; "President Kimball Speaks Out on Morality," *Ensign* 10 (November 1980): 97.

26. *Church News,* October 30, 1976, p. 2.

27. *The Church and the Proposed Equal Rights Amendment: A Moral Issue* (pamphlet circulated with Church magazines, March 1980), pp. 19-20.

Chapter 19. Joseph Fielding Smith and Harold B. Lee

1. *Conference Report,* April 1930, p. 91.

2. Quoted in *Improvement Era* 53 (April 1950): 315.

3. Joseph Fielding Smith, "History and Historical Records," *Utah Genealogical and Historical Magazine* 16 (April 1925): 52-53; "Libels of Historians," *Improvement Era* 10 (December 1906): 103-4; Leonard J. Arrington, "Joseph Fielding Smith: Faithful Historian," *Dialogue* 7 (Spring 1972): 21-24.

4. Quoted in Bryant S. Hinckley, "Joseph Fielding Smith," *Improvement Era* 35 (June 1932): 459.

5. *Conference Report,* April 1970, p. 114.

6. Joseph Fielding McConkie, *True and Faithful: The Life Story of Joseph Fielding Smith* (Salt Lake City: Bookcraft, 1971), p. 74.

7. Marion G. Romney, "Harold B. Lee, Apostle of the Lord," *Improvement Era* 56 (July 1953): 522.

8. *Report of Mexico City Area Conference,* 1972, pp. 48-49.

9. *Conference Report,* April 1952, pp. 126-27.

10. Ibid., October 1972, pp. 19-20.

11. *Church News,* July 15, 1972, p. 3.

12. Ibid., September 30, 1972, p. 3.

13. Ibid., August 28, 1971, p. 5.

14. Ibid., January 29, 1972, p. 3.

15. Address given by President Harold B. Lee, Seminar for Regional Representatives, October 1971, pp. 4-5.

16. *Church News,* February 24, 1968, p. 10.

17. *Health Services Handbook* (Salt Lake City: The Church of Jesus Christ of Latter-day Saints, 1971), pp. 2-3.

18. *Church News,* July 31, 1971, pp. 3, 12; see also July 21, 1973, p. 7; and August 18, 1973, pp. 5, 13.

19. Ibid., September 14, 1974, pp. 3, 10.

20. Ibid., October 4, 1969, p. 3.

21. *Social Services Handbook* (Salt Lake City: The Church of Jesus Christ of Latter-day Saints, 1973), p. 7.

22. Ibid., pp. 7-8.

23. Marvin J. Ashton, "The Church Focuses on Social and Emotional Problems," *Ensign* 1 (January 1971): 30-31; Robert L. Simpson, "Help Available Here," *Ensign* 3 (December 1973): 56.

24. *Church News,* October 20, 1973, p. 4.

25. Ibid., April 7, 1973, p. 4.

26. Ashton, "Problems," pp. 30-31, and Simpson, "Help," p. 56.

27. *Church News,* August 19, 1972, pp. 7-12.

28. Ibid., June 27, 1970, p. 6.

29. Harold B. Lee, *Ye Are the Light of the World* (Salt Lake City: Deseret Book Co., 1974), p. 349.

Chapter 20. Temples and Temple Work

1. James E. Talmage, *The House of the Lord* (Salt Lake City: Bookcraft, 1963), p. 17.

2. John A. Widtsoe, "Looking Toward the Temple," *Ensign* 2 (January 1972): 56-58.

3. Boyd K. Packer, *The Holy Temple* (Salt Lake City: Bookcraft, 1980), pp. 177-80.

4. Ibid., p. 45.

5. Talmage, *House of the Lord,* p. 100.

6. Joseph Smith, *History of The Church of Jesus Christ of Latter-day Saints,* 2nd ed. rev., 7 vols. (Salt Lake City: Deseret Book Co., 1960), 5:1-2; quoted in *Teachings of the Prophet Joseph Smith,* sel. Joseph Fielding Smith (Salt Lake City: Deseret Book Co., 1938), p. 237.

7. Talmage, *House of the Lord,* pp. 110-11.

8. Quoted in Richard O. Cowan, *Temple Building: Ancient and Modern* (Provo, Utah: Brigham Young University, 1971), p. 3.

9. Smith, *Teachings,* p. 179.

10. Stanley Kimball, "The Nauvoo Temple," *Improvement Era* 66 (November 1963): 974-82.

11. Quoted in Cowan, *Temple Building,* pp. 12-13.

12. *Church News,* April 11, 1953, p. 7.

13. Orson F. Whitney, *Life of Heber C. Kimball* (Salt Lake City: Bookcraft, 1973), p. 436.

14. Harold W. Burton and W. Aird MacDonald, "The Oakland Temple," *Improvement Era* 67 (May 1964): 380-81.

15. Eugene Hilton, "Temple Hill," in *Triumph,* a souvenir brochure commemorating the opening of the East Bay Interstake Center in January 1959 (published by the Hayward, Oakland-Berkeley, and Walnut Creek stakes of The Church of Jesus Christ of Latter-day Saints, 1959), pp. 10, 19.

16. *Improvement Era* 58 (November 1955): 795.

17. *Church News,* September 17, 1955, pp. 4, 10.

18. Quoted in Marba C. Josephson, "A Temple Is Risen to Our Lord," *Improvement Era* 58 (September 1955): 624-25.

19. Allie Howe, "A Temple in the South Pacific," *Improvement Era* 58 (November 1955): 811-13; Wendell B. Mendenhall in *Conference Report,* April 1955, p. 5.

20. *Church News,* March 8, 1975, p. 3.

21. *Ensign* 10 (May 1980): 99.

22. *Church News,* April 4, 1981, p. 3.

23. Ibid., March 13, 1976, p. 14; February 28, 1981, p. 3; April 11, 1981, p. 23.

24. *Ensign* 10 (May 1980): 102.

25. Smith, *Teachings,* pp. 193, 356.

26. Quoted in James R. Clark, comp., *Messages of the First Presidency,* 6 vols. (Salt Lake City: Bookcraft, 1965-75), 3:251-60.

27. Merrill S. Lofthouse, "A Glance Backward—Historical Sketch of the Genealogical Society," *Improvement Era* 72 (July 1969): 14-17.

28. Ibid., p. 15.

29. *Church News,* April 11, 1981, p. 22.

30. Ibid., January 18, 1964, pp. 8-9.

31. Ibid., March 13, 1965, p. 3.

32. *Priesthood Genealogy Handbook,* 1974, pp. 6-7.

33. *Conference Report,* April 1978, p. 4; see also *Church News,* April 22, 1978, p. 3.

34. *Church News,* July 7, 1979, p. 3.

35. *Conference Report,* October 1978, pp. 39-40.

36. *Church News,* December 31, 1978, p. 8.

37. Boyd K. Packer and Howard W. Hunter, *That They May Be Redeemed,* 1977.

Chapter 21. Spencer W. Kimball and His Administration

1. Boyd K. Packer, "President Spencer W. Kimball: No Ordinary Man," *Ensign* 4 (March 1974): 3.

2. *Conference Report,* October 1943, p. 16; Edward L. Kimball and Andrew E. Kimball, Jr., *Spencer W. Kimball* (Salt Lake City: Bookcraft, 1977), pp. 101-2, 111.

3. Kimball and Kimball, *Kimball,* pp. 169-70.

4. *Conference Report,* October 1943, p. 15.

5. Ibid., p. 16.

6. Kimball and Kimball, *Kimball,* pp. 193, 195.

7. *Conference Report,* April 1967, pp. 66-67.

8. Spencer W. Kimball, *The Miracle of Forgiveness* (Salt Lake City: Bookcraft, 1969), pp. 168-69.

9. Spencer W. Kimball, "The Lamanites: Their Burden Our Burden," an address given at BYU, April 25, 1967, quoted in Edward L. Kimball, ed., *The Teachings of Spencer W. Kimball* (Salt Lake City: Bookcraft, 1982), pp. 613-14.

10. Boyd K. Packer, "Kimball," p. 4.

11. Spencer W. Kimball, *One Silent Sleepless Night* (Salt Lake City: Bookcraft, 1975), pp. 33-35, 50-51.

12. Boyd K. Packer, "Kimball," p. 4.

13. *Conference Report,* October 1975, p. 17.

14. *Church News,* January 5, 1974, p. 14; *Conference Report,* April 1974, p. 4.

15. *Conference Report,* October 1977, pp. 38-39.

16. *Church News,* April 13, 1974, p. 17.

17. Ibid., September 17, 1977, p. 3.

18. Ibid., October 29, 1977, p. 3.

19. Ibid., March 31, 1979, p. 6.

20. Ibid., July 15, 1978, p. 5; August 11, 1979, pp. 8-10.

21. Bruce R. McConkie, "The New Revelation on Priesthood," *Priesthood* (Salt Lake City: Deseret Book Co., 1981), pp. 126-27.

22. *Church News,* January 6, 1979, p. 4.

23. Bruce R. McConkie, "New Revelation," p. 128.

24. Ibid.

25. *Conference Report,* April 1978, p. 4.

26. Bruce R. McConkie, "A New Commandment," *Ensign* 6 (August 1976): 8.

27. Ibid., p. 7.

28. *Ensign* 12 (November 1982): p. 53.

29. *Conference Report,* April 1974, pp. 6-7.

30. Ibid., April 1974, pp. 7-9; October 1974, pp. 7-10.

31. *Church News,* December 8, 1979, p. 4.

32. Ibid., September 23, 1978, pp. 3, 10.

Chapter 22. The General Authorities

1. Joseph Fielding Smith, "The First Presidency and the Council of the Twelve," *Improvement Era* 69 (November 1966): 977-79.

2. *Speeches of the Year 1974* (Provo, Utah: Brigham Young University Press, 1975), pp. 8-23.

3. Joseph Smith, *History of The Church of Jesus Christ of Latter-day Saints,* 2nd ed. rev., 7 vols. (Salt Lake City: Deseret Book Co., 1960), 2:176.

4. For a discussion see Joseph Fielding Smith, *Doctrines of Salvation,* 3 vols. (Salt Lake City: Bookcraft, 1954-56), 1:211-22.

5. Joseph Fielding Smith, "First Presidency," pp. 977-79.

6. *Instructor* 95 (August 1960): 257.

7. *Conference Report,* October 1970, p. 109.

8. Ibid., October 1976, p. 10.

9. Ibid., April 1941, pp. 94-95.

10. *Church News,* June 7, 1961, p. 3.

11. *Conference Report,* October 1975, pp. 3-4.

12. Ibid., October 1976, p. 10.

13. See D. Michael Quinn, "The Evolution of the Presiding Quorums of the LDS Church," *Journal of Mormon History* 1 (1974): 32-38.

14. Joseph L. Wirthlin, "History and Functions of the Presiding Bishopric," *Improvement Era* 59 (November 1956): 794, 830.

15. Joseph Fielding Smith, *Essentials in Church History,* 25th ed. (Salt Lake City: Deseret Book Co., 1972), pp. 142-43; Joseph Smith, Jr., *Teachings of the Prophet Joseph Smith,* sel. Joseph Fielding Smith (Salt Lake City: Deseret Book Co., 1938), p. 151.

16. John A. Widtsoe, *Priesthood and Church Government* (Salt Lake City: Deseret Book Co., 1954), pp. 269-70; *Suggestions to Patriarchs,* 1970, p. 2.

17. *Conference Report,* October 1979, p. 25.

18. Ibid., September 1978, p. 23.

19. *Ensign* 14 (May 1984): 4-5.

20. J. Reuben Clark, Jr., address to seminary and institute teachers at BYU, July 7, 1954; in *Church News,* July 31, 1954, p. 2ff.

21. Ibid.

22. *Conference Report,* April 1945, p. 90.

23. Ibid., April 1946, p. 68.

24. BYU assembly address, May 14, 1968.

Chapter 23. Administering the Worldwide Church

1. *Conference Report,* October 1967, pp. 103-4.

2. Dean L. Larsen, "The Challenges of Administering a Worldwide Church," *Ensign* 3 (July 1974): 20, 21.

3. *Church News,* October 31, 1970, pp. 3, 5.

4. Andrew Jenson, *An Encyclopedic History of the Church* (Salt Lake City: Deseret News Publishing Co., 1941), pp. 237-38.

5. *Church News,* July 1, 1961, p. 6.

6. Ibid., June 19, 1965, pp. 3-5.

7. Ibid., December 28, 1963, p. 6.

8. *Conference Report,* October 1967, pp. 25-26.

9. *Church News,* July 1, 1972, p. 3; November 2, 1974, p. 12.

10. Ibid., May 3, 1975, pp. 3, 12; May 17, 1975, p. 3.

11. Ibid., June 26, 1976, p. 7.

12. *Conference Report,* April 1979, p. 119.

13. *Church News,* April 10, 1976, p. 19.

14. *Ensign* 9 (November 1979): 101.

15. *Church News,* Feb. 5, 1977, pp. 8-9.

16. Ibid., November 2, 1974, p. 13.

17. *Ensign* 7 (February 1977): 91.

18. *Church News,* April 1, 1978, p. 4.

Chapter 24. The Destiny of the Church

1. *Conference Report,* April 1980, pp. 97-99.

2. Joseph Smith, Jr., *History of The Church of Jesus Christ of Latter-day Saints,* 2nd ed. rev., 7 vols. (Salt Lake City: Deseret Book Co., 1960), 4:537.

3. Paul F. Royal, "Every Man in His Place," BYU fireside address, January 3, 1965, p. 12.

4. *Conference Report,* September 1961, p. 81.

5. *Relief Society Magazine,* April 1967, pp. 246-47.

6. *Conference Report,* October 1967, pp. 115-16.

7. *Journal of Discourses,* 26 vols. (London: Latter-day Saints' Book Depot, 1855-86), 18:110.

8. *Conference Report,* October 1962, p. 83.

Index

European Mission, administrative responsibilities, 439–40, 415–16
Evacuation of missionaries, 176–82
Evans, Richard L.: radio announcer, 288; on correlated curriculum, 310
"Every Member a Missionary," 237, 281
Evolution, organic: statement on, 57–58; controversy over, 116–17
Expansion, geographical: following World War I, 95–102; following World War II, 257–74; challenges posed by, 270–74
External communications. *See* Public Communications
Extraction of names for temple work, 376–77

— F —

Fairs: during depression, 166–67; postwar, 287
Family: based of righteous life, 169; postwar emphasis, 219–20; emphasized by David O. McKay, 239–40; emphasized in Priesthood Correlation effort, 307; teaching gospel in, 318–26, 397
Family Home Evening: origin and benefits, 84, 322–36; emphasized following World War II, 323; supported by auxiliaries, 323–24; manuals published for, 324; promises regarding, 325
Far West, Missouri, property purchased in, 49
Fast day, shifted to Sunday, 69–70
"Father and the Son, The," a First Presidency exposition, 58–59
Felt, Louie B., Primary president, 74
Fiji, visited by David O. McKay, 243
Finances, importance of, 294

Financial and Statistical Reports Department, 303
Finland, mission opened, 210
Firesides, inaugurated, 115
First Presidency: immediate reorganization of, 8–11; functions and history of, 399–403; succession in, 8–11, 400–403; additional counselors in, 401–403; inspired authority of, 411
First Presidency statements: on gospel doctrines, 57–59; on fast day, 69–70; on ward priesthood meetings, 76–77; on Church centennial, 103; on moral issues, 124–25; on upholding community morals, 126–27; on gambling, 127; on Sunday observance, 127–28; on federal aid to education, 135; on prohibition of alcohol, 136; on labor unions, 136–37; on Welfare Plan, 141–46; on Communism, 143–44; on Welfare accomplishments, 146–47; on correlation, 168–69; on Assistants to the Twelve, 172–73; on war and military service, 188–89; on pioneer virtues, 228–29; on home evening, 323; on pornography, 326–27; on birth control, 327; on abortion, 328, 396; on Equal Rights Amendment, 331, 397; on emeritus General Authorities, 408–9; on Regional Representatives, 417–18; on delineation of ecclesiastical and temporal authority, 420
France, reduction of missionaries in, 163
Freeman, Joseph, Jr., first black to receive priesthood blessings, 392
Friedrichs, Wilhelm, preaches in Argentina, 100
Friend, magazine for children, 315

Fudge, George, microfilms in England, 218–19

Fyans, J. Thomas, on refinements in genealogy work, 377

— G —

Gambling, opposed by Church leaders, 127

Gates, Crawford, composer, 227

Gathering, new understanding of in the Church, 21–24

Genealogical Society: occupies LDS College buildings, 109; postwar programs, 218–19; led by Joseph Fielding Smith, 335; history and programs, 373–77

Genealogy: magazine, 81; Joseph Smith on importance of, 372; society and programs, 373–77; Saints' responsibility toward, 375

Genealogy Committee, part of correlation organization, 308

General Authorities: called from outside of America, 266; growing administrative load, 274; organization and functions, 399–411; emeritus status, 408–9; short-term appointments, 408–9; role as prophets, 409–11

General conference: broadcasts, 288; importance of, 409, 411; schedule changed, 422–23

Germany: Mormons suppressed, 36; Saints in World War I, 62; elders as Olympic judges, 163, 175; Church exhibit at health fair, 166; Nazis' attitude toward, 174–76; missionaries evacuated, 180; Saints' faith during World War II, 183–84; Ezra Taft Benson visits, 205

Girls Program, LDS, origin and progress, 220

Glad, A.P.A., works with inactive adults, 160–61

Goodwin, Charles C., praises Joseph F. Smith, 40

Gospel Doctrine, a compilation of Joseph F. Smith's teachings, 57

Gospel Doctrine Class: name adopted, 156; systematic scripture study, 347

Granite Stake: sponsors first Seminary, 107; early welfare projects, 140; develops girls program, 220; inaugurated home evenings, 322

Grant, Heber J.: life and character, 86–90; mission to Japan, 18–19; managed *Improvement Era,* 79; on tithing, 92; on Word of Wisdom, 92–93; on keeping the commandments, 92–93; interest in golf, 93; nominates Melvin J. Ballard as Apostle, 94–95; dedicates temples, 98; concern over education expense, 108–9; on political matters, 125–26; supports League of Nations, 126; stand on prohibition, 128–32; opposes dole, 134–35; on inspiration in Welfare Plan, 151–52; visits Europe, 169; on teaching in the home, 319

Great Britain: clergy harass Saints, 37; Churchill answers false reports, 40

Groves, William S., finances hospital, 50, 350

— H —

Handicapped, programs for the, 81–82, 355

Hansen, Harold I., produces Cumorah pageant, 167–68

Hawaii: stake formed in, 98; Laie to become educational center, 235–36; educational programs, 252–53

— M —